CRIMINALISTICS

An Introduction to Forensic Science

RICHARD SAFERSTEIN

Chief Forensic Chemist, New Jersey State Police
Lecturer at Trenton State College and Ocean County College

Prentice-Hall, Inc., Englewood Cliffs, New Jersey

Library of Congress Cataloging in Publication Data

Saferstein, Richard
    Criminalistics: an introduction to forensic science.

    Includes bibliographies and index.
    1. Criminal investigation. 2. Forensic ballistics.
3. Chemistry, Forensic. I. Title.
HV8073.S2   364.12   76-6051
ISBN 0-13-193359-0

Printed in the United States of America

10 9 8 7 6 5 4 3 2

Prentice-Hall International, Inc., *London*
Prentice-Hall of Australia Pty. Limited, *Sydney*
Prentice-Hall of Canada, Ltd., *Toronto*
Prentice-Hall of India Private Limited, *New Delhi*
Prentice-Hall of Japan, Inc., *Tokyo*
Prentice-Hall of Southeast Asia Ptd. Ltd., *Singapore*

To the Memory of Fran and Michael

Contents

Preface

Making science relevant and pertinent to the interests and goals of the student is a desirable, but often elusive goal pursued by educators. *Criminalistics* is written with such lofty objectives in mind. The book has several purposes: First and foremost is a presentation of the techniques, skills, and limitations of the modern crime laboratory for a reader who has no background in the forensic sciences. The nature of physical evidence is emphasized along with the limitations that technology and knowledge impose on its individualization and characterization.

A major portion of the text centers on discussions of the common items of physical evidence encountered at crime scenes. These chapters include updated techniques describing forensic analysis, as well as procedures and practices relating to the proper collection and preservation of evidence at crime scenes. Particular attention is paid to the meaning and role of probability in interpreting the evidential significance of scientifically evaluated evidence.

In selecting the subject matter for the book, I have drawn upon my experience both as an active forensic scientist and as an instructor of forensic science at the college level. No prior knowledge about scientific principles or techniques is assumed of the reader. He/she is introduced to those areas of chemistry and biology relating to the analysis of physical evidence with a minimum of scientific terminology and equations. It is not the intent of this book to make scientists or forensic experts of the reader. For this reason, the chemistry and biology discussed is limited to a minimum core of facts and principles that will make the subject matter comprehensible and meaningful to the nonscientist. Nevertheless, it will certainly be gratifying if this effort motivates some students to seek further scientific knowledge, and perhaps direct their education toward a career in forensic science.

Though *Criminalistics* is an outgrowth of a one-semester course offered as part of a criminal justice program at many New Jersey colleges, its subject matter is not limited to the college student. Optimum utilization of crime laboratory services requires that criminal investigators have a knowledge of the techniques and capabilities of the laboratory that extends beyond any summary that may be gleaned from departmental brochures dealing with the collection and packaging of physical evidence. Only by combining a knowledge of the principles and techniques of forensic science with logic and common sense will the investigator gain a comprehensive insight into the meaning and significance of physical evidence and its role in criminal investigations. Forensic science begins at the crime scene. If the investigator cannot recognize, collect, and package evidence properly, no amount of equipment or expertise will salvage the situation.

Likewise, there is a dire need to bridge the "communication gap" that presently exists between lawyers, judges, and the forensic scientist. An intelligent evaluation of the scientist's data and any subsequent testimony that may follow will again depend on the familiarity of the underlying principles of forensic science. Too many practitioners of the law profess ignorance of the subject or at best attempt to gain a superficial understanding of its meaning and significance minutes before meeting the expert witness. To this end, it is hoped that the book will provide a painless route to comprehending the nature of the science.

In order to merge theory with practice, a number of actual forensic case histories are included in the text. It is intended that these illustrations will remove forensic science from the domain of the abstract and make its applications relevant to the real world of criminal investigation.

I am indebted to many people for their assistance and advice in the preparation of this book. Many faculty members, colleagues, and friends have read and commented on various portions of the text. I want to particularly thank the following people for their critical reading and discussions of the manuscript:

Jeffrey Bockol, Wayne Dunning, Jew-Ming Chao, James Chickos,

Frank Creveling, Peter DeForest, Robert Epstein, David Garin, John Lintott, Raymond Murray, Vincent Peterson, Richard Tidey, and Charles Tindall.

I'm appreciative of the time and talent given by Peggy Cole and my production editor, Cheryl Smith, for converting the manuscript into a finished book.

I would also like to give credit to John Bartek, Linda Jankowski, and the New Jersey State Police Photography Laboratory for the special photographic skills that they so generously gave to this book. In addition, I am indebted to the New Jersey State Police, as well as those law enforcement agencies, governmental agencies, private individuals, and equipment manufacturers cited in the text for their contributing photographs and illustrations.

Anyone who expects to write a textbook must be prepared to contribute countless hours to the task, often at the expense of family obligations. This effort was no exception. My efforts would have fallen well short of completion without the patience and encouragement of my wife, Gail. Her typing, and critical readings of the manuscript, as well as her strength of character under circumstances that were less than ideal, will always be remembered.

The views and opinions expressed in this book are those of the author, and do not necessarily represent those of the New Jersey State Police or any other governmental agency.

Introduction

chapter 1

DEFINITION AND SCOPE OF
FORENSIC SCIENCE

Forensic science in its broadest definition is the application of science to law. As our society has grown more complex it has become more dependent on rules of law to regulate the activities of its members. Forensic science offers the knowledge and technology of science to the definition and enforcement of such laws.

Each year, as government finds it increasingly necessary to regulate those activities that most intimately influence our daily lives, science merges more closely with civil and criminal law. Consider, for example, the laws and agencies that regulate the quality of our food, the nature and potency of drugs, the extent of automobile emissions, the kind of fuel oil we burn, the purity of our drinking water, and the pesticides we use on our crops and plants. It would be difficult to conceive of any food and drug regulation or any environmental protection act that could be effectively monitored and enforced without the assistance of scientific technology and the skill of the scientific community.

In the arena of criminal justice, laws are continually being broadened and revised to counter the alarming increase in crime rates. In response to public concern, law enforcement agencies have expanded their patrol and investigative functions, hoping to stem the rising tide of crime. At the same time they are looking more and more to the scientific community for advice and technical support in their efforts. Can the technology that put man on the moon, split the atom, and eradicated man's most dreaded diseases be enlisted in this critical battle? Unfortunately, science cannot offer final and authoritative solutions to problems that stem from a maze of social and psychological factors. However, as the contents of this book will attest, science does occupy an important and unique role in the criminal justice system—a role that relates to the scientist's ability to supply accurate and objective information that reflects the events that have occurred at a crime. It will also become apparent to the reader that a good deal of work remains to be done if the full potential of science as it is applied to criminal investigations is to be realized.

Considering the vast array of civil and criminal laws that regulate society, forensic science, in its broadest sense, has become so comprehensive a subject as to make a meaningful introductory textbook treatment of its role and techniques most difficult, if not overwhelming. For this reason, we must find practical limits that narrow the scope of the subject. Fortunately, common usage provides us with such a limited definition: **Forensic science is the application of science to those criminal and civil laws that are enforced by police agencies in a criminal justice system.**

Even within this limited definition we will restrict our discussion in this book to only those areas of chemistry, biology, physics, and geology that are useful for determining the evidential value of crime-scene and related evidence, omitting any references to the subject of medicine and the law. Forensic pathology, psychology, and odontology certainly encompass important and relevant areas of knowledge and practice in law enforcement, each being an integral part of the total forensic science service that is provided to any up-to-date criminal justice system. However, these subjects go beyond the intended range of the book and the reader is referred elsewhere for discussions of their applications and techniques.[1] Instead, we will attempt to focus on the services of what has popularly become known as the crime laboratory. It is here that the principles and techniques of the physical and natural sciences are practiced and applied to the analysis of crime-scene evidence.

For many, the term "criminalistics" seems more descriptive for describing the services of a crime laboratory. However, it will serve

---

[1]Two excellent references are: Andre A. Moenssens, Ray E. Moses, and Fred E. Inbau, *Scientific Evidence in Criminal Cases* (Mineola, N.Y.: The Foundation Press, Inc., 1973) and Werner U. Spitz and Russell S. Fisher, eds., *Medicolegal Investigation of Death* (Springfield, Ill.: Charles C. Thomas, 1973).

no useful purpose to rationalize whether the subject matter included in this book can best be classified as criminalistics or forensic science, if indeed this distinction can be made at all. For all intents and purposes the two terms are taken to be one and the same, and will be used interchangeably in the text. Regardless of title, criminalist or forensic scientist, the trend of events has made the scientist in the crime laboratory an active participant in the criminal justice system.

HISTORY AND DEVELOPMENT OF FORENSIC SCIENCE

Forensic science owes its origins first to those individuals who developed the principles and techniques needed to identify or compare physical evidence, and second to those who recognized the necessity of merging these principles into a coherent discipline that could be practically applied to a criminal justice system.

Today, many believe that Sir Arthur Conan Doyle had a considerable influence on popularizing scientific crime-detection methods through his fictional character Sherlock Holmes. It was Holmes who first applied the newly developing principles of serology, fingerprinting, firearm identification, and questioned-document examination long before their value was first recognized and accepted by real-life criminal investigators. Holmes' feats excited the imagination of an emerging generation of forensic scientists and criminal investigators. Even in the first Sherlock Holmes novel, *A Study in Scarlet*, published in 1887, we find examples of Doyle's uncanny ability to describe scientific methods of detection years before they were actually discovered and implemented. For instance, here Holmes is probing and recognizing the potential usefulness of forensic serology to criminal investigation:

> "I've found it. I've found it," he shouted to my companion, running towards us with a test tube in his hand. "I have found a reagent which is precipitated by hemoglobin and by nothing else. . . . Why, man, it is the most practical medico-legal discovery for years. Don't you see that it gives us an infallable test for blood stains? . . . The old gracium test was very clumsy and uncertain. So is the microscopic examination for blood corpuscles. The latter is valueless if the stains are a few hours old. Now, this appears to act as well whether the blood is old or new. Had this test been invented, there are hundreds of men now walking the earth who would long ago have paid the penalty of their crimes. . . . Criminal cases are continually hinging upon that one point. A man is suspected of a crime months perhaps after it has been committed. His linen or clothes are examined and brownish stains discovered upon them. Are they blood stains, or rust stains, or fruit stains, or what are they? That is a question which has puzzled many an expert, and why? Because there was no reliable test. Now we have the Sherlock Holmes test, and there will no longer be any difficulty."

There are many who can be cited for their specific contribution to the field of forensic science. The following is just a brief list of those who made the earliest contributions to formulating the disciplines that now constitute forensic science:

Alphonse Bertillon (1853-1914). The first scientific system of personal identification was devised by Alphonse Bertillon. In 1879, Bertillon began to develop the science of anthropometry, a systematic procedure of taking a series of body measurements as a means of distinguishing one individual from another. For nearly two decades this system was considered the most accurate method of personal identification. Though anthropometry was eventually replaced by fingerprinting in the early 1900s, Bertillon's early efforts have earned him the distinction of being known as the father of criminal identification.

Francis Galton (1822-1911). This scientist undertook the first definitive study of fingerprints and developed a methodology of classifying them for filing. In 1892, he published a book entitled *Finger Prints* which contained the first statistical proof supporting the uniqueness of his method of personal identification. His work went on to describe the basic principles that form the present system of identification by fingerprints.

Leone Lattes (1887-1954). In 1901, Dr. Karl Landsteiner discovered that blood can be grouped into different categories. These blood groups or types are now recognized as A, B, AB, and O. The possibility that blood grouping could be a useful characteristic for the identification of an individual intrigued Dr. Leone Lattes, a professor at the Institute of Forensic Medicine at the University of Turin in Italy. In 1915, he devised a relatively simple procedure for determining the blood group of a dried bloodstain, a technique which he immediately applied to criminal investigations. Even to this day Dr. Lattes' procedure is utilized often by forensic scientists.

Calvin Goddard (1891-1955). To determine whether or not a particular gun has fired a bullet requires a comparison of the bullet with one that has been test-fired from the suspect's weapon. Calvin Goddard, a U.S. Army colonel, refined the techniques of such an examination by utilizing the comparison microscope. Goddard's expertise established the comparison microscope as the indispensable tool of the modern firearms examiner.

Albert S. Osborn (1858-1946). Osborn's development of the fundamental principles of document examination was responsible for the acceptance of documents as scientific evidence by the courts. In 1910, Osborn authored the first significant text in this field,

Questioned Documents; this book is still considered the primary reference for document examiners.

Hans Gross (1847–1915). The first treatise describing the application of scientific disciplines to the field of criminal investigation was written by Hans Gross in 1893. Gross, a public prosecutor and judge in Graz, Austria, spent many years studying and developing principles of criminal investigation. In his classic book, *Handbuch für Untersuchungsrichter*, (later published in English under the title *Criminal Investigation*), he detailed the assistance that investigators could expect from the fields of microscopy, chemistry, physics, mineralogy, zoology, botany, anthropometry, and fingerprinting. He later introduced the forensic journal *Kriminologie*, which still serves as a medium for reporting improved methods of scientific crime detection.

Edmond Locard (1877–1966). Though Gross was a strong advocate of the use of the scientific method in criminal investigation, he did not make any specific technical contributions to this philosophy. It was left instead to a Frenchman, Edmond Locard, to demonstrate how the principles enunciated by Gross could be incorporated within a workable crime laboratory. Locard's formal education was in both medicine and law. In 1910, he persuaded the Police Department in Lyons to give him two attic rooms and two assistants to start a police laboratory.

During his first years of work, the only instruments available to Locard were a microscope and a rudimentary spectrometer. However, his enthusiasm quickly overcame the technical and monetary deficiencies he encountered. From these modest beginnings Locard's research and accomplishments became known throughout the world by forensic scientists and criminal investigators. Eventually he became the founder and director of the Institute of Criminalistics at the University of Lyons; this quickly developed into a leading international center for study and research in forensic science.

Locard believed strongly that every criminal can be connected to his crime by dust particles carried from the crime scene. This belief was reinforced by a series of successful and well-publicized investigations. In one case, confronted with counterfeit coins and the names of three suspects, Locard urged the police to bring the suspects' clothing to his laboratory. Upon careful examination, he located small metallic particles in all the garments. Chemical analysis revealed that the particles and coins were composed of exactly the same metallic elements. Confronted with this evidence, the suspects were arrested and soon confessed to the crime.

During the post–World War I period, Locard's successes served as an impetus for the formation of police laboratories in Vienna, Berlin, Sweden, Finland, and Holland. It was in the United States, however, that the most ambitious commitment to forensic science was undertaken. In 1932, the Federal Bureau of Investigation, under the directorship of J. Edgar Hoover, organized a national laboratory that aimed to offer forensic services to all law enforcement agencies in the country. During its formative stages extensive consultations were made with businessmen, manufacturers, and scientists whose knowledge and experience were useful in guiding the new facility through its infancy. The FBI Laboratory is now the world's largest forensic laboratory, performing nearly 500,000 examinations every year. Its accomplishments have earned it worldwide recognition, and its structure and organization has served as a model for newly formed forensic laboratories at the state and local levels in the United States, as well as in other countries.

The oldest forensic laboratory in the United States is that of the Los Angeles Police Department, created in 1923 by August Vollmer, a former police chief of Berkeley, California. In the 1930s, Vollmer headed the first U.S. university institute for criminology and criminalistics at the University of California at Berkeley. However, this institute lacked any official status in the university until 1948, when a school of criminology was formed. The famous criminalist Paul Kirk (Figure 1-1) was selected to head its criminalistics department. Many of the graduates of this school have gone on to become actively engaged in the development of forensic laboratories in other parts of the state and country. Presently, California has a total of twenty-nine federal, state, county, and city crime laboratories. Though the majority of these facilities operate independently of one another, an exchange of information and expertise is facilitated through a regional professional society, the California Association of Criminalists.

Another important milestone marking the development of forensic science was the creation of the Central Research Establishment in Aldermaston, England in 1966. This laboratory is the first of its kind in the world to be solely dedicated to performing basic research in forensic science. In contrast to the American system of independent local laboratories, England has developed a national system of regional laboratories under the direction of the government's Home Office. With the exception of London and southeastern England, which are served by The Metropolitan Police Laboratory, the entire country is serviced by eight regional laboratories. The Central Research Establishment is the research arm of this national system.

Relieved of the necessity of performing routine analyses, the

FIGURE 1-1. Paul Leland Kirk, 1902–1970
Courtesy Blackstone-Shelburne, N.Y.

Central Research Establishment's staff is making substantial progress in developing new forensic procedures, gathering statistical data, and collecting and disseminating vital information relating to all facets of forensic science.

THE ORGANIZATION OF A CRIME LABORATORY

The development of crime laboratories in the United States has been characterized by rapid growth accompanied by a lack of national and regional planning and coordination. At present, there are more than two hundred public crime laboratories operating at various levels of government—federal, state, county, and municipal. This represents almost a doubling of such facilities since 1966.

The size and diversity of crime laboratories makes it impossible to select any one model that can best describe a typical crime laboratory. While the majority of these facilities function as elements of police departments, others have been placed under the direction of the prosecutor's or district attorney's office, and some have had their functions combined with laboratories of the medical examiner or coroner. Far fewer are affiliated with universities or exist as independent agencies in government. Laboratory staff sizes may range from one person to over a hundred, and their services may be diverse or specialized, depending on the responsibilities of the agency that houses the laboratory.

For the most part, crime laboratories have been organized by those agencies that either foresaw their potential application to criminal investigation or were pressed by the increasing demands of casework. There is little doubt that Supreme Court decisions designed to protect the rights of suspects have encouraged the criminal investigator to place a greater reliance on the scientific examination and evaluation of physical evidence collected at crime scenes. However, a far more significant impetus for the creation and growth of crime laboratories has been the staggering increase in the demand for drug analysis. The impact of this trend can be gauged by the experiences of the New Jersey State Police Laboratory. Since 1968, this organization has seen a steady and dramatic rise in drug cases. For 1975, 17,000 drug-related cases were analyzed; a 200 percent increase over 1968. To cope with this increase it has been necessary to add some 40 chemists to the laboratory's staff and to expand its facilities to include two new regional laboratories. The demand for laboratories to perform drug analyses has probably been the single most important factor in the recent expansion of forensic services in New Jersey and elsewhere in the United States.

Historically, the desire for local control has produced a variety of independent laboratories in the United States that precludes the creation of a national system of crime laboratories. Furthermore, political jurisdiction and budget limitations will prevent this situation from changing in the forseeable future. In recognition of this fact, but realizing the need for cooperation, the National Advisory Commission on Criminal Justice Standards and Goals has wisely recommended that "every State by 1982 should establish a consolidated criminal laboratory system composed of local, regional, or state facilities capable of providing the most advanced forensic science services to police agencies."[2]

Crime laboratories to a large extent mirror the law enforcement structure that exists on the national, state, and local levels. The federal government has no single law enforcement or investigative agency that has unlimited jurisdiction. Four major federal crime laboratories have been created for the purpose of assisting in the investigation and enforcement of criminal laws that extend beyond

[2]National Advisory Commission on Criminal Justice Standards and Goals: Police (Washington, D.C.: U.S. Government Printing Office, 1973).

the jurisdictional boundaries of state and local forces. The FBI (Department of Justice) maintains the largest crime laboratory in the world. Its expertise and technology support its broad investigative powers. The Drug Enforcement Administration Laboratories (Department of Justice) are responsible for the analysis of drugs seized in violation of federal laws regulating the production, sale, and transportation of drugs. The laboratories of the Bureau of Alcohol, Tobacco, and Firearms (Department of the Treasury) have responsibility for analyzing alcoholic beverages and documents relating to tax law enforcement, as well as for weapons and explosive devices received in conjunction with enforcement of the Gun Control Act of 1968 and the Organized Crime Control Act of 1970. The U.S. Postal Inspection Service maintains laboratories concerned with criminal investigations relating to the postal service. Each of these federal facilities will offer its expertise to any local agency that requests assistance in relevant investigative matters.

Most state governments maintain a crime laboratory to service state and local law enforcement agencies that do not have ready access to a laboratory. Some states, such as Alabama, Illinois, Michigan, New Jersey, Virginia, and Florida, have developed a comprehensive statewide system of regional or satellite laboratories. These operate under the direction of a central facility and provide forensic services to most areas of the state. The concept of a regional laboratory operating as part of a statewide system has successfully increased the accessibility of many local law enforcement agencies to a crime laboratory, while at the same time minimizing the duplication of services and assuring maximum interlaboratory cooperation through the sharing of expertise and equipment.

Local laboratories provide services to county and municipal agencies. Generally, these facilities operate independently of the state crime laboratory and are financed directly by local government. However, as costs have risen some counties have found it desirable to combine resources and create multi-county laboratories to service their jurisdictions. At this time many of the larger cities in the United States maintain their own crime laboratories, usually under the direction of the local police department. Frequently, high population and crime rates combine to make a municipal facility, such as New York City's or Chicago's, the largest crime laboratory in the state.

Like the United States, most countries in the world have created and now maintain forensic facilities. Reference has already been made to the British regional laboratory system. For the most part, Canadian forensic services are provided by three government-funded institutes: (1) six Royal Canadian Mounted Police regional laboratories, (2) the Centre of Forensic Sciences in Toronto, and (3) the

Institute of Legal Medicine in Montreal. In all, eighty countries are known to have at least one laboratory facility offering services in the field of forensic science.

SERVICES OF THE CRIME LABORATORY

Bearing in mind the independent development of crime laboratories in the U.S., the wide variation in total services offered in different communities is not surprising. There are many reasons for this, among which are: (1) variation in local laws, (2) the different capabilities and functions of the organization to which a laboratory is attached, and (3) budgetary and manpower limitations. Indeed, some crime laboratories have recently been created solely for the purpose of processing drug specimens in response to the ever-increasing number of arrests in this one area of law enforcement.

We can best outline the services of crime laboratories by dividing them into two general groups: (1) basic services offered by all comprehensive crime laboratories, and (2) services that are provided by many but not all crime laboratories. Because crime laboratories have no uniform organizational charts I have taken the liberty of arbitrarily designating units and assigning their responsibilities in the following manner.

Services Provided by All Comprehensive Crime Laboratories

Physical Science Unit. This type of unit applies principles and techniques of chemistry, physics, and geology to the identification and comparison of crime-scene evidence. It is staffed by criminalists who have the expertise to utilize chemical tests and modern analytical instrumentation for the examination of items as diverse as drugs, glass, paint, explosives, and soil. In a laboratory that has a staff large enough to permit specialization, the responsibilities of this unit may be further subdivided into sections devoted to drug identification, soil and mineral analyses, and the examination of a variety of trace physical evidence (see Figure 1–2).

Biology Unit. This group is staffed with biologists and serologists who apply their knowledge to the identification and grouping of dried bloodstains and other body fluids, the comparison of hairs and fibers, and the identification and comparison of botanical materials such as wood and plants.

Firearms Unit. The examination of firearms, discharged bullets, cartridge cases, shotgun shells, and ammunition of all types is con-

FIGURE 1-2. Work area of the chemistry section of the Metropolitan Police Laboratory, London, England

Courtesy Metropolitan Police Laboratory

ducted by this unit. Garments and other objects are also examined in order to detect firearm discharge residues, and to approximate the distance from its target at which a weapon was fired. The basic principles of firearm examination are also applied here to the comparison of marks made by tools.

Document Examination Unit. The handwriting and typewriting on questioned documents is studied by this group to ascertain authenticity and/or source. Related responsibilities also include analysis of paper and ink, as well as examination of indented writings (the term usually applied to the partially visible depressions appearing on a sheet of paper underneath the one on which the visible writing appears), obliterations, erasures, and burned or charred documents.

Photography Unit. A complete photographic laboratory is maintained by this unit to examine and record physical evidence. These procedures may require the use of highly specialized photographic techniques, such as infrared, ultraviolet, and X-ray photography, to make invisible information visible to the naked eye. This unit also aids in the preparation of photographic exhibits for courtroom presentation.

Services Provided by Many Comprehensive Crime Laboratories

Toxicology Unit. Body fluids and organs are examined by this group to determine the presence or absence of drugs and poisons. Frequently, such functions are shared with or may be the sole responsibility of a separate laboratory facility placed under the direction of the medical examiner's or coroner's office.

In most jurisdictions field instruments such as the Breathalyzer are used to determine the amount of alcoholic consumption of individuals. Often the toxicology section has the responsibility of training operators, as well as maintaining and servicing these instruments.

Latent Fingerprint Unit. The responsibility for processing and examining evidence for latent fingerprints when they are submitted in conjunction with other laboratory examinations belongs to this unit.

Polygraph Unit. The polygraph, or lie detector, has come to be recognized as an essential tool of the criminal investigator rather than the forensic scientist. However, during the formative years of polygraph technology many police agencies incorporated this unit into the laboratory's administrative structure, where it sometimes remains today. In any case, its functions are handled by people trained in the techniques of criminal investigation and interrogation.

Voiceprint Analysis Unit. In cases involving telephoned threats or tape-recorded messages, investigators may require the skills of this unit to tie the voice to a particular suspect. To this end a good deal of casework has been performed by the sound spectrograph, an instrument that transforms speech into a visual graphic display called a voiceprint. The validity of this technique as a means of personal identification rests on the premise that the sound patterns produced in speech are unique to the individual and that the voiceprint displays this uniqueness.

Evidence Collection Unit. The concept of incorporating crime-scene evidence collection into the total forensic science service is slowly gaining recognition in the United States. This unit dispatches specially trained personnel (civilian and/or police) to the crime scene to collect and preserve physical evidence that will later be processed at the crime laboratory.

THE FUNCTIONS OF THE FORENSIC SCIENTIST

Analysis of Physical Evidence

First and foremost the forensic scientist must be skilled in applying the principles and techniques of the physical and natural sciences to the analysis of the many types of evidence that may be recovered during crime investigation. However, in doing this the scientist must also be aware of the demands and constraints that are imposed by the judicial system. The procedures and techniques that are utilized in the laboratory must not only rest on a firm scientific foundation, but must also satisfy the criteria of admissibility that has been established by the courts.

In rejecting the scientific validity of the lie detector (polygraph), the District of Columbia Circuit Court in 1923 set forth what has since become the standard guideline for determining the judicial admissibility of scientific examinations. In *Frye* v. *United States*[3] the court stated the following:

> Just when a scientific principle or discovery crosses the line between the experimental and demonstrable stages is difficult to define. Somewhere in this twilight zone the evidential force of the principle must be recognized, and while the courts will go a long way in admitting expert testimony deduced from a well-recognized scientific principle or discovery, the thing from which the deduction is made must be sufficiently established to have gained general acceptance in the particular field in which it belongs.

Courts have usually interpreted the "general acceptance" principle of *Frye* most liberally, and have allowed testimony by experts on a wide range of scientific principles and techniques, leaving it instead

[3] 293 Fed 1013 (1923).

to the jury to weigh the conclusions that the expert derives from the data. It is only when a new technique is introduced into evidence that its relevancy to the criteria of *Frye* is questioned; thus, in some cases the courts have found it necessary to interpret and expand the meaning of *Frye*. For example, a California appellate court in *People* v. *Williams*,[4] when considering a new test for determining narcotic addiction (the Nalline test), weighed the argument that because most physicians had no knowledge of the test this meant that it was not accepted by the *entire* medical profession and therefore did not meet the *Frye* definition of "general acceptance." In rejecting this argument the court recognized the existence and need for specialization within a given field of endeavor. It concluded,

> All of the medical testimony points to the reliability of the test. It has been generally accepted by those who would be expected to be familiar with its use. In this age of specialization no more should be required.

A further refinement of *Frye* was undertaken in 1968 in *Coppolino* v. *Florida*.[5] Here a medical examiner testified to his finding that the victim had died of an overdose of a drug known as succinylcholine chloride. This drug had never before been detected in the human body. The medical examiner's findings were dependent on a toxicological report that identified an abnormally high concentration of succinic acid, a breakdown product of the drug, in the victim's body. The defense argued that this test for the presence of succinylcholine chloride was new and the absence of corroborative experimental data by other scientists meant that it had not yet gained general acceptance in the toxicology profession. The court, in rejecting this argument, recognized the necessity that exists for devising new scientific tests to solve the special problems that are continually arising in the forensic laboratory. It emphasized, however, that though these tests may be new and unique they are admissible only if they are based on scientifically valid principles and techniques:

> The tests by which the medical examiner sought to determine whether death was caused by succinylcholine chloride was novel and devised specifically for this case. This does not render the evidence inadmissible. Society need not tolerate homicide until there develops a body of medical literature about some particular lethal agent.

Provision of Expert Testimony

Because their work product may ultimately be a factor in determining a person's guilt or innocence, forensic scientists may be re-

[4] 164 Cal. App. 2d Supp 848, 331 P. 2d 251 (1958).
[5] 223 So. 2d 68 (Fla. App. 1968), app. dismissed 234 So. 2d (Fla., 1969), cert. denied 399 U.S. 927.

quired to testify with respect to their methods and conclusions at a trial or hearing. Trial courts have broad discretion in accepting an individual as an expert witness on any particular subject. Generally, if a witness can establish to the satisfaction of a trial judge that he or she possesses a particular skill, or has knowledge in a trade or profession that will aid the court in determining the truth of the matter at issue, that individual will be accepted as an expert witness. Depending on the subject area in question the court will usually consider that knowledge acquired through experience or education or a combination of both is sufficient grounds for qualification as an expert witness.

In court, the qualifying questions that are asked of the expert by counsel are often directed toward demonstrating the witness' ability and competence pertaining to the matter at hand. Competency may be established by having him or her cite educational degrees, participation in special courses, membership in professional societies, and any professional articles or books published. Also important to the issue is the number of years of occupational experience in which the witness has engaged in areas related to the matter before the court.

Unfortunately, there are few schools that confer degrees in forensic science. Most chemists, biologists, geologists, or physicists usually prepare themselves for careers in forensic science by combining training under an experienced examiner with independent study. Of course, formal education provides the scientist with a firm foundation for learning and understanding the principles and techniques of forensic science. At present there are no uniform tests or licensing boards for the accreditation or certification of forensic scientists. For the most part, courts must rely on education and years of experience as a measurement of the knowledge and ability of the expert.

Most courts are very reluctant to disqualify an individual as an expert even when presented with someone whose background is only remotely associated with the issue at hand. The question of what credentials are suitable for qualification as an expert is one that is obviously ambiguous and highly subjective, and one that the courts wisely try to avoid. However, the weight that a judge or jury will assign to "expert" testimony in subsequent deliberations is quite another matter. Undoubtedly, education and experience are factors that have considerable bearing on the value assigned to the expert's opinions. Just as important may be the witness' demeanor and ability to explain scientific data and conclusions clearly, concisely, and logically to a judge and jury composed of nonscientists. The problem of sorting out the strengths and weaknesses of expert testimony falls to prosecution and defense counsels, who themselves must endeavor to adequately prepare themselves for this undertaking.

While all other witnesses presented to the court must restrict their testimony to pertinent facts relating to the issue at hand, the expert's testimony is based solely on opinion. Normally, such a witness is called upon to report the results of an examination of some piece of evidence and to express a conclusion to the judge and jury. But this conclusion is accepted as representing the opinion of the expert witness; and this may be an opinion that is later accepted or ignored in their deliberations.

It must be recognized that it is not possible for the expert to render any conclusion with absolute certainty. At best, one may only be able to offer an opinion that is based on a reasonable scientific certainty derived from training and experience. Obviously, the expert is expected to vigorously defend the techniques and conclusions of the analysis, but at the same time there must be no reluctance to discuss impartially those findings that could minimize the significance of the analysis. The forensic scientist should not be an advocate of one party's cause, but only an advocate of truth. An adversary system of justice must give the prosecutor and defense ample opportunity to offer expert opinions and to argue the merits of such testimony. Ultimately, it will be the duty of the judge or jury to weigh the pros and cons of all the information presented in deciding guilt or innocence.

Furnishes Training in the Proper Recognition, Collection, and Preservation of Physical Evidence

The competence of a laboratory staff and the sophistication of its analytical equipment have little or no value if relevant evidence cannot be properly recognized, collected, and preserved at the site of a crime. For this reason, it is important that the forensic staff have responsibilities that will influence the conduct of the crime-scene investigation.

The most direct and effective response to this problem has been to dispatch specially trained evidence-collection technicians to the crime scene. A growing number of crime laboratories and the police agencies they service have recognized the necessity of having trained "evidence technicians" on 24-hour call to aid criminal investigators in retrieving evidence. These technicians are trained by the laboratory staff to recognize and gather pertinent physical evidence at the crime scene. They are administratively assigned to the laboratory to facilitate their continued exposure to forensic techniques and procedures. They have at their disposal all the proper tools and supplies that will make possible the proper collection and packaging of evidence for future scientific examination.

Unfortunately, many police forces have still not adopted this approach. All too often a uniformed officer or detective is charged with the responsibility of collecting the evidence. His (or her) effectiveness in this role will be dependent on the extent of his training and working relationship with the laboratory. If maximum utilization is to be made of the skills of the crime laboratory, training of the crime-scene investigator must go beyond superficial classroom lectures to involve extensive personal contact with the forensic scientist. Each must become aware of the other's problems, techniques, and limitations.

The training of police officers in evidence collection and their familiarization with the capabilities of a crime laboratory should not be restricted to a select group of personnel on the force. Every officer engaged in fieldwork, whether it be traffic, patrol, investigation, or juvenile control, will often have to process evidence for laboratory examination. Obviously, it would be a difficult and time-consuming operation to give everyone the in-depth training and attention that a qualified criminal investigator requires. However, a familiarity with crime laboratory services and capabilities can be facilitated through periodic lectures, laboratory tours, and the dissemination of manuals prepared by the laboratory staff which outline the proper methods for collecting and submitting physical evidence to the laboratory. Examples of such manuals are shown in Figure 1–3.

FIGURE 1-3

A brief outline describing the proper collection and packaging of common types of physical evidence is found in Appendix I. The procedures and information summarized in this guide will be discussed in greater detail in forthcoming chapters.

REVIEW QUESTIONS

1. The application of science to law describes _____ .

2. The fictional exploits of _____ excited the imagination of an emerging generation of forensic scientists and criminal investigators.

3. A system of personal identification using a series of body measurements was first devised by _____ .

4. _____ is responsible for developing the first statistical study proving the uniqueness of fingerprints.

5. The Italian scientist _____ devised the first workable procedure for typing dried bloodstains.

6. The comparison microscope became an indispensable tool of firearm examination through the efforts of _____ .

7. Early efforts at applying scientific principles to document examination are associated with _____ .

8. The application of science to criminal investigation was advocated by the Austrian magistrate _____ .

9. One of the first functional crime laboratories to be formed existed in Lyons, France under the direction of _____ .

10. The state of _____ is an excellent example of a geographical area in the United States that has created a large network of federal, state, county, and city crime laboratories.

11. In contrast to the United States, England's crime laboratory system is characterized by a national system of _____ laboratories.

12. The increasing demand for _____ analyses has been the single most important factor in the recent expansion of crime laboratory services in the United States.

13. Four important agencies offering forensic service at the Federal level are _____ , _____ , _____ , and _____ .

14. A decentralized system of crime laboratories presently exists in the U.S. under the auspices of various governmental agencies at the _____ , _____ , _____ , and _____ levels of government.

15. The application of chemistry, physics and geology to the identi-

fication and comparison of crime scene evidence is the function of the _____ of a crime laboratory.

16. The examination of blood, hairs, fibers and vegetative materials is conducted in the _____ of a crime laboratory.

17. The examination of bullets, cartridge cases, shotgun shells, and ammunition of all types is the responsibility of the _____ _____.

18. The examination of body fluids and organs for drugs and poisons is a function belonging to the _____ _____.

19. The _____ dispatches trained personnel to the scene of a crime to retrieve evidence for laboratory examination.

20. The "general acceptance" principle, which serves as a criterion for the judicial admissability of scientific evidence, was set forth in the case of _____.

21. In the case People v. Williams the court recognized the existence and need for _____ within a given field of endeavor in evaluating the admissability of scientific evidence.

22. In the case of _____ new and unique test results were ruled admissable so long as they were based on scientifically valid principles and techniques.

23. An _____ is one who can demonstrate a particular skill, or has knowledge in a trade or profession that will assist the court in determining the truth of the matter at issue.

24. The witnesses' courtroom demeanor may play an important role in deciding what weight the court will assign to an expert's opinions. (True, False)

25. The ability of the investigator to recognize and collect crime scene evidence properly is dependent on the amount of _____ received at the crime laboratory.

FURTHER READINGS

Berg, Stanton O., "Sherlock Holmes: Father of Scientific Crime Detection," *Journal of Criminal Law, Criminology and Police Science*, 61, no. 3 (1970), pp. 446-52.

Brunelle, Richard L., "Novel Techniques for the Examination of Physical Evidence," *Journal of the Association of Official Analytical Chemists*, 56 (1973), 1391.

Conrad, Edwin, "Landmarks and Hallmarks in Scientific Evidence," in *Sourcebook in Criminalistics*, Carroll Hormachea, ed. Reston, Va.: Reston Publishing Co., 1974.

Doyle, Sir Arthur Conan, *The Complete Sherlock Holmes*, vol. 1. New York: Doubleday, 1956.

Huber, R. A., "I Give You Yesterday," *Journal of the Canadian Society of Forensic Science*, 8 (1975), 1.

Kirk, Paul L., and Lowell W. Bradford, *The Crime Laboratory, Organization and Operation*. Springfield, Ill.: Charles C. Thomas, 1965.

Osterberg, James O., "The Investigative Process," in *Sourcebook in Criminalistics*, Carroll Hormachea, ed. Reston, Va.: Reston Publishing Co., 1974.

Thorwald, Jürgen, *Crime and Science*. New York: Harcourt, Brace and World, 1967.

Thorwald, Jürgen, *The Century of the Detective*. New York: Harcourt, Brace and World, 1964.

Walls, H. J., *Forensic Science*, 2nd ed. New York: Praeger, 1974.

Physical Evidence

chapter 2

RECOGNITION OF PHYSICAL EVIDENCE

As automobiles run on gasoline, crime laboratories "run" on **physical evidence**. Physical evidence encompasses any and all objects that can establish that a crime has been committed or can provide a link between a crime and its victim or a crime and its perpetrator. But if physical evidence is to be effectively used for aiding the investigator, its presence first must be recognized at the crime scene. If *all* the natural and commercial objects within a reasonable distance of a crime were gathered so that the scientist could uncover significant clues from them, the deluge of material would quickly immobilize the laboratory facility. Physical evidence can only achieve its optimum value in criminal investigations when its collection is performed with a selectivity governed by the collector's thorough knowledge of the crime laboratory's techniques, capabilities, and limitations.

It would be impossible to list all the objects that could conceivably be of importance to a crime; every crime scene obviously has to be treated on an individual basis, having its own peculiar history, circumstances, and problems. It is practical, however, to list those items whose scientific examination are likely to yield significant results in ascertaining the nature and circumstances of a crime. The investigator who is thoroughly familiar with the recognition, collection, and analysis of these items, as well as with laboratory procedures and capabilities, can make logical decisions when the uncommon and unexpected are encountered at the crime scene. Just as important, a qualified evidence collector cannot rely on collection procedures memorized from a pamphlet, but must be able to make innovative, on-the-spot decisions at the crime scene.

Common Types of Physical Evidence

1. *Blood, Semen, and Saliva*— All suspected blood, semen, or saliva—liquid or dried, animal or human—present in a form to suggest a relation to the offense or persons involved in a crime. These fluids are subjected to serological and biochemical analysis for determination of identity and possible origin.

2. *Documents*— Any handwriting and typewriting submitted so that authenticity or source can be determined. Related items include paper, ink, indented writings, obliterations, and burned or charred documents.

3. *Drugs*— Includes any substance seized in violation of laws regulating the sale, manufacture, distribution, and use of drugs.

4. *Explosives*— Any device containing an explosive charge, as well as all objects removed from the scene of an explosion that are suspected to contain the residues of an explosive.

5. *Fibers*— Any natural or synthetic fiber whose transfer may be useful in establishing a relationship between objects and/or persons.

6. *Fingerprints*— All prints of this nature, latent and visible, are included.

7. *Firearms and Ammunition*— Any firearm, as well as discharged or intact ammunition, suspected of being involved in a criminal offense.

8. *Glass*— Any glass particle or fragment that may have been transferred to a person or object involved in a crime. Windowpanes containing holes made by a bullet or other projectile are included in this category.

9. *Hair*— Any animal or human hair present that could link a person with a crime.

10. *Impressions*— Includes tire markings, shoe prints, depressions in soft soils, and all other forms of tracks. Glove and other fabric prints are also in this category.

11. *Organs and Physiological Fluids*— Body organs and fluids submitted for toxicology to detect possible existence of drugs and poisons. This category includes blood to be analyzed for the presence of alcohol and other drugs.

12. *Paint*— Any paint, liquid or dried, that may have been transferred from the surface of one object to another during the commission of a crime. A common example is the transfer of paint from one vehicle to another during an automobile collision.

13. *Petroleum Products*— Any petroleum product removed from a suspect or recovered from a crime scene. The most common examples are gasoline residues removed from the scene of an arson, or grease and oil stains whose presence may suggest involvement in a crime.

14. *Powder Residues*— Any item suspected of containing firearm discharge residues.

15. *Serial Numbers*— Includes all stolen property submitted to the laboratory for the restoration of erased identification numbers.

16. *Soils and Minerals*— All items containing soil or minerals that could link a person or object to a particular location. Common examples are soil imbedded in shoes, and safe insulation found on garments.

17. *Toolmarks*— Includes any object suspected of containing the impression of another object that served as a tool in a crime. For example, a screwdriver or crowbar could produce toolmarks by being impressed into or scraped along a surface of a wall.

18. *Wood and other Vegetative Matter*— Any fragments of wood, sawdust, shavings, or vegetative matter discovered on clothing, shoes, or tools, that could link a person or object to a crime location.

SEARCHING FOR PHYSICAL EVIDENCE

The search for physical evidence at a crime scene must be thorough and systematic. Where to search and what to search for will be determined by the particular circumstances of the crime. For a factual, unbiased reconstruction of the crime, the investigator, through his training and experience, must not overlook any pertinent evidence. Even in those cases in which suspects are immediately seized and the motives and circumstances of the crime are readily apparent, it is imperative that a thorough search for physical evidence be conducted at once. Failure in this, even though it may seem at the time to be unnecessary, can lead to accusations of negligence, or charges that the investigative agency knowingly "covered up" evidence that would be detrimental to its case.

Assigning those responsible for searching a crime scene is a function of the investigator in charge. Except in major crimes, or where the evidence is very complex, it is usually not necessary to have the assistance of a forensic scientist at the crime scene; his or her role appropriately begins with the submission of evidence to the crime laboratory. As has already been observed, some police agencies do have trained field evidence technicians to conduct the search for physical evidence at the crime scene. They have the equipment and skill to photograph the scene and examine it for the presence of fingerprints, footprints, toolmarks, or any other type of evidence that may be relevant to the crime.

The actual technique of a search depends to a large degree on the size of the crime scene and the circumstances of the crime. Before starting a search, the crime-scene investigator surveys the scene, noting its dimensions and all probable areas of entry and exit that the perpetrator(s) may have used. Then all major evidence items are photographed, sketched to show relationship to the crime scene, and recorded in notes kept by the investigator, before being appropriately packaged for laboratory examination (Figure 2-1). In the case of a homicide, all obvious evidential material on or near the body is processed before the body is removed for medical examination. After processing the more obvious evidence, the search for and collection of the less obvious trace evidence begins.

Where and how to search for physical evidence is often deter-

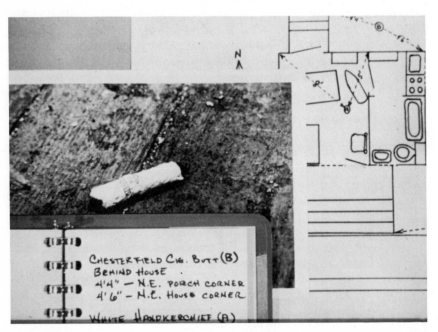

FIGURE 2-1. The finding of an evidential cigarette butt at the crime scene requires photographing it, making a sketch showing its relation to the crime scene, and recording the find in field notes.

Courtesy Police Science Services

mined by the type of evidence the investigator is seeking. For example, in the case of homicides the search will be centered on the weapon and any type of evidence left as a result of contact between the victim and assailant. For a burglary the point of entry must be established and then examined for possible toolmarks. In most crimes a thorough and systematic search for latent fingerprints is required. The investigator may choose to subdivide the scene into segments and search each segment individually. The search may start at a central location and move outward in an ever-widening circle, or it may move from one end of the room or segment to the other, until the entire area has been covered.

Vehicle searches must be carefully planned and systematically carried out. The nature of the case determines how detailed the search must be. In hit-and-run cases the outside and undercarriage of the car must be examined with care. Particular attention is paid to looking for any evidence resulting from a cross-transfer of evidence between the car and the victim—this includes blood, hair, fibers, and fabric impressions. Traces of paint or broken glass may be located on the victim. In cases of homicide, burglary, kidnapping, etc., all areas of the vehicle, inside and outside, are searched with equal care for physical evidence.

Physical evidence can be anything from massive objects to microscopic traces. Often, many of the items described in the previous section are obvious in their presence, while others can only be detected through examination in the crime laboratory. For example, minute traces of blood may be discovered in garments only after a thorough search in the laboratory; or the presence of hairs and fibers may be revealed in vacuum sweepings only after close laboratory scrutiny. For this reason, it is important to collect *possible* carriers of trace evidence in addition to more discernible items. Hence, it may be necessary to take custody of all clothing worn by the participants in a crime. Each clothing item should be handled carefully and wrapped separately to avoid loss of trace materials. All of it should be sent to the laboratory for examination. In the case of a deceased victim, arrangements must be made with the medical examiner or coroner to obtain such things as clothing, fingernail scrapings, and blood, head, and pubic hairs if the nature of the case warrants it. Additionally, critical areas of the crime scene should be vacuumed and the sweepings submitted to the laboratory for analysis. The sweepings from different areas must be collected and packaged separately. A portable vacuum cleaner equipped with a special filter attachment is suitable for this purpose (see Figure 2-2).

In recent years many police departments have gone to the ex-

FIGURE 2-2. Vacuum Sweeper Attachment. Constructed of clear plastic in two pieces that are joined by a threaded joint. A metal screen is mounted in one half to support a filter paper to collect debris. The unit attaches to the hose of the vacuum sweeper.

Courtesy Sirchie Laboratories, Inc.

FIGURE 2-3. Evidence Collection Vehicle

Courtesy Sirchie Laboratories, Inc.

pense of purchasing and equipping "mobile crime laboratories" (see Figure 2-3) for their evidence technicians. However, the term "mobile crime laboratory" is a misnomer. These vehicles carry the necessary supplies to protect the crime scene, collect and package physical evidence, and perform latent print development. They are not designed to carry out the functions of a chemical laboratory. "Crime-scene search vehicle" would be a more appropriate, but perhaps less dramatic name for such a vehicle.

COLLECTING AND PRESERVING PHYSICAL EVIDENCE

The forensic scientist seldom personally supervises the collection of evidence at the crime scene; he must depend on the field investigator's ability to recognize, collect, and preserve relevant evidence. It is important that the investigator takes care to maintain the scientific integrity of recovered evidence. Furthermore, he or she must be well aware of the requirements that will arise out of the future utilization of such evidence in a legal proceeding.

Physical evidence must be handled and processed in a way that prevents any change from taking place between the time it is removed from the crime scene and the time it is received by the crime laboratory. Changes can arise through such things as contamination, breakage, evaporation, accidental scratching or bending, or loss through improper or careless packaging. The integrity of evidence is best maintained when it is kept in its original state unless size prohibits convenient transportation to the laboratory. Whenever possible, no alterations are made in any item that is or may be evidence; blood, hairs, fibers, soils, and other types of trace evidence are best not removed from the objects that bear them.

The well-prepared evidence collector will arrive at a scene with a large assortment of packaging material and tools ready to encounter any type of situation. Tweezers, forceps, and similar tools may have to be used to pick up small items and place them in appropriate containers. Unbreakable plastic pill bottles with pressure lids are excellent containers for hairs, fibers, glass, and various types of small or trace evidence. Trace quantitites of evidence may also be conveniently packaged in a carefully folded paper, using what is known as a "druggist fold." This consists of folding the paper over one-third, then folding the other third over that, and repeating the process on the sides. After being completely folded in this manner, the edges are tucked into each other to produce a closed container that keeps the specimen from falling out. Plastic envelopes of various shapes and sizes also make versatile evidence containers; however, the accumulation of moisture in airtight containers may encourage the growth of mold that can destroy the evidential value of blood-stained materials. In these instances, wrapping paper or paper bags are recommended packaging material. Charred debris recovered from the scene of a suspicious fire *must* be sealed in an airtight container, however, to prevent the evaporation of petroleum residues. New paint cans or tightly sealed jars are recommended in such situations.

A detailed description of the proper collection and packaging of various types of physical evidence will be discussed in forthcoming chapters; additionally, most of this information is summarized in the Evidence Guide found in Appendix I.

The examination of evidence, whether it is soil, blood, glass, hair, fibers, etc., often requires comparison with a known standard or a control. Although most investigators have little difficulty in recognizing and collecting relevant crime-scene evidence, few seem aware of the like necessity and importance of providing the crime lab with a thorough sampling of control materials. Such materials may be obtained from the victim, a suspect, or other sources. Because they have equal value with actual physical evidence, they must be treated with equal care. Therefore, thorough and proper collection and packaging of accompanying control specimens is the mark of a skilled investigator.

Continuity of possession, or the chain of custody, must be established whenever evidence is presented in court as an exhibit. Adherence to standard procedures in recording the location of evidence, marking it for identification, and properly completing evidence submission forms for laboratory analysis, is the best guarantee that the evidence will withstand inquiries of what happened to it from the time of its findings to its presentation in court.

The discovery of each item must be accompanied by detailed notes reflecting the description and location of the item; by whom and when it was discovered; and how it was packaged, marked, and transported to the laboratory for examination. In many cases, it is convenient to supplement these notes with photographs and sketches of the undisturbed evidence. Such pictures should show the location of the evidence as well as the evidence itself.

The marking of physical specimens serves to identify them and should be done with utmost care to avoid destroying their evidential value or restricting the number and kind of examinations to which they will be subjected by the criminalist. If at all possible, the evidence should be marked for identification with the collector's initials and the date of collection. In all cases in which physical evidence is packaged, the container must also be marked or tagged for identification. A minimum record would show the collector's initials, location of the evidence, and date of collection.

Frequently, all of the investigators involved in the collection and transportation of the evidence may be requested to testify in court. Thus, to avoid confusion and to retain complete control of the evidence at all times, the chain of custody should be kept to a minimum. It is desirable that a single individual collect, mark, and transport the evidence to the crime laboratory.

THE NATURE OF PHYSICAL EVIDENCE

The examination of physical evidence by a forensic scientist is usually undertaken for identification or comparison.

Identification

Identification has as its purpose the determination of the physical or chemical identity of a substance with as near absolute certainty as existing analytical techniques will permit. For example, the crime laboratory is frequently requested to identify the chemical composition of an illicit drug preparation that may contain heroin, cocaine, barbiturates, etc. It may be asked to identify residues recovered from the debris of a fire, or it may have to identify the nature of explosive residues—e.g., dynamite or TNT. Each of these requests requires the analysis and ultimate identification of a specific chemical substance to the exclusion of all other possible chemicals.

The process of identification first requires the adoption of testing procedures that give characteristic results for specific standard materials. Once these test results have been established, they may be permanently recorded and used repeatedly to prove the identity of suspect materials. For example, if one wants to ascertain that a particular suspect powder is heroin, the test results on the powder must be identical to those that have been previously obtained from a known heroin sample. Secondly, identification requires that the number and type of tests needed to identify a substance be sufficient to exclude all other substances. This means that the examiner must devise a specific analytical scheme that will eliminate all but one chemical substance from consideration. Hence, if a conclusion is reached that a white powder contains heroin, the examiner's test results must have been comprehensive enough to have excluded all other drugs, or for that matter all other substances, from consideration.

Simple rules cannot be devised for defining what constitutes a thorough and foolproof analytical scheme. Each type of evidence obviously requires different tests, and each test has a different degree of specificity. Thus, one substance could conceivably be identified by one test, while another may require the combination of five or six different tests to arrive at an identification. In a science in which the practitioner has little or no control over the quality and quantity of the specimens received, a standard series of tests cannot encompass all possible problems and pitfalls. So, it is left to the forensic scientist to determine at what point the analysis can be concluded and the criteria for positive identification satisfied; for this, he/she must rely on knowledge gained through education and experience. Ultimately, the conclusion will have to be substantiated beyond any reasonable doubt in a court of law.

Comparison

A comparative analysis subjects a suspect and a control specimen to the same tests and examinations for the ultimate purpose of determining whether or not they have a common origin. For example, the forensic scientist may assist in placing a suspect at a particular location by noting the similarities of a hair found at the crime scene to hairs removed from a suspect's head. Or a paint chip found on a hit-and-run victim's garment may have to be compared with paint removed from a vehicle suspected of being involved in the incident. The forensic comparison is actually a two-step procedure: first, a combination of select properties are chosen from the suspect and the control specimen for comparison. The question of which and how many properties are to be selected will obviously depend on the type of materials being examined. (This is a subject that will receive a good deal of discussion in forthcoming chapters.) The overriding consideration must be the ultimate evidential value of the conclusion. This brings us to the second objective: once the examination has been completed, the forensic scientist must be prepared to render a conclusion with respect to the origin of the specimen. Do they or do they not come from the same source? Certainly if one or more of the properties selected for comparison do not agree, the analyst will not hesitate in concluding that the specimens are not the same, and hence could not originate from the same source. Suppose, on the other hand, that all the properties do compare and the specimens, as far as the examiner can determine, are indistinguishable. Does it logically follow that they come from the same source? Not necessarily so.

In order to comprehend the evidential value of a comparison, one must appreciate the role that probability has in ascertaining the origin of two or more specimens. Simply defined, probability is the frequency of occurrence of an event. If a coin is flipped one hundred times, in theory we can expect heads to come up fifty times. Hence, the probability of the event (heads) occurring is fifty in a hundred. In other words, probability defines the odds at which a certain event will occur.

Individual and Class Characteristics. Evidence that can be associated with a common source with an extremely high degree of probability is said to possess **individual characteristics**. Examples of this are the matching ridge characteristics of two fingerprints, the comparison of random striation markings on bullets or toolmarks, the comparison of irregular and random wear patterns in tire or footwear impressions, the comparison of handwriting characteristics, or the fitting together of the irregular edges of broken objects in the manner of a jigsaw puzzle (Figure 2-4). In all of these cases it is not possible to state with mathematical exactness the probability that the specimens are of common origin; it can only be concluded that this probability is so high as to defy mathematical calculations or human comprehension. Furthermore, the conclusion of common origin must be substantiated by the practical experience of the examiner. For example, the French scientist Victor Balthazard has mathematically determined that the probability of two individuals having the same fingerprints is one out of 1×10^{60}, or 1 followed by 60 zeros. This number is so small as to exclude the possibility of any two individuals having the same fingerprints. This contention is also supported by the experience of fingerprint examiners who,

FIGURE 2-4. The body of a woman was found with evidence of beating about the head and a stab-like wound in the neck. Her husband was charged with the murder. The pathologist found a knife blade tip in the wound in the neck. The knife blade tip was compared with the broken blade of a pen knife found in the trousers pocket of the accused. Note that in addition to the fit of the indentations on the edges there are scratch marks running across the blade tip corresponding in detail to those on the broken blade.

Courtesy Centre of Forensic Sciences

after classifying millions of prints over the past seventy years, have never found any two to be exactly alike.

One of the disappointments awaiting the investigator unfamiliar with the limitations of forensic science is the frequent inability of the laboratory to relate physical evidence to a common origin with a high degree of probability. Such evidence possesses **class characteristics**, because it can only be associated with a group and never with a single source. Here again probability is a determining factor. For example, if we were to compare two one-layer automobile paint chips of a similar color, the chances of their having originated from the same car is not nearly as great as when we compare two paint chips each having *seven* similar layers of paint, not all of which were part of the car's original color. The former will have class characteristics and could only be associated at best to one car model (which may number in the thousands), while the latter may be judged to have individual characteristics and to have a high probability of originating from one specific car.

Blood offers another good example of evidence that has class characteristics. For example, two blood specimens are compared; both are found to be of human origin, and both are typed as O. The frequency of occurrence in the population of type O blood is 43 percent—hardly offering a basis for establishing the common origin of the stains. However, if other blood factors are also determined in each stain and are found to compare, the probability that the two stains originated from a common source increases. The following types may be used as an illustration:

Type	Frequency
O	43%
D	85%
PGM 2	5.5%
Ak 2-1	9%
N	22%
EAP A	13%

The product of all the frequencies shown above will determine the probability that any one individual will possess such a combination of blood types. In this instance, 0.005 percent or 5 in 100,000 would be expected to have this particular combination of blood types. Although the forensic scientist has still not individualized the bloodstains to one person, data has been provided that will permit the investigator and the court to better assess the evidential value of the two stains.

One of the present weaknesses of forensic science is the inability of the examiner to assign exact or even approximate probability values to the comparison of most class evidence. For example, what is the probability that a red nylon fiber originated from a particular sweater, or that a glass chip came from a particular window broken during the commission of a burglary, or that a red paint chip came from a suspect car involved in a hit-and-run accident? There is very little statistical data available from which to derive this information, and in a society that is increasingly dependent on mass-produced products the gathering of such data is becoming an increasingly elusive goal. One of the primary endeavors of forensic scientists must be to create and update statistical data bases for class evidence. Of course, when such information—e.g., the population frequency of blood types—is available, it is utilized; but for the most part the forensic scientist must rely on personal experience when he is called upon to interpret the significance of class evidence. Nevertheless, its value must not be underestimated. In an era in which criminal investigators have come to rely less on suspect interrogation and more on physical evidence, scientifically evaluated evidence can provide corroboration of events that is as nearly as possible free of human error and bias.

Physical evidence may also serve to exclude or exonerate a person from suspicion. For instance, if type A blood is linked to the suspect, all individuals that have types B, AB, and O blood can be eliminated from consideration. Because it is not possible to assess at the crime scene what value, if any, the scientist will find in the evidence collected, or what significance such findings will ultimately have to a jury, it is imperative that the thorough collection and scientific evaluation of physical evidence become a routine part of all criminal investigations.

Just when physical evidence crosses the line that distinguishes class from individual is a most difficult question to answer and is often the source of heated debate and honest disagreement among forensic scientists. How many striations are necessary to individualize a mark to a single tool and no other? How many color layers will individualize a paint chip to a single car? How many ridge characteristics individualize a fingerprint, and how many handwriting characteristics will tie a person to a signature? These are all questions that defy simple solutions. It is the task of the forensic scientist to find as many characteristics as possible to distinguish one substance from another. The significance that is attached to the findings is a matter that is decided by the quality of the evidence, case history, and the examiner's experience. Ultimately, the conclusion can range from mere speculation to near certainty.

There are practical limits to the properties and characteristics the forensic scientist can select for comparison. Carried to the extreme, no two things in this world are alike in every detail. Modern analytical techniques have become so sophisticated and sensitive that the criminalist must be careful to define the limits of natural variation that exist among materials when interpreting the data gathered from a comparative analysis. For example, we will learn in the next chapter that two properties, density and refractive index, are best suited for comparing glass. Yet the latest techniques that have been developed to measure these properties are so sensitive that they can detect small variations over a single pane of window glass. Certainly, this goes beyond the desires of the criminalist who is just trying to determine whether two glass particles originated from the same window. Similarly, if the surface of a paint chip is magnified 1600 times with a powerful scanning electron microscope, it is apparent that the fine details that are revealed could not be duplicated in any other paint chip. Under these circumstances no two paint chips could ever compare in the true sense of the word. Therefore, practicality dictates that such examinations be conducted at a less revealing, but more meaningful, magnification (see Figure 2–5(a) and (b)).

Distinguishing evidential variations from natural variations is not always an easy task. Learning how to properly use the microscope and all the other modern instruments in a crime laboratory is one thing; gaining the proficiency needed to interpret the observations and data is another. As new crime laboratories are created and others expand to meet the requirements of the law enforcement community, many individuals are starting new careers in forensic science. They must be cautioned that merely reading relevant textbooks and journals is not and cannot be a substitute for experience in this most practical of sciences.

REVIEW QUESTIONS

1. The term _____ encompasses all objects that can establish whether a crime has been committed or can provide a link between a crime and its victim or perpetrator.

2. The forensic scientist's role in a criminal investigation usually begins after a properly trained crime scene investigator retrieves the physical evidence. (True, False)

3. One of the first tasks of the crime scene investigator is to _____ all relevent physical evidence as well as to _____ their location relative to the entire crime site.

4. A detailed search of the crime scene for physical evidence must be conducted in a _____ manner.

5. Besides the more obvious items of physical evidence possible

FIGURE 2-5a. Two layer paint chip magnified 244 times with a scanning electron microscope.

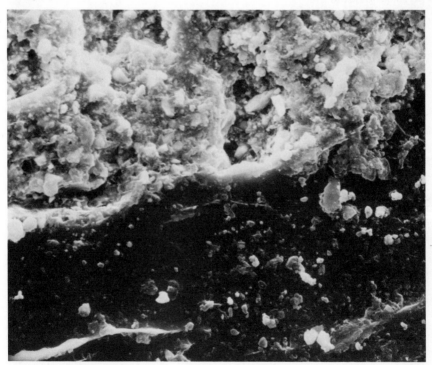

FIGURE 2-5b. The same paint chip as viewed at a magnification of 1600 times.

Courtesy Jeff Albright

_____ of trace evidence must be collected and properly packaged by the crime scene investigator.

6. In cooperation with the medical examiner or coroner, what type of evidence retrieved from a deceased victim is to be submitted to the crime laboratory for examination? _____

7. Recovered evidence must be protected from change between the time of its recovery and submission to the laboratory so as to protect its _____.

8. An air tight container (is, is not) recommended packaging material for bloodstained garments.

9. Charred debris recovered from the scene of an arson is best placed in a porous container. (True, False)

10. Whenever possible, trace evidence (is, is not) to be removed from the object that bears it.

11. Most physical evidence collected at the crime site will require the accompanying submission of _____ material for comparison purposes.

12. The possibility of future legal proceedings requires that a _____ _____ be established with respect to the possession and location of physical evidence.

13. Evidence should be marked without any consideration for the ultimate effect this will have on its evidential value. (True, False)

14. The process of _____ determines a substance's physical or chemical identity with as near absolute certainty as existing analytical techniques will permit.

15. A _____ analysis subjects a suspect and control specimen to the same tests and examination for the ultimate purpose of determining whether they have a common origin.

16. _____ is the frequency of occurrence of an event.

17. Evidence that can be traced to a common source with an extremely high degree of probability is said to possess _____ characteristics.

18. Evidence associated with a group and not to a single source is said to possess _____ characteristics.

19. One of the major deficiencies of forensic science is the inability of the examiner to assign exact or approximate probability values to the comparison of most class evidence. (True, False)

20. Modern analytical techniques have become so sensitive that the forensic examiner must be aware of the _____ that exists among materials when interpreting the significance of comparative data.

FURTHER READINGS

Fox, Richard H., and Carl L. Cunningham, *Crime Scene Search and Physical Evidence Handbook*. Washington, D.C.: U.S. Government Printing Office, 1973.

O'Hara, Charles E., and James W. Osterburg, *An Introduction to Criminalistics*, 2nd ed. Bloomington, Ind.: University Press, 1972.

Parker, Brian, and Joseph L. Peterson, *Physical Evidence Utilization in the Administration of Criminal Justice*. Washington D.C.: U.S. Government Printing Office, 1972.

Peterson, Joseph L., *The Utilization of Criminalistic Services by the Police*. Washington, D.C.: U.S. Government Printing Office, 1974.

Svensson, Arne, and Otto Wendel, *Techniques of Crime Scene Investigation*, 2nd American ed., New York: American Elsevier, 1965.

Weston, Paul B., and Kenneth M. Wells, *Criminal Investigation*, 2nd ed. Englewood Cliffs, N.J.: Prentice-Hall, 1974.

Audiovisual Presentations

Physical Evidence (eighty 35 mm slides and audio tape). Police Science Services, Arlington, Va.

The Crime Scene (filmstrip and audio tape). Robert J. Brady Co., Bowie, Md.

Care, Custody and Control (filmstrip and audio tape). Robert J. Brady Co., Bowie, Md.

Physical Properties :
Glass and Soil

chapter 3

The forensic scientist must constantly determine those properties that impart distinguishing characteristics to matter, giving it a unique identity. The search for distinctive properties is a continuing one and ends only when the scientist has completely individualized a substance, thereby leading to the one correct person or source. Properties are the identifying characteristics of substances. In this and succeeding chapters we will examine properties that are most useful for characterizing soil, glass and other physical evidence. However, before we begin this task, our understanding of the nature of properties can be made easier by classifying them into two broad categories, **physical and chemical**.

Physical properties describe a substance without reference to any other substance. For example, weight, volume, color, boiling point, and melting point are typical physical properties that can be measured for a particular substance without reference to other materials; they are associated only with the physical existence of that substance. A chemical property describes the behavior of a substance when it reacts or combines with another substance. For example, when wood burns, it chemically combines with the oxygen in air to form new substances; this transformation describes a chemical property of wood. In the crime laboratory a routine procedure for determining the presence of heroin in a suspect specimen is to react it with a chemical reagent known as Marquis reagent. In the presence of heroin, Marquis reagent turns purple. This color transformation thus becomes a chemical property of heroin and provides a convenient test for its identification.

Which physical and chemical properties the forensic scientist ultimately chooses to observe and measure depends on the type of material that is being examined. Logic requires, however, that if the property can be assigned a numerical value, it must be one that relates to a standard system of measurement accepted throughout the scientific community.

THE METRIC SYSTEM

Although scientists throughout the world have been using the metric system of measurement for more than a century, the United States still uses the cumbersome "English System" to express length in inches, feet, or yards; weight in ounces or pounds; and volume in pints or quarts. The inherent difficulty of this system is that no simple numerical relationship exists between the various units of measurement. For example, to convert inches to feet one must know that one foot is equal to twelve inches; the conversion of ounces to pounds requires the knowledge that sixteen ounces is equivalent to one pound. In 1791, the French Academy of Science devised the simple system of measurement known as the metric system. This system uses a simple decimal relationship so that a unit of length, volume, or mass can be converted into a subunit by simply multiplying or dividing by a multiple of ten—e.g., 10, 100 or 1,000.

Even though the United States has not yet adopted the metric system, its system of currency is decimal and hence analogous to the metric system. The basic unit of currency is the dollar, a dollar is divided into ten equal units called dimes, and each dime is further divided into ten equal units of cents.

The metric system has **basic units** of measurement for length, mass, and volume; they are the **meter, gram,** and **liter,** respectively. These three basic units can be converted into subunits that are decimal multiples of the basic unit by simply attaching a prefix to the unit name. The following are common prefixes and their equivalent decimal value:

Prefix	Equivalent Value
deci	1/10 or 0.1
centi	1/100 or 0.01
milli	1/1,000 or 0.001
micro	1/1,000,000 or 0.000001
nano	1/1,000,000,000 or 0.000000001
kilo	1,000
mega	1,000,000

Hence, 1/10 or 0.1 of a gram is the same as a **deci**gram (dg), 1/100 or 0.01 of a meter is equal to a **centi**meter (cm), and 1/1000 of a liter is a **milli**liter (ml). A metric conversion is simply carried out by moving the decimal point to the right or left and inserting the proper prefix to show the direction and number of places that the decimal point has been moved. For example, if the weight of a powder is 0.0165 gram it may be more convenient to multiply this value by 100 and express it as 1.65 centigrams or by 1,000 to show it as its equivalent value of 16.5 milligrams. Similarly, an object that weighs 264,450 grams may be expressed as 264.450 kilograms simply by dividing it by 1,000. It is important to remember that in any of these conversions the value of the measurement has not changed; 0.0165 gram is still equivalent to 1.65 centigrams, just as one dollar is still equal to 100 cents. We have simply adjusted the position of the decimal and shown the extent of the adjustment with a prefix.

One interesting aspect of the metric system is that volume can be defined in terms of length. A liter by definition is the volume of a cube, each side having a length of 10 centimeters. One liter is therefore equivalent to a volume of 10cm × 10cm × 10cm, or 1,000 cubic centimeters (cc). Thus, one-thousandth of a liter or one milliliter (ml) is equal to one cubic centimeter (cc). It is common for scientists to use the subunits ml and cc interchangeably to express volume.

At times, it may be necessary to convert units from the metric system into the English system, or vice versa (see Figure 3–1). In order to accomplish this, we must consult references that list English units and their metric equivalents. Some of the more useful equivalents are shown below:

        1 inch   = 2.54 centimeters
        1 meter   = 39.37 inches
        1 pound   = 453.6 grams
        1 liter   = 1.06 quarts
        1 kilogram   = 2.2 pounds

The general mathematical procedures for converting from one system to another can be illustrated by the conversion of 12 inches into centimeters. To change inches into centimeters we need to know that there are 2.54 centimeters per inch. Hence, if we multiply 12 inches by 2.54 centimeter/inch (12 in × 2.54 cm/in), the unit of inches will cancel out, leaving the product 30.48 cm. Similarly, applying the conversion of grams to pounds, 227 grams is equivalent to 227 gm × 1 lb/453.6 gm or 0.5 lb.

PHYSICAL PROPERTIES

Temperature

The determination of the physical properties of any material will often require the measurement of temperature. For instance, the temperatures at which a substance melts or boils are readily determinable characteristics that will help identify a substance. Temperature is a measure of heat energy, or the hotness or coldness of a substance. Temperature is usually measured by causing a thermometer to come into contact with a substance. The familiar mercury-in-glass thermometer functions because mercury expands more than glass when heated and contracts more than glass when cooled. Thus, the length of the mercury column in the glass tube provides a measure of the surrounding environment's temperature. The construction of a temperature scale requires two reference points and a choice of units. The reference points most conveniently chosen are the freezing point and boiling point of water. The two most common temperature scales used are the Fahrenheit and Celsius (formerly called Centigrade) scales.

The Fahrenheit scale is based on the assignment of the value 32°F to the freezing point of water and 212°F to its boiling point. The difference between the two points is evenly divided into 180 units. Thus, a degree Fahrenheit is 1/180th of the temperature change between the freezing point and boiling point of water. The Celsius scale is derived by assigning the freezing point of water a value of

FIGURE 3–1. Comparison of the metric and English systems of length measurement; 2.54 centimeters = 1 inch.

0°C and its boiling point a value of 100°C. A degree Celsius is thus 1/100th of the temperature change between the two reference points. Scientists in most countries use the Celsius scale to measure temperature. A comparison of the two scales is shown in Figure 3-2.

Weight and Mass

The force with which gravity attracts a body is called weight. If your weight is 180 lbs, this means that earth's gravity is pulling you down with a force of 180 lbs; on the moon, where the force of

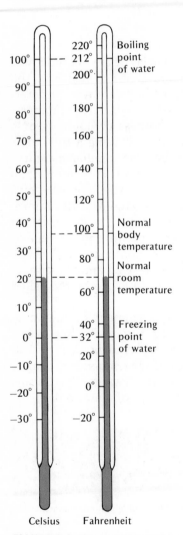

FIGURE 3-2. Comparison of Celsius and Fahrenheit Temperature Scales.

gravity is one-sixth that of earth, your weight would be 30 lbs. Mass differs from weight because it refers to the amount of matter an object contains, and is independent of its location on earth or any other place in the universe. The mathematical relationship between weight (w), and mass (m) is shown in Equation 3-1, where g is the acceleration imparted to a body by the force of gravity.

$$W = mg \qquad\qquad (3\text{-}1)$$

The weight of a body is seen to be directly proportional to its mass; hence, a large mass weighs more than a small mass.

In the metric system it is always the mass of an object rather than its weight that is specified. The basic unit of mass is the gram. An object that has a mass of 40 grams on earth will have a mass of 40 grams anywhere else in this universe. Normally however, the terms "mass" and "weight" are used interchangeably, and we often speak of the weight of an object when we really mean its mass.

The mass of an object is determined by comparing it against the known mass of standard objects. This comparison is confusingly called weighing and the standard objects are called weights (masses would be a more correct term). The comparison is performed on a *balance*. The simplest type of balance for weighing is the equal-arm balance shown in Figure 3-3. The object to be weighed is placed on the left pan and the standard weights are placed on the right pan; when the pointer between the two pans is at the center mark, the

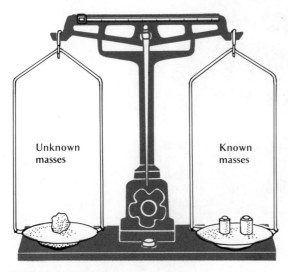

FIGURE 3-3. The Measurement of Mass.

total mass on the right pan is equal to the mass of the object on the left pan.

The modern laboratory has progressed beyond the simple equal-arm balance, and either the top-loading balance or the single-pan analytical balance (Figure 3-4) is now likely to be used. The choice depends on the accuracy required and the amount of material being weighed. Each works on the same counterbalancing principle as the simple equal-arm balance, only here the second pan, the one on which the standard weights are placed, is hidden from view within the balance's housing. Once the object whose weight is to be determined is placed on the visible pan, the operator selects the proper standard weights (also contained within the housing) by manually turning a set of knobs located on the front side of the balance. At the point of balance, the weights selected are automatically recorded on digital and optical readout scales. The top-loading balance can accurately weigh an object to the nearest one milligram or 0.001 gram; the analytical balance is even more accurate, weighing to the nearest tenth of a milligram or 0.0001 gram.

FIGURE 3-4a. Top-loading Balance.
Courtesy Mettler Instrument Corp.

FIGURE 3-4b. Single-pan Analytical Balance.
Courtesy Mettler Instrument Corp.

Density

A most important physical property of matter with respect to the analysis of certain kinds of physical evidence is density. Density is defined as mass per unit volume (Equation 3-2).

$$\text{density} = \frac{\text{mass}}{\text{volume}} \tag{3-2}$$

Density is an intensive property of matter—that is, it is the same regardless of the size of a substance; thus, it is a characteristic property of a substance and can be used as an aid in identification. Solids tend to be more dense than liquids, and liquids more dense than gases. The densities of some common substances are shown in Table 3-1.

A simple procedure for determining the density of a solid is il-

TABLE 3-1. Densities of Selected Materials
(at 20°C unless otherwise stated)

Substance	Density (g/ml)
Solids	
Silver	10.5
Lead	11.3
Iron	7.8
Aluminum	2.7
Window Glass	2.47–2.56
Ice (0°C)	0.92
Liquids	
Mercury	13.6
Benzene	0.88
Ethyl Alcohol	0.79
Gasoline	0.68
Water at 4°C	1.00
Water at 20°C	0.998
Gases	
Air (0°C)	0.0013
Chlorine (0°C)	0.0032
Oxygen (0°C)	0.0014
Carbon Dioxide (0°C)	0.0020

lustrated in Figure 3-5. First, the solid is weighed on a balance against known standard gram weights and its mass is determined. The solid's volume is then determined from the volume of water it displaces. This is easily measured by filling a cylinder with a known volume of water, (V_1) adding the object, and measuring the new water level (V_2). The difference V_2 - V_1 in ml is equal to the volume of the solid. Density can now be calculated from Equation 3-2, in the unit of grams per milliliter.

The volumes of gases and liquids vary considerably with temperature; hence, when determining density it is important to control and record the temperature at which the measurements are made. For example, one gram of water occupies a volume of one milliliter at 4°C and thus has a density of 1.0 g/ml. However, as the temperature of water increases, its volume will expand. Therefore, at 20°C (room temperature) one gram of water will occupy a volume of 1.002 ml and will have a density of 0.998 g/ml.

The observation that a solid object will either sink, float, or remain suspended when immersed in a liquid is one that can be ac-

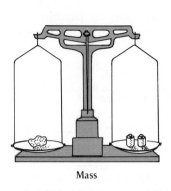

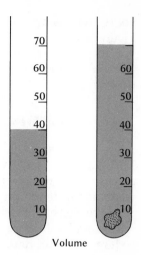

FIGURE 3-5. A simple procedure for determining the density of a solid is to first weigh it and then measure its volume by noting the volume of water it displaces.

counted for by the property of density. For instance, if the density of a solid is greater than the liquid medium in which it is immersed, the object will sink; if the solid has a density that is less than the liquid, it will float; and when the solid and liquid both have equal densities, the solid will remain suspended in the liquid medium. As we will shortly see, these observations provide the criminalist with a convenient technique for comparing the densities of solid objects.

Refractive Index

Light, as we will learn in the next chapter, can have the property of a wave. Lightwaves travel in air at a constant velocity of nearly 300,000,000 meters per second until they penetrate another medium, such as glass or water, at which point they are suddenly slowed, causing the rays to bend. The bending of a lightwave because of a change in velocity is called **refraction**.

The phenomenon of refraction is apparent when we view an object that is immersed in a transparent medium; because we are accustomed to thinking that light travels in a straight line, we often forget to take refraction into account. For instance, suppose a ball is observed at the bottom of a pool of water; the light rays reflected from the ball will travel through the water and into the air to reach the eye. As the rays leave the water and enter the air, their velocity suddenly increases, causing them to be refracted. However, because of our assumption that light travels in a straight line, our eyes deceive us and make us think we see an object lying at a higher point than is actually the case. This phenomenon is illustrated in Figure 3-6.

The ratio of the velocity of light in a vacuum to that in any medium determines the refractive index of that medium and is expressed as:

$$\text{Refractive index} = \frac{\text{velocity of light in vacuum}}{\text{velocity of light in medium}} \qquad (3\text{-}3)$$

For example, at 25°C the refractive index of water is 1.333. This means that light travels 1.333 times faster in a vacuum than it does in water at this temperature.

Like density, refractive index is an intensive physical property of matter and will serve to characterize a substance. However, any procedure used to determine a substance's refractive index must be performed under carefully controlled temperature and lighting conditions, because the refractive index of a substance varies with its temperature and the frequency or wavelength of light passing through it. Nearly all tabulated refractive indices are determined at a standard wavelength, usually 589.3 nanometers; this is the predominant wavelength emitted by sodium light and is commonly known as the sodium D line.

When a transparent solid is immersed in a liquid having a similar refractive index, light will not be refracted as it passes from the liquid into the solid. For this reason, the eye will not be able to distinguish the liquid-solid boundary and the solid seems to disappear from view. This observation, as we will see, offers the forensic

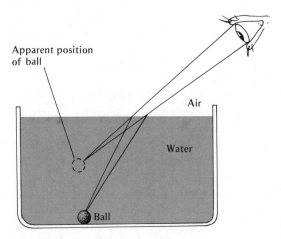

FIGURE 3-6. Light is Refracted When it Travels Obliquely From One Medium to Another.

scientist a rather simple method for comparing the refractive indices of transparent solids.

Normally, a solid or a liquid would be expected to exhibit only one refractive index value for each frequency of light; however, many solids that are crystalline in nature will have two refractive indices whose values in part depend on the direction in which the light enters the crystal with respect to the crystal axis. Solids that are crystalline have definite geometric forms because of the orderly arrangement of the fundamental particle of a solid, the atom. In any type of crystal the relative location and distance between its atoms is repetitive throughout the solid. Figure 3-7 shows the crystalline structure of sodium chloride, or ordinary table salt. Sodium chloride is an example of a cubic crystal in which each sodium is surrounded by six chloride atoms and each chloride by six sodium atoms, except at the crystal surface. Not all solids are crystalline in nature; some, such as glass, have their atoms arranged randomly throughout the solid; these materials are known as **amorphous solids.**

Most crystals, excluding those that have cubic configurations, will refract a single frequency of light into two different light-ray components. This phenomenon is known as double refraction and can be illustrated by studying the behavior of the crystal calcite. When calcite is laid on a printed page, the observer sees not one but two images of each word covered. The two light rays that give rise to the double image are refracted at different angles, and each has a different refractive index value. The indices of refraction for calcite are 1.486 and 1.658, and subtracting the two values yields a difference of 0.172; this difference is also known as **birefringence.** The

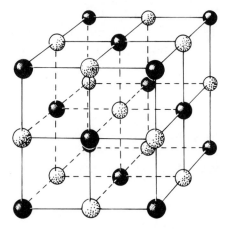

FIGURE 3-7. Diagram of a sodium chloride crystal. Sodium is represented by the black spheres, chlorine by the white spheres.

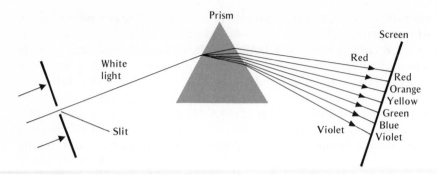

FIGURE 3-8. Representation of the Dispersion of Light by a Glass Prism.

optical properties of crystals provide points of identification that will help characterize a crystal.

Many of us have at one time or another had the experience of holding a glass prism up toward the sunlight and watching it transform light into the colors of the rainbow. This observation serves to demonstrate that visible "white light" is not homogeneous but is actually composed of many different component colors. The process of separating light into component colors is called **dispersion**. The ability of a prism to disperse light into its component colors is explained by the property of refraction. Each color component of light, on passing through the glass, will be slowed to a speed slightly different from the others, thus causing each to bend at a different angle as it emerges from the prism. As shown in Figure 3-8, the component color of visible light extends from red to violet. We will learn in Chapter 4 that each color actually corresponds to a different range of frequencies or wavelengths of light. Dispersion thus separates light into its component frequencies and demonstrates that glass has a slightly different index of refraction for each frequency of light passing through it.

GLASS AND SOIL

Now that we have investigated various physical properties of objects, we are ready to apply such properties to the characterization of two substances—glass and soil—that commonly must be examined by the criminalist.

Comparing Glass Fragments

Glass that is broken and shattered into fragments and minute particles during the commission of a crime can be used to place a suspect at the crime scene. For example, chips of broken glass from a window may be lodged in a suspect's shoes or garments during the act of a burglary, or particles of headlight glass found at the scene of a hit-and-run accident may offer clues that can confirm the identity of a suspect vehicle. All of these possibilities require the comparison of glass fragments found on the suspect, whether a person or vehicle, to the shattered glass remaining at the crime scene.

Glass is a hard, brittle amorphous substance that is composed of silicon oxides mixed with various metal oxides. The forensic scientist is often requested to analyze soda-lime glass, which is used for manufacturing most window and bottle glass. The common metal oxides found in this type of glass are of sodium, calcium, magnesium, and aluminum. In addition, a wide variety of special glasses can be made by substituting in whole or in part other metal oxides for the silica, sodium, and calcium oxides. For example, automobile headlights and heat-resistant glass, such as Pyrex, are manufactured by adding boron oxide to the oxide mix. These glasses are therefore known as borosilicates.

For the forensic scientist the problem of glass comparison is one that depends on the need to find and measure those properties that will associate one glass fragment to another while minimizing or eliminating the possible existence of other sources. Needless to say, considering the prevalency of glass in our society, it is easy to develop an appreciation for the magnitude of this analytical problem. Obviously, glass will possess its greatest evidential value when it can be individualized to one source. Such a determination, however, can only be made when the suspect and crime-scene fragments are assembled and physically fitted together. Comparisons of this type will require piecing together irregular edges of broken glass as well as the matching of all irregularities and striations on the broken surfaces (see Figure 3–9). The possibility that two pieces of glass originating from different sources will fit exactly together is so unlikely as to exclude all other sources from practical consideration.

Unfortunately, the majority of glass evidence presented to the criminalist is either too fragmentary or minute to permit a comparison of this type. In such instances, the search for individual properties has proven to be a fruitless one. For example, the general chemical composition of window glasses within the capability of current analytical methods has so far been found to be relatively uniform among various manufacturers and thus offers no basis for individualization. However, as more sensitive analytical techniques are developed, trace elements present in glass may eventually prove to be distinctive and measurable characteristics. At this time, the physical properties of density and refractive index are used most successfully for characterizing glass particles. However, these prop-

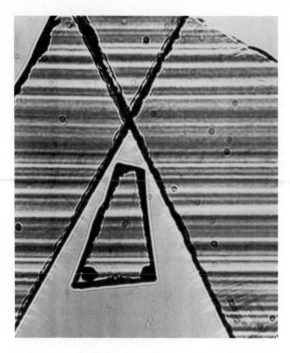

FIGURE 3-9. Match of Broken Glass. Note that in addition to the physical fit of the edges, glass ream patterns are used to establish a relationship between the fragments. The normally invisible reams are visualized by focusing a point light source on the glass so that it casts a shadow of the sample on photographic film.

Courtesy The Centre of Forensic Sciences

erties are class characteristics and as such will not provide the sole criteria for individualizing glass to a common source. They do, however, give the analyst sufficient data to evaluate the significance of a glass comparison, and the absence of comparable density and refractive index values will certainly serve to exclude those glass fragments that originate from different sources.

It was previously indicated that a solid particle will either float, sink, or remain suspended in a liquid depending on its density relative to the liquid medium. This knowledge gives the criminalist a rather precise and rapid method for comparing densities of glass. In a method known as **flotation** a control glass particle is immersed in a liquid; a mixture of bromoform and bromobenzene may be used. The composition of the liquid is carefully adjusted by the addition of small amounts of bromoform or bromobenzene until the glass chip remains suspended in the liquid medium. At this point, the control glass and liquid each have the same density. Glass chips of approximately the same size and shape as the control are now added to the liquid for comparison. If both the unknown and the control particles remain suspended in the liquid, their densities are equal to each other and to that of the liquid. Particles of different densities will either sink or float, depending on whether they are more or less dense than the liquid.

The sensitivity of this method may be enhanced by slowly heating the liquid medium to a higher temperature. As this is done its volume expands and its density decreases, causing the glass particles to sink. (Increasing the temperature has a negligible effect on the density of the glass particles.) Similarly, as the liquid is allowed to cool to room temperature its volume contracts, causing its density to increase; the fragments will now slowly start to rise. Glasses that have comparable densities will sink and rise together.

It is interesting to note that the density of a sheet of plate glass is not completely homogeneous throughout. It has a range of values that can differ by as much as 0.0003 g/ml. Therefore, in order to distinguish between the normal internal density variations of a single sheet of glass and those glasses of different origins, it is advisable to let the comparative density approach but not exceed a sensitivity value of 0.0003 g/ml. The flotation method meets this requirement and can adequately distinguish glass particles that differ in density by 0.001 g/ml.

Once glass has been distinguished by a density determination, different origins are immediately concluded. Comparable density results, however, require the added comparison of refractive indices. This determination is best accomplished by an **immersion method**. For this, glass particles are immersed in a liquid medium whose refractive index is varied until it is equal to that of the glass particles. At this point, known as the **match point**, the observer will note the disappearance of the **Becke line** and minimum contrast between the glass and liquid medium. The Becke line is a bright halo that is observed near the border of a particle that is immersed in a liquid of a different refractive index. This halo disappears when the medium and fragment have similar refractive indices.

The refractive index of an immersion fluid is best varied by adjusting the temperature of the liquid. Temperature control is of course critical to the success of the procedure and is accomplished by heating the liquid in a special apparatus known as a hot stage. The glass is immersed in a high boiling liquid, usually a silicone oil, and heated at the rate of 0.2 °C per minute until the match point is reached. Increasing the temperature of the liquid has a negligible effect on the refractive index of glass, while the liquid's index decreases at the rate of approximately 0.0004 per degree Celsius. The hot stage, as shown in Figure 3–10, is designed to be used in conjunction with a microscope, through which the examiner can observe the disappearance of the Becke line on minute glass particles that are illuminated with sodium D light or at other wavelengths of light. If all the glass fragments examined have similar match points, it can be concluded that they have comparable refractive indices (see Figure 3–11).

As with density, glass fragments removed from a single sheet of plate glass may not have one refractive index value; instead, their values may vary by as much as 0.0003. Hence, for comparison purposes, the difference in refractive index between a control and questioned glass must exceed this value. This allows the examiner to differentiate between the normal internal variation present in a sheet of glass and those glasses which originate from completely different sources.

At present, there is little statistical data available in the United States to permit an accurate assessment for the evidential value of glass comparisons. A recent study, involving fifty-two window glasses

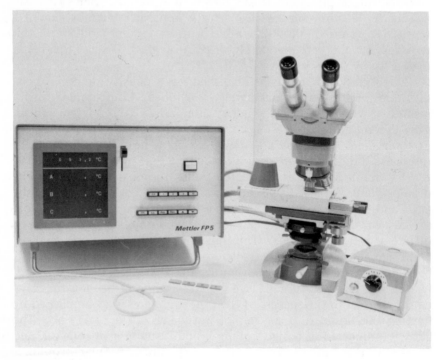

FIGURE 3-10. Hot-Stage Microscope
Courtesy New Jersey State Police

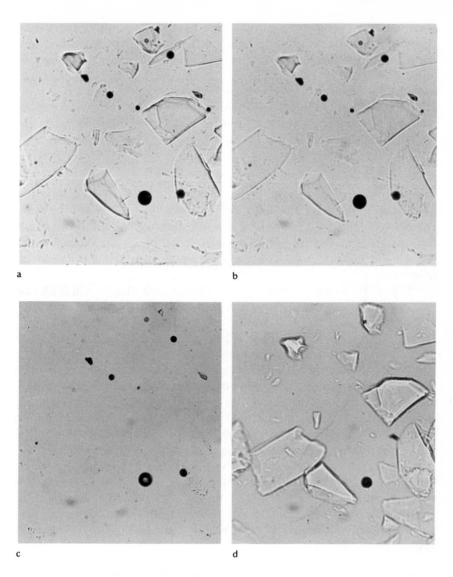

FIGURE 3-11. Determination of the refractive index of glass. (a) Glass particles are immersed in a liquid of a much higher refractive index at a temperature of 77°C. (b) At 87°C the liquid still has a higher refractive index than the glass. (c) The refractive index of the liquid is closest to that of the glass at 97°C as shown by the disappearance of the glass and the Becke lines. (d) At the higher temperature of 117°C the liquid has a much lower index than the glass, and the glass is plainly visible.

Courtesy Walter C. McCrone

submitted as evidence to a California forensic laboratory, conservatively estimated that there is only one chance in fifty of finding two glass particles from different sources that have comparable densities and refractive indices.[1] However, a far greater number of glasses will have to be examined before more definitive conclusions are drawn. Until this statistical data is available, it will be necessary for American forensic scientists to continue to base such interpretations on personal experiences.

Glass Fractures

Glass bends in response to any force that is exerted on any one of its surfaces; when the limit of its elasticity is reached the glass fractures. Frequently, fractured window glass will reveal information that can be related to the force and direction of an impact; such knowledge may be useful for reconstructing events at a crime-scene investigation.

The penetration of glass by a projectile, whether it is a bullet or stone, produces a familiar fracture pattern in which cracks both radiate outward and encircle the hole, as shown in Figure 3-12. The radiating lines are appropriately known as **radial fractures** and the circular lines are termed **concentric fractures**.

When it penetrates glass, a high-velocity projectile, such as a bullet, leaves a round crater-shaped hole that is surrounded by a nearly symmetrical pattern of radial and concentric cracks. The hole is inevitably wider at the exit side (Figure 3-13), and hence its examination is an important factor in determining the direction of impact. However, as the velocity of the penetrating projectile decreases, the irregularity of the shape of the hole and its surrounding cracks increases, so that at some point the hole shape will provide no assistance for determining the direction of impact. At this time information derived from an examination of the radial and concentric fracture lines may prove a useful alternative for determining the direction of impact.

When a force pushes on one side of a pane of glass, the elasticity of the glass permits it to bend in the direction of the force applied. Once the elastic limit is exceeded, the glass begins to crack. As shown in Figure 3-14, the first fractures form on the surface opposite that of the penetrating force, and these fractures develop into radial lines.

---

[1] Wilkaan Fong, "Value of Glass as Evidence," *Journal of Forensic Sciences*, 18 (1973), 398–404.

FIGURE 3-12. Radial and Concentric Fracture Lines in a Sheet of Glass
Courtesy New Jersey State Police.

The continued motion of the force places tension on the front surface of the glass, resulting in the formation of concentric cracks. An
examination of the edges of the radial and concentric cracks frequently reveals stress markings whose shape can be related to the side
on which the window first cracked.

Stress marks, shown in Figure 3-15, are shaped like arches that
are perpendicular to one glass surface and curved nearly parallel to
the opposite surface. The importance of stress marks stems from the
observation that the perpendicular edge always faces the surface on

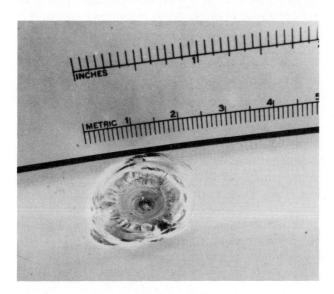

FIGURE 3-13. Crater shaped hole made by a pellet passing through glass. The upper surface of glass is the exit side of the projectile.
Courtesy New Jersey State Police.

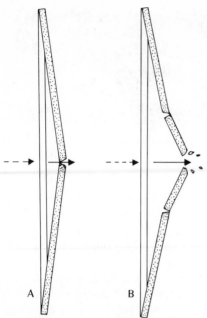

FIGURE 3-14. Diagram showing the production of radial and concentric fracture in glass. A: radial cracks are formed first, commencing on the side of the glass opposite to the destructive force; B: concentric cracks occur afterwards, starting on the same side as the force.

which the crack originated. Thus, in examining the stress marks on the edge of a radial crack near the point of impact, the perpendicular end is always found to be located opposite the side from which the force of impact was applied. For a concentric fracture the perpendicular end always faces the surface on which the force originated. A convenient way for remembering these observations is the 3R rule—*R*adial cracks form *R*ight angle on the *R*everse side of the force. These facts will enable the examiner to readily determine the side on which a window was broken.

When there have been successive penetrations of glass, it is frequently possible to determine the sequence of impact by observing the existing fracture lines and their points of termination. **A fracture always terminates at an existing line of fracture.** In Figure 3-16, the fracture on the left preceded that on the right; we know this because the latter's radial fracture lines terminated at the cracks of the former.

Collection and Preservation of Glass Evidence

The gathering of glass evidence at the crime scene and from the suspect must be thorough if the examiner is to have any chance to individualize the fragments to a common source. If even the remotest

FIGURE 3-15. Stress marks on the edge of a radial glass fracture. Arrow indicates direction of force

Courtesy New Jersey State Police

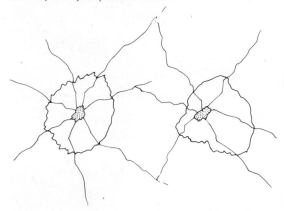

FIGURE 3-16

possibility exists that fragments may be pieced together, every effort must be made to collect all the glass found. For example, collection of evidence at hit-and-run scenes must include all the broken parts of the headlight and reflector lenses. This evidence may ultimately prove to be an invaluable means of placing a suspect vehicle at the accident scene through a physical match with glass remaining in the headlight or reflector shell of the suspect vehicle. In addition, an examination of the headlight's filaments may resolve any questions regarding whether or not an automobile's headlights were on or off before the impact (see Figure 3-17).

When an individual fit is thought improbable, the evidence collector must submit all glass evidence found in the possession of the suspect along with representative samples of broken glass remaining at the crime scene. If the suspect's shoes or clothing are to be examined for the presence of glass fragments, they should be individually wrapped in paper and transmitted to the laboratory. It is best that the field investigator avoid removing such evidence from garments unless it is thought absolutely necessary for its preservation. Control glass should always be taken from any remaining glass in the window or door frames, as close as possible to the point of breakage.

When a determination of the direction of impact is desired, all broken glass must be recovered and submitted for analysis. Wherever possible, the exterior and interior surfaces of the glass must be indicated. In cases in which this is not immediately apparent, the presence of dirt, paint, grease, or putty may provide an indication as to the exterior surface of the glass.

FIGURE 3-17. Presence of oxides on the lower filament indicates the filament was hot when it was exposed to air. Thus, the filament must have been on prior to impact
Courtesy New Jersey State Police

The Forensic Characteristics
of Soil

There are many definitions for the term "soil"; however, for forensic purposes soil may be thought of as including any disintegrated surface material, both natural and artificial, that lies on or near the earth's surface. Therefore, the forensic examination of soil is not only concerned with the analysis of naturally occurring rocks, minerals, vegetation, and animal matter—it also encompasses the detection of such manufactured objects as glass, paint chips, asphalt, brick fragments, and cinders, whose presence may impart soil with characteristics that will make it unique to a particular location. When this material is collected accidentally or deliberately in a manner that will associate it with a crime under investigation, it now becomes valuable physical evidence.

The value of soil as evidence rests with its prevalence at crime scenes and its transferability between the scene and the criminal. Thus, soil or dried mud found adhering to a suspect's clothing, shoes, or to an automobile, when compared to soil samples collected at the crime site, may provide associative evidence that can link a suspect or object to the crime scene. As with most types of physical evidence, forensic soil analysis is comparative in nature; soil found in the possession of the suspect must be carefully collected to be compared to soil samplings from the crime scene and the surrounding vicinity.

Most soils can be differentiated and distinguished by their gross appearance. A side-by-side visual comparison of the color and texture of soil specimens is easy to perform and provides a most sensitive property for distinguishing soils that originate from different locations. It is important to remember that the color of soil is darker when it is wet; therefore, color comparisons must always be made when all the samples are dried under identical laboratory conditions. It is estimated that there are nearly 1,100 distinguishable soil colors; hence the comparison of color offers a logical first step in a forensic soil comparison.

Low-power microscopic examination of soil will reveal the presence of plant and animal materials as well as man-made debris. Further high-power microscopic examination will aid in the characterization of minerals and rocks present in earth materials. Although this approach to the forensic identification of soil requires the expertise of an investigator trained in geology, it does provide the most varied and significant points of comparison between soil samples. Only through a careful examination and comparison of the minerals and rocks naturally present in soil can one take advantage of the large number of variations that exist between soils and thus add to the evidential value of a positive comparison. A mineral is a natu-

rally occurring crystal, and like any other crystal its physical properties—e.g., color, geometric shape, density and refractive index or
birefringence—are most useful for identification. More than 2,200
minerals are known to exist; however, most of these are so rare that
the forensic geologist will usually encounter only about forty of the
more common ones. Rocks are composed of a combination of
minerals and therefore exist in thousands of varieties on the earth's
surface. Their identification is usually made by characterizing their
mineral content and grain size.

Considering the vast variety of minerals, rocks, and the possible
occurrence of man-made debris that may be present in soil, the
forensic geologist is presented with many points of comparison between two or more specimens. The number of comparative points
and their frequency of occurrence must all be taken into consideration before similarity between specimens is concluded and the
probability of common origin judged.

Rocks and minerals are not only present in earth materials, they
are also used by man to manufacture a wide variety of industrial
and commercial products. For example, it is not uncommon to find
that the tools and garments of an individual suspected of breaking
into a safe will contain traces of safe insulation. Safe insulation may
be made from a wide combination of mineral mixtures that can
provide significant points of identification. Similarly, building
materials, such as brick, plaster, and concrete blocks, are combinations of minerals and rocks that can easily be recognized and compared microscopically to similar minerals found perhaps on the
breaking and entering suspect.

Many forensic laboratories presently rely on the **density-gradient
tube technique** to compare soil specimens. Typically, glass tubes 6 to
10 millimeters in diameter and from 25 to 40 cm in length are filled
with layers of two liquids mixed in varying proportions so that each
layer has a different density value. For example, tetrabromoethane
(density 2.96 g/ml) and ethanol (density 0.789 g/ml) may be mixed
so that the ratios of the two liquids in each layer are such that each
successive layer has a lower density than the preceding one, from the
bottom to the top of the tube. The simplest gradient tube may have
from six to ten layers in which the bottom layer is pure tetrabromethane and the top layer is pure ethanol, with corresponding variations of concentration in the layers between these two extremes.
When soil is added to the density-gradient tube its particles will sink
to the portion of the tube that has a density of equal value; the
particle will remain suspended in the liquid at this point. In this way,
a density distribution pattern of soil particles can be obtained and
compared to other specimens treated in a similar manner (Figure 3-

18). Though this procedure is extensively used in crime laboratories, its value as an analytic technique for the forensic comparison of soil is questioned by some. At this time, little experimental data is available to either confirm or refute its reliability.

The ultimate forensic value of soil evidence depends on its variation at the crime scene. If, for example, soil is indistinguishable for miles surrounding the location of a crime with the methods used in the examination, it will have limited value in associating soil found on the suspect to that particular site. Significant conclusions relating the suspect to a particular crime-scene location through a soil comparison may be made when variations in soil composition occur every 10 to 100 yards from the crime site. However, even when such variations do exist it is usually not possible for the forensic geologist to individualize soil to any one location unless an unusual combination of rare minerals, rocks, or man-made debris can be located.

Up to this time, there have been no statistically valid forensic studies on the variability of soil evidence. A pilot study recently conducted in southern Ontario, Canada seems to indicate that this

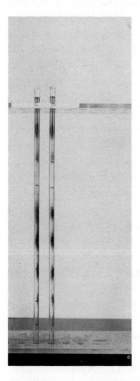

FIGURE 3-18. A Soil Comparison by Density-Gradient Tubes
Courtesy Philadelphia Police Dept. Laboratory

part of the country has soil showing extensive diversity. It was found that the probability is smaller than one in fifty of finding two soils that are indistinguishable in both color and mineral properties, but that originate in two different locations separated by a distance in the order of 1,000 feet. Based on these preliminary results, similar diversity may be expected in the northern U.S., Canada, northern Europe and much of the U.S.S.R. However, such probability values can only serve as a general indication of the variation of soil within these geographical areas. It must be emphasized that each crime scene must be evaluated separately to establish its own soil variation probabilities.

Collection and Preservation of Soil Evidence

The importance of establishing the variation of soil at the crime-scene area must be given primary consideration when the evidence collector gathers soil specimens. For this reason, control soils are to be collected at various intervals within a 100–yard radius of the crime scene, as well as at the site of the crime, for comparison to the questioned soil. Obviously, sampling locations should be determined by the terrain of the area. It is important that the specimens gathered be representative of the soil that was removed by the suspect. In most cases this means that only the top-surface layer of soil will be picked up during the commission of a crime. Thus, control specimens must be removed from the surface without digging too deeply into the unrepresentative subsurface layers. Additionally, soil specimens should also be collected at all possible alibi locations that the suspect may claim. A quantity of soil equal to approximately a tablespoon or two is required by the laboratory for a thorough comparative analysis. All specimens collected are packaged in individual containers, such as plastic vials. Each vial is marked to indicate the location at which the sampling was made.

Soil found on a suspect must be carefully preserved for analysis. If it is found adhering to an object, as in the case of soil on a shoe, the investigator must not remove it. Instead, each object is individually wrapped in paper with the soil intact and transmitted to the laboratory. Similarly, no effort should be made to remove loose soil adhering to garments; these items should be carefully wrapped individually in paper bags and sent to the laboratory for analysis. Care must be taken that all particles that may accidently fall off the garment during transportation will remain within the paper bag.

When a lump of soil is found, it should be collected and preserved intact. For example, an automobile tends to collect and build up layers of soil under fenders, body, etc. In some situations the impact of an automobile with another object may jar some of this soil loose. Once the suspect car has been apprehended, a comparison of the soil left at the scene with soil remaining on the automobile may help establish that the car was present at the accident scene. In these situations separate samples are collected from under all the fender and frame area of the vehicle; care is taken to remove the soil in lump form in order to preserve the order in which the soil was deposited onto the car. Undoubtedly, during the normal use of an automobile, soil will be picked up from numerous locations over a period of months and years. This layering effect may serve to impart soil with greater variation, and hence greater evidential value, than that which is normally associated with loose soil.

The prevalence of glass and soil in our environment makes them common types of physical evidence at crime scenes. Their proper collection and preservation by the criminal investigator will help insure that a proper scientific examination can support investigative conclusions placing a suspect or object at the crime scene. Equally important is that glass and soil, like other types of physical evidence, when properly collected and examined may serve to exonerate the innocent from involvement in a crime.

REVIEW QUESTIONS

1. A _____ property describes the behavior of a substance without reference to any other substance.

2. A _____ property is one that describes the behavior of a substance when it reacts or combines with another substance.

3. The _____ system of measurement was devised by the French Academy of Science in 1791.

4. The basic units of measurement for length, mass, and volume in the metric system are the _____ , _____ , and _____ , respectively.

5. A centigram is equivalent to _____ of a gram.

6. A milliliter is equivalent to _____ of a liter.

7. 0.2 grams is equivalent to _____ milligrams.

8. One cubic centimeter (cc) is equivalent to one _____ .

9. One meter is slightly longer than a yard. (True, False)

10. The equivalent of one pound in grams is _____ .

11. A liter is slightly larger than a quart. (True, False)

12. _____ is a measure of a substance's heat energy.

13. There are _____ degrees Fahrenheit between the freezing and boiling points of water.

14. There are _____ degrees Celsius between the freezing and boiling points of water.

15. The amount of matter an object contains determines its _____ .

16. The simplest type of balance for weighing is the _____ .

17. Mass per unit volume defines the property of _____ .

18. If an object is immersed in a liquid of greater density it will (sink, float).

19. The bending of a light wave because of a change in velocity is called _____ .

20. The physical property of _____ is determined by the ratio of the velocity of light in a vacuum to light's velocity in a substance.

21. Solids having an orderly arrangement of their constituent atoms are crystalline. (True, False)

22. Solids which have their atoms randomly arranged are said to be _____ .

23. The crystal calcite has two indices of refraction. The difference between these two values is known as _____ .

24. The process of separating light into its component colors or frequencies is known as _____ .

25. A hard, brittle amorphous substance composed mainly of silicon oxides is _____ .

26. Glass that can be physically pieced together has _____ characteristics.

27. The two most useful physical properties of glass for forensic comparisons are _____ and _____ .

28. Comparing the relative densities of glass fragments is readily accomplished by a method known as _____ .

29. When glass is immersed in a liquid of similar refractive index its _____ will disappear and minimum contrast between the glass and liquid will be observed.

30. The fracture lines radiating outward from a crack in glass are known as _____ fractures.

31. A crater-shaped hole in glass is (narrower, wider) on the side where the projectile entered the glass.

32. Stress marks on the edge of a radial crack are always perpendicular to the edge of the surface on which the crack originated. (True, False)

33. A fracture line (will, will not) terminate at an existing line fracture.

34. The vast majority of soils have indistinguishable color and texture. (True, False)

35. Naturally occurring crystals commonly found in soils are _____ .

36. A comparison of the density of soil particles is readily accomplished through the use of _____ tubes.

37. The ultimate value of soil as evidence is dependent on its variation at the crime scene. (True, False)

FURTHER READINGS

Dabbs, M. D. G., and E. F. Pearson, "The Variation in Refractive Index and Density Across Two Sheets of Window Glass," *Journal of The Forensic Science Society*, 10 (1970), 139-48.

——, "The Hot Stage Microscope," Home Office Central Research Establishment Report No. 26, Aldermaston, England (1969).

——, "Some Physical Properties of a Large Number of Window Glass Specimens," *Journal of Forensic Sciences*, 17 (1972), 70-78.

McJunkins, Steven P., and John L. Thornton, "Glass Fracture Analysis—A Review," *Forensic Science*, 2 (1973), 1-27.

Murray, Raymond C., and John C. F. Tedrow, *Forensic Geology*. New Brunswick, N.J.: Rutgers University Press, 1975.

Nelson, D. F., "The Examination of Glass Fragments," in *Methods of Forensic Science*, vol. 4, A. S. Curry, ed. New York: Wiley & Sons, 1965.

Svensson, Arne, and Otto Wendel, *Techniques of Crime Investigation*, 2nd American ed. New York: American Elsevier, 1965.

Walls, H. J., *Forensic Science*, 2nd ed. New York: Praeger, 1974.

Audiovisual Presentations

Basic Principles in Chemistry Measurement, Series 820 (35 mm slides and audio tapes). Communications Skills Corp., Fairfield, Conn.

Organic Analysis
chapter 4

In the previous chapter some physical properties were described and used to characterize glass and soil evidence. Before we can apply other physical properties, as well as chemical properties, to the identification and comparison of evidence, we need to gain an insight into the composition of matter. Beginning with knowledge of the fundamental building block of all substances—the element—it will be convenient for us to classify all evidence as either organic or inorganic. The procedures used to measure the properties associated with each class are distinctly different and merit separate chapters for their description. In later chapters we will continually return to these procedures as we discuss the examination of the various kinds of physical evidence. This chapter will be devoted, in large part, to reviewing a variety of techniques and instruments that have become the indispensable tools of the forensic scientist for examining organic evidence.

ELEMENTS AND COMPOUNDS

Matter is anything that has a mass and occupies space. As we examine the world that surrounds us and consider the countless variety of materials that we encounter, we must consider it one of man's most remarkable accomplishments to have searched for and found the fundamental model that explains the composition of all matter. This search had its earliest contributions from the ancient Greek philosophers, who suggested air, water, fire, and earth as matter's fundamental building blocks. It culminated with the development of the atomic theory and the discovery of matter's simplest identity, the element.

An element is the simplest substance known to man and provides the building block from which all matter is composed. At present, 105 elements have been identified; of these 88 occur naturally on earth, and the remainder have been created in the laboratory. In Figure 4-1 all the elements are listed by name and symbol in a form that has become known as the **periodic table**. This table is most useful to chemists because it systematically arranges elements with similar chemical properties in the same vertical row or group.

For convenience, chemists have chosen letter symbols to represent the elements. Many of these symbols come from the first letter of the element's English name—for example, carbon (C), hydrogen (H), and oxygen (O). Others are two-letter abbreviations of the English name—calcium (Ca), zinc (Zn). Some of the symbols are derived from the first letters of Latin or Greek names. Thus, the symbol for silver, Ag, comes from the Latin name *argentum*, copper, Cu, from the Latin *cuprium*, and helium, He, from the Greek name *helios*.

The smallest particle of an element that can exist and still retain its identity as that element is the atom. When we write the symbol C we mean one atom of carbon; the chemical symbol for carbon dioxide, CO_2, signifies one atom of carbon combined with two atoms of oxygen. When two or more elements are combined to form a substance, as with carbon dioxide, there is created a new substance, different in its physical and chemical properties from its elemental components. This new material is called a **compound**. Compounds contain at least two elements. Considering that there are eighty-eight natural elements, it is not difficult to imagine the large number of possible elemental combinations that may exist to form compounds. Not surprisingly, over three million known compounds have already been identified.

Just as the atom is the basic particle of an element, the molecule is the smallest unit of a compound. Thus, a molecule of carbon dioxide is represented by the symbol CO_2, and a molecule of table salt is symbolized by NaCl, representing the combination of one atom of the element sodium (Na) with one atom of the element chlorine (Cl).

As we look around us and view the materials that comprise our home planet, Earth, it becomes an awesome task even to attempt to estimate the number of different kinds of matter that exist. A much more logical approach is to classify matter according to the physical form it takes. These forms are called **physical states**. There are three

LIST OF ELEMENTS WITH THEIR SYMBOLS AND ATOMIC MASSES

Element	Symbol	Atomic Mass[a] (amu)	Element	Symbol	Atomic Mass[a] (amu)
Actinium	Ac	(227)	Mercury	Hg	200.59
Aluminum	Al	26.9815	Molybdenum	Mo	95.94
Americium	Am	(243)	Neodymium	Nd	144.24
Antimony	Sb	121.75	Neon	Ne	20.179
Argon	Ar	39.948	Neptunium	Np	237.0482
Arsenic	As	74.9216	Nickel	Ni	58.71
Astatine	At	(210)	Niobium	Nb	92.9064
Barium	Ba	137.34	Nitrogen	N	14.0067
Berkelium	Bk	(247)	Nobelium	No	(253)
Beryllium	Be	9.01218	Osmium	Os	190.2
Bismuth	Bi	208.9806	Oxygen	O	15.9994
Boron	B	10.81	Palladium	Pd	106.4
Bromine	Br	79.904	Phosphorus	P	30.9738
Cadmium	Cd	112.40	Platinum	Pt	195.09
Calcium	Ca	40.08	Plutonium	Pu	(244)
Californium	Cf	(251)	Polonium	Po	(209)
Carbon	C	12.011	Potassium	K	39.102
Cerium	Ce	140.12	Praseodymium	Pr	140.9077
Cesium	Cs	132.9055	Promethium	Pm	(145)
Chlorine	Cl	35.453	Protactinium	Pa	231.0359
Chromium	Cr	51.996	Radium	Ra	226.0254
Cobalt	Co	58.9332	Radon	Rn	(222)
Copper	Cu	63.546	Rhenium	Re	186.2
Curium	Cm	(247)	Rhodium	Rh	102.9055
Dysprosium	Dy	162.50	Rubidium	Rb	85.4678
Einsteinium	Es	(254)	Ruthenium	Ru	101.07
Erbium	Er	167.26	[Rutherfordium][b]	[Rf]	(261)
Europium	Eu	151.96	Samarium	Sm	150.4
Fermium	Fm	(253)	Scandium	Sc	44.9559
Fluorine	F	18.9984	Selenium	Se	78.96
Francium	Fr	(223)	Silicon	Si	28.086
Gadolinium	Gd	157.25	Silver	Ag	107.868
Gallium	Ga	69.72	Sodium	Na	22.9898
Germanium	Ge	72.59	Strontium	Sr	87.62
Gold	Au	196.9665	Sulfur	S	32.06
Hafnium	Hf	178.49	Tantalum	Ta	180.9479
[Hahnium][b]	[Ha]	(260)	Technetium	Tc	98.9062
Helium	He	4.00260	Tellurium	Te	127.60
Holmium	Ho	164.9303	Terbium	Tb	158.9254
Hydrogen	H	1.0080	Thallium	Tl	204.37
Indium	In	114.82	Thorium	Th	232.0381
Iodine	I	126.9045	Thulium	Tm	168.9342
Iridium	Ir	192.22	Tin	Sn	118.69
Iron	Fe	55.847	Titanium	Ti	47.90
Krypton	Kr	83.80	Tungsten	W	183.85
Lanthanum	La	138.9055	Uranium	U	238.029
Lawrencium	Lr	(257)	Vanadium	V	50.9414
Lead	Pb	207.2	Xenon	Xe	131.30
Lithium	Li	6.941	Ytterbium	Yb	173.04
Lutetium	Lu	174.97	Yttrium	Y	88.9059
Magnesium	Mg	24.305	Zinc	Zn	65.37
Manganese	Mn	54.9380	Zirconium	Zr	91.22
Mendelevium	Md	(256)			

[a]Based on the assigned relative atomic mass of C = exactly 12; parentheses denote the mass number of the isotope with the longest half-life.
[b]Name and symbol not officially approved.

PERIODIC CHART OF THE ELEMENTS

Group	IA	IIA	IIIB	IVB	VB	VIB	VIIB	VIII			IB	IIB	IIIA	IVA	VA	VIA	VIIA	O
Period																		
1	1 H																	2 He
2	3 Li	4 Be											5 B	6 C	7 N	8 O	9 F	10 Ne
3	11 Na	12 Mg											13 Al	14 Si	15 P	16 S	17 Cl	18 Ar
4	19 K	20 Ca	21 Sc	22 Ti	23 V	24 Cr	25 Mn	26 Fe	27 Co	28 Ni	29 Cu	30 Zn	31 Ga	32 Ge	33 As	34 Se	35 Br	36 Kr
5	37 Rb	38 Sr	39 Y	40 Zr	41 Nb	42 Mo	43 Tc	44 Ru	45 Rh	46 Pd	47 Ag	48 Cd	49 In	50 Sn	51 Sb	52 Te	53 I	54 Xe
6	55 Cs	56 Ba	57 La ᵃ	72 Hf	73 Ta	74 W	75 Re	76 Os	77 Ir	78 Pt	79 Au	80 Hg	81 Tl	82 Pb	83 Bi	84 Po	85 At	86 Rn
7	87 Fr	88 Ra	89 Ac ᵇ	104 Rf	105 Ha													

a Lanthanide series

58 Ce	59 Pr	60 Nd	61 Pm	62 Sm	63 Eu	64 Gd	65 Tb	66 Dy	67 Ho	68 Er	69 Tm	70 Yb	71 Lu

b Actinide series

90 Th	91 Pa	92 U	93 Np	94 Pu	95 Am	96 Cm	97 Bk	98 Cf	99 Es	100 Fm	101 Md	102 No	103 Lw

FIGURE 4-1. The Periodic Table

71

such states: **solid, liquid,** and **gas (vapor).** A solid is rigid and therefore has a definite shape and volume. A liquid also occupies a specific
volume, but its fluidity causes it to take the shape of the container
in which it is residing. A gas has neither a definite shape nor volume,
and will completely fill any container into which it is placed.

Substances can change from one state to another. For example,
as water is heated it is converted from a liquid form into a vapor. At
a high enough temperature ($100°C$), water boils and is rapidly
changed into steam. Similarly, at $0°C$ water solidifies or freezes into
ice. Under certain conditions some solids can be converted directly
into a gaseous state. For instance, a piece of dry ice (solid carbon
dioxide) left standing at room temperature will quickly form carbon
dioxide vapor and disappear. This change of state from a solid to a
gas is called **sublimation.**

In each of these examples it is important to recognize that no
new chemical species are formed; matter is simply being changed
from one physical state to another. Water, whether it is in the form
of liquid, ice, or steam, remains chemically, H_2O. Simply, what has
been altered are the attractive forces that exist between the water
molecules. In a solid these forces are very strong, and the molecules
are held closely together in a rigid state. In a liquid the attractive
forces are not as strong, and the molecules have more mobility.
Finally, in the vapor state there are no longer appreciable attractive
forces between the molecules; thus they are permitted to move in
any and all directions at will.

Chemists are forever combining different substances, no matter
whether they are in the solid, liquid, or gaseous states, hoping to
create new and useful products. Our everyday observations should
make it apparent that not all attempts at mixing matter can be
productive. For instance, oil spills testify to the fact that oil and
water do not mix. Whenever a situation exists in which substances
can be distinguished by a visible boundary, different **phases** are said
to exist. Thus, oil floating on water is an example of a two-phase
system. The oil and water each constitute a separate liquid phase,
clearly distinct from each other. Similarly, when sugar is first added
to water it will not dissolve and there exist two distinctly different
phases, the solid sugar and the liquid water. However, after stirring
all the sugar will dissolve leaving just one liquid phase.

SELECTING AN ANALYTICAL TECHNIQUE

Now that the basic components of matter have been defined, the
proper selection of analytical techniques that will allow the forensic
scientist to identify or compare matter can best be understood by

categorizing all substances into one of two broad groups: **organics** and **inorganics**.

Organic substances contain the element carbon, commonly in combination with one or more of the following elements: hydrogen, oxygen, nitrogen, sulfur, phosphorus, chlorine, and bromine. Inorganic substances encompass all other chemical substances known to man. Each of these two broad groups has properties that are quite distinctive and characteristic. Thus, once the analyst has determined whether a material is organic or inorganic, the properties to be measured and the choice of analytical techniques to be used will generally be the same for all materials falling into each group.

Another consideration in selecting an analytical technique is the need for either a **qualitative** or a **quantitative** determination. The former relates just to the identity of the material, while the latter requires the determination of the percent composition of the components of a mixture. Hence, a qualitative identification of a powder may reveal the presence of heroin and quinine, while a quantitative analysis will conclude the presence of 10 percent heroin and 90 percent quinine. Obviously, a qualitative identification must precede any attempt at quantitation, for little value is served by attempting to quantitate a material without first determining its identity. Essentially, a qualitative analysis of a material will require the determination of numerous properties using a variety of analytical techniques. On the other hand, a quantitative measurement is usually accomplished by the precise measurement of a single property of the material.

The majority of the evidence currently received by crime laboratories requires the identification of organic compounds. These include evidence such as commonly abused drugs (e.g., alcohol, marihuana, heroin, amphetamines, and barbiturates) synthetic fibers, petroleum products, paint binders, and high-energy explosives. As we have already observed, organic compounds are composed of a combination of a relatively small number of elements that must include carbon; fortunately, the nature of the forces or bonds that exist between these elements is such that the resultant compounds can readily be characterized by their absorption of light. The study of the absorption of light by chemical substances is known as **spectrophotometry** and serves as a basic tool for the characterization and identification of organic materials. Though spectrophotometry is most applicable to organic analysis, its optimum utilization requires that a material be in a relatively pure state. Because the purity of physical evidence is almost always beyond the control of the criminalist, this criterion often is not met. For this reason, the analytical technique of **chromatography** is widely applied for the analysis of physical evidence. Chromatography is a means of separating and identifying the components of a mixture. We will discuss both of these techniques in this chapter.

CHROMATOGRAPHY

Theory of Chromatography

Chromatography as a technique for purifying substances is particularly useful for analyzing the multi-component specimens that are frequently received in the crime laboratory. For example, illicit drugs sold on the street are not manufactured to meet government labeling standards; instead, they may be diluted with practically any material that is at the disposal of the drug dealer in order to increase the quantity of the product that is made available to prospective customers. Hence, the task of identifying an illicit drug preparation would be an arduous one without the aid of chromatographic methods to first separate the mixture into its components.

The theory of chromatography has as its basis the observation that chemical substances have a tendency to partially escape into the surrounding environment when dissolved in a liquid or absorbed on a solid surface. This is best illustrated by a gas dissolved in a beaker of water kept at a constant temperature. It will be convenient for us to characterize the water in the beaker as the liquid phase and the air above it as the gas phase. If the beaker is covered with a bell jar, as shown in Figure 4-2, some of the gas molecules (represented by the dark balls) will escape from the water into the surrounding enclosed air. The molecules remaining behind are said to be in the liquid

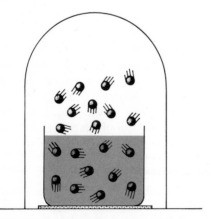

FIGURE 4-2. Evaporation of a Liquid.

phase; those molecules that have found their way into the air are said to be in the gas phase. As the gas molecules continue their escape into the surrounding air they will begin to accumulate above the water; here, random motion will carry some of them back into the water. Eventually, a point will be reached at which the number of molecules leaving the water will be equal to the number returning. At this time the liquid and gas phases are said to be in **equilibrium**. If the temperature of the water is increased, the equilibrium state will readjust itself to a point where more gas molecules will move into the gas phase.

This behavior was first observed in 1803 by a British chemist, William Henry. His explanation of this phenomenon is known appropriately as Henry's Law and may be stated as follows: When a volatile chemical compound is dissolved in a liquid and is brought to equilibrium with air, there is a fixed ratio between the concentration of the volatile compound in air and its concentration in the liquid, and this ratio remains constant for a given temperature.

The distribution or partitioning of a gas between the liquid and gas phases is determined by the solubility of the gas in the liquid. The higher its solubility, the greater the tendency of the gas molecules to remain in the liquid phase. If two different gases are now simultaneously dissolved in the same liquid, each will reach a state of equilibrium with the surrounding air independently of the other. For example, as shown in Figure 4-3, gas A (black balls) and gas B (clear balls) are both dissolved in water. At equilibrium, gas A has a greater number of its molecules dissolved in the water as compared to B. This is so because A is more soluble in water than B.

Now returning to the concept of chromatography: In the illustra-

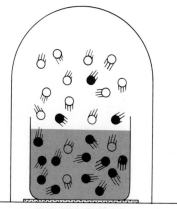

FIGURE 4-3. At equilibrium there are a greater number of gas A molecules (black balls) in the liquid phase than there are gas B molecules (white balls).

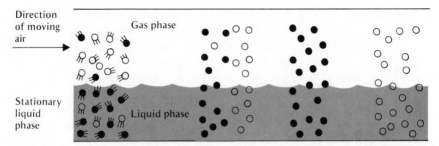

Direction
of moving
air

Stationary
liquid
phase

Gas phase

Liquid phase

FIGURE 4-4. In this illustration of chromatography the molecules represented by the white balls have a greater affinity for the upper phase and hence will be pushed along at a faster rate by the moving air. Eventually, the two sets of molecules will separate from each other, completing the chromatographic process.

tions cited above, both phases—the liquid and gas—were kept stationary; that is, they were not moving. During a chromatographic process this is not the case; instead, one phase is always made to move continuously in one direction over a stationary or fixed phase. For example, in the illustration showing the two gases, A and B, dissolved in water, chromatography will occur only when the air is forced to move continuously in one direction over the water. Because B has a greater percentage of its molecules in the moving gas phase as compared to A, its molecules will travel over the liquid at a faster pace than those of A. Eventually, when the moving phase has advanced a reasonable distance, B will become entirely separated from A and the chromatographic process will be complete. This process is illustrated in Figure 4-4.

Simply, we can think of chromatography as being analogous to a race between chemical compounds. At the starting line all the participating substances are mixed together; however, as the race progresses, those materials that have a preference for the moving phase will slowly pull ahead of those substances that prefer to remain in the stationary phase. Finally, at the completion of the race, all the participants will be separated, each crossing the finish line at different times.

The different types of chromatographic systems that can exist are as varied as the possible number of stationary and moving-phase combinations that can be devised. However, two chromatographic processes, gas chromatography (GC) and thin-layer chromatography (TLC), are found to be most applicable for solving many of the analytical problems encountered in the crime laboratory.

Gas Chromatography (GC)

Gas chromatography (GC) separates mixtures on the basis of their distribution between a stationary liquid phase and a moving-gas phase. This technique is widely utilized because of its ability to resolve a highly complex mixture into its components within a time period that is usually measured in minutes.

In gas chromatography the moving phase is actually a gas that flows through a column constructed of stainless steel or glass. The stationary phase is a thin film of liquid that is fixed onto smaller granular particles packed into the column. As the gas flows through the column, it carries along with it the components of a mixture that has been injected onto the column. Those components having a greater affinity for the moving-gas phase will travel through the column at a faster rate as compared to those having a greater affinity for the stationary liquid phase. Eventually, after the mixture has traversed the length of the column, it will emerge separated into its components.

A simplified scheme of the gas chromatograph is shown in Figure 4-5. The operation of the instrument can be summed up briefly as follows: A gas stream, the so-called carrier gas, is fed into the column

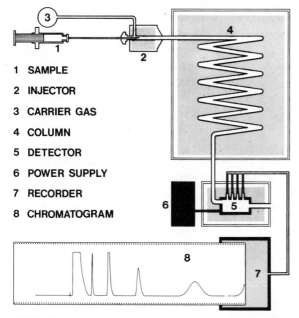

1 SAMPLE

2 INJECTOR

3 CARRIER GAS

4 COLUMN

5 DETECTOR

6 POWER SUPPLY

7 RECORDER

8 CHROMATOGRAM

FIGURE 4-5. Basic gas chromatography. Gas chromatography permits the rapid separation of complex mixtures into individual compounds and allows identification and quantitative determination of each compound. As shown, a sample is introduced by a syringe (1) into a heated injection chamber (2). A constant stream of nitrogen gas (3) flows through the injector carrying the sample into the column (4) packed with a coated powdered material. The sample is separated in the column, and the carrier gas and separated components emerge from the column and enter the detector (5). Signals developed by the detector activate the recorder (7) which makes a permanent record of the separation by tracing a series of peaks on the chromatograph (8). The time of elution identifies the component present and the peak area identifies the concentration.

Courtesy Varian Instruments

at a constant rate. The carrier gas is chemically inert and is generally nitrogen or helium. The sample under investigation is injected as a liquid into a heated injection port with a syringe where it is immediately vaporized and swept into the column by the carrier gas. The column itself is heated in an oven in order to keep the sample in a vapor state as it travels through the column. In the column, the components of the sample travel in the direction of the carrier gas flow at speeds that are determined by their distribution between the stationary and moving phases. Assuming that the analyst has selected the proper liquid phase and has made the column long enough, the components of the sample will be completely separated as they emerge from the column.

As each component emerges from the column it enters a detector. One type of detector uses a flame to ionize the emerging chemical substance, thus generating an electrical signal. The signal is recorded onto a strip-chart recorder as a function of time. This written record of the separation is called a **chromatogram**. A gas chromatogram is a plot of the recorder response (vertical axis) versus time (horizontal axis). A typical chromatogram will show a series of peaks, each peak corresponding to one component of the mixture. The time required for a component to emerge from the column from the time of its injection onto the column is known as the **retention time**. This serves as a useful identifying characteristic of a material. Figure 4-6a shows the chromatogram of two barbiturates; each barbiturate has tentatively been identified by comparing its retention time to those of known barbiturates, shown in Figure 4-6(b). (See Appendix II for chromatographic conditions.) However, because it is always possible that other substances may have comparable retention times under similar chromatographic conditions, gas chromatography cannot be considered an absolute means of identification. Conclusions derived from this technique must be confirmed by other testing procedures.

Gas chromatography has an added advantage in that it is extremely sensitive and can yield quantitative results. The amount of substance passing through the GC detector is proportional to the peak area recorded; therefore, by chromatographing a known concentration of a material and comparing it to the unknown, the amount of the sample may be determined by proportion. Gas chromatography has sufficient sensitivity to detect and quantitate materials at the nanogram (0.000000001 gram or 1×10^{-9} level.[1]

---

[1] For ease of handling large or small numbers, the power of 10 notion is quite useful and simple. The power of ten expresses the number of places that the decimal point must be moved. If it is positive, the decimal point is moved to the right; if it is negative, the decimal point is moved to the left. Thus, to express 1×10^{-9} as a number, the decimal point is simply moved nine places to the left of 1.

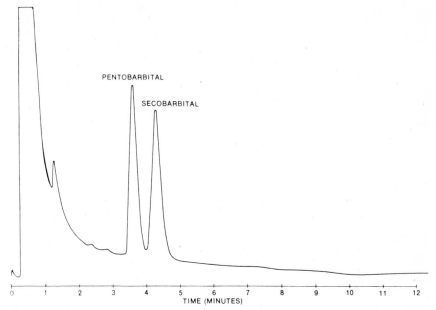

FIGURE 4-6a. An unknown mixture of barbiturates is identified by comparing its retention times to (b).

Courtesy Varian Instruments

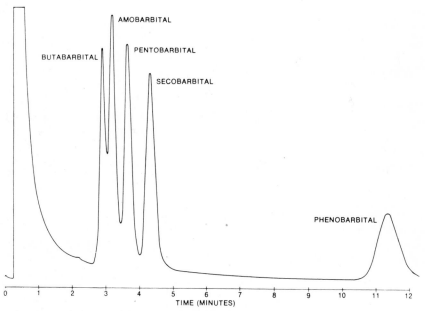

FIGURE 4-6b. A Known Mixture of Barbiturates

Courtesy Varian Instruments

   An important extension of the application of gas chromatography to forensic science is the technique of **pyrolysis gas chromatography.** Many solid materials commonly encountered as physical evidence— e.g., paint chips, fibers, and plastics—cannot be readily dissolved in a solvent for injection into the gas chromatograph. Thus, under normal conditions these substances cannot be subjected to gas chromatographic analysis. However, materials such as these can be heated or pyrolyzed to high temperatures (500–1000°C) so that they will decompose into numerous gaseous products. Pyrolyzers have been designed to permit these gaseous products to enter the carrier gas stream where they flow into and through the GC column. The pyrolyzed material can then be characterized by the pattern produced by its chromatogram or **pyrogram.** As an example, Figure 4–7 illustrates the pyrogram of a paint chip. The complexity of the paint pyrogram in essence serves as a "fingerprint" of the material and gives the examiner many points to compare with other paints that are analyzed in a similar fashion.

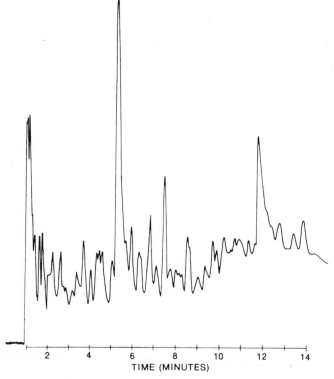

FIGURE 4–7. Pyrogram of a 1973 GM Automobile Paint

Courtesy Varian Instruments

Thin-Layer Chromatography (TLC)

This technique incorporates a solid stationary phase and a moving liquid phase to effect the separation of the constituents of a mixture. A thin-layer plate is prepared by coating a glass plate with a thin film of a granular material. Commonly, silica gel or aluminum oxide is used. This granular material serves as the solid stationary phase. If the sample to be analyzed is a solid, it first must be dissolved in a suitable solvent and a few microliters of the solution spotted with a capillary tube onto the granular surface near the lower edge of the plate. A liquid sample may be applied directly to the plate in the same manner. The plate is then put into a closed chamber which contains a selected liquid, with care that the liquid does not touch the sample spot.

The liquid will slowly begin to rise up the plate by capillary action. It is the rising liquid that serves as the moving phase in thin-layer chromatography. As it moves past the sample spot, the components of the sample will become distributed between the stationary solid phase and the moving liquid phase. Those components with the greatest affinity for the moving phase will travel up the plate at a faster speed as compared to those that have greater affinity for the stationary phase. When the liquid front has moved a sufficient distance (usually 10cm) the development is complete and the plate is removed from the chamber and dried.

Because most compounds are colorless, no separation will be noticed after development unless the materials are *visualized*. To accomplish this the plates are placed under ultraviolet light, revealing those materials that fluoresce as bright spots on a dark background. When a fluorescent dye has been incorporated into the solid phase, nonfluorescent substances appear as dark spots against a fluorescent background when exposed to the ultraviolet light. A second method of visualization is accomplished when the plate is sprayed with a chemical reagent that reacts with the separated substances and causes them to form colored spots. Figure 4–8 shows the chromatogram of a marihuana extract that has been separated into its components by TLC and visualized by having been sprayed with a chemical reagent.

Once the components of a sample have been separated, their identification must follow. For this, the questioned sample must be developed alongside an authentic or standard sample on the same TLC plate. If both the standard and the unknown are found to travel the same distances up the plate from their origins, they can tentatively be identified as being the same. For example, a sample suspected of containing heroin and quinine is chromatographed alongside known heroin and quinine standards, as shown in Figure 4-9. A confirmation of the identity of the suspect material is made by comparing the

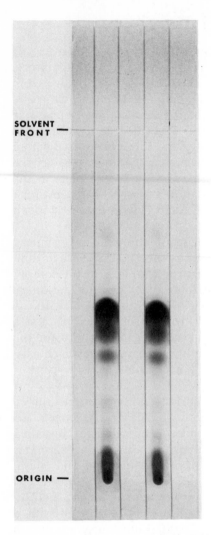

SOLVENT FRONT —

ORIGIN —

FIGURE 4-8. Chromatogram of a Marihuana Extract

migration distances of the heroin and quinine standards against those of the components of the unknown material. If they are the same, a tentative identification can be made. However, it must be cautioned that such an identification cannot be considered definitive, for the possibility always exists that numerous other substances can migrate the same distance up the plate when chromatographed under similar conditions. Thus, thin-layer chromatography cannot by itself provide an absolute identification; it must be utilized in conjunction with other testing procedures to prove absolute identity.

The distance a spot has traveled up a thin-layer plate can be assigned a numerical value known as the R_f value. This value is defined as the distance traveled by the component divided by the distance traveled by the moving liquid phase. For example, in Figure 4-9 the moving phase was allowed to travel 10 cm up the plate before the plate was removed from the tank. After visualization, the heroin spot moved 8 cm and thus has an R_f value of 0.8; the quinine migrated 4 cm, and has an R_f value of 0.4.

There are literally thousands of possible combinations of liquid and solid phases that can be chosen from in thin-layer chromatography. Fortunately, years of research have produced much published data relating to the proper selection of TLC conditions for

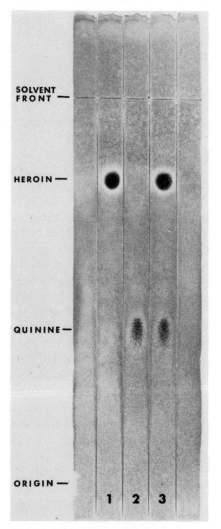

FIGURE 4-9. Chromatograms of known heroin (1) and quinine (2) standards alongside suspect sample (3).

separating and identifying specific classes of substances—e.g., drugs, dyes, and petroleum products. These references, along with the personal experiences of the analyst, will aid in the proper selection of TLC conditions for specific problems.

Thin-layer chromatography is a powerful tool for solving many of the analytical problems presented to the forensic scientist. The method is both rapid and sensitive; moreover, less than 100 micrograms of suspect material are required for the analysis. In addition, the equipment necessary for TLC work has minimal cost and space requirements. And numerous samples can be analyzed simultaneously on one thin-layer plate. The principle application of this technique is the detection and identification of components in complex mixtures.

Electrophoresis

Electrophoresis is somewhat related to thin-layer chromatography in that it separates materials according to their migration rates on a stationary solid phase. However, it does not utilize a moving-liquid phase to move the material; instead, an electrical potential is placed across the stationary medium. The nature of this medium can vary; most forensic applications call for a starch or agar gel coated onto a glass plate. Under these conditions only substances that possess an electrical charge will migrate across the stationary phase. The technique is particularly useful for separating and identifying complex biochemical mixtures. In forensic science it finds its most successful application in the characterization of proteins in dried blood.

Because many of the substances in blood carry an electrical charge, they can be separated and identified by electrophoresis. Forensic serologists have developed several electrophoretic procedures for characterizing dried blood. Many enzymes present in blood are actually composed of distinct proteins that can be separated by electrophoresis on starch gel. These proteins will migrate on the plate at speeds that vary according to their electrical charge and size. After completion of the electrophoresis run, the separated proteins are stained with a suitable developing agent for visual observation. In this manner, characteristic band patterns are obtained that are related to the enzyme type present in the blood. This technique will be discussed in further detail in Chapter 11.

SPECTROPHOTOMETRY

Theory of Light

We have already seen that when white light passes through a glass prism it is dispersed into a continuous spectrum of colors. This phenomenon demonstrates the fact that white light is not homogeneous but is actually composed of a range of colors that extends from red through violet. Similarly, the observation that a substance has a color is also consistent with this description of white light. For example, when light is passed through a red glass, all the component colors of light are absorbed by the glass except for red, which passes through or is transmitted by the glass. Likewise, one can determine the color of an opaque object by observing its ability to absorb some of the component colors of light while reflecting others back to the eye. Color is thus a visual indication of the fact that objects absorb certain portions of visible light and transmit or reflect others. Scientists have long recognized this phenomenon and have learned to characterize different chemical substances by the type and quantity of light they absorb.

To understand why materials absorb light, one must first comprehend the nature of light. Two simple models have been developed to explain light's behavior. The first model describes light as a continuous wave; the second depicts it as a stream of discrete energy particles. Together, these two very different descriptions can explain all of the observed properties of light; but by itself, no one model can explain all the facets of the behavior of light.

The wave concept depicts light as having an up and down motion of a continuous wave, as shown in Figure 4-10. Several terms are used to describe such a wave. The distance between two consecutive crests (or one trough to the next trough) is called the **wavelength**; the Greek letter *lambda* (λ) is used as its symbol and the unit of nanometers is frequently used to express its value. The number of crests (or troughs) passing any one given point in a unit of time is defined as the **frequency** of the wave. Frequency is normally designated by the letter f, and is expressed in cycles per second (cps). The speed of light in a vacuum is a universal constant at 300,000,000 meters per second, and is designated by the symbol c. Frequency and wavelength are inversely proportional to one another, as shown by the relationship expressed in Equation 4-1.

$$f = \frac{c}{\lambda} \qquad (4\text{-}1)$$

Actually, visible light is only a small part of a large family of radiation waves known as the **electromagnetic spectrum**. All electromagnetic radiations travel at the speed of light (c) and are only distinguishable from one another by their different wavelengths or frequencies. (Figure 4-11 illustrates the various types of electromagnetic radiations in the order of decreasing frequency.) Hence, the only property that distinguishes X-rays from radio waves is the different frequencies they possess. Similarly, the range of colors that

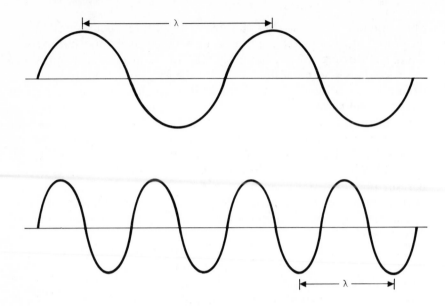

FIGURE 4-10. The frequency of the lower wave is twice that of the upper wave.

Electromagnetic spectrum

Gamma rays	X rays	Ultraviolet rays	Visible light	Infrared rays	Microwave rays	Radio waves

Decreasing frequency ⟶
Increasing wavelength ⟶

FIGURE 4-11. Electromagnetic Spectrum

comprise the visible spectrum can be correlated with frequency. For instance, the lowest frequencies of visible light are red in color, with those waves having a somewhat lower frequency falling into the invisible infrared region. The highest frequencies of visible light are violet in color, while those radiations having a somewhat higher frequency extend into the invisible ultraviolet region. No definite boundary exists between any one color or any one region of the electromagnetic spectrum; instead, each region is comprised of a continuous range of frequencies, each blending into the other.

As long as electromagnetic radiation is moving through space, its behavior can be explained as that of a continuous wave; however, once radiation is absorbed by a substance, the model of light as a stream of discrete particles must be invoked to best describe its behavior. Here, light is depicted as consisting of energy particles that are known as **photons**. Each photon has a definite amount of energy associated with its behavior. This energy is related to the frequency of light, as shown by Equation 4-2:

$$E = hf \qquad (4\text{-}2)$$

E specifies the energy of the photon, f the frequency of radiation, and h is a universal constant called Planck's constant. As shown by Equation 4-2, the energy of a photon is directly proportional to its frequency. Therefore, the photons of ultraviolet light will be more energetic than the photons of visible or infrared light, and exposure to the more energetic photons of X-rays presents more danger to human health than the photons of radio waves.

Absorption of Electromagnetic Radiation

Just as a substance can absorb visible light to produce color, many of the invisible radiations of the electromagnetic spectrum are likewise absorbed. This absorption phenomenon is the basis for spectrophotometry, an important analytical technique in chemical identification. Spectrophotometry measures the quantity of radiation that a particular material absorbs as a function of wavelength or frequency.

We have already observed in the description of color that an object will not absorb all the visible light it is exposed to; instead, it will selectively absorb some of the component frequencies and reflect or transmit others. Similarly, the absorption of other types of electromagnetic radiation by chemical substances is also found to be selective. The key questions that must be asked is why does a particular substance absorb only at certain frequencies and not at others, and are these frequencies predictable? The answers are not simple ones. Scientists find it most difficult to predict with certainty all the frequencies at which any one substance will absorb in a particular region of the electromagnetic spectrum. What is known, however, is that a chemical substance will absorb photons of radiation that have a frequency that corresponds to an energy requirement of the substance, as defined by Equation 4-2. Different materials have different energy requirements and therefore absorb at different frequencies. What is most important to the analyst is that these absorbed frequencies are measurable and they can be used to characterize a material.

The selective absorption of a substance is measured by an instrument called the **spectrophotometer**. It produces a graph or **absorption spectrum** that depicts the absorbance of light as a function of wavelength or frequency. The absorption of ultraviolet (UV), visible, and infrared (IR) radiations are particularly applicable for obtaining qualitative data pertaining to the identification of organic substances.

Absorption at a single wavelength or frequency of light is not one hundred percent complete—there will always be some radiation transmitted or reflected by the material. Just how much radiation a substance will absorb is defined by a fundamental relationship known as Beer's Law (Equation 4-3):

$$A = kc \qquad \qquad (4\text{-}3)$$

Here, A symbolizes the absorbance or the quantity of light taken up at a single frequency, c is the concentration of the absorbing material, and k is a proportionality constant. From this relationship, it is seen that the quantity of light absorbed at any frequency is directly proportional to the concentration of the absorbing species; the more material you have, the more radiation it will absorb. By defining the relationship between absorbance and concentration, Beer's Law permits spectrophotometry to be used as a technique for quantitation.

The Spectrophotometer

The spectrophotometer is the instrument used to measure and record the absorption spectrum of a chemical substance. The basic components of a simple spectrophotometer are the same regardless of whether it is designed to measure the absorption of UV, visible, or IR radiation. These components are illustrated diagramatically in Figure 4-12. They include: (1) a radiation source, (2) a monochromator or frequency selector, (3) a sample holder, (4) a detector to convert electromagnetic radiation into an electrical signal, and (5) a recorder to produce a record of the signal.

The choice of a source will vary with the type of radiation desired. For visible radiation, an ordinary tungsten bulb provides a convenient source of radiation. In the UV region, a hydrogen or deuterium discharge lamp is normally used, and a heated molded rod containing a mixture of rare-earth oxides is a good source of IR light.

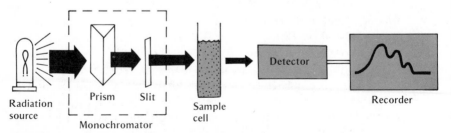

FIGURE 4-12. Parts of a Simple Spectrophotometer

The function of the monochromator is to select a single wavelength or frequency of light from the source. In some inexpensive spectrophotometers this may be accomplished when the light is caused to pass through colored glass filters that will remove all radiation from the beam except for a desired range of wavelengths. More precise spectrophotometers may employ a prism or diffraction gratings to disperse radiation into its component wavelengths or frequencies.[2] The desired wavelength is obtained when the dispersed radiation is focused onto a narrow slit that permits only selected radiations to pass through.

Sample preparation varies with the type of radiation being studied. Absorption spectra in the UV and visible regions are usually obtained from samples that have been dissolved in an appropriate solvent. Because the cells holding the solution must be transparent to the light being measured, glass cells are used in the visible region and quartz cells in the ultraviolet region. Practically all substances absorb in some region of the IR spectrum, so sampling techniques must be modified to measure absorption in this spectral region; special cells made out of sodium chloride or potassium bromide are commonly utilized, because they will not absorb light over a wide range of the IR portion of the electromagnetic spectrum.

The detector measures the quantity of radiation that passes through the sample by converting it to an electrical signal. UV and visible spectrophotometers employ photoelectric tube detectors. A signal is generated when the photons strike the tube surface to produce a current that is directly proportional to the intensity of the light transmitted through the sample. When this signal is compared to the intensity of light that is transmitted to the detector in the absence of an absorbing material, the absorbance of a substance can be determined at each wavelength or frequency of light selected. The signal from the detection system is then fed into a recorder, which plots absorbance as a function of wavelength or frequency. Modern spectrophotometers are designed to trace an entire absorption spectrum automatically.

Ultraviolet, Visible, and Infrared Spectrophotometry

Ultraviolet (UV) and visible spectrophotometry measures the absorbance of UV and visible light as a function of wavelength or frequency. For example, the illustrated UV absorption spectrum of heroin shows a maximum absorption band at a wavelength of 278

---

[2]Present-day spectrophotometers use diffraction gratings to disperse light into its component wavelengths. A diffraction grating is made by scratching many thousands of parallel lines on a transparent surface such as glass. As light passes through the narrow spacings between the lines, it spreads out and produces a spectrum similar to that formed by a prism.

nanometers (Figure 4-13). From this it can readily be seen that the simplicity of a UV spectrum facilitates its use as a tool for determining a material's probable identity. For instance, a white powder may have a UV spectrum comparable to heroin, and therefore may be tentatively identified as such. (Fortunately, sugar and starch, common diluents of heroin, do not absorb UV light.) However, this technique will not provide for a definitive result; the possibility always exists that there are other drugs or materials that have a UV absorption spectrum similar to that of heroin. But, this lack of specificity does not diminish the value of the technique, for the analyst has quickly eliminated thousands of other possible drugs from consideration and can now proceed to conduct other confirmatory tests, such as thin-layer or gas chromatography, to complete the identification.

In contrast to the simplicity of a UV spectrum, absorption in the infrared region provides a far more complex pattern. Figure 4-14 depicts the IR spectra of heroin and secobarbital. Here the absorption bands are so numerous that each spectrum can provide enough characteristics to specifically identify a substance. Different materials always have distinctively different infrared spectra; each IR spectrum is therefore equivalent to being a "fingerprint" of that substance and no other. This technique is one of the few tests available to the

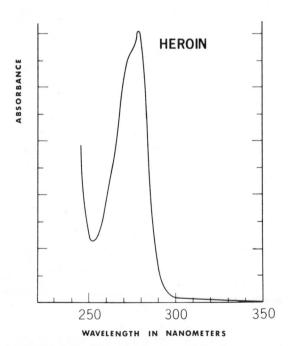

FIGURE 4-13. Ultraviolet Spectrum of Heroin

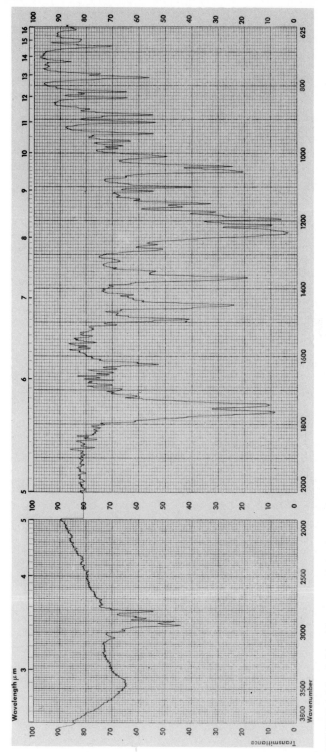

FIGURE 4-14a. Infrared Spectrum of Heroin

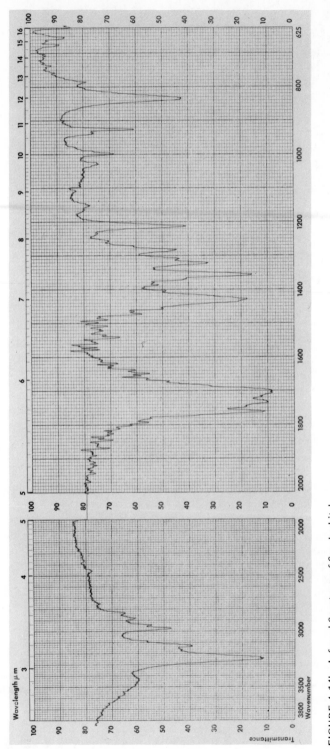

FIGURE 4-14b. Infrared Spectrum of Secobarbital

92

forensic scientist that can be considered specific in itself for identification. The IR spectra of thousands of organic compounds have been collected, indexed, and catalogued to serve as invaluable references for identifying organic substances.

MASS SPECTROMETRY

Though chromatography and spectrophotometry have become well-established analytical techniques in the crime laboratory, forensic scientists continue their search for methods that will provide them with additional information to aid in the identification of organic compounds. In the assessment of the potential of other methods, it has become quite apparent that mass spectrometry is rapidly taking its place as an indispensable analytical technique in the crime laboratory. It is sensitive to minute concentrations, and under proper conditions will provide a specific identification of an organic substance. At present, mass spectrometry finds its widest application in areas relating to the identification of drugs; however, further research is expected to yield significant applications with respect to the identification of other types of physical evidence.

Mass spectrometry is performed by the introduction of a very small amount of material into a high-vacuum chamber in which a beam of high-energy electrons is aimed at the sample's molecules. The electrons collide with the molecules, causing them to lose electrons and to acquire a positive charge (commonly called ions). These positively charged molecules or ions are very unstable or are formed with excess energy and almost instantaneously decompose into numerous smaller fragments. The fragments are then passed through an electric or magnetic field which separates them according to their mass. The unique feature of mass spectroscopy is that under carefully controlled conditions no two substances produce the same fragmentation pattern. The technique thus offers itself as a specific means for identifying a chemical structure. Figure 4-15 illustrates the mass spectrum of heroin; here, each line represents a fragment of a different mass (actually the ratio of mass to charge), and the line height reflects the relative abundance of each fragment.

The production of meaningful mass spectra requires that pure samples be introduced into the spectrometer, because the presence of only the slightest impurities can significantly change the fragmentation pattern. Thus, in the analysis of complex organic mixtures it is desirable and convenient to interface a gas chromatograph to the mass spectrometer. The separation of a mixture's components is first accomplished on the gas chromatograph. A direct connection between the GC column and the mass spectrometer then allows each

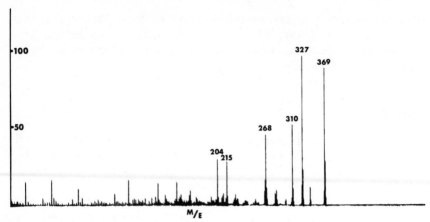

FIGURE 4-15. Mass Spectrum of Heroin.

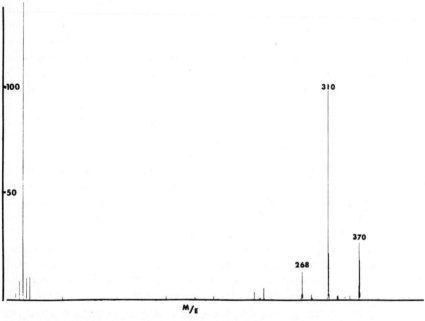

FIGURE 4-16. Chemical Ionization Mass Spectrum of Heroin

component to enter the spectrometer as it emerges from the gas chromatograph. This combination is further enhanced when a computer is added to the system. The integrated gas chromatograph/ mass spectrometer/ computer system provides the ultimate in speed, accuracy, and sensitivity. With the ability to record and store several hundred mass spectra, such a system can detect and identify substances present in only one-millionth of a gram quantities. Furthermore, the computer can be programmed to compare an unknown spectrum against a comprehensive library of mass spectra stored in the computer's memory.

Recently, a new variation of mass spectrometry known as **chemical ionization mass spectrometry** has been developed. This technique is particularly applicable to the forensic scientist, because it allows the analyst to tentatively identify the components of a mixture without resorting to prior chromatographic separation. The major advantage of the technique is that it simplifies the mass spectral fragmentation pattern that is produced by a substance. This is exemplified by the relatively simple chemical ionization mass spectrum of heroin shown in Figure 4-16, as contrasted with its conventional mass spectrum, shown in Figure 4-15.

REVIEW QUESTIONS

1. Anything that has mass and occupies space is defined as _____ .

2. The basic building blocks of all substances are the _____ .

3. The number of elements known today is _____ .

4. An arrangement of elements by similar chemical properties is accomplished in the _____ table.

5. An _____ is the smallest particle of an element that can exist.

6. Substances composed of two or more elements are called _____ .

7. A _____ is the smallest unit of a compound formed by the union of two or more atoms.

8. The physical state that retains a definite shape and volume is a _____ .

9. A gas (has, has no) definite shape or volume.

10. During the process of _____ solids will go directly to the gaseous state, bypassing the liquid state.

11. The attraction forces between the molecules of a liquid are (more, less) than those in a solid.

12. Different _____ are separated by definite visible boundaries.

13. Carbon-containing substances are classified as _____ .

14. _____ substances encompass all non-carbon containing materials.

15. A _____ analysis describes the identity of a material, while a _____ analysis relates to a determination of the quantity of a substance in a sample.

16. The study of the absorption of light by chemical substances is known as _____ .

17. The separation of a mixture's components can be accomplished utilizing the technique of _____ .

18. Henry's Law describes the distribution of a volatile chemical compound between its liquid and gas phases. (True, False)

19. The (higher, lower) the solubility of a gas in a liquid the greater will be its tendency to remain dissolved in that liquid.

20. In order for chromatography to occur, one phase must be made to move continuously in one direction over a stationary phase. (True, False)

21. A technique that separates mixtures on the basis of their distribution between a stationary liquid phase and a moving gas phase is _____ .

22. The time required for a substance to travel through the gas chromatographic column is a useful identifying characteristic known as _____ .

23. Solid materials that are not readily dissolved in solvents for injection into the gas chromatograph can be _____ into numerous gaseous products prior to entering the gas chromatograph.

24. A technique that utilizes a moving liquid phase and a stationary solid phase to separate mixtures is _____ .

25. Since most chemical compounds are colorless the final step of the thin-layer development usually requires that they be _____ by spraying with a chemical reagent.

26. The distance a spot has traveled up a thin-layer plate can be assigned a numerical value known as the _____ value.

27. Thin-layer chromatography yields the positive identification of a material. (True, False)

28. The migration of materials along a stationary phase under the influence of an electrical potential describes the technique of _____ .

29. Color is a usual indication that substances selectively absorb light. (True, False)

30. The distance between two successive identical points on a wave is known as _____ .

31. Frequency and wavelength are directly proportional to one another. (True, False)

32. Light, X-rays, and radiowaves are all members of the _____ spectrum.

33. Red light is (higher, lower) in frequency than violet light.

34. One model of light depicts it as consisting of energy particles known as _____ .

35. The energy of a light particle (photon) is directly proportional to its frequency. (True, False)

36. Red light is (more, less) energetic than violet light.

37. The selective absorption of electromagnetic radiation by materials (can, cannot) be used as an aid for identification.

38. The amount of radiation a substance will absorb is directly proportional to its concentration as defined by _____ Law.

39. The _____ is the instrument used to measure and record the absorption spectrum of a chemical substance.

40. The function of the _____ is to select a single frequency of light emanating from the spectrophotometer's source.

41. An (ultraviolet, infrared) absorption spectrum provides an unique "fingerprint" of a chemical substance.

42. The technique of _____ exposes molecules to a beam of high energy electrons in order to fragment them.

FURTHER READINGS

Connor, Kenneth A., *A Textbook of Pharmaceutical Analysis*, 2nd ed. New York: Wiley & Sons, 1975.

Howard, Patrick Y., *Forensic Analysis by Gas Chromatography*. Palo Alto, Cal.: Varian Instrument Division, 1974.

Saferstein, Richard, Jew-Ming Chao, and J. Manura, "Identification of Drugs by Chemical Ionization Mass Spectroscopy—Part II," *Journal of Forensic Sciences*, 19, no. 3 (1974), 463.

Walls, H. J., *Forensic Science*, 2nd ed. New York: Praeger, 1974.

Williams, Ray L., "Forensic Science—The Present and Future," *Analytical Chemistry*, 45, no. 13 (1973), 1076A.

Audiovisual Presentations

Colorimetric Analysis (Thirty-nine 35 mm slides and audio tape). Communication Skills Corp., Fairfield, Conn.

Gas Chromatography—Basic Relationships and Instrumentation (Forty-three 35 mm slides and audio tape). Communication Skills Corp., Fairfield, Conn.

Inorganic Analysis
chapter 5

INTRODUCTION

In the previous chapter, analytical techniques were described for characterizing a class of matter known as organics. Generally, these materials contain the element carbon in their chemical composition. Though organic substances do constitute a substantial portion of the physical evidence submitted to crime laboratories, the element carbon does not appear among the earth's most abundant elements. It is perhaps rather surprising to observe that about three-quarters of the weight of the earth's crust is composed of only two elements—oxygen and silicon. In fact, only ten elements make up approximately 99 percent of the earth's crust (see Table 5-1). The remaining elements may be considered almost as impurities, though exceedingly important ones. Carbon, the element that is a constituent of most chemical compounds, comprises less than 0.1 percent of the earth's crust.

Considering these facts, it is certainly reasonable to expect that non-carbon-containing substances—that is, inorganics—will be encountered as physical evidence at crime scenes. One only has to consider the prevalence of metallic materials, such as iron, steel, copper, and aluminum, in our society to understand the possibilities of finding tools, coins, weapons, and metal scrapings at crime scenes.

TABLE 5-1. Elemental Abundance as Percentages in the Earth's Crust

Element	Percentage by Weight
Oxygen	47.3
Silicon	27.7
Aluminum	7.9
Iron	4.5
Calcium	3.5
Sodium	2.5
Potassium	2.5
Magnesium	2.2
Titanium	0.5
Hydrogen	0.2
Other Elements	1.2

Less well-known, but perhaps almost as significant to the criminalist, is the utilization of inorganic chemicals as pigments in paints and dyes, the incorporation of inorganics into explosive formulations, and the prevalence of inorganic poisons such as mercury, lead, or arsenic.

To fully appreciate the role that inorganic analysis has in forensic science we must first examine its application to the basic objectives of the crime laboratory—the identification and comparison of physical evidence. The identification of inorganic evidence is exemplified by a typical request to examine an explosive formulation suspected of containing the inorganic chemical potassium chlorate, or perhaps to examine a poisonous powder thought to be arsenic. In each case, the forensic scientist must perform tests that will ultimately determine the specific chemical identity of the suspect materials to the exclusion of all others. Only after tests are completed and their results found to be identical to tests previously recorded for a known potassium chlorate or a known arsenic can a valid conclusion as to the chemical identity of the evidence be reached.

However, in a situation that requires a comparison of two or more objects in order to ascertain their common origin, a different problem is presented to the analyst. For example, a criminalist may be requested to determine whether or not a piece of brass pipe found in the possession of a suspect compares to a broken pipe found at the crime scene. The condition of the two pipes might not allow for their comparison by the physical fitting together of broken edges. Under these circumstances, the only alternative will be to attempt a comparison through a chemical analysis. Here, it is not enough for the analyst to conclude that both pipes are alike because they are brass (an alloy of copper and zinc). After all, hundreds of thousands of brass pipes are known to exist, a situation that is hardly conducive to proving that these two particular pipes were at one time a single unit. The examiner must go a step further to try and distinguish these pipes from all others. Although this may not be possible, a comparison of the pipes' trace elements—that is, elements present in small quantities—will provide a meaningful criterion for at least increasing the probability that the two pipes originated from the same source.

Considering the fact that most of our raw materials originate from the earth's crust, it is not surprising to observe that they are rarely obtained in pure form; instead, they include numerous elemental impurities that usually have to be eliminated through industrial processing. However, in most cases it is not economically feasible to completely exclude all such minor impurities, especially in light of the fact that their presence will have no effect on the appearance or performance of the final product. For this reason, we find that many of our manufactured products, and even most natural materials, contain small quantities of elements present in concentrations of less than 1 percent. For the criminalist, the presence of trace elements is particularly useful because they provide "invisible" markers that may establish the source of a material or at least provide additional points for comparison. Table 5-2 illustrates how two types of brass alloys can readily be distinguished by their elemental composition. Similarly, the comparison of trace elements present in

TABLE 5-2. Elemental Analysis of Brass Alloys

Element	High-Tensile Brass %	Manganese Brass %
Copper	57.0	58.6
Aluminum	2.8	1.7
Zinc	35.0	33.8
Manganese	2.13	1.06
Iron	1.32	0.90
Nickel	0.48	1.02
Tin	0.64	1.70
Lead	0.17	0.72
Silicon	0.08	Nil

Source: R. L. Williams, "An Evaluation of the SEM with X-Ray Microanalyzer Accessory for Forensic Work," in Scanning Electron Microscopy/1971, O. Johari and I. Corvin, eds. (Chicago: IIT Research Institute, 1971), p. 541.

paint or other types of metallic specimens may provide particularly meaningful data with respect to source or origin. Currently, forensic investigators are examining the evidential value of trace elements known to be present in hair, soil, fibers, and glass, as well as all types of metallic objects.

A variety of analytical instruments are available to forensic scientists for identifying inorganic compounds and for detecting their minor constituents. The remainder of this chapter will be devoted to describing those techniques that are most applicable for the identification or comparison of inorganic physical evidence.

THE EMISSION SPECTRUM OF ELEMENTS

We have already observed that organic molecules can readily be characterized by their selective absorption of ultraviolet, visible, or infrared radiations. Equally significant to the analytical chemist is the knowledge that the elements will also selectively absorb and emit light. These observations form the basis of two important analytical techniques designed to determine the elemental composition of materials—emission spectroscopy and atomic absorption spectrophotometry.

The statement that elements emit light should not come as a total surprise, for one need only observe the common tungsten incandescent light bulb or the glow of a neon light to confirm this observation. When the light emitted from a bulb or any other light source is passed through a prism, it is separated into its component colors or frequencies. The resulting display of colors is called an **emission spectrum.**

When sunlight or the light from an incandescent bulb is passed through a prism we have already observed that a range of rainbow colors is produced. This emission spectrum is called a **continuous spectrum** because all the colors merge or blend into one another to form a continuous band. However, not all light sources produce such a spectrum. For example, if the light from a sodium lamp, or a mercury arc lamp, or a neon light were passed through a prism the resultant spectrum would consist not of a continuous band, but of several individual colored lines separated by dark spaces. Here, each line represents a definite wavelength or frequency of light that is separate and distinct from all others present in the spectrum. This type of spectrum is called a **line spectrum.** Figure 5-1 shows the line spectra of several elements.

Hydrogen

Helium

Mercury

FIGURE 5-1. Some Characteristic Emission Spectra

It is important to realize that heated matter in a solid or liquid state produces a continuous spectrum that is not very indicative of its composition. However, if this same matter is vaporized and "excited" by exposure to high temperature, each element present will emit light that is composed of select frequencies that are characteristic of the element. This spectrum is in essence a "fingerprint" of an element and offers itself as a very practical method of identification. Sodium vapor, for example, always shows the same line spectrum, which differs from the spectrum of all other elements.

An **emission spectrograph** is an instrument used to obtain and record the line spectra of elements. Essentially, this instrument requires a means for vaporizing and exciting the atoms of elements so that they emit light, a means for separating this light into its component frequencies, and a means of recording the resultant spectrum. A simple emission spectrograph is depicted in Figure 5-2.

Excitation of the specimen under investigation is accomplished when it is inserted between two carbon electrodes through which a direct current arc is passed. The arc produces a sufficient amount of heat to vaporize and excite the specimen's atoms. The resultant emitted light is collected by a lens and focused onto a prism that disperses it into component frequencies. The separated frequencies are then directed toward a photographic plate, where they are recorded as line images. Normally, a specimen consists of numerous elements; hence, the typical emission spectrum contains many lines.

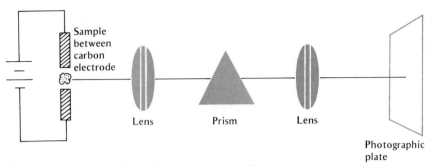

FIGURE 5-2. Parts of a Simple Emission Spectrograph

Each element present in the spectrum can be identified when it is compared to a standard chart that shows the position of the principal spectral lines of all the elements. However, the more common situation in forensic analysis simply requires a rapid comparison. of the elemental composition of two or more specimens. This can readily be accomplished when the emission spectra are matched line for line, an approach illustrated in Figure 5-3. Here the emission spectra of two paint chips are shown to compare.

A recent advancement in emission spectroscopy has been the utilization of a laser beam to vaporize a small portion of the specimen. The laser beam is focused onto a selected area of the specimen through a microscope. The intense energy of laser radiation is sufficient to vaporize the specimen, causing it to rise between two carbon electrodes situated just above the sample. As the vapor passes between the electrodes, it triggers an electrical discharge that excites the atoms and causes them to emit light (see Figure 5-4). In this manner it is possible to determine the elemental composition of a specimen that is no larger than the size of the period at the end of this sentence. Trace elements present in concentrations of 0.1 to 0.01 percent are readily detected by this procedure.

FIGURE 5-3. A comparison of paint chips 1 and 2 by emission spectrographics analysis. A line for line comparison shows both paints have the same elemental composition.

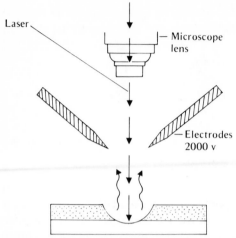

FIGURE 5-4. Laser Microprobe

ATOMIC ABSORPTION SPECTROPHOTOMETRY

When an atom is vaporized it will absorb many of the same frequencies of light that it emits in an excited state. The selective
absorption of light by atoms is the basis for a technique known as
atomic absorption spectrophotometry. A simple atomic absorption
spectrophotometer is illustrated in Figure 5-5.

In atomic absorption spectrophotometry the specimen is heated
to a temperature that is hot enough to vaporize its atoms while
leaving a substantial number of atoms in an unexcited state. Normally, the specimen is inserted into an air-acetylene flame to achieve
this temperature. The vaporized atoms are then exposed to radiation
emitted from a light source. In practice, the technique achieves great

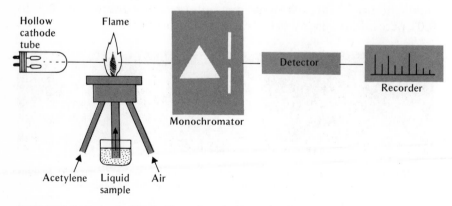

FIGURE 5-5. Parts of a Simple Flame Atomic Absorption Spectrophotometer

specificity by using as its radiation source a discharge tube made of the very same element being analyzed in the specimen. When the discharge lamp is turned on, it emits only those frequencies of light that are present in the emission spectrum of the element. Likewise, the sample will only absorb these frequencies when it contains this very same element. Therefore, if one wanted to determine the presence of the element antimony in a specimen, the atomic absorption spectrophotometer would have to be fitted with a discharge lamp that is constructed of antimony. Under these conditions the sample will only absorb light when it contains antimony.

Once the radiation has passed through the sample, a monochromator, consisting of a prism or a diffraction grating and a slit, isolates the desired radiation frequency and transmits it to a detector. The detector converts the light into an electrical signal, the intensity of which is recorded on a strip-chart recorder.

The absorption of light by the element of interest is the phenomenon that is being measured in atomic absorption spectrophotometry. The concentration of the absorbing element will be directly proportional to the quantity of the light absorbed. The higher the concentration of the element, the more light absorbed. For this reason, atomic absorption spectroscopy has its most useful application in providing an accurate determination of an element's concentration in a sample. Furthermore, the technique is sufficiently sensitive as to find wide application in detecting and quantitating elements that are present at trace levels. However, the technique does have one drawback, in that the analyst can only determine one element at a time, each time having to select the proper lamp to match the particular element under investigation.

Though atomic absorption spectrophotometry has been utilized for chemical analysis since 1955, it has not yet found wide application for solving forensic problems. However, a recent modification in the design of the instrument promises to change this situation. By substituting a heated graphite furnace or a heated strip of metal (tantalum) for the flame, analysts have succeeded in achieving a more efficient means of atomic volatilization and as a result have produced a substantial increase in the sensitivity of the technique. Many elements can now be detected at levels that approach one-trillionth of a gram.

The high sensitivity of "flameless" atomic absorption now equals or surpasses that of any known analytical procedure. Considering the relative simplicity and low cost of the technique, atomic absorption spectrophotometry has become an attractive method for detecting and measuring the smallest levels of trace elements present in physical evidence.

TABLE 5-3. Antimony Concentration in .38 Special Lead Bullets Determined
by Atomic Absorption Spectrophotometry

Manufacturer	Antimony %
Remington	0.89 ± 0.10
Federal	1.63 ± 0.18
Winchester	2.20 ± 0.26

Source: R. L. Brunelle, C. M. Hoffman, and K. B. Snow, "Comparison of Elemental Composition of Pistol Bullets by Atomic Absorption: Preliminary Study," *Journal of the Association of Official Analytical Chemists,* 53 (1970), 470.

Crime laboratories are often required to compare bullets or bullet fragments to determine the relationship between questioned and known specimens. In some cases, adequate comparison by standard microscopic techniques is not possible because the questioned bullet is badly mutilated. When this situation exists, an analysis of the elemental composition of the bullet by atomic absorption spectrophotometry may provide information about the similarity of the specimens under investigation.

It has been shown that .38 caliber bullets produced by the three major U.S. manufacturers can be distinguished on the basis of their concentration of antimony, a hardening agent added to lead (see Table 5-3). Further analysis by atomic absorption spectrophotometry of trace elements present in bullets—i.e., copper, silver, and bismuth—will provide additional points of comparison between the questioned and known specimens.

THE ORIGIN OF EMISSION AND ABSORPTION SPECTRA

Any proposed theory that attempts to explain the origin of emission and absorption spectra must relate to the fundamental structure of the element—the atom. Scientists now know that the atom is composed of even more elementary particles that are collectively known as subatomic particles. The most important subatomic particles are the **proton, electron,** and **neutron.** The mass of the proton and neutron are each about 1,837 times the mass of an electron. The proton is a particle with a positive electrical charge; the electron has a negative charge equal in magnitude to that of the proton; and the neutron is a neutral particle having neither a positive nor a negative charge. The properties of the electron, proton, and neutron are summarized below:

Particle	Symbol	Relative Mass	Electrical Charge
Proton	P	1	+1
Neutron	n	1	0
Electron	e	1/1837	-1

A popular descriptive model of the atom, and the one that will be adopted for the purpose of this discussion, pictures an atom as consisting of electrons orbiting around a central nucleus—an image that is analogous to our solar system, in which the planets revolve around the sun.[1] The nucleus of the atom is comprised of positively charged protons and neutrons that have no charge. Because the atom has no net electrical charge, the number of protons must always be equal to the number of negatively charged electrons in orbit around the nucleus.

With this knowledge, we can now begin to describe the atomic structure of the elements; for example, hydrogen has a nucleus consisting of one proton and no neutrons, and it has one orbiting electron. Helium has a nucleus comprised of two protons and two neutrons with two electrons in orbit around the nucleus (see Figure 5-6).

The behavior and properties that distinguish one element from another must be related to those differences that exist in the atomic structure of each element. One such distinction resides in the fact that each element possesses a different number of protons. This number is called the **atomic number** of the element. As we look back at the periodic table, illustrated in Figure 4-1, we see that the elements are numbered consecutively from 1 to 105. This number represents the atomic number or number of protons associated with each element. **An element is therefore a collection of atoms, all having the same number of protons.** Thus, each atom of hydrogen has one and only one proton, each atom of helium has two protons, each atom of silver has forty-seven protons, and each atom of lead has eighty-two protons in its nucleus.

To explain the origin of atomic spectra, our attention must now focus on the orbiting electrons of the atom. As electrons move around the nucleus they are confined to a path of flight from which they cannot stray. This orbital path is associated with a definite amount of energy and is therefore called an energy level. Each ele-

---

[1] Actually, the electrons are moving so rapidly around the nucleus as to be best visualized as being in the form of an electron cloud spread out over the surface of the atom.

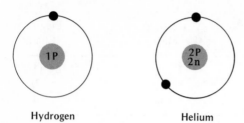

Hydrogen   Helium

FIGURE 5-6. The Atomic Structure of Hydrogen and Helium

ment has its own set of characteristic energy levels located at varying distances from the nucleus. Some of these levels are occupied by electrons, others are empty.

An atom will be in its most stable state when all of its electrons are positioned in their lowest possible energy orbitals in the atom. When an atom absorbs energy, such as heat or light, its electrons are pushed into higher energy orbitals. In this condition the atom is in an **excited state**. However, because energy levels have fixed values, only a definite amount of energy can be absorbed in moving an electron from one level to another. This is a most important observation, for it means that atoms will absorb only a definite value of energy while all other energy values will be excluded. In atomic absorption spectrophotometry a photon of light interacts with an electron, causing it to jump into a higher orbital as shown in Figure 5-7a. A specific frequency of light is required to effect this transition and its energy must correspond to the exact energy difference between the two orbitals involved in the transition. This energy difference is expressed by the relationship $E = hf$, where E represents the energy difference between the two orbitals, and f is the frequency of absorbed light. Any energy value that is more or less than this difference will not affect the transition. Hence, an element is selective in the frequency of light it will absorb, and this selectivity is determined by the electron energy levels each element possesses.

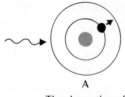   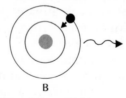

A   B

The absorption of   The emission of light
light by an atom   by an atom caused
causing an electron   by an electron falling
to jump into a   back to a lower orbital
higher orbital

FIGURE 5-7.

In the same manner, if atoms are exposed to intense heat, enough energy will be generated to push electrons into higher unoccupied energy orbitals. Normally, the electron will not remain in this excited state for long and it will quickly fall back to its original energy level. As the electron falls back it will have to release energy. An emission spectrum testifies to the fact that this energy loss comes about in the form of light emission (see Figure 5-7b). The frequency of light emitted will again be determined by the relationship $E = hf$, where E is the energy difference between the upper and lower energy levels and f is the frequency of emitted light. Because each element has its own characteristic set of energy levels, each will emit a unique set of frequency values. The emission spectrum thus provides us with a "picture" of the energy levels that surround the nucleus of each element.

Thus, we see that as far as atoms are concerned, energy is a two-way street. Energy can be put into the atom while at the same time energy is given off; what goes in must come out. The chemist has the option of studying the atom using either approach. Atomic absorption spectrophotometry carefully measures the value and amount of light energy going into the atom; emission spectroscopy collects and measures the various light energies given off. The end result is the same; atoms are identified by the existence of characteristic energy levels.

NEUTRON ACTIVATION ANALYSIS

Once scientists realized that it was possible to change the number of subatomic particles in the atom's nucleus, the unleashing of a new source of energy—nuclear energy—was inevitable. This energy has proven so awesome in its power that the very survival of civilization will depend on man's ability to refrain from using its destructive forces. Today, of course, this threat does not obscure the fact that controlled nuclear energy promises to be a source of power capable of relieving our dependency on earth's dwindling reserves of fossil fuels. For the chemist, nuclear chemistry offers itself as a new tool for identifying and quantitating the elements.

Until now, our discussion of subatomic particles has been limited to the proton and electron. However, in order to understand the principles of nuclear chemistry we must look at the other important subatomic particle, the neutron. Although the atoms of a single element must have the same number of protons, there is nothing to prevent them from having different numbers of neutrons. The total number of protons and neutrons in a nucleus is known as the **atomic**

mass number. Atoms having the same number of protons but differing solely in the number of neutrons they possess are called **isotopes.** For example, the element hydrogen actually consists of three isotopes; besides ordinary hydrogen, which has one proton and no neutrons in its nucleus, two other isotopes exist, deuterium and tritium. Deuterium (or heavy hydrogen) also has one proton, but contains one neutron as well. Tritium has one proton and two neutrons in its nucleus. The atomic structures of these isotopes are shown in Figure 5-8. Therefore, all the isotopes of hydrogen have an atomic number of one, but differ in their atomic mass numbers. Hydrogen has an atomic mass of one, deuterium a mass of two, and tritium a mass of three. Ordinary hydrogen makes up 99.98 percent of all the hydrogen atoms found in nature.

Like hydrogen, most elements are known to have two or more isotopes. The element tin, for example, has as many as ten. Many of these isotopes are quite stable and for all intents and purposes the isotopes of any one element have indistinguishable properties. Others, however, are not as stable and will decompose with time by a process known as **radioactive decay.** Radioactivity is the emission of radiation that accompanies the spontaneous disintegration of unstable nuclei. Radioactivity is actually comprised of three types of radiation: **alpha rays, beta rays,** and **gamma rays.**

Alpha rays have proven to be positively charged particles, each having a mass approximately four times that of a hydrogen atom. These particles are known to be helium atoms stripped of their orbiting electrons. Beta rays are actually electrons, and the gamma rays are electromagnetic radiation similar to X-rays but of a higher frequency and energy (refer to the electromagnetic spectrum in Figure 4-11). Fortunately, the vast majority of naturally occurring isotopes are not radioactive, and those that do exist—i.e., radium, uranium and thorium—are found in such small quantities in the earth's crust that their radioactivity presents no hazard to human survival.

The existence of isotopes would be of little importance to the forensic chemist were it not for the fact that scientists have mastered

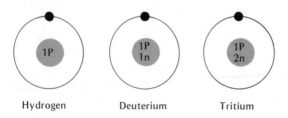

Hydrogen   Deuterium   Tritium

FIGURE 5-8. Isotopes of Hydrogen

the techniques for synthesizing radioactive isotopes. If the only distinction between isotopes of an element is the number of neutrons it possesses, is it not reasonable to assume that by bombarding atoms with neutrons, some will be captured by the nucleus to make a new isotope? This is exactly what takes place in a nuclear reactor. A nuclear reactor is simply a source of neutrons that can be used for bombarding the atoms of a specimen, thereby creating radioactive isotopes. When a neutron is captured by the nucleus of an atom, a new isotope is formed with one additional neutron. In this state the nuclei are said to be activated and many will immediately begin to decompose by emitting radioactivity.

To identify the activated isotope it is necessary to measure the energy of the gamma rays emitted as radioactivity. The gamma rays of each element can be associated with a characteristic energy value. Furthermore, once the element has been identified, its concentration can be measured by the intensity of its gamma ray radiation; intensity is directly proportional to the concentration of the element in a specimen. The technique of bombarding specimens with neutrons and measuring the resultant gamma ray radioactivity is known as **neutron activation analysis**. The process is depicted in Figure 5-9.

The major advantage of neutron activation analysis is that it offers itself as a nondestructive method for identifying and quantitating trace elements. A median detection sensitivity of one-billionth of a gram (one nanogram) makes neutron activation analysis one of the most sensitive methods available today for the quantitative detection of many elements. Further, neutron activation has the capability to perform a simultaneous analysis for twenty to thirty elements. A major drawback to the technique is its expense. Only a handful of

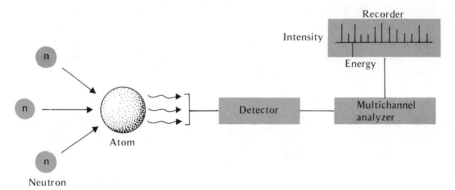

FIGURE 5-9. The neutron activation process requires the capture of a neutron by the nucleus of an atom. The new atom is now radioactive and emits gamma rays. A detector permits the identification of the radioactive atoms present by measuring the energies and intensities of the gamma rays emitted.

TABLE 5-4. Concentration of Trace Elements in Copper Wire[a]

	Selenium	Gold	Antimony	Silver
Control Wire				
A_1	2.4	0.047	0.16	12.7
A_2	3.5	0.064	0.27	17.2
A_3	2.6	0.050	0.20	13.3
A_4	1.9	0.034	0.21	12.6
Suspect Wire				
B	2.3	0.042	0.15	13.0

[a]Average concentration measured in part per million.
Source: R. K. H. Chan, "Identification of Single-Stranded Copper Wires by Nondestructive Neutron Activation Analysis," Journal of Forensic Sciences, 17 (1972), 93. Reprinted by permission of the American Society for Testing and Materials, copyright, 1972.

crime laboratories have access to a nuclear reactor; in addition, sophisticated analyzers are needed to detect and discriminate gamma ray emissions.

As far as forensic analysis is concerned, neutron activation has been employed for characterizing the trace elements present in metals, drugs, paint, soil, gunpowder residues, and hair. A typical illustration of its application occurred during the investigation of a theft of copper telegraphic wires in Canada. Four lengths of copper wire (A_1, A_2, A_3, A_4) found at the scene of the theft were compared by neutron activation with a length of copper wire (B) seized at a scrap yard and suspected of being stolen. All were bare, single-stranded wire with the same general physical appearance and a diameter of 0.28cm. Prior experiments had revealed that significant variations could be expected in the concentration levels of the trace elements selenium, gold, antimony, and silver for wires originating from different sources. A comparison of these elements present in the wires involved in the theft was undertaken. After exposing the wires to neutrons in a nuclear reactor, neutron activation analysis revealed a match between A_1 and B that was well within experimental error (see Table 5-4). The findings suggested a common origin of control and suspect wires.

X-RAY DIFFRACTION

The methods of analysis that have thus far been described have their primary application for determining trace elements present in materials. In contrast, X-ray diffraction is used to identify the major components of any crystalline material. The technique takes advantage of the fact that 95 percent of all inorganic compounds and many organic materials are crystalline in nature; that is, they have a definite geometric shape that is determined by the orderly arrangement of their atoms. The atoms are spaced at such distances that they can diffract a beam of X-rays that is directed against the surface of the crystal.

The atoms in a crystal can be thought of as being arranged in a series of parallel planes. As the X-rays penetrate the crystal, a portion of the beam is reflected by each of the atomic planes. As the reflected beams leave the crystal's planes they combine with one another to produce an interference or diffraction pattern that is the result of each wave being superimposed on the other. It is this pattern that is recorded on photographic film in the X-ray diffraction process (see Figure 5-10).

The value of X-ray diffraction as a tool for forensic identification stems from the observation that each inorganic substance produces its own characteristic diffraction pattern. Figure 5-11 shows the patterns for potassium nitrate and potassium chlorate, two common constituents of homemade explosives. A comparison of a questioned specimen with a known X-ray pattern is thus a rapid and specific means of proving chemical identity. Because of its lack of sensitivity, X-ray diffraction only has value for characterizing the major components of an inorganic substance. The forensic chemist must resort to more sensitive techniques—i.e., emission spectroscopy, atomic absorption, and neutron activation analysis—if there is a need to identify the trace elements that may be present.

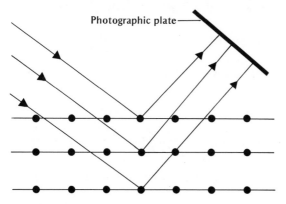

Photographic plate

FIGURE 5-10. A beam of X-rays being reflected off the atomic planes of a crystal. The interference patterns that are formed on the photographic plate are unique for each crystalline substance.

FIGURE 5-11a. X-ray Diffraction Pattern for Potassium Nitrate

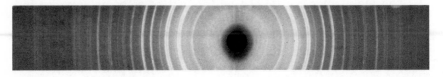

FIGURE 5-11b. X-ray Diffraction Pattern for Potassium Chlorate

REVIEW QUESTIONS

1. The elements _____ and _____ make up 75 percent of the weight of the earth's crust.

2. Only _____ elements make up about 99 percent of the weight of the earth's crust.

3. The presence of _____ elements in materials provides useful "invisible" markers when comparing physical evidence.

4. The knowledge that elements selectively _____ and _____ light provides the basis for important analytical techniques designed to detect the presence of elements in materials.

5. An _____ is a display of colors or frequencies emitted from a light source.

6. A continuous spectrum consists of a blending of colors. (True, False)

7. A _____ spectrum shows distinct frequencies or wavelengths of light.

8. A line spectrum of an element (is, is not) characteristic of the element.

9. Matter in a solid or liquid state will produce an emission spectrum that is characteristic of its composition. (True, False)

10. The _____ is an instrument used to obtain and record the line spectrum of elements.

11. A recent development in emission spectroscopy utilizes a _____ _____ in combination with an emission spectrograph.

12. The selective absorption of light by atoms is the basis for a technique known as _____ .

13. The composition of the discharge lamp (does, does not) have to be taken into consideration when performing an analysis by atomic absorption for a particular element.

14. One advantage of atomic absorption analysis is that it can simultaneously detect 20–30 elements. (True, False)

15. The element _____ is used as a hardening agent for lead.

16. Three important subatomic particles of the atom are the _____ _____ , _____ , and _____ .

17. The proton and electron (are, are not) of approximately equal mass.

18. A proton imparts the nucleus of an atom with a _____ charge.

19. The number of protons (is, is not) always equal to the number of electrons in orbit around the nucleus of an atom.

20. Each atom of the same element always has the same number of _____ in its nucleus.

21. The number of protons in the nucleus of an atom is called the _____ .

22. Each element has its own characteristic set of energy levels. (True, False)

23. To move an electron from one energy level to the next requires a definite amount of energy. (True, False)

24. As an electron falls back from a higher to lower energy level it emits _____ .

25. The total number of protons and neutrons present in a nucleus is known as the _____ .

26. Atoms differing only in the number of neutrons present in their nuclei are called _____ .

27. Deuterium has the greatest number of protons of all the isotopes of hydrogen. (True, False)

28. Radioactivity is composed of the following emissions: _____ , _____ , and _____ .

29. Beta particles are identical to _____ .

30. Electromagnetic radiations similar to X-rays but of a higher energy are _____ .

31. A nuclear reactor is a source of _____ .

32. The technique of bombarding specimens with neutrons and measuring the resultant gamma ray emissions is known as _____ .

33. X-ray diffraction patterns are obtained from (crystalline, amorphous) substances.

FURTHER READINGS

Krishnan, S. S., "Merits and Demerits of Forensic Activation Analysis when Compared to Other Analysis Methods," *Journal of Radioanalytical Chemistry*, 15 (1973), 165-72.

Singhal, S. P., "Atomic Absorption Spectroscopy in Forensic Chemistry," *Journal of the Canadian Society of Forensic Science*, 7 (1974), 7.

Walls, H. J., *Forensic Science*, 2nd ed. New York: Praeger, 1974.

Wessel, J. E., P. F. Jones, Q. Y. Kwan, R. S. Nesbitt, and E. J. Rattin, *Equipment Systems Improvement Program—Gunshot Residue Detection*. El Segundo, Cal.: The Aerospace Corp., 1974.

Willard, Hobart H., Lynne L. Merritt, and John A. Dean, *Instrumental Methods of Analysis*, 5th ed. New York: D. Van Nostrand, 1974.

Williams, Ray L., "Forensic Science—The Present and Future," *Analytical Chemistry*, 45, no. 13 (1973), 1067A.

Audiovisual Presentations

Basic Atomic Absorption Spectroscopy—Principles of Atomic Absorption (thirty-seven 35 mm slides and audio tape). Communication Skills Corp., Fairfield, Conn.

The Microscope

chapter 6

A microscope is an optical instrument that uses a lens or a combination of lenses to magnify and resolve the fine details of an object. The earliest methods for examining physical evidence in crime laboratories relied almost solely on the microscope to study the structure and composition of matter. Even the advent of modern analytical instrumentation and techniques in recent years has done little to diminish the usefulness of the microscope for forensic analysis. If anything, the development of the powerful scanning electron microscope promises to add a new dimension to forensic science heretofore unattainable within the limits of the ordinary light microscope.

The earliest and simplest microscope was the single lens commonly referred to as a magnifying glass. The hand-held magnifying glass makes things appear larger than they are because of the way light rays are refracted, or bent, in passing from air into the glass and back into the air. The magnified image is observed by looking through the lens as shown in Figure 6-1. Such an image is known as a **virtual image**; it can only be seen by looking through a lens and cannot be viewed directly. This is distinguished from a **real image**, which can be seen directly, like the image that is projected onto a motion picture screen.

The ordinary magnifying glass can achieve a magnification of about five to ten times. Higher magnifying power is obtainable only with a **compound microscope** constructed of two lenses mounted at

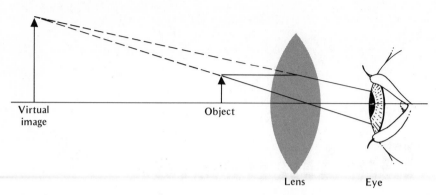

FIGURE 6-1. The Passage of Light Through a Lens Showing How Magnification is Obtained.

each end of a hollow tube. The object to be magnified is placed under the lower lens, called the **objective lens**, while the magnified image is viewed through the upper lens, known as the **eyepiece lens**. As shown in Figure 6-2, the objective lens forms a real, inverted, and magnified image of the object. The eyepiece, acting just like a simple magnifying glass, further magnifies this image into a virtual image, which is what is seen by the eye. The combined magnifying

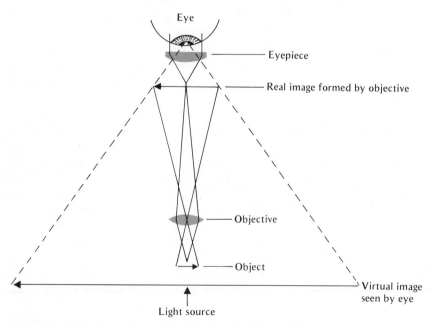

FIGURE 6-2. The principle of the compound microscope. The passage of light through two lenses forms the virtual image of the object seen by eye

power of both lenses can produce an image magnified up to 1,500 times.

The optical principles of the compound microscope are incorporated into the basic design of different types of light microscopes. Those microscopes found most applicable for examining forensic specimens are

1. The compound microscope
2. The comparison microscope
3. The stereoscopic microscope
4. The polarizing microscope

After a description of these four microscopes we will talk about a completely different approach to microscopy, the scanning electron microscope (SEM). This instrument focuses a beam of electrons instead of visible light onto the specimen to produce a magnified image. The principle and design of this microscope permits magnifying powers as high as 100,000 times.

THE COMPOUND MICROSCOPE

The parts that collectively comprise the compound microscope are illustrated in Figure 6–3a. Basically, this microscope consists of a mechanical system, which supports the microscope, and an optical system. The latter illuminates the object under investigation and passes the light through a series of lenses to form an image of the specimen on the retina of the eye. The optical path of light through a compound microscope is shown in Figure 6–3b.

The Mechanical System

1. *Base.* The support upon which the instrument rests.
2. *Arm.* A C-shaped upright structure hinged to the base which supports the microscope and acts as a handle for carrying.
3. *Stage.* The horizontal plate upon which the specimens are placed for study. The specimens are normally mounted on glass slides that are held firmly in place on the stage by means of spring clips.
4. *Body Tube.* A cylindrical hollow tube on which the objective and eyepiece lenses are mounted at opposite ends. This tube merely serves as a corridor through which light passes from one lens to another.
5. *Coarse Adjustment.* This knob serves to focus the microscope lenses on the specimen by raising and lowering the body tube.

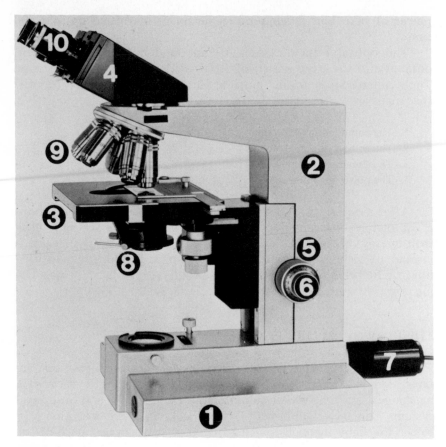

FIGURE 6–3a. Parts of the compound microscope: 1) Base, 2) Arm, 3) Stage, 4) Body tube, 5) Coarse adjust, 6) Fine adjust, 7) Illuminator, 8) Condenser, 9) Objective lens, and 10) Eyepiece lens

Courtesy Ernst Leitz

6. *Fine Adjustment.* The movements effected by this knob are similar to those of the coarse adjustment, but are of a much smaller magnitude.

The Optical System

7. *Illumination.* Most modern microscopes use artificial light supplied by a light bulb to illuminate the specimen being examined. If the specimen is transparent, the light is directed up toward and through the specimen stage from an illuminator built into the base of the microscope. This is known as **transmitted illumination**. When the object is opaque—that is, not transparent—the light source must

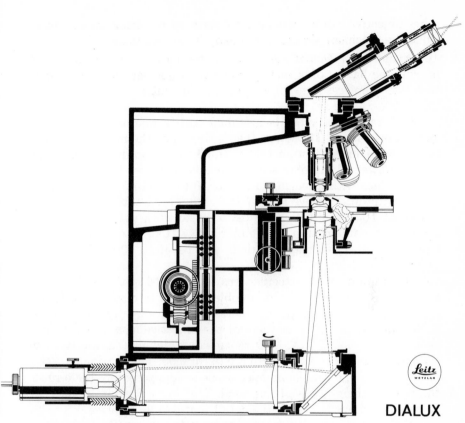

DIALUX

FIGURE 6-3b. Optics of the compound microscope
Courtesy Ernst Leitz

be placed above the specimen so that it can be reflected off the specimen's surface and into the lens system of the microscope. This type of illumination is known as **vertical** or **reflected illumination**.

8. *Condenser.* This collects light rays from the base illuminator and concentrates them on the specimen. The simplest condenser is known as the **Abbé condenser**. It consists of two lenses held together in a metal mount. The condenser also includes an iris diaphragm which can be opened or closed to control the amount of light passing into the condenser.

9. *Objective Lens.* This is the lens positioned closest to the specimen. To facilitate changing from one objective lens to another, several objectives are mounted on a revolving nosepiece or turret located above the specimen. Most microscopes are **parfocal**, meaning that when the microscope is focused with one objective in position, the

other objective can be rotated into place by revolving the nosepiece while the specimen remains very nearly in correct focus.

10. *Eyepiece or Ocular Lens.* This is the lens closest to the eye. A microscope having only one eyepiece is monocular; one constructed with two eyepieces (one for each eye) is binocular.

Each microscope lens is inscribed with a number signifying its magnifying power. The image that is viewed by the microscopist will have a total magnification that is equal to the product of the magnifying power of the objective and eyepiece lenses. For example, an eyepiece lens with a magnification of 10 times (10X) used in combination with an objective lens of 10X will have a total magnification power of 100 times (100X). Most forensic work will require a 10X eyepiece in combination with either a 4X, 10X, 20X, or 45X objective. The respective magnifications will be 40X, 100X, 200X, and 450X.

In addition, each objective lens is inscribed with its numerical aperture (N.A.) The ability of an objective lens to resolve details into separate images instead of one blurred image is directly proportional to the numerical aperture value of the objective lens. For example, an objective lens of N.A. 1.30 can separate details that are twice as close as compared to a lens with a N.A. of 0.65. The maximum useful magnification of a compound microscope is approximately 1,000 times the N.A. of the objective being used. This magnification is sufficient to permit the eye to see all the detail that can be resolved.

Although a new student of the microscope may be tempted to immediately choose the highest magnifying power available to view a specimen, the experienced microscopist realizes that a number of important factors must be weighed before the selection of magnifying power is made. A first consideration must be the size of the specimen area, or the **field of view**, that the examiner wishes to study. As magnifying power increases, the field of view decreases. Thus, it is best to first select a low magnification in which a good general overall view of the specimen is seen, and to later switch to a higher power in which a smaller portion of the specimen can be viewed in more detail.

At the same time the **depth of focus** is also a function of magnifying power. After a focus has been achieved on a specimen, the depth of focus defines the thickness of that specimen. Areas lying above and below this region will be blurred and can only be viewed when the focus is readjusted. Depth of focus decreases as magnifying power increases.

THE COMPARISON MICROSCOPE

Forensic microscopy often requires a side-by-side comparison of specimens. This kind of examination can best be performed with a comparison microscope, such as the one pictured in Figure 6-4. Basically, the comparison microscope is two compound microscopes combined into one unit. The unique feature of its design is that it uses a bridge incorporating a series of mirrors and lenses to join two independent objective lenses into a single binocular unit. When a viewer looks through the eyepiece lenses of the comparison microscope, a circular field equally divided into two parts by a fine line is observed. The specimen mounted under the left-hand objective is seen in the left half of the field, while the specimen under the right-hand objective is observed in the right half of the field. It is important that the optical characteristics of the objective lenses be closely matched to assure that each specimen is seen at equal magnification and with minimal but identical lens distortions.

Figure 6-5 shows the striation markings on two bullets that have

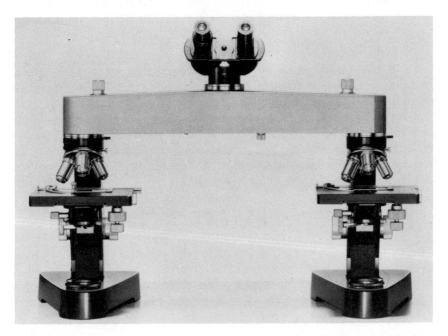

FIGURE 6-4. The comparison microscope. Two independent objective lenses joined together by an optical bridge.

Courtesy Ernst Leitz

FIGURE 6–5. Photomicrograph taken through a comparison microscope. On the left is the striation markings on test fired bullet, fired through the suspect weapon. On the right is the crime scene bullet.

Courtesy Laboratoire de L'Identite Judicaire, Paris

been placed under each of the objective lenses of a comparison microscope. Modern firearm examination can trace its origin to the introduction of the comparison microscope with its ability to give the firearms examiner a side-by-side magnified view of bullets. Bullets that are fired through the same rifle barrel will display comparable rifling markings on their surfaces. By matching the majority of striations present on each bullet, a conclusion that both bullets traveled through the same barrel is justified.

THE STEREOSCOPIC MICROSCOPE

The details that characterize the structure of many types of physical evidence do not always require examination under very high magnifications. For such specimens the stereoscopic microscope has proven quite adequate, providing magnifying powers that range from 10X to 125X. Furthermore, this microscope has the advantage of presenting a distinctive three-dimensional image of an object. The stereoscopic microscope, shown in Figure 6–6, is actually two monocular compound microscopes properly spaced and aligned to present a three-dimensional image of a specimen to the viewer who looks through both eyepiece lenses.

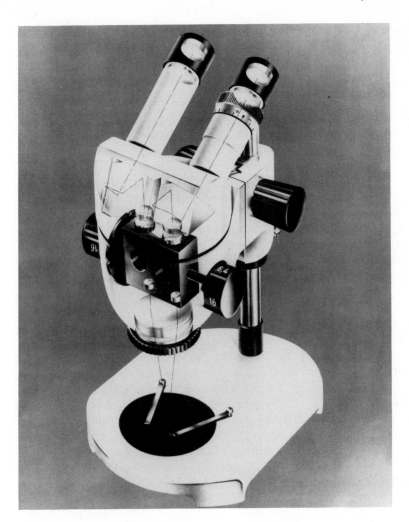

FIGURE 6-6. Stereoscopic Microscope
Courtesy Wild Herbrugg

The stereoscopic microscope is undoubtedly the most frequently used and versatile microscope found in the crime laboratory. Its wide field of view and great depth of focus make it an ideal instrument for locating trace evidence that may be present in debris, garments, weapons, or tools. Furthermore, its potentially large **working distance** (the distance between the objective lens and the specimen) makes it quite applicable for the microscopic examination of big, bulky items. When fitted with vertical illumination, the stereoscopic microscope becomes the primary tool for characterizing physical evidence as diverse as paint, soil, gunpowder residues, and marihuana.

THE POLARIZING MICROSCOPE

It will be recalled from the discussion in Chapter 4 that light's wave-like motion in space can be invoked to explain many facets of its behavior. The waves that comprise a beam of light can be pictured as vibrating in all directions perpendicular to the direction in which the light is traveling. However, it is a familiar observation that when a beam of light passes through certain types of specially fabricated crystalline substances it emerges vibrating in only one plane. Light that is confined to a single plane of vibration is said to be **plane-polarized**. The device that polarizes light in this manner is called a **polarizer**. A common example of this phenomenon is the passage of sunlight through polaroid sunglasses. By transmitting light vibrating in the vertical plane only, these sunglasses will have the effect of eliminating or reducing light glare. Most glare consists of partially polarized light that has been reflected off horizontal surfaces and thus is vibrating in a horizontal plane.

Because polarized light appears no different to the eye than ordinary light, special means must be devised for detecting it. This is simply accomplished by placing a second polarizing crystal, called an **analyzer**, in the path of the polarized beam. As shown in Figure 6-7, if the polarizer and analyzer are aligned parallel to each other, the polarized light will pass through and be seen by the eye. If, on the other hand, the polarizer and analyzer are set perpendicular to one another, or are "crossed," no light will penetrate and the result will be total darkness or extinction.

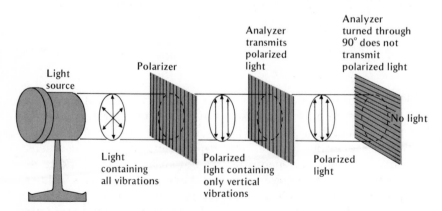

FIGURE 6-7. Polarization of Light

In this manner the design of a compound or stereoscopic microscope can be modified to be outfitted with a polarizer and analyzer so as to be capable of allowing the viewer to detect polarized light. Such a microscope is known as a **polarizing microscope**. Essentially, the polarizer is placed between the light source and the sample stage to polarize the light before it passes through the specimen. The polarized light penetrating the specimen must then pass through an analyzer before it reaches the eyepiece and finally the eye. Normally, the polarizer and analyzer are "crossed," so that when no specimen is in place, the field appears dark. However, the effect of introducing a specimen that polarizes light will be to reorient the polarized light, allowing it to pass through the analyzer. This result produces vivid colors and intensity contrasts that makes the specimen readily distinguishable.

The most obvious and important applications of this microscope relates to studying materials that polarize light. For example, scientists have long known that crystals that are birefringent or doubly refractive (see page 49) will produce two planes of polarized light, each perpendicular to the other. Utilizing this knowledge, polarizing microscopy has found wide application for the examination of birefringent minerals present in soil. By utilizing the immersion method (see page 53) and selecting the proper immersion liquid, a refractive index corresponding to each plane of polarized light can be determined. Thus, when a mineral is viewed under polarized light in a liquid that matches one of its refractive indices, the Becke Line will no longer be visible. In this manner both indices can readily be determined. This information plus observations on crystal color, form, etc., makes it possible for the microscopist to identify the mineral. Similarly, criminalists take advantage of the fact that many synthetic fibers are birefringent in order to characterize them with a polarizing microscope.

THE SCANNING ELECTRON MICROSCOPE (SEM)

All the microscopes described thus far utilize light coming off the specimen to produce a magnified image. The scanning electron microscope is, however, a special case in the family of microscopes. Here, the image formation is produced by aiming a beam of electrons onto the specimen and studying electron emissions on a closed TV circuit. The beam of electrons is emitted from a hot tungsten filament and is focused by means of electromagnets onto the surface of the specimen. This primary electron beam causes the emission of electrons from the elements in the upper layers of the specimen. The emitted electrons are collected and the amplified signal is displayed on a cathode ray or TV tube. By scanning the primary electron beam across the specimen's surface in synchronization with the cathode ray tube, it is possible to convert the emitted electrons into an image of the specimen for display on the cathode tube.

The major attractions of the SEM image are its high magnification, high resolution, and great depth of focus. In its usual mode the SEM has a magnification that ranges from 10X to 100,000X. Its depth of focus is some 300 times better than optical systems at similar magnifications and the resultant picture is almost stereoscopic in appearance. Its great depth of field and magnification is exemplified by the magnification of cystolith hair on the marihuana leaf, as shown in Figure 6-8.

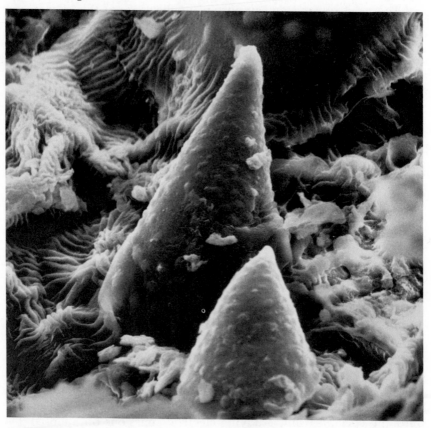

FIGURE 6-8. The cystolithic hairs on the marihuana leaf as viewed with a scanning electron microscope (800X)

Courtesy Jeff Albright

Undoubtedly, as the SEM becomes available at lower cost, the technique will rapidly become accepted as a routine instrument in the crime laboratory. Already, some manufacturers are offering SEMs that are small compact table models at relatively attractive prices (see Figure 6-9).

Another facet of scanning electron microscopy has been the use of X-ray production as a means of determining the elemental composition of the specimen under examination. X-rays are generated when the electron beam of the scanning electron microscope strikes a target. When the SEM is coupled to an X-ray analyzer, the emitted X-rays can be sorted according to their energy values and used to build up a picture of the elemental distribution in the specimen. Because each element emits X-rays of characteristic energy values, the X-ray analyzer can identify the elements present in a specimen. Furthermore, the element's concentration can be determined by measuring the intensity of the X-ray emission.

A relatively new application of scanning electron microscopy has been as a tool for determining whether or not a suspect recently has fired a gun. In this case, an attempt is made to remove any gunshot particles that may be remaining on a shooter's hands by lifting them

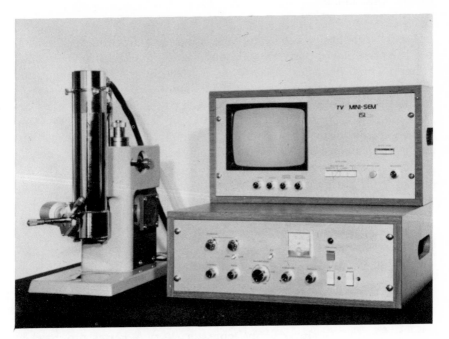

FIGURE 6-9. Scanning Electron Microscope
Courtesy International Scientific Instruments

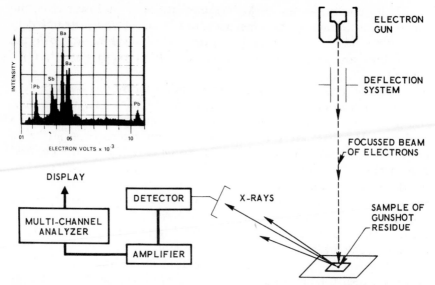

FIGURE 6-10. A schematic diagram of an X-ray analyzer detecting and displaying X-ray emissions from the elements lead (Pb), antimony (Sb), and barium (Ba) present in gunshot residue

Courtesy Aerospace Corp.

off with an adhesive tape. The tape is then examined under the SEM for the presence of particles that may have originated from the bullet primer. These particles can be characterized by their size, shape, and elemental composition. As shown in Figure 6-10, when the sample of gunshot residue is exposed to a beam of electrons from the scanning electron microscope, X-rays are emitted. These X-rays are passed into a detector where they are converted into electrical signals. These signals are sorted and displayed according to the energies of the emitted X-rays. Through the use of this technique, the elements lead, antimony, and barium, frequently found in most primers, can be rapidly detected and identified.

REVIEW QUESTIONS

1. A microscope uses a combination of _____ to magnify an image.

2. A type of image that cannot be viewed directly is called a _____ image.

3. A _____ microscope consists of two lenses mounted at each end of a hollow tube.

4. The lens closest to the specimen is called the _____ .

5. The lens nearest the viewer's eye is called the _____ .

6. The image seen through a compound microscope is (virtual, real).

7. The coarse and fine adjustments are part of the microscope's mechanical system. (True, False)

8. A transparent specimen is viewed through a microscope using _____ light.

9. An opaque object requires _____ illumination for viewing with a microscope.

10. A _____ collects light rays from the base illuminator and concentrates them on the specimen.

11. A microscope that remains in focus regardless of which objective lens is rotated into place is _____ .

12. A microscope having only one eyepiece is monocular; one having two eyepieces is _____ .

13. Each microscope lens is inscribed with a number signifying its

_____ .

14. An eyepiece lens of 10X used in combination with an objective lens of 20X will have a total magnification power of _____ .

15. The ability of an objective lens to resolve details into separate images is directly proportional to its _____ .

16. The size of the specimen area in view is known as the _____ .

17. As magnification increases, the field of view (increases, decreases).

18. The thickness of a specimen in view is known as the _____ .

19. The depth of focus (increases, decreases) with increasing magnification.

20. A side-by-side view of two specimens is best obtained with the _____ microscope.

21. A bridge is used to join two independent objective lenses into a single binocular unit to form a comparison microscope. (True, False)

22. Two monocular compound microscopes properly spaced and aligned describes the _____ microscope.

23. The stereoscopic microscope is the least frequently used microscope in a typical crime laboratory. (True, False)

24. The stereoscopic microscope offers a large _____ between the objective lens and the specimen.

25. Light confined to a single plane of vibration is said to be _____ .

26. If a polarizer and analyzer are placed (perpendicular, parallel) to each other no light will penetrate.

27. The _____ microscope allows a viewer to detect polarized light.

28. Crystals that are _____ will produce two planes of polarized light each perpendicular to the other.

29. The _____ microscope focuses a beam of electrons on a specimen to produce an image.

30. When a beam of electrons strikes a specimen _____ are emitted whose energies correspond to elements present in the specimen.

FURTHER READINGS

McCrone, Walter C., and John G. Delly, *The Particle Atlas*, vol. 1, 2nd ed. Ann Arbor, Mich.: Ann Arbor Science Publishers, 1973.

O'Hara, Charles E., and James W. Osterburg, *An Introduction to Criminalistics*, 2nd ed. Bloomington, Ind.: University Press, 1972.

Schaeffer, Harold F., *Microscopy for Chemists*. New York: Dover, 1966.

Taylor, M. E., "Scanning Electron Microscopy in Forensic Science," *Journal of the Forensic Science Society*, 13 (1973), 269.

Audiovisual Presentation

Laboratory Instrumentation (filmstrips and audio tape). Robert J. Brady Co., Bowie, Md.

Hairs, Fibers and Paint

chapter 7

The trace evidence that is transferred between individuals and objects during the commission of a crime will, if recovered, often corroborate other evidence developed during the course of an investigation. Though in most cases physical evidence cannot by itself provide for a positive identification of a suspect, laboratory examination may narrow its origin to a group that includes the suspect. Utilizing many of the instruments and techniques described in the previous three chapters, the crime laboratory has developed a variety of procedures for comparing and tracing the origins of physical evidence. It will be the purpose of this and forthcoming chapters to apply these techniques to the analysis of the types of physical evidence most often encountered at crime scenes. We will begin with a discussion of hairs, fibers, and paints.

HAIR

Morphology of Hair

Hair is encountered as physical evidence in a wide variety of crimes. However, any review of the forensic aspects of hair examination must start with the observation that it is not yet possible to individualize a human hair to any single head or body. Over the years, criminalists have tried in vain to find a way to isolate some of the physical and chemical properties of hair so that it could serve as an individual characteristic of identity. One by one these efforts have repeatedly failed to uncover any one property that remains consistent with time and is uniform throughout the head or body. It is a testimony to hair's reluctance to yield distinctive chemical properties that its color and structure, or morphology, still remains its most character-istic forensic feature.

This is not to imply that hair has no value as physical evidence. On the contrary, when it is properly collected at the crime scene and its submission to the laboratory is accompanied by an adequate number of controls, hair can provide strong corroborative evidence for placing an individual at a crime site.

Hair is an appendage of the skin that grows out of an organ known as the hair follicle. The length of a hair extends from its root or bulb embedded in the follicle, continues into a shaft, and it termi-nates at a tip end. It is the shaft, however, composed of three layers—the **cuticle**, **cortex**, and **medulla**—that is subjected to the most intense examination by the forensic scientist (see Figure 7-1).

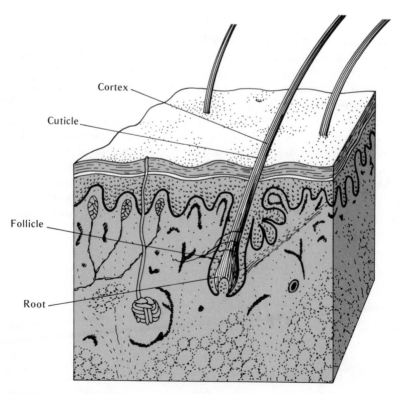

FIGURE 7-1.

Cuticle. One of the features that makes hair an attractive marker for individual identity is its resistance to chemical decomposition, and its ability to retain structural features over a long period of time. Much of this resistance and stability is attributed to the cuticle or outside covering of the hair. The cuticle is formed by overlapping scales which always point toward the tip end of the hair. The scales are formed from specialized cells which have hardened (keratinized) and flattened in progressing from the follicle. The scale of most animal hairs can best be described as having the appearance of shingles on a roof. Although this shinglelike pattern is not a distinctive characteristic among human hairs, the variety of patterns formed by animals does make it an important feature for species identification. Figure 7-2 shows the scale patterns of some animal hairs as viewed by the scanning electron microscope. Another method of studying the scale pattern of hair is to make a cast of its surface. This is readily done by embedding the hair in a soft medium, such as clear nail polish or softened vinyl. When the medium has hardened, the hair is removed and there remains a clear, distinct impression of the hair's cuticle ideal for examination with a compound microscope.

Cortex. Contained within the protective layer of the cuticle is the cortex. The cortex is actually made up of spindle-shaped cortical cells which are aligned in a regular array, parallel to the length of the hair. The cortex derives its major forensic importance from the fact that it is imbedded with the pigment granules that impart hair with color. It is the color and distribution of these granules that provide the criminalist with important points of comparison between human hairs.

The structural features of the cortex are examined microscopically after the hair has been mounted in a liquid medium that has a refractive index closely matched to that of the hair; usually, Canadian Balsam is used. Under these conditions the amount of light reflected off the hair's surface is minimized and the amount of light penetrating the hair is optimized.

Medulla. The medulla is the core or central canal that runs through the hair. In many animals this canal is a most predominant feature, occupying more than half of the hair's diameter. The **medullary index** measures the diameter of the medulla relative to the diameter of the hair shaft, and is normally expressed as a fraction. For humans the index generally has a value less than 1/3; for most other animals the value is 1/2 or greater.

It is important to stress that the presence and appearance of the medulla vary from individual to individual, and even between hairs of a given individual. Not all hairs have medullae, and when they do

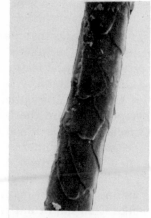

a. Human head hair (500X)

b. Dog (1000X)

c. Deer (700X)

d. Rabbit (300X)

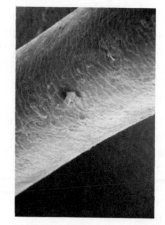

e. Cat (2000X)

f. Horse (500X)

FIGURE 7-2

Courtesy International Scientific Instruments

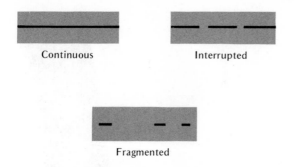

FIGURE 7-3. Medulla Patterns

exist the degree of medullation can vary. In this respect, medullae may be classified as being continuous, interrupted, fragmented, or absent (see Figure 7-3). Human head hairs generally exhibit no medullae or have fragmented ones; they rarely show continuous medullation. On the other hand, most animals have medullae that are either continuous or interrupted.

Another interesting feature of the medulla is its shape. Human beings, as well as many animals, have medullae that give a nearly cylindrical appearance. Other animals exhibit medullae that have a patterned shape. For example; the medulla of a cat can best be described as resembling a string of pearls. Figure 7-4 illustrates medullary sizes and forms for a number of common animal hairs.

Identification and Comparison of Hair

Most often when hair evidence is present in a criminal case, the prime purpose for its examination in a crime laboratory is to establish whether the hair is human or animal in origin, or to determine whether human hair of unknown origin compares with hair that is known to have come from a particular individual. While the distinction of animal hair from human hair can normally be accomplished with little difficulty, the problem of human hair comparisons is one that must be undertaken with extreme caution and with an awareness of hair's tendency to exhibit variable morphological characteristics from one person to another, as well as within a single individual.

A careful microscopic examination of hair will reveal morphological features that can distinguish human from other animal hairs. The hair of many animals differs in structure to such an extent that the examiner may often be able to identify the species of animal from which the hair originated. It is important, however, that before such a conclusion is reached the examiner has access to a comprehensive collection of reference standards and the accumulated experience of hundreds of prior hair examinations. Scale structure, medullary

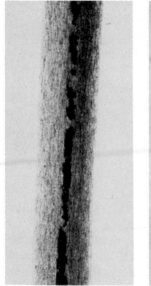  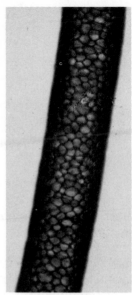

a. Human head hair (450X)   b. Dog (450X)   c. Deer (100X)

d. Rabbit (450X)   e. Cat (450X)   f. Mouse (450X)

FIGURE 7-4.

Courtesy Linda Jankowski

index, and medullary shape are features that are particularly important to this aspect of hair identification.

The most common request that is made of the laboratory when hair is used as forensic evidence is to determine whether or not hairs recovered at the crime scene compare to hairs removed from a suspect. In most cases, such a comparison relates to hairs obtained from the scalp or pubic area. Ultimately, the evidential value of the comparison will depend on the degree of probability with which the examiner can associate the questioned hairs to a particular individual.

In making a hair comparison, a comparison microscope is an invaluable tool that allows the examiner to view the questioned and known hairs together side by side. Any variations in the microscopic characteristic will thus be readily observed. Because hair from any part of the body exhibits a range of characteristics, it is necessary to have an adequate number of known hairs that are representative of all its features when making the comparison. For this reason, the evidence collector must obtain several dozen hairs randomly selected from the relevant portions of the suspect's body to compare to the unknown. A random sampling of up to 100 hairs should suffice.

Combing the head or pubic area offers the most satisfactory way of collecting hairs. In this manner, hairs representative of the variations in color, thickness, and length are normally collected. As hair may show a variation in color and other morphological features over a single strand, an effort has to be made to collect the entire hair length. Therefore, if the hairs have to be clipped, it is best that the clipping be made as close to the skin as possible.

In comparing hairs, the criminalist is particularly interested in matching their color and diameter. Other important features are the presence or absence of a medulla, and the distribution and color intensity of the pigment granules present in the cortex. A microscopic examination may also be able to distinguish dyed or bleached hair from natural hair. The cortex of dyed hairs frequently show a more uniform distribution of color when compared to undyed hairs. If there has been a growth of hair since it was bleached or dyed, the natural-end portion will be quite distinct in color. An estimate of the time since dying or bleaching can be made, because hair is known to grow at a rate of approximately one centimeter per month.

A recent study conducted by a laboratory of the Royal Canadian Mounted Police offers an interesting insight into the evidential value of a hair comparison.[1] One hundred different individuals were asked to submit a sample of eighty to one hundred hairs randomly selected

---

[1] B. D. Gaudette and E. S. Keeping, "An Attempt at Determining Probabilities in Human Scalp Hair Comparison," *Journal of Forensic Sciences*, 19 (1974), 599.

from various regions of the scalp. From these, depending on the homogeneity of the sample, 6 to 11 mutually dissimilar hairs were selected to represent the range of length, coarseness, and color present in the 80 to 100 hairs. The representative hairs were then mounted individually on glass slides and compared to one another, utilizing a comparison microscope. A total of 861 hairs from the 100 individuals were compared in this manner.

By use of a card coding system it was possible to record 366,630 hair comparisons between the 861 hairs. As a result, it was estimated that if one human head hair found at the scene of a crime is indistinguishable from a suspect's head hair, the odds against it originating from another person are about 4,500 to 1. The recovery of two dissimilar hairs at the crime site, each comparing to two dissimilar hairs from the same suspect raises the odds against their originating from another source to 20,000,000 to 1. Once the number of hair comparisons reaches three or more, the odds become so high that for all practical purposes all other possible sources are excluded. At this point, hair evidence has assumed individual characteristics.

More studies of this kind will have to be completed before conclusive statistical data can be claimed for the different race, sex, and age segments of the population. However, this initial study has confirmed what many forensic scientists have long suspected—hair, when accompanied by a thorough collection of control specimens, can be highly distinctive evidence for personal identification.

Normally, little difficulty is experienced in distinguishing human hairs from different parts of the body. Scalp hairs generally show less diameter variation and more uniform pigment distribution when compared with hairs from other body areas. Pubic hairs are often short, curly, and usually have broad continuous medullae. The age of an individual cannot be learned from a hair examination with any degree of certainty except with infant hair. Infant hairs are fine, short in length, have fine pigment, and are rudimentary in character. At present, sex cannot be determined from a hair examination. Though the presence of dye or bleach on the hair may offer some clue to sex, present hair styles make these characteristics less valuable than they were in the past.

In many instances the examiner can distinguish hair originating from members of different races; this is especially true of Caucasian and Negroid head hair. Negroid hairs are normally kinky, containing dense, unevenly distributed pigments. Caucasian hairs are usually straight or wavy with very fine to coarse pigments that are more evenly distributed when compared to Negroid hair. Sometimes a cross-sectional examination of hair may aid in the identification of race. Cross-sections of hair from Caucasians are oval to round in shape, while Negroid hair is flat to oval in shape. However, it must be emphasized that all of these observations are general in nature, with many possible exceptions. The criminalist must approach the determination of race from hair with caution and a good deal of experience.

At the present time, there is a widespread interest among forensic scientists in the possibilities of individualizing human hair through trace elemental content. The neutron activation analysis of hair has been found to be quite sensitive. However, a lot more research remains to be conducted before the technique can be judged valid for forensic comparisons. The variation of hair's elements over an individual's head, its possible variation with time, and the influence of environment and diet are all aspects of the problem that require considerable research efforts before any forensic significance can be assigned to the elemental composition of hair.

FIBERS

Just as hair left at a crime scene can serve as identification, the same logic can reasonably be extended to the fibers that comprise our fabrics and garments. Fibers may become important evidence in incidents that involve personal contact—such as homicide, assault, or sexual offenses—in which cross-transfers may occur between the clothing of suspect and victim. Similarly, it is not uncommon to find that the force of impact between a hit-and-run victim and a vehicle leaves fibers, threads, or even whole pieces of clothing adhering to parts of the vehicle. Fibers may also become fixed in screens or glass broken in the course of a breaking-and-entering attempt.

Regardless of where and under what conditions fibers are recovered, their ultimate value as forensic evidence will depend on the criminalist's ability to narrow their origin to a limited number of sources or even to a single source. Unfortunately, the mass production of our garments and fabrics has served to limit the value of fiber evidence in this respect, and it is only under the most unusual circumstances that the recovery of fibers at a crime scene will provide individual identification with a high degree of certainty.

For centuries man was dependent upon the source and forces of nature for textile fibers. Early in the twentieth century the first manufactured fiber—rayon—became a practical reality, followed in the 1920s by the introduction of cellulose acetate. Since the late 1930s scientists have produced literally dozens of new fibers. In fact, the development of fibers, fabrics, finishes, and other textile-processing techniques have made greater advances since 1900 than in the four to five thousand years of recorded history before the twentieth century. Today, such varied things as clothing, carpeting, drapes, wigs, and even artificial turf attest to the predominant role that manufactured fibers have come to play in our culture and environment.

For the purposes of discussing the forensic examination of fibers, it will be convenient to classify them into two broad groups: **natural** and **man-made.**

Natural Fibers

Natural fibers are derived in whole from animal or plant sources. Animal fibers comprise the majority of the natural fibers encountered in crime laboratory examinations. These include hair coverings from such animals as sheep (wool), goats (mohair, cashmere), camels, llamas, alpacas, and vicuñas; fur fibers include those obtained from animals such as mink, rabbit, beaver, and muskrat.

Any discussion of the forensic examination of animal fibers will merely restate procedures developed in the previous section for the forensic examination of animal hairs. The identification and comparison of such hairs relies solely on a microscopic examination of color and morphological characteristics. Again, a sufficient number of control specimens must be examined to establish the range of fiber characteristics that comprise the suspect fabric.

By far the most prevalent plant fiber is cotton. However, the wide use of undyed white cotton fibers in clothing and other fabrics has made its evidential value almost meaningless; although the presence of dyed cotton in a combination of colors has, in some cases, served to enhance its evidential significance. The microscopic view of the cotton fiber, shown in Figure 7–5, reveals its most distinguishing feature—a ribbonlike shape with twists at irregular intervals.

Man-Made Fibers

Beginning with the introduction of rayon in 1911 and the development of nylon in 1939, man-made fibers have increasingly replaced natural fibers in garments and fabrics. Today such fibers are marketed under hundreds of different trademark names. To reduce consumer confusion, the United States Federal Trade Commission has approved the following "generic" or family names for the grouping of all man-made fibers:

Acetate and Triacetate	Metallic	Rayon
Acrylic	Modacrylic	Rubber
Anidex	Nylon	Saran
Azlon	Nytril	Spandex
Glass	Olefin	Vinal
Lastrile	Polyester	Vinyon

Many of these generic classes are produced by several manufacturers and sold under a confusing variety of trademark names. For example, in the United States polyesters are marketed under names that include: Dacron®, Fortrel®, and Kodel®. The same fiber is called Terylene® in England.

The first machine-made fibers were manufactured from raw materials that were derived from cotton or wood pulp. These materials are processed and pure cellulose extracted from them. Depending on the type of fiber that is desired, the cellulose may be chemically

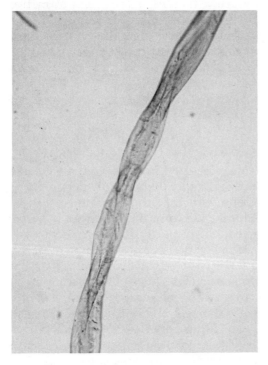

FIGURE 7-5. Photomicrograph of Cotton Fiber (450X)
Courtesy Linda Jankowski

treated and dissolved in an appropriate solvent before it is forced through the small holes of a spinning jet or spinnerette to produce the fiber. Fibers manufactured from natural raw materials in this manner are classified as **regenerated fibers** and commonly include rayon, acetate, and triacetate, all of which are produced from regenerated cellulose.

Most of the fibers presently manufactured are produced solely from synthetic chemicals and are therefore classified as **synthetic fibers**. These include nylons, polyesters, and acrylics. The creation of synthetic fibers became a reality only when scientists developed a method of synthesizing long-chained molecules called **polymers**.

In 1930, chemists discovered an unusual characteristic of one of the polymers under investigation. It was found that when a glass rod in contact with viscous material in a beaker was slowly pulled away, the substance adhered to the rod and formed a fine filament that hardened as soon as it entered the cool air. Furthermore, it was observed that the cold filaments could be stretched several times their extended length to produce a flexible, strong, and attractive fiber. The first synthetic fiber was to be improved upon and marketed as nylon. Since then fiber chemists have successfully synthesized new polymers and developed more efficient methods for manufacturing them. These efforts have produced a multitude of synthetic fibers.

The Polymer

The polymer is the basic chemical substance of all synthetic fibers. Indeed, an almost unbelievable array of household, industrial, and recreational products are manufactured from them; these include plastics, paints, adhesives, and synthetic rubber. Polymers exist in countless forms and varieties and with the proper treatment can be made to assume different chemical and physical properties.

As we have already observed, chemical substances are composed from basic structural units called molecules. The molecules of most materials are comprised of just a few atoms; for example, water, H_2O, has two atoms of hydrogen and one atom of oxygen. The heroin molecule, $C_{21}H_{23}O_5N$ contains twenty-one atoms of carbon, twenty-three of hydrogen, five atoms of oxygen, and one atom of nitrogen. Polymers, on the other hand, are formed by linking together a large number of molecules, so that it is not unusual for a polymer to contain thousands or even millions of atoms. This is why polymers are often referred to as macro-molecules, or "big" molecules.

Simply, a polymer can be pictured as resembling a long repeating chain, with each link representing the basic structure of the polymer (see Figure 7-6). The repeating molecular units in the polymer, called

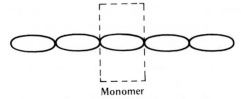

Monomer

FIGURE 7–6. The chain-link model of a segment of a polymer molecule. The actual molecule may contain as many as several million monomer units or links

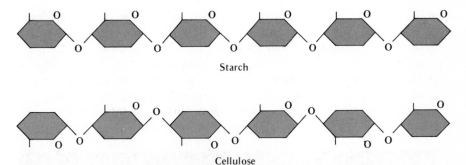

Starch

Cellulose

FIGURE 7–7. Starch and cellulose are natural carbohydrate polymers consisting of a large number of repeating units or monomers

the monomers, are joined together end to end, so that on a greatly enlarged scale thousands upon thousands are linked together to form a long chain. What makes polymer chemistry so fascinating is the countless varieties of possibilities that exist for linking different molecules together. By simply varying the chemical structure of the basic molecules, or monomers, and by devising numerous ways to weave them together, chemists have created polymers that exhibit different properties. It is this versatility that enables polymer chemists to synthesize glues, plastics, paints, and fibers.

It would be a mistake to give the impression that all polymers are synthesized in the chemical laboratory. Indeed, this is far from true, for nature has produced polymers that man has not yet been able to copy. For example, the proteins that form the basic structure of animal hairs, as well as all living matter, are polymers, composed of thousands of amino acids linked together in a highly organized arrangement and sequence. Similarly, starch, as well as cellulose, the basic ingredient of wood and cotton, are both natural polymers built by the combination of several thousand carbohydrate monomers, as shown in Figure 7–7. Hence, the synthesis of man-made fibers merely represents an extension of chemical principles that nature has successfully utilized to produce hair and vegetable fibers.

Identification and Comparison
of Man-Made Fibers

The evidential value of fibers is related to the criminalist's ability to trace their origin. Obviously, if the examiner is presented with fabrics that can be exactly fitted together at their torn edges, it is a virtual certainty that the fabrics were of common origin. Such a fit is demonstrated in Figure 7–8 for a portion of a fabric that was removed from a vehicle suspected of involvement in a hit-and-run fatality. The exact fit with the remains of the victim's trousers resulted in the direct implication of the car's driver in the incident.

However, a more common case finds the criminalist presented with a very limited number of fibers for identification and comparison. Generally, in these situations, the possibilities for obtaining a physical match are nonexistent and the examiner must resort to a side-by-side comparison of the control and crime-scene fibers.

The first and most important step in the examination will be a microscopic comparison for color and diameter. Unless there is agreement

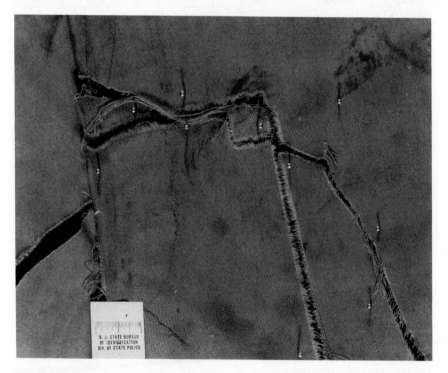

FIGURE 7–8. A piece of fabric found on a suspect hit-and-run vehicle inserted into the torn trousers of the victim

Courtesy New Jersey State Police

between these two characteristics there would be little reason to suspect a comparison. Other morphological features that could be present to aid in the comparison are lengthwise striations on the surface of some fibers, and the pitting of the fiber's surface with delustering particles (usually titanium dioxide) added in the manufacturing process to reduce shine (Figure 7-9). A cross-sectional view may also assist in characterizing the fiber.

Once this phase of the analysis is complete, and before any conclusion can be reached that two or more fibers compare, each must be shown to have the same chemical composition. In this respect, tests are performed to confirm that all the fibers involved belong to the same broad generic class. Additionally, the comparison will be substantially enhanced if it can be demonstrated that all the fibers belong to the same subclassification within their generic class. For example, when we speak of nylon we must remember that there are at least five different types of nylon available in commercial and consumer markets. These include nylon 6, nylon 6-10, nylon 11,

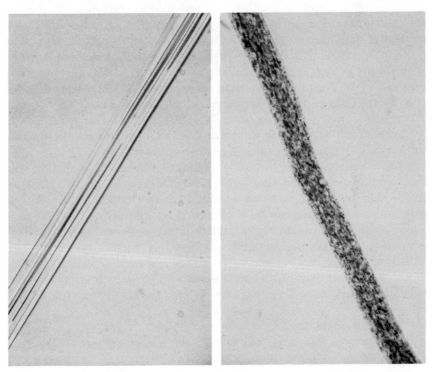

a. Cellulose triacetate (450X)   b. Nylon embedded with titanium dioxide particles (450X)

FIGURE 7-9. Photomicrographs of Synthetic Fibers

Courtesy Linda Jankowski

nylon 6-6, and Quiana®. Although all types of nylon have many properties in common, each may differ in physical shape, appearance, and dyeability owing to modifications in basic chemical structure. Similarly, a study of forty different brand-name acrylic fibers revealed that they could actually be divided into twenty-five distinguishable groups on the basis of their polymeric structure and physical characteristics.[2]

Textile chemists have devised numerous tests for determining the class of a fiber. However, unlike the textile chemist, the criminalist frequently does not have the luxury of having a substantial quantity of fabric to work with and must therefore select those tests that will yield the most information with the least amount of material. Only a single fiber may be available for analysis and often this may amount to no more than a minute strand recovered from a fingernail scraping of a homicide or rape victim.

A most useful physical property of fibers, from the criminalist's point of view, arises out of the knowledge that many manufactured fibers exhibit double refraction or birefringence (see page 49). Synthetic fibers are manufactured by melting a polymeric substance or dissolving it in a solvent and then forcing it through the very fine holes of a spinnerette. The polymer emerges as a very fine filament with its molecules aligned parallel to the length of the filament (see Figure 7-10). Just as the regular arrangement of atoms produces a crystal, so will the regular arrangement of the fiber's polymers cause crystallinity in the finished fiber. It is this crystallinity which makes a fiber stiff and strong and is responsible for its exhibiting the optical property of double refraction.

Light passing through a fiber emerges polarized, perpendicular and parallel to the length of the fiber. Depending on the class of fiber, each polarized plane of light will have a characteristic index of refraction. This value can be determined by immersing the fiber in a fluid that has a comparable refractive index and observing the disappearance of the Becke Line under a polarizing microscope. Table 7-1 lists the two refractive indices of some common classes of fibers, along with their birefringence. The virtue of this technique is that a single fiber, microscopic in size, can be characterized in a nondestructive manner.

The polymers that comprise a man-made fiber, just as in any other organic substance, will selectively absorb infrared light in a characteristic pattern. Infrared spectrophotometry thus provides a rapid and reliable method for identifying the generic class, and in

---

[2] K. W. Smalldon, "The Identification of Acrylic Fibers by Polymer Composition as Determined by Infrared Spectroscopy and Physical Characteristics," *Journal of Forensic Sciences*, 18 (1973), 69.

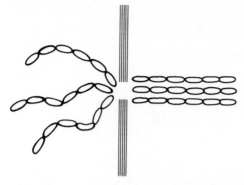

FIGURE 7-10. In the production of man-made fibers the bulk polymer is forced through small holes to form a filament in which all the polymers are aligned in the same direction.

some cases the subclasses, of a very small quantity of fiber. The infrared spectra of two types of acrylic fibers are shown in Figure 7-11.

The technique of pyrolysis gas chromatography also has the ability to characterize small quantities of polymers, such as those that comprise synthetic fibers, plastics, or paints. Here, as shown in Figure 7-12, the polymer chain is decomposed by a heated filament and the resultant products are swept into and through a

TABLE 7-1. Refractive Indices of Common Textile Fibers[a]

Fiber	Refractive Index		
	Parallel	Perpendicular	Birefringence
Acetate	1.478	1.477	0.001
Triacetate	1.472	1.471	0.001
Acrylic	1.524	1.520	0.004
Nylon			
Nylon 6	1.568	1.515	0.053
Nylon 6–6	1.582	1.519	0.063
Polyester			
Dacron	1.710	1.535	0.175
Kodel	1.642	1.540	0.102
Modacrylic	1.536	1.531	0.005
Rayon			
Cuprammonium Rayon	1.552	1.520	0.032
Viscose Rayon	1.544	1.520	0.024

[a]The listed values are for specific fibers, which warrants the highly precise values given. In identification work such precision is not practical: values within 0.02 or 0.03 of those listed will suffice.

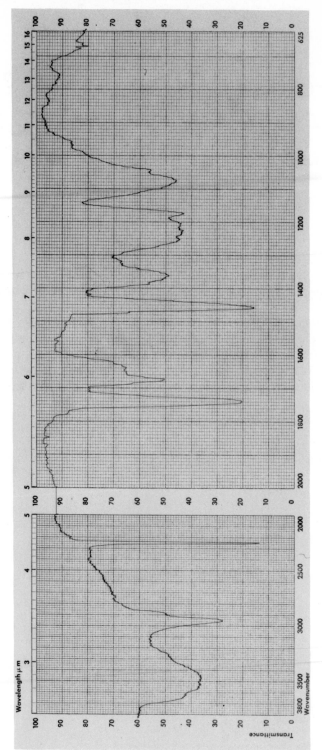

a. Orlon 42

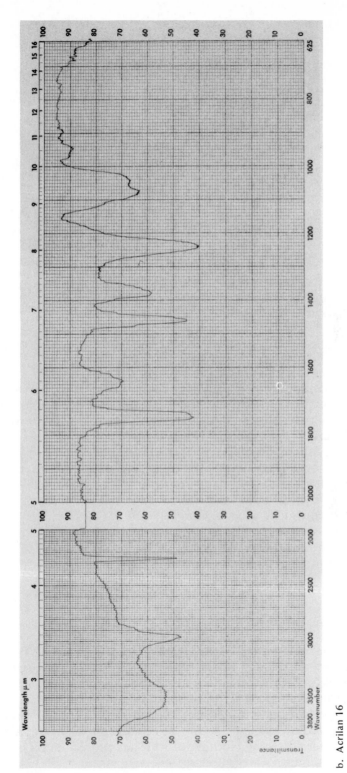

b. Acrilan 16

FIGURE 7-11. The Infrared Spectra of Two Acrylic Fibers

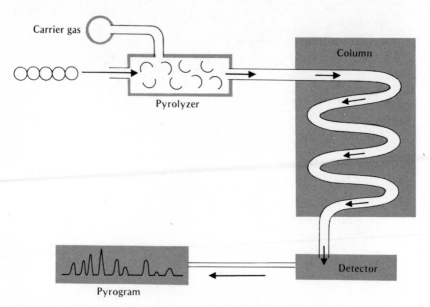

FIGURE 7-12. Schematic Diagram of Pyrolysis Gas Chromatography

gas chromatograph column. What emerge and are recorded are the separated decomposition products of the polymer. It is the pattern of this chromatogram or "pyrogram" that distinguishes one polymer from another. Figure 7-13 illustrates how pyrogram patterns distinguish various members of the acrylic class of fibers.

In reality, there is no analytical technique that will permit the criminalist to associate a fiber with any single garment. Futhermore, there is no statistical data available for determining the probability of a fiber's origin. Considering the mass distribution of synthetic fibers and the constantly changing fashion tastes of our society, it is highly unlikely that such data will be available in the foreseeable future. Except in the most unusual of circumstances, the value of fiber evidence lies in its ability to corroborate other investigative findings rather than to individualize a garment to a crime scene.

PAINT

Our environment is literally surrounded with millions of objects whose surfaces are painted. Thus, it is not surprising to observe that paint, in one form or another, is one of the most prevalent types of physical evidence received by the crime laboratory. Paint as physical evidence is perhaps most frequently encountered in hit-and-run and burglary cases. For example, a chip of dried paint or a paint smear may be transferred to the clothing of a hit-and-run victim on impact

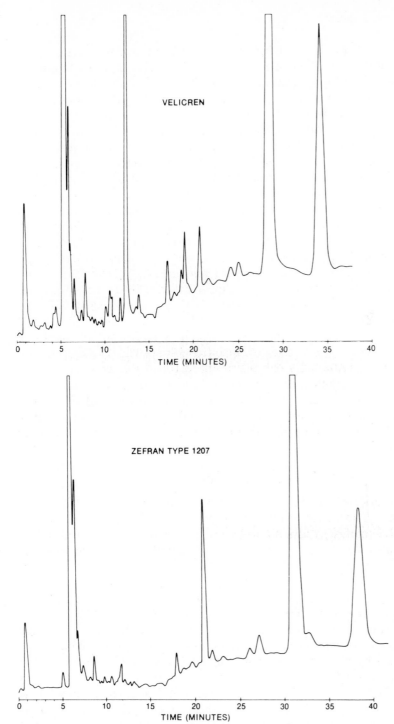

FIGURE 7-13. Pyrograms of Two Acrylic Fibers

Courtesy Varian Instruments

with an automobile, or paint smears could be transferred onto a tool during the commission of a burglary. Obviously, there exist numerous possibilities and situations under which a transfer of paint from one surface to another could impart an object with an identifiable forensic characteristic.

In most circumstances the criminalist will be required to compare two or more paints for the ultimate purpose of establishing their common origin. Through such a comparison it may be possible, for example, to associate an individual or a vehicle to the crime site. However, the criminalist need not be confined to comparisons alone. Crime laboratories can often provide valuable assistance in identifying the color, make, and model of an automobile by examining small quantities of paint recovered at an accident scene. Such requests, normally made in connection with hit-and-run cases, can lead to the apprehension of the responsible vehicle.

Paint, when spread onto a surface, will dry into a hard film that can best be described as consisting of pigments suspended in a binder. Pigments impart color to paint and are usually mixtures of different inorganic and organic compounds added to the paint by the manufacturer to produce specific colors. The binder provides the support medium for the pigments and is a polymeric substance. Paint is thus comprised of a binder and pigments, as well as other materials added for bulk, all dissolved in a suitable solvent. After the paint has been applied to a surface, the solvent evaporates, leaving behind a hard polymeric binder and any pigments that were suspended in it.

The Forensic Examination of Paints

The microscope has traditionally been and remains the most important instrument for locating and comparing paint specimens. When one considers the thousands upon thousands of paint colors and shades that are known to exist, it is quite understandable why color, more than any other property, imparts paint with its most distinctive forensic characteristic. Questioned and known specimens are best compared side by side under a stereoscopic microscope for color, surface texture, and color-layer sequence.

The importance of layer structure for evaluating the evidential significance of paint evidence cannot be overemphasized. When paint specimens possess colored layers that match with respect to number and sequence of colors, the examiner can begin to confidently think in terms of relating the paints to a common origin. How many layers must be matched before the criminalist can conclude that the paints come from the same source? There is no one accepted criterion.

Much depends on the uniqueness of each layer with respect to its color and texture, as well as the frequency with which the particular combination of colors under investigation is observed to occur. Because there are at present no books or journals that have compiled this type of information, the criminalist is left to his own experience and knowledge when making this decision.

Unfortunately, the vast majority of the paint specimens presented to the criminalist will not have a layer structure of sufficient complexity to allow them to be individualized to a single source, nor is it common to have paint chips that can be physically fitted together to prove common origin, as shown in Figure 7-14. However, the diverse chemical composition of modern paints does provide for additional points of comparison between specimens. Specifically, a thorough comparison of paint must include a chemical analysis of either the paint's pigments or its binder composition, or both.

The wide variation in binder formulations provides particularly significant information with respect to the forensic comparison of automobile finishes. At present, automobile finishes can be classified into three broad classes:

1. *Acrylic Lacquers.* The polymers that comprise these binders typi-

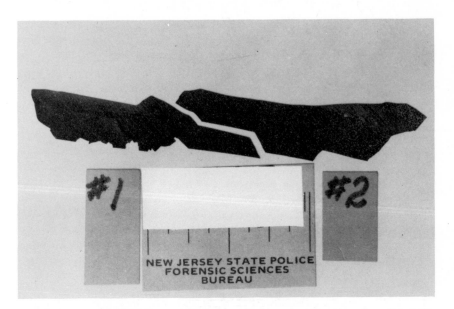

FIGURE 7-14. Paint chip no. 1 was recovered from the scene of a hit-and-run. Paint chip no. 2 was obtained from the suspect vehicle.

Courtesy New Jersey State Police

cally have long chains with few, if any, chemical bonds acting as cross-links between adjacent chains. This is shown schematically in Figure 7-15a. Such binders, when heated, become soft and more or less fluid. This is preferred by some manufacturers because local surface irregularities are smoothed out in the process. Vehicles made by General Motors have a topcoat of acrylic lacquer paint.

2. *Acrylic Enamels.* These polymers, when heated, form an extensively cross-linked network that becomes extremely hard and resistant to attack by solvents. A schematic representation of a highly cross-linked polymer using chemical bonds between adjacent polymer chains is shown in Figure 7-15b. American Motors, Ford, Chrysler, and some imported brands use acrylic enamel paints as topcoat finishes on their cars.

3. *Alkyd Enamels.* The polymers that comprise this group also produce an extensively cross-linked surface when heated. Most cars imported to the United States have alkyd enamel finishes.

Fortunately, acrylic lacquer paints can readily be distinguished from the other classes by their solubility in acetone. Thus, a paint

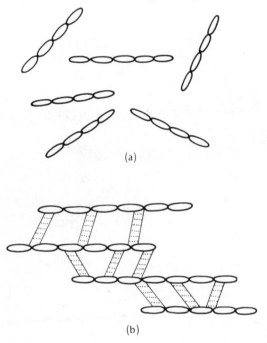

(a)

(b)

FIGURE 7-15. Schematic representation of (a) an uncross-linked polymer and (b) a highly cross-linked polymer

chip found to be soluble in acetone is immediately associated with a General Motors vehicle. However, just knowing the type of automobile finish contributes very little to the individual identity of the paint. What is more important is the knowledge that paint manufacturers make each of the three classes of automobile finishes in hundreds of varieties; a situation most helpful to the criminalist who is trying to associate a paint chip to one car as distinguished from the thousands of similar models that have been produced in any one year. Pyrolysis gas chromatography has proven to be a particularly invaluable technique for distinguishing most of these formulations. Here, paint chips as small as 20 micrograms are decomposed by heat into numerous gaseous products and sent through a gas chromatograph. What results is a pyrogram that is sufficiently detailed to reflect the chemical makeup of the binder. Figure 7-16 illustrates how the patterns produced by paint pyrograms can differentiate acrylic enamel paints removed from two different automobiles.

The elements that comprise the inorganic pigments of paints can be identified by emission spectroscopy. In most automobile paints, the spectrograph can simultaneously detect fifteen to twenty elements. Some of these elements are relatively common to all paints and have little forensic value; others are less frequently encountered and provide excellent points of comparison between paint specimens (see Figure 5-3).

Infrared spectrophotometry is another analytical technique used to provide the analyst with information about both the binder and pigment composition of paint.[3] Both of these paint components will selectively absorb infrared radiation to yield a spectrum that is highly characteristic of a paint specimen.

Presently, there is very little statistical data available to help guide the forensic examiner in assessing the evidential value of a paint comparison. One study, conducted in England, involved comparing two thousand household paint samples. It revealed that the odds against finding two randomly collected paints that matched with respect to microscopic characteristics and solvent tests was of the order of a quarter of a million to one. If pyrolysis gas chromatography and emission spectrography tests are performed as well, the odds increase to a million to one.[4] But those odds should not be applied to all household paints. Criminalists will have to examine many more thousands of paints before valid statistical data can be

[3] F. T. Tweed, R. Cameron, J. S. Deak, and P. G. Rodgers, "The Forensic Microanalysis of Paints, Plastics and Other Materials by an Infrared Diamond Cell Technique," *Forensic Science*, 4 (1974) 211-18.

[4] C. F. Tippet, V. J. Emerson, M. J. Fereday, F. Lawton, A. Richardson, L. T. Jones, and J. M. Lampert, "The Evidential Value of the Comparison of Paint Flakes from Sources other than Vehicles," *Journal of the Forensic Science Society*, 8 (1968), 61.

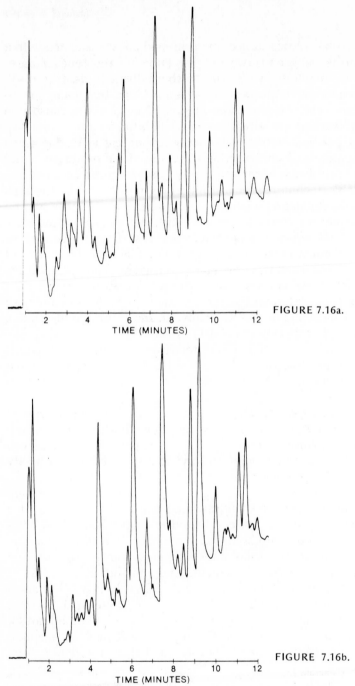

FIGURE 7.16a.

TIME (MINUTES)

FIGURE 7.16b.

TIME (MINUTES)

FIGURE 7-16. Paint pyrograms of acrylic enamel paints. (a) Paint from a Ford model. (b) Paint from a Chrysler model.

Courtesy Varian Instruments

158

accumulated for any one region of a country. Unfortunately, at this time this effort has barely begun.

It is often requested of crime laboratories to identify the make and model of a car from a very small amount of paint left behind at a crime scene. Such information is frequently of use in a search for an unknown car involved in a hit-and-run incident. Often, the questioned paint is identified when its color is compared to color chips representing the various makes and models of manufactured cars. These chips can be obtained from paint manufacturers or refinishers. Starting with the 1974 model year, the Law Enforcement Standards Laboratory at the National Bureau of Standards[5] has collected and disseminated to crime laboratories auto paint color samples from U.S. domestic passenger cars. This collection promises to further enhance the ability of the criminalist to match an unknown paint chip to a particular vehicle model.

Collection and Preservation of Paint Evidence

As has already been noted, paint chips are most likely to be found on or near persons or objects involved in hit-and-run incidents. The recovery of loose paint chips from a garment or from the road surface must be done with the utmost care to keep the paint chip intact. Paint may be picked up with a tweezer, or scooped up with a piece of paper. Paper druggist folds and glass or plastic vials make excellent containers for paint. If the paint is smeared or imbedded in garments or objects, the investigator should not attempt to remove it; instead, it is best to carefully package the item and send it on to the laboratory for examination.

When a transfer of paint occurs in hit-and-run situations, uncontaminated control paint must always be collected from undamaged areas of the vehicle(s) involved for comparison in the laboratory. It is particularly important that the collected paint be close to the area of the car that was suspected of being in contact with the victim. This is necessary because other portions of the car may have faded or been repainted. Control samples are always removed so as to include **all the paint layers** down to the bare metal. This is best accomplished by removing a painted section with a clean scalpel or knife blade. Each paint sample should be separately packaged and marked as to the exact location of its recovery. When a cross-transfer of paint occurs between two vehicles, again all the layers, including the foreign as well as the original paints, must be removed from each

---

[5] U.S. Department of Commerce, National Bureau of Standards, Washington, D.C. 20234.

vehicle. A control sample from an adjacent undamaged area must also be taken in such cases.

Tools used to gain entry into buildings or safes often contain traces of paints, as well as other substances such as wood, safe insulation, etc. Care must be taken that this type of trace evidence is not lost. It is preferable that the scene investigator avoid making any attempt to remove the paint, choosing instead to package the tool for laboratory examination. Control paint should be collected from all surfaces suspected of having been in contact with the tool. Again, all layers of paint must be removed from the surface.

In cases in which the tool has left its impression on a surface, control paint is collected from an uncontaminated area adjacent to the impression. No attempt is to be made to collect the paint from the impression itself. If this is done, the impression may be permanently altered and its evidential value lost.

REVIEW QUESTIONS

1. Hair is an appendage of the skin, growing out of an organ known as the _____ .

2. The three layers that comprise the hair shaft are _____ , _____ , and _____ .

3. The scales of most animal hairs can be described as having the appearance of shingles on a roof. (True, False)

4. The _____ contains the pigment granules that impart hair with color.

5. The central canal running through many hairs is known as the _____ .

6. The diameter of the medulla relative to the diameter of the hair shaft is the _____ .

7. Human hair generally has a medullary index of less than a _____ ; most animals have an index of _____ or greater.

8. Human head hairs generally exhibit (continuous, absent) medullas.

9. If a medulla exhibits a patterned shape the hair is (human, animal) in origin.

10. A single hair (can, cannot) be individualized to one person.

11. In making hair comparisons it is best to view the hairs side-by-side under a _____ microscope.

12. When sampling the head or pubic area for hair it is desirable to collect up to _____ hairs.

13. It (is, is not) possible to determine the time when hair was last bleached or dyed.

14. The age and sex of hair can be determined through an examination of its morphological features. (True, False)

15. The elemental composition of hair can be determined by a technique known as _____ .

16. _____ fibers are derived totally from animal or plant sources.

17. The most prevalent natural plant fiber is _____ .

18. Regenerated fibers, such as rayon and acetate, are manufactured by chemically treating cellulose and passing it through a spinnerette. (True, False)

19. Fibers manufactured solely from synthetic chemicals are classified as _____ .

20. Polyester was the first synthetic fiber. (True, False)

21. _____ are composed of a large number of atoms arranged in repeating units.

22. The basic unit of the polymer is called the _____ .

23. _____ are polymers composed of thousands of amino acids linked together in a highly organized arrangement and sequence.

24. A first step in the forensic examination of fibers will be the comparison of color and diameter. (True, False)

25. Synthetic fibers possess the physical property of _____ because they are crystalline.

26. The technique of _____ characterizes a fiber by decomposing its polymer chain and separating the resultant gaseous products.

27. The two most important components of dried paint from the criminalist's point of view are the _____ and the _____ .

28. The most important physical property of paint relating to a forensic comparison is _____ .

29. Paints can be individualized to a single source only when they have a sufficiently detailed _____ .

30. The polymeric paint binder used primarily by General Motors is

_____ .

31. A highly cross-linked polymer binder used by most American automobile manufacturers is _____ .

32. Acrylic enamels are readily dissolved by the solvent acetone. (True, False)

33. Pyrolysis gas chromatography is a particularly valuable technique for characterizing paint's (binder, pigments)

34. Emission spectroscopy can be used to identify the (inorganic, organic) components of paint's pigments.

35. Paint samples removed for examination must always include all the paint layers. (True, False)

FURTHER READINGS

Bortniak, J. P., S. E. Brown, and E. H. Sild, "Differentiation of Microgram Quantities of Acrylic and Modacrylic Fibers using Pyrolysis Gas-Liquid Chromatography," *Journal of Forensic Sciences*, 16 (1971), 380.

Crown, David A., *The Forensic Examination of Paints and Pigments*. Springfield, Ill.: Charles Thomas, 1968.

"Don't Miss a Hair," *FBI Law Enforcement Bulletin*, December 1968, p. 10.

Fouweather, C., and J. Porter, *An Appraisal of Human Head Hair as Forensic Evidence*, Home Office Central Research Establishment Report No. 98. Aldermaston, England, 1973.

Identification of Textile Materials, 6th ed. Manchester, England: The Textile Institute, 1970.

Kirk, Paul L., *Crime Investigation*, 2nd ed. John I. Thornton, ed. New York: Wiley & Sons, 1974.

Longhetti, Anthony, and George W. Roche, "Microscopic Identification of Man-Made Fibers from the Criminalist's Point of View," *Journal of Forensic Sciences*, 3 (1958), 303.

Manura, John J., and Richard Saferstein, "Examination of Automobile Paints by Laser Beam Emission Spectroscopy," *Journal of the Association of Official Analytical Chemists*, 56 (1973), 1227.

May, R. W., and J. Porter, "An Evaluation of Common Methods of Paint Analysis," *Journal of the Forensic Science Society*, 15 (1975), 137.

Moenssens, André A., Ray E. Moses, and Fred E. Inbau, *Scientific Evidence in Criminal Cases*. Mineola, N.Y.: Foundation Press, 1973.

Rowen, R. A., and V. C. Reeve, "A Comparison and Evaluation of Techniques for Identification of Synthetic Fibers," *Journal of Forensic Sciences*, 15 (1970), 410.

Stewart, W. D., "Pyrolysis-Gas Chromatographic Analysis of Automobile Paints," *Journal of Forensic Sciences*, 19 (1974), 121.

Wheals, B. B., and W. Noble, "The Pyrolysis Gas Chromatographic Examination of Car Paint Flakes as an Aid to Vehicle Characterization," *Journal of the Forensic Science Society*, 14 (1974), 23.

Drugs

chapter 8

A drug can be defined as a natural or synthetic substance that is used to produce physiological or psychological effects in man or other higher-order animals. However, this colorless clinical definition does not really tell us what drugs are; in their modern context, drugs mean something different to each person. To some, drugs are a necessity for sustaining and prolonging life; to others drugs provide an escape from the pressures of life; and to some they are a means of ending it.

Considering the wide application and acceptance of drugs in our society, it was perhaps inevitable that a segment of our population would abuse their use. During the 1960s, succeeding waves of hallucinogens, amphetamines, and barbiturates found their way out of laboratories, pharmacies, and medicine chests into the streets. During this decade, marihuana became the most widely used illicit drug in the United States, and alcohol consumption continued to rise—today 85 million Americans drink alcohol regularly and 10 million of these are hopelessly addicted to the drug or have severe problems in coping with their drinking habits.

Drug abuse has grown from a problem generally associated with members of the lower end of the social economic ladder to one that cuts across all social and ethnic classes of society. There are now millions of people addicted to alcohol, barbiturates, and heroin. In addition, there are millions more illegally using drugs such as marihuana, amphetamines, LSD, and cocaine.

In the United States, the epidemic proportions of illegal drug use has produced a situation that finds more than 75 percent of the evidence entering most crime laboratories to be drug-related. The deluge of drug specimens has forced the expansion of existing crime laboratories and the creation of new ones. For many concerned forensic scientists, the crime laboratory's preoccupation with drug evidence represents a serious distraction from time that could be devoted to the evaluation of evidence related to homicides and other types of serious crimes. However, few can deny that the increasing caseloads associated with drug evidence has provided the major, and often the sole, justification for the expansion of forensic laboratory services. Unquestionably, this expansion has had the effect of increasing the overall analytical capabilities of crime laboratories.

DRUG DEPENDENCE

In assessing the potential danger of drugs, society has become particularly conscious of their affects on human behavior. In fact, the first drugs to be regulated by law in the early years of the twentieth century were those deemed to have "habit-forming" properties. These laws were aimed primarily at controlling opium and its derivatives, cocaine, and later marihuana. Today, it is known that the ability of a drug to induce dependence after repeated use is submerged in a complex array of physiological and social factors.

Dependence on drugs exists in numerous patterns and in all degrees of intensity, depending on the nature of the drug, the route of administration, the dose, frequency of administration, and the individual's rate of metabolism. Furthermore, non-drug factors play an equally crucial role in determining the behavioral patterns associated with drug use. The personal characteristics of the user, his expectations about the drug experience, society's attitudes and possible responses, as well as the setting in which the drug is used, are all major determinants of drug effect.

The question of how to define and measure a drug's influence on the individual and the danger it poses for society is difficult to assess. To this end, the nature and significance of drug dependence must be considered from two overlapping points of view; one relates to the interaction of the drug with the individual, and the second has to do with the drug's influence on society. It will be useful when discussing the nature of the drug experience to approach the problem from two distinctly different aspects of human behavior—psychological dependency and physical dependency.

The common denominator that characterizes all types of repeated drug use is the creation of a **psychological dependence** to continue on the drug. In this context it is important to discard the unrealistic image that all drug users are hopeless "addicts" who are social drop-outs. The fact is that most users present quite a normal appearance and remain both socially and economically integrated in the life of the community.

The reasons why some people abstain from drugs while others become moderately or heavily involved are difficult if not impossible to answer. Unquestionably, psychological needs arise from numerous personal and social factors that inevitably stem from the individual's desires to create a sense of well-being and to escape from reality. In some cases, the individual may be seeking relief from personal problems or stressful situations, or may be trying to sustain a physical and emotional state that permits an improved level of performance. Whatever the reasons, it is the existence of underlying psychological needs and the desire to fulfill them that creates a conditioned pattern of drug use.

The intensity of the psychological dependence associated with a drug's use is difficult to define and to a large extent depends on the nature of the drug used. For drugs such as alcohol, heroin, amphetamines, barbiturates, and cocaine there is a significant likelihood that continued use will result in a high degree of involvement. Others, such as marihuana and codeine, appear to have a considerably lower potential for the development of psychological dependence. However, this is not to imply that the repeated abuse of drugs deemed to have a low potential for psychological dependency is safe or will always produce low psychological dependence. The fact is that we have no precise way of measuring or predicting the impact of drug abuse on the individual. Even if a system could be devised for controlling the many possible variables affecting a user's response, the unpredictability of the human personality would still have to be contended with; for it is the personal inadequacies of the drug user that represent the underlying motivation for drug use.

Our general knowledge of alcohol consumption should warn us of the fallacy of generalizing when attempting to describe the danger of drug abuse. Obviously, not all drinkers of alcohol are psychologically addicted to the drug; most are "social" drinkers who drink in reasonable amounts and on an irregular basis. Certainly there are many who have progressed beyond this stage and who consider alcohol a necessary crutch for dealing with life's stresses and anxieties. However, a wide range of behavioral patterns does exist among alcohol abusers, and to a large extent the determination of the degree of psychological dependency must be made on an individual basis. Likewise, it would be fallacious to generalize that all users of marihuana can at worst develop a low degree of dependency on the drug. A wide range of factors also influence marihuana's affect, and heavy users of the drug do expose themselves to the danger of developing a high degree of psychological dependency.

Where emotional well-being is the primary motive leading to repeated and intensive use of a drug, certain drugs, when taken in sufficient dose and frequency, are capable of producing physiological changes that encourage their continued use. Once the user abstains from such a drug, severe physical illness follows. It is the desire to avoid this withdrawal sickness or abstinence syndrome that ultimately causes **physical dependence** or addiction. Hence, for the addict who is accustomed to receiving large doses of heroin, the thought of abstaining and encountering body chills, vomiting, abdominal distress, convulsions, insomnia, pain, and hallucinations serves as a powerful inducement for continued drug use.

Interestingly, some of the more widely abused drugs have little or no potential for creating physical dependence. Drugs such as marihuana, LSD, and cocaine do create strong anxieties when their repeated use is discontinued; however, no medical evidence exists to associate these discomforts to physiological reactions that accompany withdrawal sickness. On the other hand, use of alcohol, heroin, and barbiturates can result in the development of physical dependency.

Physical dependency develops only when the drug user adheres to a regular schedule of drug intake; that is, the interval between doses must be short enough so that the effects of the drug never wear off completely. For example, the interval between injections of heroin for the drug addict probably does not exceed six to eight hours. Beyond this time the addict begins to experience the uncomfortable symptoms of withdrawal. It is well-known that many users of heroin avoid taking the drug on a regular basis for fear of becoming physically addicted to its use. Similarly, the risk of developing physical dependence to alcohol becomes greatest when the consumption is characterized by a continuing pattern of daily use in large quantities.

Table 8-1 categorizes some of the more commonly abused drugs according to their effect on the body, and summarizes their tendency to produce psychological dependency and to induce physical dependency with repeated use.

The social impact of drug dependence is directly related to the extent with which the user has become preoccupied with the drug. Here, the most important element to consider is the extent to which drug use has become interwoven in the fabric of the user's life. The more frequently the drug satisfies the person's need, the greater is the likelihood of his or her preoccupation with its use with a con-

TABLE 8-1. The Potential of Some Commonly Abused Drugs to Produce
Dependency with Regular Use

Drug	Psychological Dependence	Physical Dependence
Narcotics		
Morphine	High	Yes
Heroin	High	Yes
Methadone	High	Yes
Codeine	Low	Yes
Depressants		
Barbiturates (short-acting)	High	Yes
Barbiturates (long-acting)	Low	Yes
Alcohol	High	Yes
Methaqualone (Quaalude)	High	Yes
Meprobamate (Miltown, Equanil)	Moderate	Yes
Diazepam (Valium)	Moderate	Yes
Chlordiazepoxide (Librium)	Moderate	Yes
Stimulants		
Amphetamines	High	?
Cocaine	High	No
Caffeine	Low	No
Nicotine	High	No
Hallucinogens		
Marihuana	Low	No
LSD	Low	No

sequent neglect of individual and social responsibilities. Personal health, economic relationships, and family obligations may all suffer as the drug-seeking behavior increases in frequency and intensity and dominates the individual's life. The extreme of drug dependence may lead to behavior that has serious implications for the public safety, health, and welfare.

Drug dependence in its broadest sense involves much of the world's population. As a result there must be a complex array of individual, social, cultural, legal, and medical factors that ultimately influences society's decision to prohibit or to impose strict controls on a drug's distribution and use. Invariably, society must weigh the beneficial aspects of the drug against the ultimate harm its abuse will do to the individual and to society as a whole. Obviously, there are many forms of drug dependence that do not carry adverse social consequences, as is illustrated by the widespread use of such drug-containing substances as tobacco and coffee. Although the heavy and prolonged use of these drugs may eventually damage body organs and result in injury to an individual's health, there is no evidence that they induce physical dependence or result in antisocial behavior even upon prolonged or excessive use. Hence, society is willing to accept the widespread use of these substances.

We are certainly all aware of the disastrous failure in the United States to prohibit the use of alcohol during the 1920s, and the current intensive debate on whether or not marihuana should be legalized. Each of these issues emphasizes that the balance between individual desires and needs and society's concern with the consequences of drug abuse is a delicate one; moreover, it is one that is continuously subject to change and re-evaluation.

NARCOTIC DRUGS

The term "narcotic" is derived from the Greek word narkotikos, which implies a state of lethargy or sluggishness. Pharmacologists actually classify narcotic drugs as substances that bring relief from pain and produce sleep. Unfortunately, "narcotic" has come to be popularly associated with any drug that is socially unacceptable. As a consequence of this incorrect usage, many drugs are improperly called "narcotics." Furthermore, this confusion has produced legal definitions which are at variance with the pharmacological actions of many drugs. For example, until the early 1970s most drug laws in the United States incorrectly designated marihuana as a narcotic substance; even at the present time many drug-control laws in the United States, including the federal law, classify cocaine as a narcotic drug. Pharmacologically, cocaine is actually a powerful central nervous system stimulant possessing properties opposite to those normally associated with the depressant effects of a narcotic.

Narcotic drugs are analgesics—that is, they relieve pain by exerting a depressing action on the central nervous system. The source of most analgesic narcotics is opium, a gummy, milky juice exuded through a cut made in the unripe pod of the poppy (Papaver somniferium), a plant grown mostly in parts of Asia. Opium is brownish in color and has a morphine content that can range from 9 to 20 percent.

Although morphine is readily extracted from opium, for reasons that are not totally known, most addicts prefer to use one of its derivatives, heroin, as the drug of choice. Heroin is made rather simply by reacting morphine with acetic anhydride or acetyl chloride (see Figure 8-1). Heroin's high solubility in water makes its street preparation for intravenous administration rather simple, for it is only by injection that heroin's effects are almost instantaneously felt

FIGURE 8-1. The opium poppy and its derivatives. Shown are the poppy plant, crude and smoking opium, codeine, heroin and morphine

Courtesy Drug Enforcement Administration

and with maximum sensitivity. To prepare the drug for injection, the addict frequently dissolves it in a small quantity of water in a spoon. The process can be speeded up by heating the spoon over a candle or several matches. The solution is then drawn into a syringe or eye-dropper for injection beneath the skin. Figure 8–2 shows some of the paraphernalia typically associated with heroin's street administration.

Besides being a powerful analgesic, heroin produces a "high" that is accompanied by drowsiness and a deep sense of well-being; however, the effect is of short duration, generally lasting only three to four hours.

The contents of a typical heroin bag is an excellent example of the uncertainty attached to buying illicit drugs. For many years into the 1960s and early 1970s, the average bag contained 15 to 20 percent heroin; however, vigorous law enforcement has slowly reduced the drug's concentration to a level somewhere between 2 to 5 percent. The addict rarely knows or cares what comprises the other 95 percent or so of the material. Traditionally, quinine has been the most common diluent of heroin. Like heroin, it has a bitter taste and was probably originally used to obscure the actual potency of a

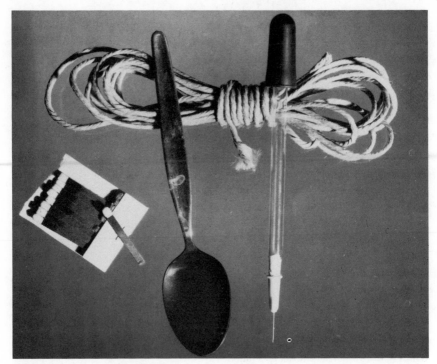

FIGURE 8-2. Heroin Paraphernalia
Courtesy New Jersey State Police

heroin preparation for those who wished to taste-test the material before buying it. Other diluents commonly added to heroin are starch, lactose, procaine (Novacaine), and mannitol.

Codeine is also present in opium, but is usually prepared synthetically from morphine. It is commonly used as a cough suppressant in cough syrup. Codeine, being only one-sixth as strong as morphine, is not an attractive street drug for addicts.

There are a number of narcotic drugs that are not derived from opium or morphine. However, because they too have the same physiological effects on the body as the opium narcotics, they are commonly referred to as "opiates." Methadone is perhaps the best-known of the synthetic opiates. In the 1960s, scientists discovered that a person receiving methadone periodically in oral doses of 80 to 120 milligrams a day would not get high if he then took heroin or morphine. Clearly, although methadone is a narcotic pharmacologically related to heroin, its administration appears to eliminate the addict's desire for heroin while producing minimal side effects. Critics of the controversial methadone maintenance programs claim that methadone is just substituting one narcotic drug for another, and supporters argue that this is the only known treatment for keeping the addict off heroin and offering some hope for eventual abstention from narcotics.

HALLUCINOGENS

Hallucinogens are drugs that can cause marked alterations in normal thought processes, perceptions, and moods. Perhaps the most popular and controversial member of this class of drugs is marihuana.

Marihuana

Marihuana refers to a preparation derived from the plant *Cannabis*. Most botanists believe there is only one species of the plant, *Cannabis sativa L.* The marihuana preparation normally consists of crushed leaves mixed in varying proportions with the plant's flower, stem, and seed. The plant secretes a sticky resin that is known as hashish. Hashish also describes the resinous material extracted from *Cannabis* when the plant is soaked in a solvent such as alcohol.

Marihuana and its related products have been in use legally and illegally for almost three thousand years. The first reference to the medical use of marihuana is in a pharmacy book written about 2737 B.C. by the Chinese Emperor, Shen Nung, who recommended it for "female weakness, gout, rheumatism, malaria, beriberi, constipation and absent-mindedness." In China, at that time and even today, the marihuana or hemp plant was also a major source of fiber for the production of rope. Marihuana's mood-altering powers probably did not receive wide attention until about 1000 B.C., when it became an integral part of Hindu culture in India. After 500 A.D., marihuana began creeping westward and references to it began to appear in the Persian and Arabian literature.

The plant was probably brought to Europe by Napoleon's soldiers returning from Egypt in the early years of the nineteenth century. In Europe the drug excited the interests of many physicians, who foresaw its application for the treatment of a wide range of ailments. At this time it also found some use as a pain-killer and mild sedative. In later years these applications were to be either forgotten or ignored.

Marihuana was first introduced into the United States around 1920. The weed was smuggled by Mexican laborers across the border into Texas. American soldiers also brought the plant in from the ports of Havana, Tampico, and Veracruz. Though its use was confined to a small segment of the population, its popularity quickly spread from the border and Gulf states into most of the major U.S. cities. By

1937, forty-six states and the federal government had laws prohibiting the use or possession of marihuana. Under most of these laws, marihuana was subject to the same rigorous penalties applicable to morphine, heroin, and cocaine, and was often erroneously designated a narcotic.

Marihuana is a weed that grows wild under most climatic conditions. The plant grows to a height of five to fifteen feet and is characterized by an odd number of leaflets on each leaf. Normally, each leaf contains five to nine leaflets, all having serrated or sawtooth edges, as shown in Figure 8-3.

It wasn't until 1964 that scientists isolated the chemical substance largely responsible for the hallucinogenic properties of marihuana. This substance is known as tetrahydrocannabinol, or THC. Its discovery has allowed researchers to measure the potency of marihuana preparations and permitted studies related to measuring the effect of marihuana's potency on man. It has also been found that the THC content of *Cannabis* varies in different parts of the plant,

FIGURE 8-3. The Marihuana Leaf
Courtesy Drug Enforcement Administration

generally decreasing in the following sequence: resin, flowers, and leaves. Little THC is found in the stem, roots, or seeds. The potency and resulting effect of the drug fluctuates, depending on the relative proportion of these plant parts in the marihuana mixture.

Most marihuana preparations available in the United States have a THC content of about 0.5 to 2.0 percent. Hashish preparations are more potent, having THC content of 5 to 10 percent. Recently, a new form of hashish, known as "liquid hashish" or "hashish oil," has appeared on the illicit market. Hashish in this form is normally a viscous substance, dark green in color, having the consistency of tar (see Figure 8-4). Liquid hashish is produced by efficiently extracting the THC-rich resin out of the marihuana plant with an appropriate solvent. The liquid hashish so far discovered has varied between 20 to 65 percent in THC content. Because of its extraordinary potency, one drop of the material can make a "high." Ordinarily, a drop is placed on a regular cigarette or on a marihuana cigarette before smoking.

Any study that relates to marihuana's effect on man must take the potency of the marihuana preparation into consideration. An interesting insight into the relationship between dosage level and marihuana's pharmacological effect was presented in the first report of the National Commission of Marihuana and Drug Abuse[1] :

> At low, usual "social" doses the user may experience an increased sense of well-being; initial restlessness and hilarity followed by a dreamy, carefree state of relaxation; alteration of sensory perceptions including expansion of space and time; and a more vivid sense of touch, sight, smell, taste and sound; a feeling of hunger, especially a craving for sweets; and subtle changes in thought formation and expression. To an unknowing observer, an individual in this state of consciousness would not appear noticeably different from his normal state.
>
> At higher, moderate doses these same reactions are intensified but the changes in the individual would still be scarcely noticeable to an observer. . . . At very high doses, psychotomimetric phenomena may be experienced. These include distortion of body image, loss of personal identity, sensory and mental illusions, fantasies and hallucinations.

Looking only at the effects on the individual, the National Commission concluded that there was no evidence that experimental or intermittent use causes physical or psychological harm. Marihuana does not cause physical dependency. However, the risk of harm lies instead in the heavy, long-term use of the drug, particularly of the

[1] *Marihuana —a Signal of Misunderstanding* (Washington, D.C.: U.S. Government Printing Office, 1972), p. 56.

FIGURE 8-4. Top to Bottom: Marihuana Vegetation, Hashish, and Liquid Hashish
Courtesy Drug Enforcement Administration

most potent preparations. The heavy user can develop a strong psychological dependence for the drug.

Other Hallucinogens

There are a substantial number of substances of widely varying chemical compositions that have become part of the drug culture because of their hallucinogenic properties. These include lysergic acid diethylamide (LSD), dimethoxymethylamphetamine (STP), dimethyltryptamine (DMT), mescaline, phencyclidine (PCP), and psilocybin. Of this family of drugs, LSD is the most potent and differs little from the other drugs except for the greater intensity of its induced reactions and side effects.

LSD is synthesized from lysergic acid, a substance derived from ergot, which is a type of fungus that attacks certain grasses and grains. Its hallucinogenic effects were first described by the Swiss chemist Albert Hofmann after he accidently ingested some of the material in his laboratory in 1943. The drug is very potent; as little as 25 micrograms is enough to start vivid visual hallucinations which may last for about twelve hours. The drug also produces marked changes in mood, leading to laughing or crying at the slightest provocation. Feelings of anxiety and tension almost always accompany LSD's use. Although physical dependence does not develop with continued use, the individual user may be prone to flashbacks and psychotic reactions even after use is discontinued.

The possibility of LSD causing chromosome damage in the children of users has been explored. At present, there is no medical evidence to substantiate this claim; however, this issue has received so much publicity that undoubtedly many have stopped experimenting with the drug for fear of maiming future offspring.

DEPRESSANTS

Alcohol (Ethyl Alcohol)

Many people tend to overlook the fact that alcohol is a drug; as such its major behavioral effects derives from its depressant action on the central nervous system. In the United States the alcohol industry annually produces over one billion gallons of spirits, wine, and beer for which 85 million consumers pay nearly $30 billion. Unquestionably, these and other statistics support the fact that alcohol is the most widely used and abused drug in the world today.

The behavioral patterns of alcohol intoxication are varied and depend in part on such factors as social setting, amount consumed, and the personal expectation of the individual with regard to alcohol. When alcohol enters the body's bloodstream, it quickly travels to the brain, where it acts to surpress the brain's control of thought processes and muscle coordination.

Low doses of alcohol tend to inhibit the mental processes of judgment, memory, and concentration. The drinker's personality becomes expansive and he or she exudes confidence. When taken in moderate doses, alcohol has been found to substantially reduce coordination and reaction times, as well as orderly thought processes and speech patterns. Under these conditions, the ability to walk or drive becomes noticeably impaired. In the next chapter we will examine in greater detail the relationship between alcohol blood levels and driving ability. Higher doses of alcohol may cause the user to become highly irritable and emotional; displays of anger and crying are not uncommon. Extremely high doses may cause an individual to lapse into unconsciousness or even into a comatose state that is a prelude to a fatal depression of circulatory and respiratory functions.

Barbiturates

Barbiturates are commonly referred to as "downers" because they relax, create a feeling of well-being, and produce sleep. Like alcohol, barbiturates act on the central nervous system to suppress its vital functions. Collectively, barbiturates can be described as derivatives of barbituric acid, which was first synthesized by a German chemist, Adolf Von Bayer, over 100 years ago. Twenty-five barbiturate derivatives are currently used in medical practice in the United States; however, only five—amobarbital, secobarbital, phenobarbital, pentobarbital, and butabarbital—seemingly suffice for most present-day medical applications. Slang terms for "barbs" usually stem from the color of the capsule or tablet (e.g., "yellow jackets," "blue devils," and "reds").

Normally, barbiturate users take these drugs by mouth. The average sedative dose is about 10 to 70 milligrams. When taken in this fashion, the drug enters the blood through the walls of the small intestine. Some barbiturates, such as phenobarbital, are absorbed more slowly than others and are therefore classified as long-acting barbiturates. Undoubtedly, it is the slow action of these drugs that accounts for their low incidence of abuse. Apparently, barbiturate abusers prefer the faster-acting ones—i.e., secobarbital, pentobarbital, and amobarbital.

When taken in prescribed amounts, barbiturates are relatively safe, but in instances of extensive and prolonged use physical dependence can develop. However, this only happens when the total daily intake of the drug exceeds a minimum level; in those instances in which this level has been determined, it definitely exceeds the normal therapeutic level prescribed by a physician. This means that patients can, for example, take barbiturates daily for sedative purposes or as an aid to sleep without developing physical dependence. For individuals who deliberately resort to maintaining high levels of barbiturate use, cessation will produce a severe withdrawal syndrome which may result in insomnia, muscle spasms, delirium, and convulsions. Consequently, withdrawal must be conducted under close medical supervision if the likelihood of death is to be minimized.

Since the early 1970s, a new nonbarbiturate depressant, methaqualone (Quaalude), has appeared on the illicit scene. Methaqualone is a powerful sedative and muscle relaxant that possesses many of the depressant properties of barbiturates. Its initial popularity before

1973 probably stemmed from the fact that the drug was not controlled by U.S. federal law or by most of the states. However, since this time the drug has been placed under strict control, causing the incidence of its abuse to decline.

Tranquilizers

In the past twenty-five years there has been a dramatic growth in the prescription of tranquilizers. Although tranquilizers can be considered depressants, they do differ from barbiturates in the extent of their actions on the central nervous system. Generally, these drugs produce a relaxing tranquility without impairment of high thinking facilities or the inducement of sleep. "Major tranquilizers" like reserpine and chlorpromazine have been successfully used to reduce the anxieties and tensions of mental patients.

There is a group of so-called "mild tranquilizers" commonly prescribed to deal with the everyday tensions of many healthy people. These drugs include: meprobamate (Miltown), chlordiazepoxide (Librium), and diazepam (Valium). There is medical evidence to show that these drugs produce psychological and physical dependency with repeated and high levels of usage. For this reason the widespread prescribing of tranquilizers as a means of overcoming the pressures and tensions of life has worried many who fear the creation of a legalized drug culture.

"Glue Sniffing"

Since the early 1960s the practice of sniffing materials containing volatile solvents (airplane glue or model cement, for example) has grown in popularity. Within recent years an added dimension has been added to the problem by the increasing number of incidents involving the sniffing of aerosol gas propellants such as freon. All materials used in sniffing contain volatile or gaseous substances which are primarily central nervous system depressants.

Though toluene seems to be the most popular solvent to sniff, there are others that can produce comparable physiological effects. These chemicals include naphtha, methyl ethyl ketone, gasoline, and trichloroethylene.

The usual immediate effects of sniffing are a feeling of exhilaration and euphoria combined with slurred speech, impaired judgment, and double vision. Finally, the user may experience drowsiness and stupor, with these depressant effects slowly wearing off as the user returns to a normal state. Most experts believe that users become physiologically dependent upon the effects achieved by sniffing.

There is, however, little evidence to suggest that the practice of solvent inhalation is addictive. But sniffers do expose themselves to the danger of liver, heart, and brain damage from the chemicals they have inhaled. Even worse, sniffing of some solvents, particularly halogenated hydrocarbons, is accompanied by a significant risk of death.

STIMULANTS

Amphetamines

Amphetamines are a group of synthetic drugs that stimulate the central nervous system. They are commonly referred to in the terminology of the drug culture as "uppers" or "speed." Ordinary therapeutic doses of 5 to 20 milligrams per day, taken orally, provide a feeling of well-being and increased alertness that is followed by a decrease in fatigue and a loss of appetite. However, these apparent benefits of the drug are accompanied by restlessness and instability or apprehension, and once the drug effects wear off, depression may set in.

In the United States, the most serious form of amphetamine abuse stems from the intravenous injection of amphetamine or its chemical derivative methamphetamine. The desire for a more intense amphetamine experience is the primary motive for this route of administration. The initial sensation of a "flash" or "rush," followed by an intense feeling of pleasure, constitutes the principal appeal of the intravenous route for the "speed freak." During a speed binge, the individual may inject 500 to 1,000 mg of amphetamines every two or three hours. Users have reported experiencing a euphoria that produces hyperactivity, with a feeling of clarity of vision, as well as hallucinations. As the effect of the amphetamines wear off, the individual lapses into a period of exhaustion and may sleep continuously for one or two days. Following this, the user often experiences a prolonged period of severe depression, lasting from days to weeks.

The repeated use of amphetamines does lead to a strong psychological dependency that encourages its continued administration. At this time there is some disagreement among medical specialists as to whether amphetamines repeated use does create physical dependence. Several investigators are of the opinion that the length of sleep, chronic fatigue, and sensation of hunger that follows amphetamines' repeated administration constitutes a withdrawal sickness.

Amphetamines are marketed in a confusing array of proprietary formulations and under different trade names. They are also called "bennies" and "dexies," street names for Benzedrine and Dexedrine, two trademark forms of amphetamine. Methamphetamine is sold under numerous trade names that include Mededrine and Desoxyn. In light of the reduced production quotas that have been imposed on amphetamine manufacturers by U.S. government regulations, an increasing percentage of the amphetamines sold on the illicit market are being synthesized in clandestine drug laboratories. It appears that the illicit production of drugs has become a profitable endeavor for both amateurs and accomplished chemists who are associated with their misuse. Some of the more knowledgeable and experienced chemists have been able to achieve clandestine production levels that approach commercial scale (see Figure 8-5).

Drugs having pharmacological properties similar to those of amphetamine, but which are chemically unrelated, are also being

FIGURE 8-5. Scene From a Clandestine Drug Laboratory
Courtesy Drug Enforcement Administration

increasingly abused. These include phenmetrazine and phendimetrazine, two drugs commonly prescribed for weight control.

Cocaine

Between 1884 and 1887, Sigmund Freud created something of a sensation in European medical circles by describing his experiments with a new drug. What he reported was a substance of seemingly limitless potential as a source of "exhilaration and lasting euphoria" that permitted "intensive mental or physical work [to be] performed without fatigue. . . . It is as though the need for food and sleep was completely banished."

The object of Freud's enthusiasm was cocaine, a drug stimulant extracted from the leaves of *Erythroxylon coca*, a plant grown in the Andes Mountains of South America and tropical Asia (see Figure 8-6). At one time cocaine had wide medical application as a local painkiller or anesthetic. However, this function has now been largely replaced by other drugs, namely procaine and lidocaine. Cocaine is also a powerful stimulant to the central nervous system, and its effects resemble that caused by the amphetamines; namely, increased alertness and vigor accompanied by the suppression of hunger, fatigue, and boredom.

Most commonly cocaine is sniffed or "snorted" and is absorbed into the body through the mucous membranes of the nose. The

FIGURE 8-6. Coca Leaves and Illicit Forms of Cocaine
Courtesy Drug Enforcement Administration

major attraction of cocaine to the drug culture is the absence of physical dependence accompanying repeated use. However, abstention from cocaine after prolonged use does bring on severe bouts of mental depression, which produces a very strong compulsion to resume the drug's use. In fact, laboratory experiments with animals have demonstrated beyond dispute that cocaine produces the strongest psychological compulsions for continued use of all the commonly abused drugs.

DRUG-ABUSE LAWS

Although the previous sections have attempted to classify drugs according to their physiological effects on the body, the practical experiences of the law enforcement community require a thorough knowledge of drug classification and definitions as they are delineated by drug laws. As may often happen, the medical and legal definition or classification of a drug bear little resemblance to one another. The provisions of drug laws are of particular interest to the criminalist, for they may impose specific analytical requirements on a drug analysis. For example, the severity of a penalty associated with the manufacture, distribution, possession, and use of a drug may depend on the weight of the drug or its concentration in a mixture. In such cases, the chemist's report must contain all information that is needed to properly charge a suspect under the provisions of the existing law.

The provisions of any drug-control law is an outgrowth of national and local law enforcement requirements and customs, as well as moral and political philosophies. These factors have combined to produce a wide spectrum of national and local drug-control laws. Although their detailed discussion is beyond the intended scope of this book, a brief description of the U.S. federal law known as the Controlled Substances Act of 1970 will serve to illustrate a legal drug-classification system that has been created to prevent and control drug abuse. The fact that many states have modeled their own drug-control laws after this act represents an important step in establishing uniform drug-control laws throughout the United States.

The federal law establishes five schedules of classification for controlled dangerous substances on the basis of a drug's potential for abuse, potential for physical and psychological dependence, and medical value. This classification system is extremely flexible in that the U.S. attorney general has the authority to add, delete, or reschedule a drug as more information becomes available. In addition, controlled dangerous substances listed in schedules I and II are subject to manufacturing quotas set by the attorney general. For example, some 8 billion doses of amphetamines were manufactured in the United States in 1971. In 1972, production quotas were established reducing amphetamine production approximately 80 percent below 1971 levels.

The criminal penalties for the unauthorized manufacture, sale, or possession of controlled dangerous substances are related to the schedules as well. The most severe penalties are associated with drugs listed in schedules I and II. For example, for narcotics included in schedules I and II, a first offense is punishable by up to 15 years in prison and up to a $25,000 fine.

Schedule I drugs are deemed to have a high potential for abuse; no currently accepted medical use in the U.S.; and/or lack accepted safety for use in treatment under medical supervision. Drugs controlled under this schedule include heroin, marihuana, and LSD.

Schedule II drugs have a high potential for abuse; a currently accepted medical use, or a medical use with severe restrictions; and a potential for severe psychological or physical dependence. Schedule II drugs include opium and its derivatives not listed in schedule I, cocaine, most amphetamine preparations, methaqualone, and most barbiturate preparations containing amobarbital, secobarbital, and pentobarbital.

Schedule III drugs have a potential for abuse less than those in schedules I and II; have a currently accepted medical use in the U.S.; and a potential for low or moderate physical dependence or high psychological dependence. Schedule III controls, among other substances, all barbiturate preparations (except phenobarbital) not covered under schedule II, phencyclidine (PCP), and certain codeine preparations.

Schedule IV drugs have a low potential for abuse relative to schedule III drugs; have a current medical use in the U.S.; and their abuse may lead to limited dependence relative to schedule III drugs. Drugs controlled in this schedule include phenobarbital and tranquilizers such as meprobamate (Miltown), diazepam (Valium), and chlordiazepoxide (Librium).

Schedule V drugs must show low abuse potential; medical use in the U.S.; and have less potential for producing dependence than schedule IV drugs. Schedule V controls certain opiate drug mixtures that also contain non-narcotic medicinal ingredients.

DRUG IDENTIFICATION

One only has to look into the evidence vaults of crime laboratories to appreciate the assortment of drug specimens that confront the criminalist. The presence of a huge array of powders, tablets, capsules, vegetable matter, liquids, pipes, cigarettes, cookers, and syringes is testimony to the vitality and sophistication of the illicit drug market. If outward appearance is not evidence enough of the difficult analytical chore facing the forensic chemist, consider the complexity of the drug preparations themselves. Usually they contain active drug ingredients of unknown origin and identity as well as additives—e.g., sugar, starch, and quinine—that dilute their potency and stretch their value on the illicit marketplace. Mind you, illicit dealers are not hampered by governmental regulations that insure the quality and consistency of their product.

When a forensic chemist picks up a drug specimen for analysis, anything can be expected to be found and all contingencies must be prepared for. To be sure, the analysis leaves no room for error, for its results will have a direct bearing on the process of determining the guilt or innocence of a defendant. There is no middle ground in drug identification—either the specimen is a specific drug or it is not—and once a positive conclusion is drawn, the chemist must be prepared to support and defend the validity of the results in a court of law.

The challenge and difficulty of forensic drug identification comes in selecting analytical procedures that will insure a specific identification of a drug. Presented with a substance of unknown origin and composition, the forensic chemist must develop a plan of action that will ultimately yield the drug's identity. This plan, or scheme of analysis, is divided into two phases: first, faced with the prospect that his or her unknown may be any one of a thousand or more commonly encountered drugs, the analyst must employ screening tests to reduce these possibilities to a small and manageable number. This objective is often accomplished by subjecting the material to a series of color tests that will produce characteristic colors for the more commonly encountered illicit drugs. Even if these tests should produce negative results, their value lies in having excluded drugs from further consideration.

Once the number of possibilities has been substantially reduced, the remainder of the analysis must be devoted to pinpointing and confirming the drug's identity. In an era in which crime laboratories are receiving voluminous quantities of drug evidence, it would certainly be impractical to subject a drug to all chemical and instrumental tests that are at the disposal of the modern criminalist. Indeed, it is more realistic to look upon these techniques as constituting a large analytical arsenal. It is up to the chemist, aided by training and experience, to selectively choose tests that will most conveniently furnish the identity of a particular drug.

In most cases, the analytical scheme will consist of a series of nonspecific or presumptive tests. Each test in itself is insufficient to prove the drug's identity; however, the proper analytical scheme will encompass a combination of test results that are characteristic of one and only one chemical substance—the drug under investigation. Furthermore, experimental evidence must exist to confirm that the probability of any other substance responding in an identical manner to the scheme selected is so small as to go beyond any reasonable scientific certainty.

There are several tests that forensic chemists normally rely upon to comprise a routine drug-identification scheme. They are color tests, microcrystalline tests, chromatography, and spectrophotometry.

Color Tests

Many drugs yield characteristic colors when brought into contact with specific chemical reagents. Not only do these tests provide a useful indicator of a drug's presence, but they are also utilized by investigators in the field to examine materials suspected of containing a drug.[2] However, it must be emphasized that color tests are useful for screening purposes only and are never taken as conclusive identification of unknown drugs.

Five primary color test reagents are listed and described below:

1. *Marquis* (2% formaldehyde in sulfuric acid). Turns purple in the presence of heroin and morphine, as well as most opium derivatives. Marquis will also become orange-brown when mixed with amphetamines and methamphetamine.

2. *Dillie-Koppanyi* (1% cobalt acetate in methanol is first added to the suspect material followed by 5% isopropylamine in methanol). A valuable screening test for barbiturates in whose presence the reagent turns violet-blue in color.

3. *Duquenois-Levine* (solution A is a mixture of 2% vanillin and 1% acetaldehyde in ethyl alcohol; solution B is concentrated hydrochloric acid; solution C is chloroform). A valuable color test for marihuana. Performed by adding solutions A, B, and C, respectively, to the suspect vegetation. A positive result is shown by a purple color in the chloroform layer.

4. *Van Urk* (1% p-dimethylaminobenzaldehyde and 10% concentrated hydrochloric acid in ethyl alcohol). Turns blue-purple in the presence of LSD. However, owing to the extremely small quantities of LSD in illicit preparation, this test is difficult to conduct under field conditions.

---

[2] Field test color kits for drugs can be purchased from various commercial manufacturers.

5. *Cobalt Thiocyanate* (2% cobalt thiocyanate in water). This reagent produces a blue flaky precipitate in the presence of cocaine. Users are cautioned that this test is extremely unreliable because many other drugs and diluents respond in the same manner.

Microcrystalline Tests

A technique considerably more specific than color tests is the microcrystalline test. Here, a drop of a chemical reagent is added to a small quantity of the drug on a microscopic slide. After a short time, a chemical reaction ensues, producing a crystalline precipitate. It is the size and shape of the crystals, under microscope examination, that are highly characteristic of the drug. Crystal tests for heroin are illustrated in Figure 8-7.

Over the years analysts have developed hundreds of crystal tests to characterize most commonly abused drugs. These tests are rapid and often do not require the isolation of a drug from its diluents; however, because diluents can sometimes alter or modify the shape of the crystal, the examiner must develop experience in interpreting the results of a test.

It is important to note that most color and crystal tests are largely empirical—that is, scientists do not fully understand why they produce the results that they do. From the forensic chemist's point of view, this is not important. The fact is that when they are properly chosen and used in proper combination, their results constitute an analytical scheme that is characteristic for one and only one drug.

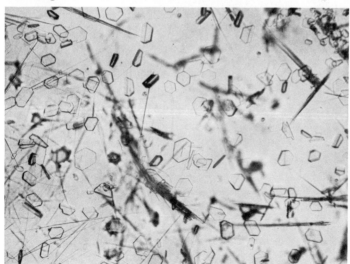

FIGURE 8-7a. A Photomicrograph of Heroin Crystals in the Presence of 10% Sodium Acetate

FIGURE 8-7b. A Photomicrograph of Heroin Crystals in the Presence of Mercuric Iodide

Chromatography

The techniques of thin-layer and gas chromatography are especially well-suited to the needs of the drug analyst, because they separate drugs from their diluents while providing for their tentative identification. The basic principles of these techniques have already been described in Chapter 4.

Because chromatography requires a comparison of either R_f or retention-time values between questioned and known drugs, the analyst must have some clue as to the identity of the illicit material before utilizing these techniques. Hence, in a typical drug analysis, chromatography accompanies and complements color and crystal tests.

Spectrophotometry

The selective absorption of light by drugs in the UV and IR regions of the electromagnetic spectrum provides a valuable technique for characterizing drugs. The ultraviolet spectrum is not conclusive for the positive identification of a drug, because other materials may very well produce an indistinguishable spectrum. Nevertheless, UV spectrophotometry is often a useful technique for establishing the *probable* identity of a drug. For example, if an unknown yields a UV spectrum that resembles amphetamine (see Figure 8-8), thousands of substances are immediately eliminated from consideration and efforts can now begin to identify the material from a relatively small number of possibilities. A comprehensive collection of UV drug spectra will give the analyst a ready index that can rapidly be searched in order to tentatively identify a drug, or failing that, to at least exclude certain drugs from consideration.

Infrared spectrophotometry is one of the few analytical techniques available to the chemist that can specifically identify a substance. The pattern of an infrared spectrum is unique for each compound and can thus be thought of as being analogous to a "fingerprint" of the compound. The combination of preliminary screening tests with a final verification by infrared spectrophotometry offers an ideal approach to drug identification. Unfortunately, the technique does present some problems to the criminalist, because the substance to be identified must be as pure as possible. This requirement often necessitates employing lengthy purification steps to prepare the sample for IR analysis. The IR spectra of heroin and secobarbital are shown in Figure 4-14.

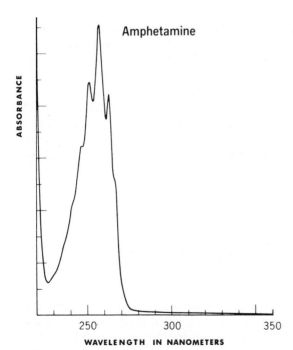

FIGURE 8-8. Ultraviolet Spectrum of Amphetamine

The Identification of Marihuana

Enforcement of laws prohibiting the sale and use of marihuana presently accounts for a high percentage of drug arrests in the United States. Any trial or hearing involving a seizure of marihuana requires an identification of the material before the issue of guilt or innocence can be decided.

Unlike most other drugs received by the crime laboratory, marihuana (*Cannabis sativa L.*) possesses botanical features that impart it with identifiable characteristics. Because the vast majority of marihuana specimens consist of small leaf fragments, their identification must be partially based upon botanical features observed under the microscope by a trained expert. This approach is further augmented with a chemical test that will independently confirm the findings of the botanical examination.

The identification of marihuana by microscopic methods depends largely on observing short hair having the shape of "bear claws" on the upper side of the leaf (see SEM photo in Figure 6-8). These hairs are known as cystolith hairs. Further verification of marihuana's presence is confirmed by the presence of longer nonglandular hairs on the opposite side of the leaf.

The Duquenois-Levine color test, described on page 184, has been found to be a highly, but not totally specific, test for marihuana. However, when used in combination with a botanical examination the results constitute a specific identification of marihuana. In addition, situations may arise in which the analyst is unable to obtain a microscopic identification of the marihuana leaf, as in the case of hashish or hashish oil. Here, the color test has to be supplemented by another examination, preferably thin-layer chromatography. This approach involves separating chemical constituents found in the suspect resin on a thin-layer plate. The separated components are compared on the same plate to those obtained from a known marihuana extract, as shown in Figure 4-8. In this manner, a positive TLC comparison, when used in conjunction with the Duquenois-Levine color test, constitutes a specific identification for marihuana.

THE COLLECTION AND PRESERVATION OF DRUG EVIDENCE

The preparation of drug evidence for submission to the crime laboratory is normally a relatively simple task, accomplished with minimal precautions in the field. The field investigator has the responsibility of insuring that the evidence is properly packaged and labeled for delivery to the laboratory. Considering the countless forms and varieties of drug evidence seized, it is not practical to prescribe any single packaging procedure for fulfilling these requirements. Generally, common sense is the best guide in such situations; keeping in mind that the package must prevent both the loss of the contents and cross-contamination between specimens. Often the original container in which the drug was seized will suffice to meet these requirements. Specimens suspected of containing volatile solvents, such as those involved in glue-sniffing cases, must be packaged in an air-tight container to prevent evaporation of the solvent.

All packages must be marked with information that is sufficient to insure identification by the officer in future legal proceedings and to establish the chain of custody.

To aid the drug analyst, it would be helpful if the investigator could supply any background information that may relate to a drug's identity. In some instances, analysis time is markedly reduced when this information is at the disposal of the chemist. For the same reason, the results of drug screening tests used in the field must also be transmitted to the laboratory. However, though these tests indicate the presence of a drug and may help the officer establish probable cause to search and arrest a suspect, they do not offer conclusive evidence of a drug's identity.

REVIEW QUESTIONS

1. Underlying emotional factors are the primary motives leading to the repeated use of a drug. (True, False)

2. Drugs such as alcohol, heroin, amphetamines, barbiturates and cocaine can lead to a (high, low) degree of psychological dependence with repeated use.

3. The development of (psychological, physical) dependence for a drug is shown by withdrawal symptoms, such as convulsions, once the user stops taking the drug.

4. Abuse of barbiturates can lead to physical dependency. (True, False)

5. The repeated use of LSD will lead to physical dependency. (True, False)

6. Physical dependency develops only when the drug user adheres to a _____ schedule of drug intake.

7. Narcotic drugs are _____ that exert a _____ action on the central nervous system.

8. _____ is a gummy, milky juice exuded through a cut made in the unripe pod of the opium poppy.

9. The primary constituent of opium is _____ .

10. _____ is a chemical derivative of morphine made by reacting morphine with acetic anhydride.

11. Methadone is classified as a narcotic drug even though it is not derived from opium or morphine. (True, False)

12. Drugs that cause marked alterations in normal thought processes, perceptions, and mood are called _____ .

13. _____ is the sticky resin extracted from the marihuana plant.

14. The active ingredient of marihuana largely responsible for its hallucinogenic properties is _____ .

15. The potency of a marihuana preparation depends on the proportion of the various plant parts in the mixture (True, False).

16. A marihuana preparation having the highest THC content is _____ .

17. LSD is a chemical derivative of _____ . This chemical is obtained from the ergot fungus which grows on certain grasses and grains.

18. Alcohol (stimulates, depresses) the central nervous system.

19. _____ are called "downers" because they depress the actions of the central nervous system.

20. Phenobarbital is an example of a (short, long) acting barbiturate.

21. _____ is a powerful sedative and muscle relaxant that possesses many of the depressant properties of barbiturates.

22. _____ are drugs used for the relief of anxiety and tension without inducing sleep.

23. Glue sniffing stimulates the central nervous system. (True, False)

24. _____ are a group of synthetic drugs that stimulate the central nervous system.

25. The most severe form of amphetamine abuse stems from its (oral, intravenous) administration.

26. An increasing percentage of amphetamines available on the illicit market originate from _____ drug laboratories.

27. _____ is extracted from the leave of the coca plant.

28. Traditionally cocaine is _____ into the nostrils.

29. The 1970 federal drug control law is known as _____ .

30. Federal law establishes _____ schedules of classification for the control of dangerous drugs.

31. Drugs that have no accepted medical use are placed in schedule
_____ .

32. Librium and Valium are listed in schedule _____ .

33. Color tests are used to identify drugs conclusively. (True, False)

34. The _____ color test turns purple in the presence of heroin.

35. The _____ color test turns orange-brown in the presence
of amphetamines.

36. The Duquenois-Levine test is a valuable color test for _____ .

37. Cobalt thiocyante reagent produces a blue flaky precipitate in
the presence of _____ .

38. _____ tests tentatively identify drugs by the size and
shape of crystals formed when the drug is mixed with specific reagents.

39. _____ provides a means of separating drugs from their
diluents while making a tentative identification.

40. The pattern of an _____ absorption spectrum is unique
for each drug and thus is a specific test for identification.

41. The microscopic identification of marihuana largely depends on
observing short hairs on the leaf known as _____ hairs.

42. All packages containing drugs must be marked for identification
by the police officer before being sent to the laboratory in order to
maintain the _____ .

FURTHER READINGS

Clarke, E. G. C., *Isolation and Identification of Drugs, Volume I.* London:
    Pharmaceutical Press, 1969.

Drug Use in America: Problem in Perspective. Washington, D.C.: U.S. Govern-
    ment Printing Office, 1973.

Fulton, Charles C., *Modern Microcrystal Tests for Drugs.* New York: Wiley—Inter-
    science, 1969.

Hofmann, Fredrick G., *A Handbook on Drug and Alcohol Abuse.* New York:
    Oxford University Press, 1975.

Marihuana and Health, Second Annual Report to Congress from the Secretary of
    Health, Education and Welfare. Washington, D.C.: U.S. Government Print-
    ing Office, 1972.

Marihuana: A Signal of Misunderstanding. Washington, D.C.: U.S. Government
    Printing Office, 1972.

Thornton, J. I., and G. R. Nakamura, "The Identification of Marijuana," *Journal
    of the Forensic Science Society,* 12 (1972), 461.

Audiovisual presentation

The Drug Scene (35 mm slides and audio tape). Police Science Services, Arling-
    ton, Va.

Forensic Toxicology

chapter 9

It is no secret that, in spite of the concerted effort that law enforcement agencies are making to prevent the distribution and sale of illicit drugs, thousands die every year from the intentional or unintentional administration of drugs, and many more innocent lives are lost as a result of the erratic and frequently uncontrollable behavior of individuals who are under the influence of drugs. However, one should not automatically attribute these occurrences to the wide proliferation of illicit drug markets. For example, in the United States alone, drug manufacturers produce enough barbiturates each year to provide every man, woman, and child with about forty pills. In a recent five-year period in New York City, there were 8,500 cases of barbiturate poisoning and 1,100 of the victims died; half were called suicide.

All the statistical and medical evidence presently available shows ethyl alcohol, a legal over-the-counter drug, to be the most heavily abused drug in Western countries. In the United States, nearly 25,000 automobile deaths each year are alcohol-related, with a rate of injury requiring hospital treatment exceeding two million persons per year. This death toll of human beings on the road, and the untold damage to life, limb, and property, is testimony in itself to the dangerous consequences of drug abuse.

At a time when the uncontrolled use of drugs has become a

worldwide problem affecting all segments of society, the role of the toxicologist has taken on new and added significance in society. Toxicologists are charged with the responsibility for detecting and identifying the presence of drugs and poisons in body fluids, tissues, and organs. Their services are not just required in such legal institutions as crime laboratories and medical examiners' offices; they reach into hospital laboratories—where the possibility of identifying a drug overdose may represent the difference between life and death—and into health facilities responsible for monitoring the intake of drugs and other toxic substances in various segments of our population. Primary examples include blood tests performed on children exposed to leaded paints, or the analysis of the urine of addicts enrolled in methadone maintenance programs.

The role of the forensic toxicologist is one limited to matters that pertain to violations of criminal law. However, the assignment of the responsibility for performing toxicological services in a criminal justice system does vary considerably throughout the United States. In those systems that have structured a crime laboratory independent of the medical examiner, this responsibility may reside with one or the other, or may be shared by both. Some systems, however, take advantage of the expertise residing in governmental health department laboratories, and assign to them this role. Nevertheless, it is a fact that whatever facility is ultimately assigned this work, its caseload will reflect the prevailing popularity of drugs that are abused in the community. In most cases, this means that the forensic toxicologist must expect to be confronted with numerous requests relating to the determination of alcohol's presence in the body.

ALCOHOL

The Fate of Alcohol in the Body

The subject of the analysis of alcohol immediately confronts us with the primary objective of forensic toxicology—the detection and isolation of drugs in the body for the express purpose of determining their influence on human behavior. In the case of alcohol, however, the problem is further complicated by practical considerations. The predominant role of the automobile in our society has mandated the imposition of laws designed to protect the public from the drinking driver. In practice, this has meant that toxicologists have had to devise rapid and specific procedures for measuring the degree of alcohol intoxication. The methods utilized must be suitably designed to annually test hundreds of thousands of motorists without causing them undue physical harm or unreasonable inconveniences, while at the same time providing reliable diagnoses that can be supported and defended within the framework of the legal system.

Alcohol, or ethyl alcohol, is a colorless liquid normally diluted with water and consumed as a beverage. Logically, the most obvious measure of intoxication would be the amount of liquor a person has consumed. Unfortunately, most arrests are made after the fact, when such information is not available to legal authorities; furthermore, even if this data could be collected, numerous related factors, such as body weight and the rate of alcohol's absorption into the body, are so extremely variable that it would be impossible to prescribe uniform standards that would yield reliable alcohol intoxication levels.

Like any other depressant, alcohol has its principal effect on the central nervous system, particularly the brain. The extent of the depression is proportional to the concentration of alcohol within the nerve cells. The nerve functions most prone to alcohol's actions are found in the surface areas of the forebrain. Later, as the subject absorbs alcohol to a greater extent, the functions of the central and rear portions of the brain are affected. The nerve functions that are most resistant, and that are the last to fail, are those centered in the brain's medulla, which regulates such vital functions as respiration and heart activity.

Theoretically, if one wanted a true determination of the quantity of alcohol that was impairing normal body functions, it would be best to remove a portion of brain tissue and perform a direct analysis on it for alcohol content. For obvious reasons this cannot be done on living subjects. Consequently, toxicologists have concentrated their efforts on the blood, for it is the blood that provides the medium for circulating alcohol throughout the body, carrying it to all tissues, including the brain. Fortunately, experimental evidence supports this approach and shows blood alcohol concentration to be directly proportional to the concentration of alcohol in the brain. From the medico-legal point of view, blood alcohol levels have become the accepted standard for relating alcohol intake to its effect on the body.

Alcohol appears in the blood within minutes after it has been taken by mouth, and slowly increases in concentration while it is being absorbed from the stomach and the small intestine into the bloodstream. When all the alcohol has been absorbed, a maximum alcohol level is reached in the blood and the post-absorption period begins. Then the alcohol concentration slowly decreases until a zero level is again reached.

There are many factors that determine the rate at which alcohol is absorbed into the bloodstream. These include the total time taken to consume the drink, the alcohol content of the beverage, the amount consumed, and the quantity and type of food that may be present in the stomach at the time of drinking. With so many variables, it is difficult to predict just how long the absorption process will require. For example, beer is absorbed more slowly than is an equivalent concentration of alcohol in water. This is apparently because of the carbohydrates present in beer. Also, alcohol consumed on an empty stomach is absorbed faster than an equivalent amount of alcohol taken with food in the stomach. The longer the total time required for complete absorption to occur, the lower will be the peak alcohol concentration in the blood (see Figure 9-1). Depending on a combination of factors, maximum blood concentration may not

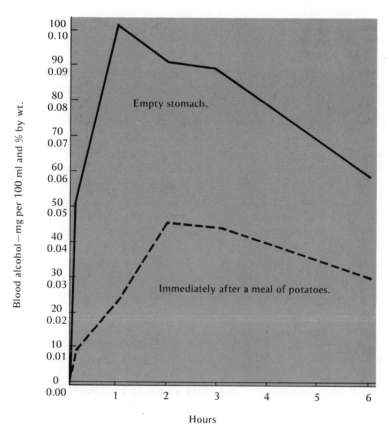

FIGURE 9-1. Blood alcohol concentrations after ingestion of 2 ounces of pure alcohol mixed in 8 ounces of water (equivalent to about 5 ounces of 80 proof vodka).

Source U.S. Dept. of Transportation

be reached until two or three hours have elapsed. However, under normal social drinking conditions, it takes anywhere from 30 to 90 minutes from the time of the final drink until the absorption process is completed.

During the absorption phase, alcohol slowly enters the body's bloodstream and is carried to all parts of the body. When the absorption period is completed, the alcohol will become distributed uniformly throughout the watery portions of the body—that is to say, throughout about two-thirds of the body volume. Fat, bones, and hair are low in water content and therefore contain little alcohol; however, alcohol's concentration in the rest of the body is fairly uniform. Hence, if blood is not available, as may be the case in some post-mortem situations, a medical examiner always has the option of selecting a water-rich organ or fluid—e.g., brain, cerbrospinal fluid, or vitreous humor—for determining the body's alcohol content to a reasonable degree of accuracy.

As the alcohol is circulated by the bloodstream, the body proceeds at once to begin the task of eliminating its presence. Elimination is accomplished through two mechanisms—oxidation and excretion. Nearly all the alcohol (90 to 95 percent) is oxidized to carbon dioxide and water. Oxidation takes place almost entirely in the liver. Here, in the presence of the enzyme alcohol dehydrogenase, the alcohol is converted into acetaldehyde and then to acetic acid. The acetic acid is subsequently oxidized in practically all parts of the body to carbon dioxide and water.

The remaining portion of alcohol is excreted unchanged in the breath, urine, and perspiration. Most significantly, extensive experimental evidence has verified that the amount of alcohol exhaled in the breath is in direct proportion to the concentration of alcohol in the blood. This observation has had a tremendous impact on the technology and procedures used for blood alcohol testing. The development of instruments to reliably measure breath for its alcohol content has made possible the testing of millions of persons in a rapid, safe, and convenient manner.

The fate of alcohol in the body is therefore relatively simple—namely, absorption into the bloodstream, distribution throughout the body's water, and finally, elimination by oxidation and excretion. The elimination or "burn-off" rate of alcohol varies in different individuals; 0.015 percent w/v per hour seems to be an average value once the absorption process is complete.[1] However, it must be emphasized that this figure is an average that may vary by as much as 30 percent between individuals.

---

[1] In the United States, laws that define blood alcohol levels almost exclusively use the unit percent weight per volume—% w/v. Hence, 0.015% w/v is equivalent to 0.015 grams of alcohol per 100 milliliters of blood, or 15 milligrams of alcohol per 100 milliliters of blood.

Alcohol in the Circulatory System

The extent to which an individual may be under the influence of alcohol is usually determined by measuring the quantity of alcohol present in the blood system. Normally, this is accomplished in one of two ways: (1) by a direct chemical analysis of the blood for its alcohol content; and (2) by a measurement of the alcohol content of breath and a subsequent relating of this value to blood alcohol concentration. In either case, the significance and meaning of the results can better be understood when the movement of alcohol through the circulatory system is studied.

Man, like all vertebrates, has a closed circulatory system, which consists basically of a heart and numerous arteries, capillaries, and veins. An **artery** is a blood vessel carrying blood away from the heart, while a **vein** is a vessel carrying blood back toward the heart. **Capillaries** are tiny blood vessels that interconnect the arteries with the veins. It is across the thin walls of the capillaries that the exchange of materials between the blood and the other tissues takes place. A schematic diagram of the circulatory system is shown in Figure 9-2.

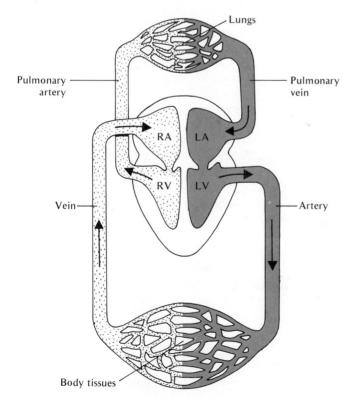

FIGURE 9-2. Simplified diagram of the human·circulatory system. Dark vessels contain oxygenated blood; light vessels contain deoxygenated blood.

Let us now proceed to trace the movement of alcohol through the human circulatory system. Alcohol is first absorbed through the gastrointestinal tract of the digestive system into the portal vein of the blood system. Here, it is carried through the liver, where the process of its destruction starts and continues as the alcohol moves up to the heart. The blood enters the upper right chamber of the heart, called the right atrium (or auricle), and is forced into the lower right chamber of the heart, known as the right ventricle. Having returned to the heart from its circulation through the tissues, the blood at this time contains very little oxygen and much carbon dioxide. Consequently, the blood must be pumped up to the lungs, through the pulmonary artery, to be replenished with oxygen.

It is in the lungs that the respiratory system bridges with the circulatory system so that oxygen can enter the blood and carbon dioxide leave it. As shown in Figure 9–3a, the pulmonary artery

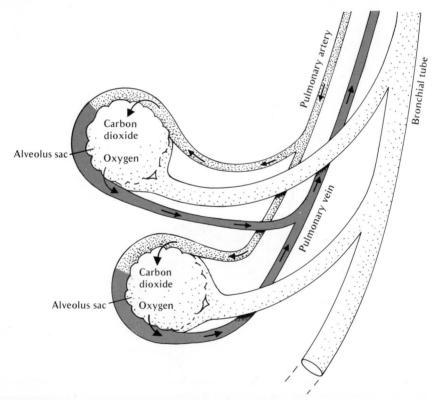

FIGURE 9–3a. Gas exchange in the lungs. Blood flows from the pulmonary artery into vessels that lay close to the walls of the alveoli sacs. Here the blood gives up its carbon cioxide and absorbs oxygen. The oxygenated blood leaves the lungs via the pulmonary vein, and returns to the heart.

branches into capillaries lying in close proximity to tiny pear-shaped sacs called **alveoli**. There are about 250 million alveoli in the lungs, all located at the end of the bronchial tubes. The bronchial tubes themselves connect into the windpipe (trachea), which leads up to the mouth and nose (Figure 9–3b). It is at the surface of an alveolar sac that blood flowing through the capillaries comes in contact with fresh oxygenated air in the sac. A rapid exchange now proceeds to take place between the fresh air in the sac and the spent air in the blood. Oxygen passes through the walls of the alveoli into the blood while carbon dioxide is discharged from the blood into the air (see Figure 9–3a). If, while this exchange is taking place, alcohol or any other volatile substance happens to be in the blood, it too will pass into the alveoli. During the act of breathing, the carbon dioxide and alcohol are expelled through the nose and mouth and the alveoli sacs are replenished with fresh oxygenated air breathed into the lungs, thus allowing the process to begin all over again.

The distribution of alcohol between the blood and alveolar air is

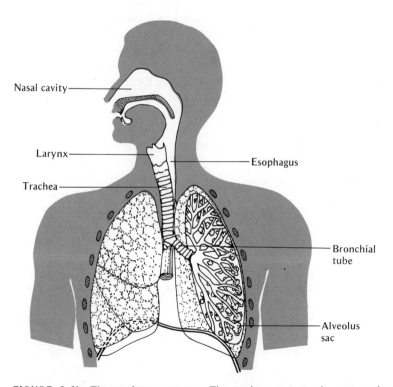

FIGURE 9–3b. The respiratory system. The trachea connects the nose and mouth to bronchial tubes. The bronchial tubes divide into numerous branches which terminate in the alveoli sacs in the lungs.

very much analagous to the example of a gas dissolved in an enclosed beaker of water that was described on page 75. Here again, one can use Henry's Law to explain how the alcohol will partition itself between the air and blood. Henry's Law may now be restated as follows: When a volatile chemical (alcohol) is dissolved in a liquid (blood) and is brought to equilibrium with air (alveolar breath), there is a fixed ratio between the concentration of the volatile compound (alcohol) in air (alveolar breath) and its concentration in the liquid (blood), and this ratio is constant for a given temperature.

The temperature at which the breath leaves the mouth is normally 34°C. At this temperature, experimental evidence has shown that the ratio of alcohol in the blood to alcohol in alveoli air is approximately 2,100 to 1. In other words, one milliliter of blood will contain nearly the same amount of alcohol as 2,100 milliliters of alveolar breath. Henry's Law thus becomes a basis for relating breath to blood alcohol concentration.

Now let's return to the circulating blood. After emerging from the lungs, the oxygenated blood is rushed back to the upper left chamber of the heart (left atrium) by the pulmonary vein. When the left atrium contracts, it forces the blood through a valve into the left ventricle, which is the lower left chamber of the heart. The left ventricle then pumps the freshly oxygenated blood into the arteries, which carry the blood to all parts of the body. Each of these arteries, in turn, branches into smaller arteries, until eventually they connect with the numerous tiny capillaries embedded in the tissues. Here the alcohol moves out of the blood and into the tissues. The blood then runs from the capillaries into tiny veins which fuse to form larger and larger veins. These veins eventually lead back to the heart to complete the circuit.

During the period of absorption, the concentration of alcohol in the arterial blood will be considerably higher as compared to the venous blood. One typical study revealed a subject's arterial alcohol blood level to be 41 percent higher than the venous level 30 minutes after the last drink.[2] This difference is thought to exist because of the rapid diffusion of alcohol into the body tissues from venous blood during the early phases of absorption. Because the administration of a blood test requires drawing venous blood from the arm, this test is clearly to the advantage of a subject who may still be in the absorption stage. However, once absorption is complete, the alcohol will become equally distributed throughout the blood system. Likewise, a breath test reflects the alcohol concentration in the pulmonary artery. Breath-test results obtained during the absorption phase may

[2] Forney, R. B., F. W. Hughes, R. M. Harger, and A. B. Richard, *Quarterly Journal of Studies on Alcohol*, 25 (1964), 205.

be higher than results obtained from a simultaneous direct analysis of venous blood. However, the former are more reflective of the concentration of alcohol reaching the brain and therefore more accurately reflect the effects of alcohol on the subject. Again, once absorption is complete, the difference between a blood and breath test should be minimal.

The Breathalyzer

From a practical point of view, the idea of drawing blood from a vein to test motorists suspected of being under the influence of alcohol simply does not offer itself as a convenient method to police authorities. The need to have the suspect transported to a location where a medically qualified person can draw blood would be a costly and time-consuming operation, considering the many hundreds of thousands of tests that the average police department must conduct every year. Thus, breath analysis serves a very useful purpose in providing an easily obtainable specimen along with a rapid and accurate result.

Though there are a number of breath-testing instruments that are presently commercially available, the Breathalyzer has become the instrument most widely employed for this application. The Breathalyzer was first developed in 1954 by R. F. Borkenstein, who at that time was a captain in the Indiana State Police. Although it has since undergone several modifications, the basic theory and design of the instrument has not changed. The Breathalyzer and an accompanying schematic diagram of its parts is illustrated in Figure 9–4a and b.

Simply, the Breathalyzer is a device for collecting and measuring the alcohol content of alveolar breath. When the valve is in the TAKE position, the subject is required to blow into a mouthpiece that leads into a metal cylinder. As the subject is blowing, the pressure of the exhaled breath raises a piston to a height that exposes two vent holes near the top of a heated cylinder. When the last breath has been expired, the piston settles down to a predetermined position covering the vent holes and trapping the last portion of air (alveolar breath) in the cylinder. The amount of breath collected in this manner is 52.5 ml or 1/40th of 2,100 ml.[3]

When the valve is placed in the ANALYZE position, the piston drops, causing the trapped sample of alveolar air to pass into a glass ampoule that contains 3 ml of a 0.025 percent potassium dichromate

[3] Actually, the collection cylinder is designed to hold 56.5 ml of breath. This is because having left the mouth at 34°C, the breath will expand when heated to 50°C in the cylinder. Furthermore, added breath is needed to compensate for the air that remains in the delivery tube leading to the test ampoule.

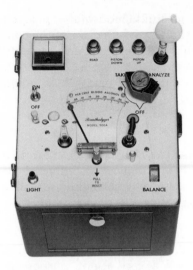

FIGURE 9-4a. The Breathalyzer.
Courtesy Smith & Wesson Electronics Co.

and 0.025 percent silver nitrate in sulfuric acid and water. Any alcohol present in the breath immediately dissolves in the dichromate solution and is oxidized to acetic acid. In the oxidation process, potassium dichromate is also destroyed. It is the extent of this destruction that is measured by the Breathalyzer and related to the quantity of alcohol passed into the ampoule.

Basically, the Breathalyzer is a spectrophotometer (see Chapter 4) that has been specially designed to measure the absorption of light passing through the potassium dichromate solution at a single wavelength. To better understand its operation, let's examine what is happening in the ampoule when alcohol is converted to acetic acid. Whenever a chemical reaction takes place between two or more substances, chemists use a chemical equation as a shorthand method to describe the changes taking place. The equation serves two purposes. It identifies the participants, and it describes the quantitative aspects of the reaction.

The following equation depicts the chemical reaction taking place in the ampoule:

$$2K_2Cr_2O_7 + 3C_2H_5OH + 8H_2SO_4 \rightarrow 2Cr_2(SO_4)_3 + 2K_2SO_4 +$$

Potassium   + Ethyl   + Sulfuric yields Chromium   + Potassium +
Dichromate   Alcohol   Acid   Sulfate   Sulfate

$$3CH_3COOH + 11H_2O$$

Acetic   + Water
Acid

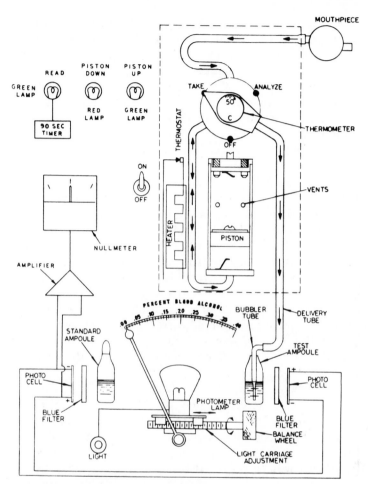

FIGURE 9-4b. Schematic diagram of breathalyzer.
Courtesy Smith & Wesson Electronics Co.

From this chemical equation we can see that there is always a fixed relationship between the number of potassium dichromate molecules reacting with the alcohol. Two molecules of potassium dichromate always combine with three molecules of ethyl alcohol. Hence, by determining the amount of potassium dichromate consumed, one has an indirect way of determining the quantity of alcohol that was originally present. Silver nitrate is also present in the Breathalyzer ampoule; however, this substance acts only as a catalyst to speed up the rate of reaction between potassium dichromate and ethyl alcohol. As a catalyst, silver nitrate undergoes no net change itself during the reaction.

Potassium dichromate is yellow in color and is known to absorb visible light in the wavelength region of 420 nanometers. In accordance with Beer's Law (see page 88). $A = kc$, the quantity of light absorbed by potassium dichromate is directly proportional to its concentration. As the reaction proceeds, the concentration and hence the light absorbance of potassium dichromate will diminish in proportion to the amount of alcohol consumed. **The Breathalyzer indirectly determines the quantity of alcohol consumed by measuring the absorption of light by potassium dichromatic before and after its reaction with alcohol.**

Because the Breathalyzer determines alcohol concentration by measuring a change in light absorption, its operation entails two measurements. First, referring to the schematic diagram in Figure 9-4b, the light source is positioned somewhere between a test ampoule and a sealed standard ampoule, both having a similar chemical composition, so that the intensity of the light passing through each is the same. At this time, there will be an equal electrical signal coming from each of the photocells located behind the ampoules as shown by a zero reading on the null meter. The light source is mechanically connected to a pointer that is located above a scale calibrated to read directly in blood alcohol percentage. The pointer is now manually set to read zero. The filters incorporated into the design of the Breathalyzer will allow only a narrow band of wavelengths in the region of 420 nanometers to pass through the ampoules and reach the photocells.

The captured alveolar air is now bubbled into the test ampoule in the manner previously described and the operator must wait 90 seconds for the chemical reaction to be complete. If alcohol was present in the breath, its oxidation to acetic acid will be accompanied by a corresponding decline in the potassium dichromate concentration, and this in turn will be reflected by a decrease in light absorption in the test ampoule. To compensate for this decrease, the operator must move the light source away from the test ampoule toward the standard ampoule in order to return the null meter to a zero reading. When the light source is moved to its new position, the pointer moves a distance that reflects the blood alcohol percentage as read off the scale.

It is well-recognized that almost the only volatile substances encountered in significant concentrations in the blood or breath of subjects operating a motor vehicle are acetone, acetaldehyde, methanol, isopropyl alcohol, and paraldehyde. Acetone, which might be present on the breath of an untreated diabetic, does not give a test result under the reaction conditions of the Breathalyzer. Isopropyl alcohol and paraldehyde have a distinct odor that can be recognized on the breath. However, it must be emphasized that all of these interfering substances are highly toxic and their presence in the blood in concentrations sufficient to give an apparent blood alcohol reading of 0.04 to .05 percent w/v would be associated with severe poisoning or death.

The Analysis of Blood for Alcohol

Before the widespread use of the Breathalyzer, toxicologists had to rely extensively on a direct chemical analysis of the blood for quantitating alcohol levels. Today, many of these procedures are still used in toxicology laboratories. Almost all of them take advantage of alcohol's volatility and first require the separation of the alcohol from the blood by distillation. Alcohol's concentration in the distillate can be determined when a measured volume of potassium dichromate solution of known concentration is slowly added until all the alcohol is completely consumed. In this process, known as **titration**, the potassium dichromate is added from a graduated buret, as shown in Figure 9-5. A colored indicator is used to detect the

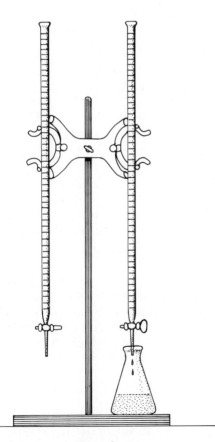

FIGURE 9-5. A typical titration setup.

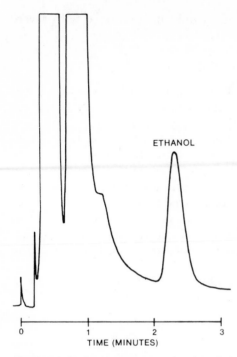

FIGURE 9-6. Gas chromatogram showing ethyl alcohol (ethanol) in whole blood.

Courtesy Varian Instruments

point at which all of the alcohol has been oxidized to acetic acid. A change in the color of the indicator signals when the analyst should stop the addition of potassium dichromate.

A more recent procedure developed for alcohol analysis involves the oxidation of alcohol in the presence of the enzyme alcohol dehydrogenase and a co-enzyme diphosphopyridine nucleotide (DPN). As the oxidation proceeds, DPN is converted into another chemical species, DPN-H_2. The extent of this conversion is measured spectrophotometrically and related to alcohol concentration.

Gas chromatography offers the toxicologist another approach for determining alcohol levels in blood. When proper gas chromatographic conditions are used, alcohol can be separated from other volatiles that may be present in blood. By comparing the resultant alcohol peak area to ones obtained with known blood alcohol standards, the investigator can calculate the alcohol level with a high degree of accuracy (see Figure 9-6).

Preservation of Blood

Once blood is removed from an individual, its preservation will be best insured when it has been sealed in an airtight container after an anticoagulant and a preservative have been added. The blood should be stored in a refrigerator until delivery to the toxicology laboratory. The addition of an anticoagulant, such as EDTA or potassium oxalate, will prevent clotting. A preservative, such as sodium fluoride, will inhibit the growth of micro-organisms capable of destroying alcohol.

A recent study[4] performed to determine the stability of alcohol in blood found that the most significant factors affecting alcohol's stability in blood are storage temperature, the presence of a preservative, and the time of storage. It is worth noting that not a single blood specimen examined showed an increase in alcohol level with time. Failure to keep the blood refrigerated or to add sodium fluoride resulted in a substantial decline in alcohol concentration. Longer storage times also reduced blood alcohol levels. Hence, failure to adhere to all or any of the proper preservation requirements for blood will work toward the benefit of the suspect and to the detriment of society.

Alcohol and the Law

Constitutionally, every state in the United States is charged with the responsibility of establishing and administrating statutes regulating the operation of motor vehicles. Though it might be expected that such an arrangement would encourage diverse laws defining permissible blood alcohol levels, this has not been the case. Both the American Medical Association and the National Safety Council have been able to exert considerable influence in convincing the states to establish uniform and reasonable blood alcohol standards.

Between 1939 and 1964, thirty-nine states and the District of Columbia enacted legislation that followed the recommendations of the American Medical Association and the National Safety Council in specifying that a person having a blood alcohol concentration in excess of 0.15 percent w/v was to be considered under the influence of alcohol.[5] However, continued experimental studies have since shown that there is a clear correlation between drinking and driving impairment for blood alcohol levels much below 0.15 percent w/v. As a result of these studies, in 1960 the American Medical Association and in 1965 the National Safety Council recommended lowering the presumptive level at which an individual was considered to be under the influence of alcohol to 0.10 percent w/v. In 1969, the National Highway Traffic Safety Administration, an arm of the U.S.

---

[4]G. A. Brown, D. Neylan, W. J. Reynolds, and K. W. Smalldon, "The Stability of Ethanol in Stored Blood," *Analytica Chimica Acta*, 66 (1973), 271.
[5]0.15% w/v is equivalent to 0.15 grams of alcohol per 100 milliliters of blood, or 150 milligrams per 100 milliliters.

Department of Transportation, mandated the states to set the presumptive impairment limit of blood alcohol concentration at a value no higher than 0.10 percent w/v or face the prospect of receiving a reduced share of federal highway construction funds. As can be seen from the map in Figure 9-7, all the states, as well as the District of Columbia, and most possessions of the United States have complied with this recommendation. The reader may *estimate* the relationship of blood alcohol levels to body weight and the quantity of 80 proof liquor consumed by referring to Figure 9-8.

The trend toward lowering the presumptive impairment level continues; in 1972, the Committee on Alcohol and Drugs of the National Safety Council suggested that a blood concentration of 0.08 percent w/v indicates impairment in driving performance. Already, two states—Idaho and Utah—have adopted such a standard.

Several Western countries have also set .08 percent w/v as the blood level above which it is an offense to drive a motor vehicle. These countries include Great Britain, Canada, Austria, and Switzerland. In addition, a few countries have even lower levels: Norway and Sweden designate 0.05 percent w/v and Czechoslovakia has an allowable limit of 0.03 percent w/v.

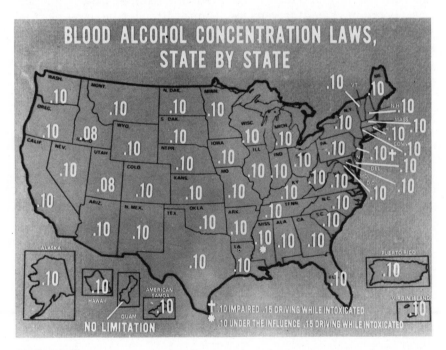

FIGURE 9-7.
Courtesy U.S. Dept. of Transportation

HOW TO TELL WHAT YOUR BLOOD ALCOHOL LEVEL IS AFTER DRINKING

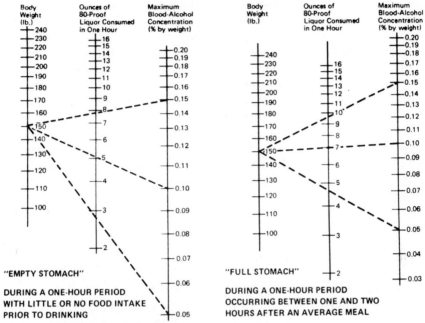

"EMPTY STOMACH"

DURING A ONE-HOUR PERIOD
WITH LITTLE OR NO FOOD INTAKE
PRIOR TO DRINKING

"FULL STOMACH"

DURING A ONE-HOUR PERIOD
OCCURRING BETWEEN ONE AND TWO
HOURS AFTER AN AVERAGE MEAL

Lay a straightedge across your weight and number of
ounces of liquor you've consumed on empty or full
stomach. The point where the edge hits the righthand
column is your blood alcohol level.

FIGURE 9-8.

In order to prevent a person's refusal to take a test for alcohol
intoxication on the constitutional grounds of self-incrimination, the
National Highway Traffic Safety Administration recommended an
"implied consent" law. By 1973, all the states had complied with
this recommendation. In accordance with this statute, the operation
of a motor vehicle on a public highway automatically carries with it
the stipulation that the driver will have the choice of either submitting
to a test for alcohol intoxication if requested, or be subject to loss of
the license for some designated period—usually six months to one year.

The leading case relating to the constitutionality of collecting a
blood specimen for alcohol testing, as well as for obtaining other types
of physical evidence from a suspect without consent, is *Schmerber*
v. *California.*[6] While being treated at a Los Angeles hospital for
injuries sustained in an automobile collision, Schmerber was arrested
on a charge of having driven under the influence of alcohol. A blood
sample was subsequently obtained from Schmerber by a physician at
the direction of the police over the objection of the defendant. On

[6] 384 U.S. 757 (1966).

appeal to the U.S. Supreme Court, the defendant argued that his privilege against self-incrimination had been violated by the introduction of the results of the blood test at his trial. The Court ruled against the defendant, reasoning that the Fifth Amendment only prohibits compelling a suspect to give "testimonial" evidence that may prove to be self-incriminating; furnishing "physical" evidence such as fingerprints, photographs, measurements, and blood samples, the Court ruled, was protection not afforded by the Fifth Amendment.

Furthermore, it was the Court's opinion that Schmerber was entitled in this instance to Fourth Amendment privileges against unreasonable search. However, it held that there was no violation of this privilege because the arrest had been made on probable cause and the search (taking a blood sample) had been conducted in a reasonable manner.

THE ROLE OF THE TOXICOLOGIST

Once the forensic toxicologist ventures beyond the analysis of alcohol, he immediately confronts an encyclopedic maze of drugs and poisons. Only a cursory discussion of the problem and handicaps imposed on the toxicologist is enough to develop a sense of appreciation for the accomplishments and ingenuity of the scientists who occupy this branch of forensic science. To begin with, the toxicologist is presented with body fluids and/or organs and is normally requested to examine them for the presence of drugs and poisons. If he or she is fortunate, which is not often, some clue as to the type of toxic substance present may develop from the victim's symptoms, a post-mortem pathological examination, an examination of the victim's personal effects, or the nearby presence of empty drug containers or house chemicals. Without such supportive information, the toxicologist is forced into using general screening procedures with the hope of narrowing thousands of possibilities to one.

If this task in itself does not seem monumental, consider that the toxicologist is not dealing with drugs at the concentration levels found in powders and pills. By the time a drug specimen reaches the toxicology laboratory, it has been dissipated and distributed throughout the body. Where the drug analyst may have gram or milligram quantities of material to work with, the toxicologist must be satisfied with nanogram or at best microgram amounts, and these are only acquired after careful extraction from body fluids and organs.

Furthermore, the body is an active chemistry laboratory, and no one can appreciate this observation more than a toxicologist. Few substances enter and completely leave the body in the same chemical state. The drug that is injected is not always the substance extracted from the body tissues. A thorough understanding of how the body alters or metabolizes the chemical structure of a drug is essential in ultimately detecting the presence of a drug. It would, for example, be a futile and frustrating effort on the part of any toxicologist to undertake an exhaustive search for heroin in the human body. This drug is almost immediately metabolized to morphine on entering the bloodstream. Even with this information, the search may still prove impossible unless the examiner is also aware of the fact that only a small percentage of morphine is excreted unchanged in urine. For the most part, morphine becomes chemically bonded to body carbohydrates before its elimination in urine. Thus, the successful detection of morphine requires that its extraction be planned in accordance with a knowledge of its chemical fate in the body.

Last, when and if the toxicologist has surmounted all these obstacles and has finally detected, identified, and quantitated a drug or poison, he must be prepared to assess the substance's toxicity. Unfortunately, there is very little published information relating to the toxic levels of most drugs. Even when such data is available, its interpretation must be predicated on the assumption that the victim's physiological behavior is in agreement with that experienced by the subjects of previous studies. In some cases, such an assumption may not be entirely valid without knowing the subject's case history. No experienced toxicologist would be terribly surprised to find an individual walking around with a toxic level of a drug that would have killed most others.

Toxicology is made infinitely easier once it is recognized that the toxicologist's capabilities are directly dependent on the input received from the attending physician, medical examiner, and police investigator. It is a tribute to forensic toxicologists, who must often labor under conditions that do not afford such cooperation, that they can achieve the high level of proficiency that they do.

Generally, with a deceased person, the medical examiner is in a position to make the necessary decisions regarding what biological specimens must be shipped to the toxicology laboratory for analysis. The living person suspected of being under the influence of a drug presents the police investigator with few choices. Urine is the specimen of choice and must be obtained from any suspected drug user. The entire void is to be collected and submitted for toxicological analysis. Preferably, two consecutive voids should be collected in separate specimen containers. When a licensed physician or registered nurse is available, a sample of blood should also be collected as well. The amount of blood taken is dependent upon the type of examination to be conducted. Routine toxicological analysis for drugs and poisons requires approximately 20 to 25 cc of blood. A determination solely for the presence of alcohol will require much less—approximately 5 cc of blood. However, it must be emphasized that many therapeutic drugs, such as tranquilizers and barbiturates, when taken in combination with a small, nonintoxicating amount of alcohol, will produce behavioral patterns resembling alcohol intoxication. For this reason, it is particularly important that the toxicologist be given an adequate amount of blood so he will have the option of performing a comprehensive analysis for drugs in cases of low alcohol concentrations.

TECHNIQUES USED IN TOXICOLOGY

For the toxicologist, the upsurge in drug use and abuse has meant that the overwhelming majority of fatal and nonfatal toxic agents are drugs. Not surprisingly, it is a relatively small number of drugs— namely, those discussed in Chapter 8, that comprise nearly all the toxic agents encountered. Of these, alcohol and the barbiturates normally account for 90 percent or more of the drugs encountered in a typical toxicology laboratory. Unfortunately, owing to low concentration levels, there are at present no methods suitable for detecting the presence of marihuana or LSD in human fluids and organs. Although intense research in this area has produced procedures that may ultimately offer solutions, these methods are presently unsuitable for routine use in most toxicology laboratories.

Like the drug analyst, the toxicologist must devise an analytical scheme that will successfully detect, isolate, and specifically identify a toxic substance. In doing so, the first chore will be to selectively remove and isolate drugs and other toxic agents from the biological materials submitted as evidence. Because drugs do constitute a large portion of the toxic materials found, a good deal of effort will necessarily have to be devoted to their extraction and detection. The procedures used are numerous, and their description is too detailed for inclusion in an introductory text such as this is intended to be. We can best understand the underlying principal of drug extraction by observing that a very large number of drugs fall into the categories of **acids** and **bases**.

Although there are a number of definitions for these two classes, a reasonably simple one states that an acid is a compound that sheds a hydrogen ion (or a hydrogen minus its electron) with reasonable ease. Conversely, a base is a molecule that can pick up a hydrogen ion shed by an acid. The idea of acidity and basicity can be expressed in terms of a simple numerical value which relates to the concentration of the hydrogen ion (H^+) in a liquid medium such as water. Chemists use what is called the pH scale to do this. This scale runs from 0 to 14.

pH = 0 1 2 3 4 5 6 7 8 9 10 11 12 13 14
————————————————————↑————————————————————
← Increasing — Neutral — Increasing →
Acidity   Basicity

Normally, water is neither acid or basic—in other words, it is neutral, and has a pH of 7. However, when an acidic substance—e.g., sulfuric acid or hydrochloric acid—is added to the water, it adds excess hydrogen ions and the pH value becomes less than 7. The lower the number, the more acidic the water. Similarly, when a basic substance—e.g., sodium hydroxide or ammonium hydroxide—is added to water, it removes hydrogen ions, thus making water basic. The more basic the water, the higher its pH value.

By controlling the pH of a water solution into which blood or tissues are dissolved, the toxicologist can conveniently control the type of drug that will be recovered. For example, acid drugs are easily extracted from an acidified water solution (pH less than 7), with organic solvents such as chloroform. Similarly, basic drugs are readily removed from a basic water solution (pH greater than 7) with organic solvents. This relatively simple approach gives the toxicologist a general technique for extracting and categorizing drugs. Some of the more commonly encountered drugs may be classified as follows:

Acid Drugs	Basic Drugs
Barbiturates	Morphine
Acetylsalicylic Acid (Aspirin)	Methadone
	Amphetamines
	Cocaine

Once the specimen has been extracted and separated into acidic and basic fractions, the toxicologist can proceed to identify the drugs present in a manner similar to that described in Chapter 8. The techniques of color tests, microcrystalline tests, chromatography, and spectrophotometry are all at the disposal of the toxicologist to be used in appropriate combination to complete the identification process. In addition, many toxicology laboratories have added the mass spectrometer (see Chapter 4) to their arsenal of instruments.

The high sensitivity and specificity of this technique makes it highly suitable for identifying small concentration of drugs. The combination gas chromatograph/mass spectrometer/computer promises the toxicologist a one-step identification procedure of unequalled sensitivity (see pg. 94).

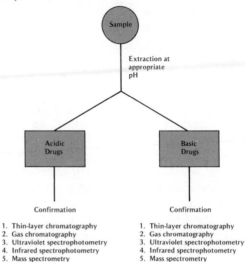

It is obviously difficult to define any specific time period following the administration of a given drug during which its presence in the body may be detected by the analytical methods normally available to the toxicologist. There are many individual factors that one would have to take into consideration before arriving at such a time limit. These would include the type of drug taken, the dosage level, the route of administration, and the frequency of drug intake. As a matter of practicality, the finding of a drug in the blood or urine of an individual suspected of being under the influence can best be utilized in a criminal justice system to verify the observations and tests performed by a police officer at the time of arrest.

These days the forensic toxicologist only occasionally encounters a group of poisons known as "heavy metals." They include arsenic, bismuth, antimony, mercury, and thallium. To screen for many of these metals, the investigator may dissolve the suspect body fluid or tissue in a hydrochloric acid solution and insert a copper strip into the solution (the Reinsch test). The appearance of a silvery or dark coating on the copper is indicative of the presence of a heavy metal. Such a finding must be confirmed by the use of analytical techniques suitable for inorganic analysis; namely, atomic absorption spectro-photometry, emission spectroscopy, or X-ray diffraction.

Carbon monoxide still represents one of the most common poisons encountered in a forensic laboratory. When carbon monoxide enters the human body, it is primarily absorbed by the red blood cells, where it combines with hemoglobin to form carboxyhemoglobin. An average red blood cell contains about 280 million molecules of hemoglobin. It is with this chemical that oxygen normally combines, allowing the blood to transport the oxygen throughout the body. Once a high percentage of the hemoglobin combines with carbon monoxide, not enough is left to carry sufficient oxygen to the tissues and death by asphyxiation shortly follows.

There are two basic methods for measuring the concentration of carbon monoxide in the blood. Spectrophotometric methods examine the visible spectrum of blood to determine the relative amount of carboxyhemoglobin to oxyhemoglobin or total hemoglobin; or, a volume of blood can be treated with a reagent to liberate the carbon monoxide, which is then measured by gas chromatography.

The amount of carbon monoxide in blood is generally expressed as "percent saturation." This actually represents the extent to which the available hemoglobin has been converted to carboxyhemoglobin. The transition from normal or occupational levels of carbon monoxide to toxic levels is not sharply defined. It depends, among other things, upon the age, health, and general fitness of each individual. In a healthy middle-aged individual, a carbon monoxide blood saturation greater than 50 to 60 percent is considered fatal. However, in combination with alcohol or other depressants, fatal levels become significantly lower. For instance, a carbon monoxide saturation of 35 to 40 percent may prove fatal in the presence of a blood alcohol concentration of 0.20 percent w/v. Interestingly, chain smokers may have a carbon monoxide level of 8 to 10 percent from the carbon monoxide in cigarette smoke.

Inhalation of automobile fumes is a relatively common way chosen by people to commit suicide. A garden or vacuum cleaner hose is often used to connect the tailpipe with the vehicle's interior, or the engine is allowed to run in a closed garage. A level of carbon monoxide sufficient to cause death accumulates in five to ten minutes in a closed single-car garage. The level of carbon monoxide in the blood of a victim found dead at the scene of a fire is of significance in ascertaining whether or not foul play has occurred. The presence of high levels of carbon monoxide in the blood is proof that the victim breathed the combustion products of the fire and was therefore alive when the fire began. Many attempts at covering up a murder by setting fire to a victim's house or car have been uncovered in this manner.

REVIEW QUESTIONS

1. The most heavily abused drug in the Western world is _____.

2. Toxicologists are only employed by crime laboratories. (True, False)

3. The amount of alcohol present in the blood (is, is not) directly proportional to the concentration of alcohol in the brain.

4. Blood levels have become the accepted standard for relating alcohol intake to its effect on the body. (True, False)

5. Alcohol is absorbed into the blood from the _____ , and _____ .

6. Alcohol consumed on an empty stomach is absorbed (faster, slower) than an equivalent amount of alcohol taken with food in the stomach.

7. Under normal drinking conditions alcohol concentration in the blood peaks in _____ to _____ minutes.

8. In the post-absorption period alcohol is distributed uniformly between the _____ portions of the body.

9. Elimination of alcohol from the body is accomplished by _____ and _____ .

10. Ninety to ninety-five percent of the alcohol is _____ to carbon dioxide.

11. Alcohol's oxidation take place almost entirely in the _____ .

12. The amount of alcohol exhaled in the _____ is directly proportional to the concentration of alcohol in the blood.

13. Alcohol is eliminated from the blood at an average rate of _____ percent w/v.

14. An _____ carries blood away from the heart; a _____ carries blood back to the heart.

15. The _____ artery carries deoxygenated blood from the heart to the lungs.

16. Alcohol passes from the blood capillaries into the _____ sacs located in the lungs.

17. One milliliter of blood will contain the same amount of alcohol as approximately _____ milliliters of alveolar breath.

18. During the period of alcohol's absorption into the blood, alcohol

concentration in venous blood will be (higher, lower) than that in arterial blood.

19. The most widely used instrument for breath testing is the _____ .

20. In a Breathalyzer ampoule the ethyl alcohol reacts with _____ in a fixed ratio.

21. The Breathalyzer measures the (absorption, emission) of light by potassium dichromate before and after its reaction with alcohol.

22. Silver nitrate is present in a Breathalyzer ampoule as a _____ to speed up the rate of reaction.

23. Alcohol can be separated from other volatiles present in blood and quantitated by the technique of _____ .

24. Failure to add a preservative, such as sodium fluoride, to blood may lead to a(n) (increase, decline) in alcohol concentration.

25. Most states have established _____ percent w/v as the presumative impairment limit for blood alcohol concentration.

26. In the case of _____ the Supreme Court ruled that the taking of nontestimonial evidence, such as a blood sample, was not in violation of a suspect's Fifth Amendment privileges.

27. Heroin is changed upon entering the body into _____ .

28. The body fluids _____ and _____ are both desirable for the toxicological examination of a living person suspected of being under the influence of a drug.

29. At present, the drugs _____ and _____ cannot routinely be detected in human fluids and organs.

30. A large number of drugs can be classified chemically as _____ and _____ .

31. Water having a pH value (less, greater) than seven is basic.

32. Barbiturates are classified as _____ drugs.

33. Drugs are extracted from body fluids and tissues by carefully controlling the _____ of the medium in which the sample has been dissolved.

34. The finding of a drug in blood or urine is always a conclusive indication that an individual was under its influence. (True, False)

35. The gas _____ will combine with hemoglobin in the blood to form carboxyhemoglobin thus interfering with blood's transportation of oxygen.

36. The amount of carbon monoxide present in blood is usually expressed as _____ .

218   Criminalistics

FURTHER READINGS

Clarke, E. G. C., *Isolation and Identification of Drugs.* Volume I. London: The Pharmaceutical Press, 1969.

Clarke, E. G. C., *Isolation and Identification of Drugs.* Volume 2. London: The Pharmaceutical Press, 1975.

Cravey, Robert H., and Naresh C. Jain, "Current Status of Blood Alcohol Methods," *Journal of Chromatographic Science*, 12 (1974), 209.

Curry, A. S., *Advances in Forensic and Clinical Toxicology.* Cleveland, Ohio: CRC Press, 1972.

——, *Poison Detection in Human Organs*, 3rd ed. Springfield, Ill.: Charles C. Thomas, 1976.

Freimuth, Henry C., "Forensic Aspects of Alcohol," in *Medicological Investigation of Death*, Werner U. Spitz and Russell S. Fisher, eds. Springfield, Ill.: Charles C. Thomas, 1973.

Harger, R. N., *Recently Published Analytical Methods for Determining Alcohol in Body Materials—Alcohol Countermeasures Literature Review.* Springfield, Va.: National Technical Information Source, 1974.

Jain, Naresh C., and Robert H. Cravey, "Analysis of Alcohol. I. A Review of Chemical and Infrared Methods," *Journal of Chromatographic Science*, 10 (1972), 257.

——, "Analysis of Alcohol. II. A Review of Gas Chromatographic Methods," *Journal of Chromatographic Science*, 10 (1972), 263.

Mason, M. F., and K. M. Dubowski, "Alcohol, Traffic, and Chemical Testing in the United States: A Résume and Some Remaining Problems," *Clinical Chemistry*, 20, (1974), 126.

Muehlberger, Clarence W., "Chemical Tests to Determine Alcoholic Influence," in *Chemical Tests and the Law*, 2nd ed., Robert L. Donigan, Evanston, Ill.: Traffic Institute, Northwestern University, 1966.

Forensic Aspects of Arson and Explosive Investigations

chapter 10

Arson and explosions often present the criminal investigator with complex and difficult circumstances to investigate. Normally, these incidents are committed at the convenience of a perpetrator who has thoroughly planned the criminal act and left the crime scene long before any official investigation is launched. Furthermore, proof of the commission of the offense is rendered more difficult to obtain because of the extensive destruction that frequently dominates the crime scene. The contribution of the criminalist is only one aspect of a comprehensive and difficult investigative process that must establish a motive, the modus operandi, and a suspect.

In practice, the criminalist's function is a rather limited one; usually he is expected only to detect and identify relevant chemical materials collected at the scene, and to reconstruct and identify ignitors or detonating mechanisms. Although a chemist can identify trace amounts of gasoline or kerosene in debris, there is no scientific test that will determine whether or not an arsonist may have ignited a pile of rubbish or paper to start the fire. Furthermore, a fire can have many accidental causes, including faulty wiring, overheated electric motors, improperly cleaned and regulated heating systems, and cigarette smoking—and these usually leave no chemical traces. Thus, the final determination as to the cause of a fire or explosion must take numerous factors into consideration and requires an extensive on-site investigation. The ultimate determination must be made by an investigator whose training and knowledge has been augmented by the practical experiences of fire and explosive investigation.

FIRE

The Chemistry of Combustion

Man's early search to explain the physical concepts underlying the behavior of matter always bestowed a central and fundamental role on fire. To ancient Greek philosophers, fire was one of the four basic elements from which all matter was derived. The alchemist thought of fire as an instrument of transformation to be used for changing one element into another. One ancient recipe expresses its mystical power as follows:

> Now the substance of cinnabar is such that the more it is heated the more exquisite are its sublimations. Cinnabar will become mercury, and passing through a series of other sublimations, it is again turned into cinnabar, and thus it enables man to enjoy eternal life.

Today, man knows of fire not as an element of matter, but as a transformation process during which oxygen is united with some other substance to produce noticeable quantities of heat and light (a flame). Therefore, any insight into why and how a fire is initiated and sustained must begin with the knowledge of the fundamental chemical reaction of fire – oxidation.

A simple description of oxidation is one that has oxygen combining with other substances to produce new products. Thus, we may write the chemical equation for the burning of methane gas, a major component of natural gas, as follows:

$$CH_4 + 2O_2 \rightarrow CO_2 + 2H_2O$$

Methane + Oxygen   yields   Carbon + Water
Dioxide

However, not all oxidation proceeds in the manner that one associates with fire. For example, oxygen combines with many metals to form oxides. Thus, iron forms a red-brown iron oxide, the familiar rust:

$$4\,Fe + 3O_2 \rightarrow 2Fe_2O_3$$

Iron + Oxygen yields Iron Oxide

Yet chemical equations do not give us the complete insight into the oxidation process. Other factors must be taken into consideration if we are to understand all the implications of oxidation, or, for that matter, any other chemical reaction. We know that when methane unites with oxygen it burns, but the mere mixing of methane and oxygen will not produce a fire, nor will, for example, gasoline burn when it is simply exposed to air. However, light a match in the presence of any one of these fuel-air mixtures (assuming proper proportions), and you have an instant fire. What are the reasons behind these differences? Why do some oxidations proceed with the outward appearances that we associate with a fire, while others do not? Why do we need a match to initiate some oxidations while others proceed at room temperature? The explanation lies in a fundamental but abstract concept—energy.

Energy can be defined as the capacity for doing work. Energy takes many forms such as heat energy, electrical energy, mechanical energy, nuclear energy, light energy, or chemical energy. For example, when methane is burned, the stored chemical energy in methane is converted to energy in the form of heat and light. This heat may be used to boil water, or to provide high-pressure steam to turn a turbine. This is an example of converting chemical energy to heat energy to mechanical energy. The turbine can then be used to generate electricity, involving a transformation from mechanical to electrical energy. Electrical energy may then be used to turn a motor. In other words, energy can enable work to be done; heat is energy.

The quantity of heat evolved from a particular chemical reaction arises out of the breaking and formation of chemical bonds. For instance, methane is a molecule composed of one atom of carbon bonded with four hydrogen atoms:

$$\begin{array}{c} H \\ | \\ H - C - H \\ | \\ H \end{array}$$

Oxygen is a molecule that is formed by bonding two atoms of the element oxygen:

$$O = O$$

In chemical changes, atoms are not lost, but are merely redistributed during the chemical reaction; thus, the products of methane's oxidation will be carbon dioxide

$$O = C = O$$

and water.

$$H - O - H$$

This rearrangement, however, means that the bonds holding the atoms together must be broken and new bonds formed. We now have arrived at a fundamental observation in our dissection of a chemical reaction—that molecules must absorb energy to break apart their chemical bonds, and that they will liberate energy when their bonds are re-formed. The amount of energy needed to break a bond and the quantity of energy liberated when a bond is formed is a characteristic of the type of chemical bond involved. Hence, a chemical reaction involves a change in energy content; energy is going in and energy is given off. The quantities of energies involved are different for each reaction and are determined by the participants of the chemical reaction.

All oxidation reactions, including the combustion of methane, are examples of reactions in which more energy is liberated than what is required to break the various bonds. This excess energy is liberated as heat and often as light and is known as the **heat of combustion**. Such reactions are said to be **exothermic**. Table 10-1 summarizes the heats of combustion of a few of the more important fuels from the standpoint of fire investigation.

TABLE 10-1. Heats of Combustion of Fuels

Fuel	Heat of Combustion[a]
Crude Oil	19,650 BTU/gal
Diesel Fuel	19,550 BTU/lb
Gasoline	19,250 BTU/lb
Methane	995 BTU/cu ft
Natural Gas	128–1868 BTU/cu ft
Octane	121,300 BTU/gal
Wood	7,500 BTU/gal
Coal—Bituminous	11,000–14,000 BTU/lb
Anthracite	13,351 BTU/lb

[a]BTU (British Thermal Unit) is defined as the quantity of heat required to raise the temperature of 1 pound of water $1°F$ at or near its point of maximum density.
Source: Paul L. Kirk, *Fire Investigation* (New York: Wiley & Sons, 1969).

Though we will not be concerned with them, there are reactions that require more energy than what they will eventually liberate. These reactions are known as **endothermic** reactions.

It is apparent from the above considerations that all reactions require an energy input to start them. We can perhaps think of this requirement as an invisible energy barrier that has been erected between the reactants and the products of a reaction (see Figure 10-1). The higher this barrier, the more energy will be required to initiate the reaction. Where does this initial energy come from? There are many sources of energy; however, for the purpose of this discussion it will only be necessary to look at one—heat.

The energy barrier that exists in the conversion of iron to rust is a relatively small one, and it can be surmounted with the help of heat energy present in the surrounding environment at normal outdoor temperatures. Not so for methane or gasoline—here the energy barriers are quite high and a high temperature must be applied to start its oxidation. Hence, before any fire can result, the temperature of these fuels must be raised to a value that will allow the heat energy input to exceed the energy barrier. Table 10-2 shows that this temperature, known as the **ignition temperature**, is quite high for common fuels. Once the combustion starts, a sufficient amount of heat is liberated to keep the reaction going by itself. In essence, the fire becomes a chain reaction, absorbing a portion of its own liberated heat in order to generate even more heat. The fire will continue to burn until either the supply of oxygen or the fuel is exhausted.

Normally, an ordinary lighted match offers itself as a convenient ignitor of fuels. However, the fire investigator must also consider other potential sources of heat—e.g., electrical discharges, sparks, and chemicals—while reconstructing the initiation of a fire. All of these sources have temperatures in excess of what is needed to meet the ignition temperature requirement of most fuels.

Although the liberation of energy explains many important features of oxidation, it does not offer a complete explanation for

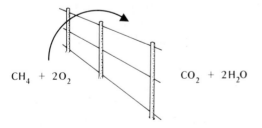

$CH_4 + 2O_2$ $CO_2 + 2H_2O$

FIGURE 10-1. An energy barrier must be hurdled before reactants such as methane and oxygen can combine with one another to form the products of carbon dioxide and water.

TABLE 10-2. Ignition Temperatures of Some Common Fuels

Fuel	Ignition Temperature °F
Acetone	1000
Acetylene	635
Benzene	1076
Ethyl Alcohol	799
Gasoline	495
Kerosene (fuel oil #1)	490
Methane	999
Methyl Alcohol	878
Naphtha (Stoddard solvent)	450-500
Naphtha (V.M. and P.)	450-500
n-Octane	450
Petroleum Ether	475
Propane	874
Toluene	1026
Turpentine	488

Source: Paul L. Kirk, Fire Investigation (New York: Wiley & Sons, 1969).

all the characteristics of the reaction. Obviously, although all oxidations liberate energy, they are not all accompanied by the presence of a flame; witness the oxidation of iron to rust. There is, therefore, one other important consideration that must be taken into account before our understanding of oxidation and fire is complete. This additional factor is the rate or speed at which the reaction takes place.

Simply, we can picture a chemical reaction, such as oxidation, taking place when molecules combine or collide with one another. Essentially, the faster the molecules move, the greater will be the number of collisions taking place between them and the faster will be the rate of reaction. There are many factors that influence the rate at which these collisions take place. In our description of fire and oxidation we need only be concerned with two; the physical state of the fuel and temperature.

A fuel will only achieve a reaction rate with oxygen sufficient to produce a flame when it is in the gaseous state, for it is only in this state that molecules can collide frequently enough to support a flaming fire. This remains true even though the fuel that may be feeding the flame is a solid—e.g., wood, paper, cloth, plastic, or a liquid, such as gasoline or kerosene. How then does a liquid or solid maintain a gaseous reaction? In the case of a liquid fuel, the temperature must be high enough to vaporize the fuel. The vapor that forms burns when it mixes with oxygen and combusts as a flame. The **flash point** is the *lowest* temperature at which a liquid gives off sufficient vapor to form a mixture with air that will support combustion. Once the flash point is reached, the fuel can be ignited by some outside source of temperature to start a fire. The ignition temperature is always considerably higher than the flash point. For example, gasoline has a flash point of $-50°F$; however, it takes an ignition temperature of $495°F$ to start a gasoline fire. With a solid fuel, the process of generating vapor is more complex. Wood, or any other solid fuel, will only burn when it is exposed to heat that is hot enough to decompose the solid into gaseous products. This chemical breakdown of solid material is known as **pyrolysis**. It is the numerous gaseous products of pyrolysis that combine with oxygen to produce a fire. Here again fire can be described as a chain reaction. A match or other source of heat initiates the pyrolysis of the solid fuel, the gaseous products react with oxygen in the air to produce heat and light, and this heat in turn is used to pyrolyze more solid fuel into volatile gases.

Although a flaming fire will only be supported by a gaseous fuel, there are instances in which a fuel can burn without the presence of a flame. Witness the burning cigarette or the red glow of hot charcoals. These are examples of a phenomenon known as **glowing combustion**. Here combustion is taking place on the surface of a solid fuel in the absence of heat sufficiently high enough to pyrolyze the fuel. Interestingly, this phenomenon generally ensues long after a flaming fire. Wood, for example, tends to burn with a flame until all of its pyrolyzable components have been expended; however, wood's carbonaceous residue will continue to smoulder long after the flame has extinguished itself.

We may now consider the conversion of iron to rust to be an example of an extremely slow oxidation process; a situation that exists because of the inability of the iron atoms to achieve a gaseous state. For this reason, the combination of oxygen with iron to produce rust is restricted to the surface area of the metal exposed to air, a limitation that severely reduces the rate of reaction. On the other hand, the reaction of methane and oxygen is an example of oxidation in which all the reactants are in the gaseous state. Hence, this reaction proceeds at a rapid rate as reflected by the production of noticeable quantities of heat and light (a flame).

Most typically, the rate of a chemical reaction increases when the temperature is raised. The magnitude of the increase in rate with temperature varies from one reaction to another and also from one temperature range to another. For most reactions a $10°C$ $(18°F)$

rise in temperature doubles or triples the reaction rate. This observation in part explains why burning is so rapid. As the fire spreads, it raises the temperature of the fuel-air mixture, thus increasing the rate of reaction; this in turn generates more heat, again increasing the rate of reaction. It is only when the fuel or oxygen is depleted that this vicious cycle will come to a halt.

Until now we have only referred to oxidation reactions that rely on air as the sole source of oxygen. However, we need not restrict ourselves to this type of situation. For example, explosives are substances that undergo a rapid exothermic oxidation reaction with the production of large quantities of gases. It is this sudden buildup of gas pressure that constitutes the nature of an explosion. Detonation frequently occurs so rapidly that oxygen in the air cannot participate in the reaction; thus, many explosives must have their own source of oxygen. Chemicals that supply oxygen are known as **oxidizing agents**. Black powder, a low-energy explosive, is composed of a mixture of the following chemical ingredients:

75% Potassium Nitrate (KNO_3)
15% Charcoal (C)
10% Sulfur (S)

In this combination, oxygen containing potassium nitrate acts as an oxidizing agent toward the charcoal and sulfur fuels. As heat is applied to black powder, oxygen is liberated from potassium nitrate and simultaneously combines with charcoal and sulfur to produce heat and gases (symbolized by ↑), as represented in the following chemical equation:

$$3C + S + 2KNO_3 \rightarrow 3CO_2 \uparrow + N_2 \uparrow + K_2S + heat$$

Carbon + Sulfur + Potassium   yields   Carbon   + Nitrogen   + Potassium
Nitrate   Dioxide   Sulfide

Some explosives have their oxygen and fuel components combined within one molecule. For example, nitroglycerin, the major constituent of dynamite, has a chemical structure that combines carbon, hydrogen, nitrogen, and oxygen.

$$
\begin{array}{ccccc}
H & & H & & H \\
| & & | & & | \\
H-C & - & C & - & C-H \\
| & & | & & | \\
O & & O & & O \\
| & & | & & | \\
NO_2 & & NO_2 & & NO_2
\end{array}
$$

When nitroglycerin detonates, large quantities of energy are released as the molecule decomposes and the oxygen recombines to produce large volumes of carbon dioxide, nitrogen, and water.

In summary, three requirements must be satisfied if combustion is to be initiated and sustained:

1. A fuel must be present
2. Oxygen must be available in sufficient quantity to combine with the fuel
3. Heat must be applied to initiate the combustion and sufficient heat must be generated to sustain the reaction

Searching the Fire Scene

It is important that the arson investigator begin a search for a fire's origin immediately after the fire goes out. It is this area that will prove most productive in any search for an apparatus or device that may have been used to start the fire. However, there are no fast and simple rules for locating a fire's origin. Normally, a fire has a tendency to move in an upward direction, and thus the probable origin will most likely be located closest to the lowest point that shows the most intense characteristics of burning. However, there are many factors that can contribute to the deviation of a fire from normal behavior. Prevailing drafts and winds, secondary fires due to collapsing floors and roofs, the physical arrangement of the burning structure, stairways, elevator shafts, holes in the floor, wall, or roof, and the effects of the fire fighter in suppressing the fire, are all factors that the knowledgeable fire investigator must consider before determining conclusive findings.

Once located, the point of origin should be protected as necessary to permit careful investigation. As at any crime scene, nothing should be touched or moved before notes, sketches, and photographs are taken. Examination of the debris at the point of origin must be made with great care. An examination must be made for possible accidental causes, as well as for evidence of arson. The most common materials used by an arsonist to assure the rapid spread and intensity of a fire are gasoline, kerosene, or, for that matter, any volatile flammable liquid. Fortunately, only under the most ideal of conditions will combustible liquids be entirely consumed during a fire. When the liquid is poured over a large area, it is highly likely that a portion of it will seep into a porous surface, such as cracks in the floor, upholstery, rags, plaster, wallboards, or carpet, where enough of it remains unchanged so that it can be detected in the crime laboratory. In addition, when a fire has been extinguished with water, the rate of evaporation of volatile fluids may have been slowed down, because water cools and covers materials through which the combustible liquid may have soaked. Fortunately the presence of water does not interfere with laboratory methods utilized to detect and characterize flammable liquid residues.

The fire investigator's search for traces of flammable liquid residues may be aided by the use of a highly sensitive portable vapor detector or "sniffer" (Figure 10-2). This device can rapidly screen suspect materials for the presence of volatile residues by sucking in the air surrounding the questioned sample. The air is passed over a heated filament; if a combustible vapor is present, it ignites and immediately increases the temperature of the filament. The rise in filament temperature is then registered as a deflection on the detector's meter. Of course, such a device is not a conclusive test for a flammable vapor, but it does provide the investigator with an excellent screening device for checking suspect samples at the fire scene.

As a matter of routine, two to three quarts of ash and soot debris must be collected at the point of origin of a fire when arson is suspected. The collection should include all porous materials and all other substances thought likely of containing flammable residues.

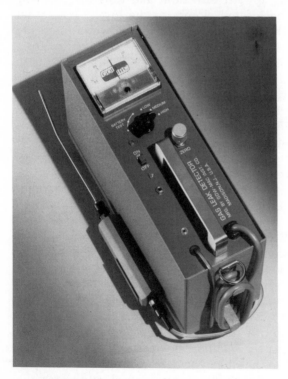

FIGURE 10-2. Portable hydrocarbon detector.

Courtesy Gow-Mac Instrument Co.

Specimens are to be immediately packaged in an airtight container so no loss can occur through evaporation. New clean paint cans are low-cost, airtight, unbreakable containers and are available in a variety of sizes. Wide-mouthed glass jars are also useful for packaging suspect specimens, provided that they contain airtight lids. If need be, large bulky samples will have to be cut to size at the scene so they will fit into available containers. Plastic bags are not suitable for packaging specimens because they are porous and will permit volatile hydrocarbon vapors to escape.

It is important that the collection of all materials suspected of containing volatile liquids be accompanied by a thorough sampling of similar but uncontaminated control specimens from another area of the fire scene. For example, if he collects carpeting at the point of origin, the investigator must sample the same carpet from another part of the room where he is reasonably sure that no flammable substance was placed. In the laboratory, the criminalist will check the control to be sure that it is free of any flammables. This procedure will reduce the possibility and subsequent argument that the carpet was exposed to a flammable liquid, such as a cleaning solution, during the normal course of its maintenance.

Needless to say, fluids found in open bottles or cans must be collected and sealed. Even when such containers appear to be empty, the investigator is wise to seal and preserve them in case they contain trace amounts of liquids or vapors. At the same time, a thorough search of the scene should be undertaken for ignitors. The most common ignitor is the match. Normally, the match is completely consumed during a fire and is impossible to locate. However, there have been cases in which, by force of habit, matches have been blown out and tossed aside only to be recovered later by the investigator. This evidence may prove valuable if the criminalist can successfully fit the match to a book found on the possession of a suspect, as shown in Figure 10-3, a and b. There are, in addition, many other types of devices that an arsonist can construct to start a fire. These might include a burning cigarette, firearms, ammunition, a mechanical match striker, electrical sparking devices, and a "Molotov cocktail." Relatively complex mechnical devices are much more likely to survive the fire for later discovery. The broken glass and wick of the Molotov cocktail, if recovered, must be preserved as well.

One rather interesting phenomenon that is often invoked by arson suspects as being the cause of a fire is spontaneous combustion. Actually, the conditions under which spontaneous combustion can develop are rather limited and in fact rarely account for the cause of a fire. Spontaneous combustion is the result of a natural heat-producing process in poorly ventilated containers or areas. For example,

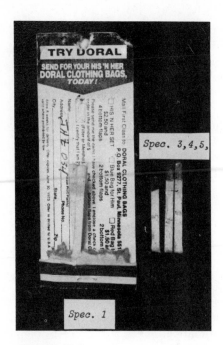

FIGURE 10-3a.

FIGURE 10-3b. Three matches discarded at the scene of an arson are each shown to fit into a match book found in the suspect's possession. Such evidence provides a strong link between the crime scene and suspect.

Courtesy New Jersey State Police

hay stored in barns offers itself as an excellent growing medium for bacteria whose activities will generate heat. If the hay is not properly ventilated, the heat will build to a level that will support other types of heat-producing chemical reactions in the hay. Eventually, as the heat rises, the ignition temperature of hay is reached, spontaneously setting off a fire.

Another known example of spontaneous combustion involves the ignition of improperly ventilated containers containing rags wetted with certain types of highly unsaturatured oils, such as linseed oil. It is conceivable that heat will build up to the point of ignition as a result of a slow heat-producing chemical oxidation between air and the oil. Of course, storage conditions will have to encourage the accumulation of the heat over a prolonged period of time. However, spontaneous combustion will not occur with hydrocarbon lubricating oils, and it is not expected to occur with most of the fats and oils that are found in a household.

The Analysis of Flammable Residues

Criminalists are unanimous in judging the gas chromatograph the most sensitive and reliable instrument for detecting the characterizing flammable residues. The vast majority of arsons are initiated by petroleum distillates, such as gasoline and kerosene; these liquids are actually composed of a complex mixture of hydrocarbons. Basically, the gas chromatograph separates the hydrocarbon components and produces a chromatographic pattern characteristic of a particular petroleum product.

The criminalist in the laboratory places a representative sample of the collected debris material in a glass bottle and seals it with a rubber septum. When the container is heated, any volatile residue present in the debris will be driven off and trapped in the bottle's enclosed air space.[1] The vapor is removed with a syringe, as shown in Figure 10-4. When the vapor is injected into the gas chromatograph, it is separated into its components and each peak is recorded on the chromatogram. The identity of the volatile residue is determined when the pattern of the resultant chromatogram is compared to patterns produced by known petroleum products. For example, in Figure 10-5 a and b a gas chromatographic analysis of soil recovered from a fire site shows a chromatogram similar to a known gasoline standard, thus proving the presence of gasoline. In the absence of any recognizable pattern the individual peaks can be identified when the

[1] An alternate approach to the recovery of hydrocarbon residues is to immerse the debris in water and steam distill off the volatile residues.

FIGURE 10-4. Removal of vapor from an enclosed container prior to gas chromatographic analysis.

Courtesy New Jersey State Police

investigator compares their retention times to known hydrocarbon standards (e.g., hexane, benzene, toluene, and xylenes).

One of the primary advantages of the gas chromatograph is its extreme sensitivity. Gasoline vapor as low as ten parts per million in concentration is detected and identified in this manner, far surpassing all other techniques known to the criminalist.

Though the gas chromatograph can readily distinguish gasoline from other flammable liquids, such as kerosene, turpentine, and naphtha, it offers no solution for the identification of gasoline by brand name. In an era of uncertain gasoline markets, exchange agreements among the various oil companies makes such an identification uncertain at best anyway. However, a procedure that has proven quite useful for associating a *liquid* gasoline sample to a particular brand stems from the knowledge that most brands of gasoline are distinguishable from one another by the colored dye additives that manufacturers put into them. These dyes are readily separated into characteristic patterns on a thin-layer chromatographic plate. But, the failure of some oil companies to consistently add the same dyes does limit the utility of the procedure.

Even with this limitation, the above technique has proven a useful investigative tool for tentatively identifying a source of gasoline, or for at least eliminating a suspected source. For example, an investigator may request of the crime laboratory to undertake such an analysis in order to pinpoint a gasoline to a particular gas station. Here, it is important that the criminalist be supplied with known gasoline samples from all local and suspect stations for comparison to the unknown. These specimens must be collected as quickly as possible in order to minimize the possibility that the dye composition at the pumps will be altered by fresh gasoline deliveries.

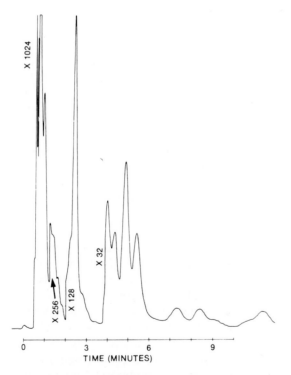

FIGURE 10-5a. Gas chromatograph of vapors from Esso regular gasoline.

Courtesy Varian Instruments

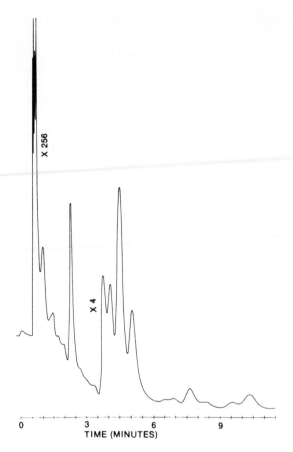

FIGURE 10-5b. Gas chromatograph of vapors from soil recovered at fire site. Note the similarity to known gasoline standard shown on the preceeding page.

Courtesy Varian Instruments

EXPLOSIVES

The ready accessibility of potentially explosive laboratory chemicals, dynamite, and in some countries, an assortment of military explosives, has provided a criminal element of society with a very lethal weapon. Although worldwide politically motivated bombings have received considerable publicity, it is a fact that in the United States the vast majority of bombing incidents are perpetrated by isolated individuals rather than organized terrorists. Unfortunately for society, explosives have become attractive weapons to be used by the criminal bent on revenge, the destruction of commercial operations, or just plain mischief.

Most bombing incidents that confront police agencies today involve the use of homemade explosives and incendiary devices. The design of such weapons is limited only by the imagination and ingenuity of the bomber. Like arson investigation, bomb investigation requires the close cooperation of a group of highly specialized individuals trained and experienced in bomb disposal, bomb-site investigation, forensic analysis, and criminal investigation. To the criminalist falls the responsibility of detecting and identifying explosive chemicals recovered from the crime scene, as well as identifying detonating mechanisms. It is this special responsibility that will concern us for the remainder of this chapter.

Definition and Classification of Explosives

Like fire, an explosion is the product of combustion accompanied by the creation of gases and heat. However, the distinguishing characteristic of an explosion is the rapid rate at which the reaction proceeds. It is the sudden buildup of expanding gas pressure at the origin of the explosion that produces the violent physical disruption on the surrounding environment. Consider, for example, the effect of confining an explosive charge to a relatively small enclosed container. Upon detonation, the explosive almost instantaneously produces large volumes of gases that begin to exert enormously high pressures on the interior walls of the container. In addition, the heat energy released by the explosion serves to expand the gases, causing them to push on the walls with an even greater force. If we could observe the effects of an exploding lead pipe in slow motion, we would first see the pipe's walls stretch and balloon under pressures as high as several hundred tons per square inch. Finally, the walls would fragment and fly outward in all directions. It is this flying debris that constitutes the greatest danger to life and limb in the immediate vicinity of an explosion.

Upon release from confinement, the gaseous products of the explosion suddenly expand and compress layers of surrounding air as they move outward from the origin of the explosion. This blast effect or outward rush of gases, at a rate that may be as high as 7,000 miles per hour, creates an artificial gale that can overthrow walls, collapse roofs, and disturb any object in its path. If a bomb is sufficiently powerful, the more serious damage will be inflicted on life and property by the blast effect rather than by fragmentation debris.

The speed at which explosives detonate or decompose varies greatly from one to another and permits their classification as high- and low-energy explosives. **Low-energy** explosives, such as black and smokeless powders, decompose relatively slowly at rates that vary up to 1,000 meters per second. Because of their slow burning rates, they produce a propelling or throwing action that makes them suitable as propellants for ammunition or skyrockets. However, the danger of this group of explosives must not be underestimated, for when any one of them is confined to a relatively small container, it can explode with a force as lethal as any known explosive. **High-energy** explosives include dynamite, TNT, PETN, and RDX. They detonate almost instantaneously at rates from 1,000 to 8,500 meters per second, producing a smashing or shattering effect upon their target.

Low-Energy Explosives. The most widely used explosives in this group are black powder and smokeless powder. The popularity of these two explosives is enhanced by their accessibility to the public. Both are available in any gun store, and black powder can easily be made from ingredients purchased at any chemical supply house as well. Black powder is a relatively stable mixture of potassium or sodium nitrate, charcoal, and sulfur. Unconfined, it merely burns and is, in fact, used as a medium for carrying a flame to the explosive charge. A safety fuse usually consists of black powder wrapped in a fabric or plastic casing. When ignited, a sufficient length of fuse will burn at a rate slow enough to allow an individual adequate time to leave the site of the pending explosion. Black powder, like any other low-energy explosive, only becomes explosive and lethal when it is confined.

Actually, the only ingredient required for a low-energy explosive is a fuel and a good oxidizing agent. Thus, the oxidizing agent potassium chlorate, for example, when it is mixed with sugar, produces a popular and accessible explosive mix. When it is confined to a small container—e.g., a pipe—and ignited by the flame of a safety fuse, this mixture can explode with a force equivalent to a stick of 40 percent dynamite. Some other commonly encountered ingredients that may be combined with chlorate to produce an explosive are carbon, sulfur, starch, phosphorous, and magnesium filings. Chlorate mixtures may also be ignited by the heat generated from a chemical reaction. For instance, sufficient heat can be generated to initiate combustion when concentrated sulfuric acid comes in contact with a sugar-chlorate mix.

The safest and most powerful low-energy explosive is smokeless powder. This explosive usually consists of nitrated cotton or nitrocellulose (single-base powder) or nitroglycerin mixed with nitrocellulose (double-base powder). The powder is manufactured in a variety of grain sizes and shapes depending on the desired application.

Another common low-order explosive is created when a considerable quantity of natural gas escapes into a confined area and mixes with a sufficient amount of air. If ignited, this mixture will result in a simultaneous combustion, with the sudden production of large volumes of gases and heat. In a building, walls are forced outward by the expanding gases, causing the roof to fall into the interiors while objects are thrown outward and scattered in erratic directions with no semblance of pattern.

Mixtures of air and a gaseous fuel will only explode or burn within a limited concentration range. For example, the concentration limits for methane in air ranges from 5.3 to 13.9 percent. In the presence of too much air, the fuel will become too diluted and will not respond to efforts to ignite it; on the other hand, if the fuel becomes too concentrated, ignition will be prevented because there is not enough oxygen to support the combustion. Mixtures at or near the upper concentration limit ("rich" mixtures) will explode; however, some gas will remain unconsumed because there is not enough oxygen to complete the combustion. As air rushes back into the origin of the explosion, it combines with the residual hot gas and a fire is produced that is characterized by a "whoosh" sound. Often this fire may prove to be more destructive than the explosion that preceded it. Mixtures near the lower end of the limit ("lean" mixtures) generally cause an explosion without accompanying damage due to fire.

High-Energy Explosives. The sensitivity of a high-energy explosive provides a convenient basis for its classification into two groups. **Initiating explosives** are ultrasensitive to heat, shock, or friction, and under normal conditions will detonate violently instead of burning. For this reason, they are used to detonate other explosives through a chain reaction and are often referred to as primers. Initiating explosives provide the major ingredient of a blasting cap and include lead azide, lead styphnate, and mercury fulminate. Because of their extreme sensitivity, these explosives are rarely used by bombers as the main charge of a homemade bomb.

Noninitiating explosives are relatively insensitive to heat, shock, or friction and will normally burn rather than detonate if they are ignited in small quantities in the open air. This group comprises the majority of high-energy explosives used for commercial and military blasting. Some common examples of noninitiating explosives are: dynamite, TNT (trinitrotoluene), PETN (pentaerythritol tetranitrate), RDX (cyclotrimethylenetrinitramine), and tetryl (2,4,6-trinitrophenylmethylnitramine).

It is an irony of history that the prize most symbolic of man's search for peace should bear the name of the developer of one of man's most lethal discoveries, dynamite. In 1867, the Swedish chemist Alfred Nobel, searching for a method to desensitize nitroglycerin, found that when kieselguhr, a variety of diatomaceous earth, absorbed a large portion of nitroglycerin, it became far less sensitive but still retained its explosive force. Nobel later decided to use pulp as an absorbent, because kieselguhr was a heat-absorbing material. Thus, pulp dynamite was the beginning of what is now known as the straight dynamite series, the gradations of which are specified according to the percentage of nitroglycerin used. These dynamites are used when a quick shattering action is desired. Present-day straight dynamites also include sodium nitrate, which serves to furnish oxygen for complete combustion, along with a small percentage of a stabilizer—e.g., calcium carbonate. The strength rating of a straight dynamite is designated by the weight percentage of nitroglycerin in the formula; a 40 percent straight dynamite contains 40 percent, a 60 percent grade contains 60 percent, and so forth. However, the concept that the actual blasting power developed by different strengths is in direct proportion to the percent markings is erroneous. Actually, a 60 percent straight dynamite, rather than being three times as strong as a 20 percent, is only one and one-half times as strong.

Today, there are hundreds of dynamite formulations commercially available that can perform a variety of blasting tasks. In some types of dynamites the proportion of nitroglycerin is reduced by substituting other strength-imparting ingredients, such as ammonium nitrate. Ammonium nitrate intensifies the explosive action of dynamite by furnishing oxygen, but the resulting blast is accompanied by less of a shattering action as compared to straight dynamites. This type of dynamite has a definite advantage in quarry operations and on construction projects in which the material to be blasted is of medium hardness.

Gelatin dynamites are formulated by the dissolving of nitrocellulose in the nitroglycerin to form a rubberlike gel. Gelatin dynamites are characterized by their water-resistant nature and are employed for all types of blasting under wet conditions.

No discussion of high explosives would be complete without a mention of military high explosives. In many countries outside the United States, their accessibility to terrorist organizations makes them very common constituents of homemade bombs. RDX is the most popular and powerful of the military explosives. This explosive is often encountered in the form of a pliable plastic of doughlike consistency known as composition C-4 (a U.S. military designation).

TNT was produced and used on an enormous scale during World War II, and may be considered the most important military bursting charge explosive. Alone or in combination with other explosives, it has found wide application in shells, bombs, grenades, demolition explosives, and propellent compositions. Interestingly, military "dyna-mite" contains no nitroglycerin, but is actually composed of a mix-ture of RDX and TNT. Like other military explosives, TNT is rarely encountered in bombings in the United States.

PETN is used by the military in TNT mixtures for small-caliber projectiles and grenades. Commercially, the chemical is used as the explosive core in detonating fuse or primacord. Instead of the slower-burning safety fuse, a detonating fuse is often used to interconnect a series of explosive charges so that they will detonate simultaneously.

Unlike low-energy explosives, bombs made of high-energy explo-sives must be detonated by an initiating explosion. In most cases, detonators are blasting caps composed of copper or aluminum cases filled with lead azide as an initiating charge and PETN or RDX as a detonating charge. Blasting caps can be initiated by means of a burning safety fuse or by an electrical current (see Figure 10-6).

Homemade bombs camouflaged in packages, suitcases, etc. are for the most part usually initiated with an electrical blasting cap wired to a battery. An unlimited number of switching-mechanism designs have been devised for setting off these devices; favored are clocks and mercury switches. There are certain situations in which bombers prefer to employ outside electrical sources. For instance, most automobile bombs are detonated when the ignition switch of a car is turned on.

Collection and Analysis of Explosives

The single most important step in the detection and analysis of explosive residues is the collection of appropriate samples from the explosion scene. Invariably, there remains at the site of the explosion undetonated residues of the explosive. The ultimate detection and identification of these in the laboratory will depend on the bomb-scene investigator's skill and ability to recognize and sample areas most likely to contain such materials.

The most obvious characteristic of a high-energy or a contained low-energy explosion is the presence of a crater at the origin of the blast. Once the crater has been located, all loose soil and other debris must immediately be removed from the interior of the hole and pre-served for laboratory analysis. Other good sources of explosive residues are objects located near the origin of detonation. Wood, insulation, rubber or other soft materials which are readily penetrated, often collect traces of the explosive. However, nonporous objects in

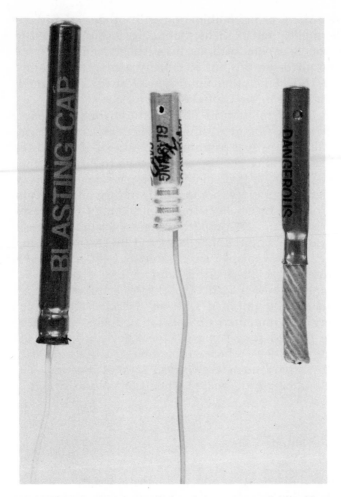

FIGURE 10-6. Blasting caps. Left and center caps are initiated by an electrical current, the right cap is initiated by a safety fuse.

close proximity to the blast must not be overlooked. For instance, experience has shown that residues can be located on the surfaces of metal objects found near the site of an explosion.

The entire area must be systematically searched with great care to recover any trace of a detonating mechanism or any other item foreign to the explosion site. Material blown away from the blast's origin should be recovered, because it, too, may retain explosive residues. Wire-mesh screens are best utilized for sifting through debris. In pipe bomb explosions, for example, particles of the explosive are frequently found adhering to the pipe cap or to the pipe threads, as a result of either being impacted into the metal by force of the explosion or being deposited in the threads during the construction of the bomb.

All materials collected for examination by the laboratory must be placed in sealed containers and labeled with all pertinent information. Soil and other soft, loose materials are best stored in metal containers or plastic bags. Care is required when packaging metal or other hard objects in plastic bags so that sharp edges will be prevented from piercing the plastic wrapper. Particles dislodged from the sample during its transportation to the laboratory are readily recovered if the packaging material remains tightly sealed.

When the bomb-scene debris and other material arrives in the laboratory, it is first examined microscopically so that particles of unconsumed explosive can be detected. Portions of the recovered debris and detonating mechanism, if found, are carefully viewed under a low-power stereoscopic microscope in a painstaking effort to locate particles of the explosive. In this manner, black and smokeless powder are relatively easy to locate in debris because of their characteristic shape and colors (see Figure 10-7). However, dynamite

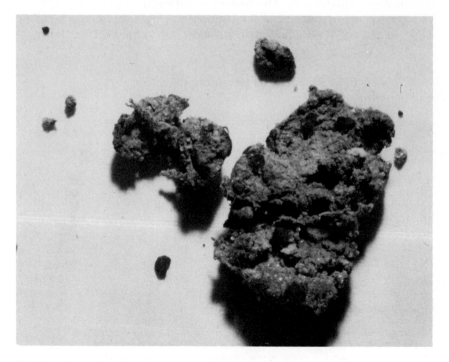

FIGURE 10-7. Black powder imbedded in soil.

Courtesy Bureau of Alcohol, Tobacco and Firearms, U.S. Treasury Dept.

and other high-energy explosives present the microscopist with a much more difficult task and more often than not have to be detected by other means.

Following microscopic examination, the recovered debris is thoroughly rinsed with acetone. The high solubility of most explosives in acetone will assure their quick removal from the debris. Once collected, the acetone extract is concentrated and analyzed utilizing color spot tests and thin-layer chromatography. The presence of an explosive will be indicated by a well-defined spot on a TLC plate with an R_f value corresponding to a known explosive—e.g., nitroglycerin, RDX, or PETN. When a low-order explosion is suspected, the debris is rinsed with hot water so that any water-soluble inorganic substances that are common constituents of low-energy explosives (e.g., nitrates and chlorates) will be extracted.

Table 10-3 lists a number of simple color tests the examiner can perform on the acetone and water extracts in order to screen for the presence of organic and inorganic explosives, respectively.

When sufficient quantities of explosives are recoverable, confirmatory tests may be performed by either infrared spectrophotometry or X-ray diffraction. The former produces a unique "fingerprint" pattern for an organic explosive, as shown by the IR spectrum of RDX in Figure 10-8. The latter provides an unique diffraction pat-

TABLE 10-3. Color Spot Tests for Common Explosives

Substance	Griess[a]	Diphenylamine[b]	Alcoholic KOH[c]
Chlorate	No color	Blue	No color
Nitrate	Pink to red	Blue	No color
Nitrocellulose	Pink	Blue-black	No color
Nitroglycerin	Pink to red	Blue	No color
PETN	Pink to red	Blue	No color
RDX	Pink to red	Blue	No color
TNT	No color	No color	Red
Tetryl	Pink to red	Blue	Red-violet

[a]*Griess Reagent*
   Solution 1—Dissolve 1 g sulfanilic acid in 100 ml of 30% acetic acid.
   Solution 2—Dissolve 1 g alpha-napthylamine in 230 ml of boiling distilled water. Cool. Decant the colorless supernatant liquid and mix with 110 ml of glacial acetic acid. Add solutions 1 and 2 and a few milligrams of zinc dust to the suspect extract.
[b]*Diphenylamine Reagent*
   Dissolve 1 g diphenylamine in 100 ml concentrated sulfuric acid.
[c]*Alcoholic KOH Reagent*
   Dissolve 10 g of potassium hydroxide in 100 ml of absolute alcohol.

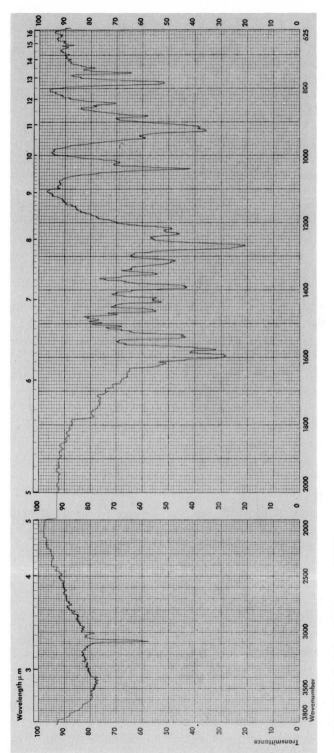

FIGURE 10-8. Infrared spectrum of RDX.

243

tern for inorganic substances, as exemplified by the diffraction pattern for potassium nitrate and potassium chlorate shown in Figure 5-11 (page 114).

If an investigator is fortunate enough to arrive at the scene of a suspected natural gas explosion in time to smell the odor of gas, he must make an effort to collect air samples. One of the simplest and most effective ways of accomplishing this is to take a bottle full of water to the area where the odor is strongest and pour the water out of the container. The surrounding air will immediately fill the bottle. If it is then tightly sealed, the bottle will confine any natural gas that was present in the surrounding air for an extended period of time. Once submitted to the laboratory, the bottle's contents can be analyzed and identified by gas chromatographic analysis.

REVIEW QUESTIONS

1. The absence of chemical residues always rules out the possibility of arson. (True, False)

2. The combination of oxygen with other substances to produce new chemical products is called _____ .

3. All oxidation reactions produce noticeable quantities of heat and light. (True, False)

4. _____ is the capacity for doing work.

5. Burning methane for the purpose of heating water to steam in order to drive a turbine is an example of converting _____ energy to _____ energy.

6. The quantity of heat evolved from a chemical reaction arises out of the _____ and _____ of chemical bonds.

7. Molecules must (absorb, liberate) energy to break their bonds and will (absorb, liberate) energy when their bonds are reformed.

8. All oxidation reactions (absorb, liberate) heat.

9. Reactions which liberate heat are said to be _____ .

10. Excess heat energy liberated by an oxidation reaction is called the _____ .

11. A chemical reaction in which heat is absorbed from the surroundings is said to be _____ .

12. All reactions require an energy input to start them. (True, False)

13. The minimum temperature at which a fuel will burn is known as the _____ temperature.

14. A fuel will only achieve a sufficient reaction rate with oxygen to produce a flame when it is in the (gaseous, liquid) state.

15. The lowest temperature at which a liquid fuel will produce enough vapor to burn is the _____ .

16. _____ is the chemical breakdown of a solid material to gaseous products.

17. _____ is a phenomenon in which a fuel will burn without the presence of a flame.

18. The rate of a chemical reaction (increases, decreases) as the temperature rises.

19. Oxidizing agents supply _____ to a chemical reaction.

20. Three ingredients of black powder are _____ , _____ , and _____ .

21. The probable origin of a fire will most likely be located closest to the lowest point that shows the most intense characteristics of burning. (True, False)

22. The collection of debris at the origin of a fire should include all (porous, nonporous) materials.

23. _____ containers must be used to package all materials suspected of containing hydrocarbon residues.

24. _____ describes a fire caused by a natural heat-producing process.

25. The most sensitive and reliable instrument for detecting and characterizing flammable residues is the (gas chromatograph, infrared spectrophotometer).

26. The criminalist (can, cannot) identify gasoline residues by brand name.

27. Gasoline dyes are best separated by the technique of _____ .

28. Combustion accompanied by the creation of large volumes of gases describes an _____ .

29. Explosives that decompose at relatively slow rates are classified as _____ explosives.

30. _____ explosives detonate almost instantaneously to produce a smashing or shattering effect.

31. The most widely used low energy explosives are _____ and _____ .

32. A low energy explosive only becomes explosive and lethal when it is _____ .

33. Air and a gaseous fuel will burn when mixed at any concentration range. (True, False)

34. High energy explosives can be classified either as _____ or _____ explosives.

35. The blasting power of different dynamite strengths (is, is not) in direct proportion to the weight percentage of nitroglycerin.

36. The most widely used explosive in the military is _____ .

37. The explosive core in detonating cord is _____ .

38. A high energy explosive is normally detonated by an _____ explosive contained within a blasting cap.

39. An obvious characteristic of a high energy explosive is the presence of a _____ at the origin of the blast.

40. The single most important step in the detection of explosive residues is the _____ of appropriate samples from the explosion scene.

41. Unconsumed explosive residues may be detected in the laboratory through a careful _____ examination of the debris.

42. Debris recovered from the site of an explosion is routinely rinsed with _____ in an attempt to recover high energy explosive residues.

43. Once collected, the acetone extract is initially analyzed by _____ and _____.

44. The technique of _____ produces a unique absorption spectrum for an organic explosive.

45. The technique of _____ provides a unique diffraction pattern for the identification of the inorganic constituents of explosives.

FURTHER READINGS

Hoffman, C. M., and E. B. Byall, "Identification of Explosive Residues in Bomb Scene Investigations," *Journal of Forensic Sciences*, 19 (1974), 54.

Kirk, Paul L., *Fire Investigation*. New York: Wiley & Sons, 1969.

Stoffel, J. F., *Explosives and Homemade Bombs*, 2nd ed. Springfield, Ill.: Charles C. Thomas, 1972.

Yates, C. E., "Recovery and Identification of Residues of Flammable Liquids from Suspected Arson Debris," in *Forensic Science*, Geoffrey Davies, ed. Washington, D.C.: American Chemical Society, 1975.

Forensic Serology

chapter 11

In 1901, Karl Landsteiner announced one of the most significant scientific discoveries of this century, a finding that twenty-nine years later was to earn for him a Nobel Prize. For years before the new century, physicians had attempted to transfuse blood from one individual to another. Their efforts often ended in failure, because the transfused blood had a tendency to coagulate in the body of the recipient, causing instantaneous death. It was Landsteiner who first recognized that all human blood was not the same; instead, he found blood to be distinguishable by its group or type. Out of Landsteiner's work came the classification system that we presently call the A-B-O system. Now for the first time physicians had the key for properly matching the blood of a donor to a correct recipient. One blood type cannot be mixed with a different blood type without disastrous consequences. While this discovery of course had important implications for blood transfusion and the millions of lives it has since saved, Landsteiner's findings opened up a completely new field of research in the biological sciences. Now others were to pursue the identification of other characteristics that could further differentiate blood. By 1937, the Rh factor in blood was demonstrated, and shortly thereafter, numerous blood factors or groups were discovered. At present, more than 100 different blood factors have been shown to exist. However, of all the known blood factors, those belonging to the A-B-O system are still by far the most important for properly matching a donor and recipient for a transfusion.

The intriguing aspect of all these findings, as far as forensic science is concerned, is that in theory no two individuals, except for identical twins, can be expected to have the same combination of blood factors. In other words, blood factors are controlled genetically and have the potential of being a highly distinctive feature for personal identification. What makes this observation so relevant is the high frequency of occurrence of bloodstains at crime scenes; especially crimes of the most serious nature—i.e., homicides, assaults, and rapes. Consider, for example, the situation in which a transfer of blood takes place between the victim and assailant during a struggle; that is, the victim's blood is transferred to the suspect's garment or vice versa. If, as has been suggested, the criminalist can individualize human blood by identifying all of its known factors, the result could be evidence of the strongest kind for linking the suspect to the crime scene.

Unfortunately, we must separate theory from reality. The goal of truly individualizing human blood is still many years away. The problem of identifying most blood factors in whole blood is in itself a difficult task; however, in the crime laboratory the task is further complicated by the fact that practically all blood evidence is received in the form of dried stains. As blood dries, some of its characteristic blood factors are destroyed, and as the stain continues to age, the destruction slowly extends to most of the other factors. Even a task as relatively simple as determining the A-B-O classification of blood becomes much more difficult when applied to dried bloodstains.

During the past decade, chiefly owing to research efforts of the Metropolitan Police Laboratory in London, the individualization of dried blood has become one of the most exciting and promising research areas in forensic science. As forensic serologists pursue the detection and identification of various blood characteristics, their ability to associate a bloodstain to a particular individual with a known degree of probability has increased dramatically. The fact is that the individualization of bloodstains now has become a distinct possibility—but one that can only be achieved through the willingness of crime laboratories to commit time, brainpower, and money to unravel the mysteries of blood.

BLOOD

Antigens and Antibodies

The word "blood" actually refers to a highly complex mixture of cells, enzymes, proteins, and inorganic substances. The fluid portion of blood is called **plasma**. It is composed principally of water and accounts for 55 percent of blood content. Suspended in the plasma are solid materials consisting chiefly of cells—i.e., red blood cells (erythrocytes), white blood cells (leukocytes), and platelets. The solid portion of blood accounts for 45 percent of its content. Blood clots when a protein in the plasma known as fibrin traps and emeshes red blood cells. If one were to remove the clotted material, remaining behind would be a pale yellowish liquid known as **serum**.

Obviously, considering the complexity of blood, any discussion of its functions and chemistry would have to be an extensive one, extending beyond the scope of this text. It is certainly far more relevant at this point to concentrate our discussion on those blood components that are directly pertinent to the forensic aspects of blood identification—the red blood cells and the blood serum.

Functionally, red blood cells transport oxygen from the lungs to the body tissues and in turn remove carbon dioxide from tissues by transporting it back to the lungs, where it is exhaled. However, for reasons unrelated to the red blood cell's transporting mission, there resides on the surface of each cell millions of characteristic chemical structures called **antigens**. It is these antigens that impart blood-type characteristics to the red blood cells. Blood antigens are grouped into systems, depending on their relationship to each other. More than fifteen blood antigen systems have been identified to date; of these, the A-B-O, M-N, and Rh systems are the most important.

If an individual is type A, this simply indicates that each red blood cell has A antigens located on its surface; similarly, all type B persons have B antigens, while the red blood cells of type AB contain both A and B antigens. Type O persons will have neither A or B antigens on their cells. Hence, it is the presence or absence of the A and B antigen on the red blood cells that determines a person's blood type in the A-B-O system.

Another important blood antigen has been designated as the Rh factor, or D antigen. Those people having the D antigen are said to be Rh positive; those not having this antigen are Rh negative. In routine blood banking, it is the presence or absence of the three antigens, A, B, and D that are always determined in testing for the compatibility of the donor and recipient.

Serum is important because it contains, among other proteins, some known as antibodies. **The fundamental principle of blood typing is that for every antigen there exists a specific antibody.** Each antibody symbol contains the prefix "anti," followed by the name of the antigen for which it is specific. Hence, anti-A is specific only for A antigen, anti-B for B antigen, and anti-D for the D antigen. The serum-containing antibody is referred to as **antiserum**, meaning a serum that reacts against something (antigens).

An antibody will only react with its specific antigen and no other. Thus, if serum containing anti-B is added to red blood cells carrying the antigen B, the two will immediately combine, causing the antibody to attach itself to the cell. Antibodies are normally bivalent—that is, they have two reactive sites. This means that each antibody can simultaneously be attached to antigens located on two red blood cells. This creates a vast network of cross-linked cells usually seen as **clumping** or **agglutination**. (see Figure 11–1).

Let's look a little more closely at this phenomenon. In normal blood, shown in Figure 11–2a, antigens on red blood cells and antibodies can co-exist without destroying each other because the

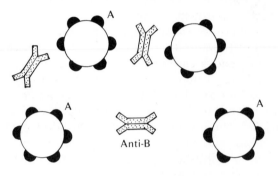

Red blood cells containing A antigens
will not combine with B antibodies

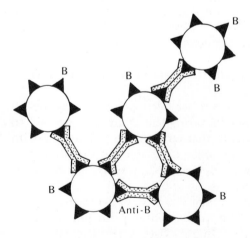

Red blood cells containing B antigens
are agglutinated or clumped together
in the presence of B antibodies

FIGURE 11–1.

antibodies present are not specific toward any of the antigens. However, suppose a foreign serum added to the blood introduces a new antibody. The occurrence of a specific antigen-antibody reaction will immediately cause the red blood cells to link together, or agglutinate, as shown in Figure 11–2b.

Evidently, nature has taken this situation into account, for when we examine the serum of type A blood we find anti-B and no anti-A. Similarly, type B blood contains only anti-A, type O blood has both anti-A and anti-B, and type AB blood contains neither anti-A nor anti-B. The antigen and antibody components of normal blood are summarized below:

Blood Type	Antigens on Red Blood Cells	Antibodies in Serum
A	A	Anti-B
B	B	Anti-A
AB	AB	Neither anti-A nor anti-B
O	Neither A nor B	Both anti-A and anti-B

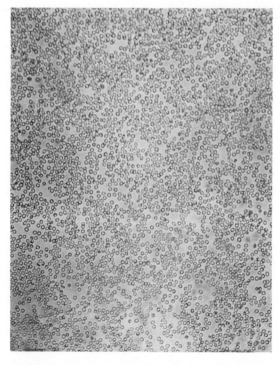

FIGURE 11–2a. Microscopic view of normal red blood cells (225X).
Courtesy Linda Jankowski

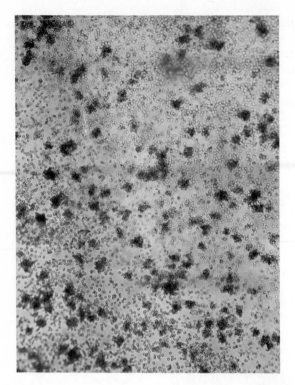

FIGURE 11-2b. Microscopic view of agglutinated red blood cells (225X).
Courtesy Linda Jankowski

The reasons for the fatal consequences of mixing incompatible blood during a transfusion should now be quite obvious. For example, the transfusion of type A blood into a type B patient will cause the natural anti-A in the blood of the type B patient to react promptly with the incoming A antigens, resulting in agglutination. In addition, the incoming anti-B of the donor will react with the B antigens of the patient.

The concept of a specific antigen-antibody reaction is one that is finding applications in other areas unrelated to the blood typing of individuals. Most significantly, this approach has been extended to the detection of drugs in blood and urine. Antibodies that are capable of reacting with drugs do not naturally exist; however, they can be produced in animals such as rabbits by first combining the drug with a protein and injecting this combination into the animal. This drug-protein complex now acts as an antigen stimulating the animal to produce antibodies. The recovered blood serum of the animal will now contain antibodies that are specific or nearly specific toward the drug.

There are at present a number of immunological assay techniques commercially available for detecting drugs through an antigen-antibody reaction. Their primary advantage is speed and sensitivity. Many forensic toxicologists believe that this approach offers the best hope for the eventual routine detection of low levels of LSD and THC in body fluids.

Blood Typing

The term "serology" is used to describe a broad scope of laboratory tests that utilize specific antigen and serum antibody reactions. The most widespread application of serology is the typing of whole blood for its A-B-O identity. In determining the A-B-O blood type, only two antiserums are needed—anti-A and anti-B. For routine blood typing, both of these antiserums are commercially available.

Table 11-1 summarizes how the identity of each of the four blood groups is established when the blood is tested with anti-A and anti-B serum. Blood of type A will be agglutinated by anti-A serum; blood of type B will be agglutinated by anti-B serum; AB blood will be agglutinated by both anti-A and anti-B serum; and blood of type O will not be agglutinated at all by the anti-A or anti-B serum.

The identification of natural antibodies present in blood offers another route to the determination of blood type. Testing blood for the presence of anti-A and anti-B requires using red blood cells that have known antigens. Again, these cells are commercially available. Hence, when A cells are added to a blood specimen, agglutination will only occur in the presence of anti-A. Similarly, B cells will only agglutinate in the presence of anti-B. All four A-B-O types can be identified in this manner by testing blood with known A and B cells as summarized in Table 11-2.

TABLE 11-1. Identification of Blood with Known Antiserum

Anti-A Serum + Whole Blood	Anti-B Serum + Whole Blood	Antigen Present	Blood Type
+	–	A	A
–	+	B	B
+	+	AB	AB
–	–	O	O

+ shows agglutination
– shows absence of agglutination

TABLE 11-2. Identification of Blood with Known Cells

A Cells + Blood	B Cells + Blood	Antibody Present	Blood Type
+	–	Anti-A	B
–	+	Anti-B	A
+	+	Both anti-A and anti-B	O
–	–	Neither anti-A nor anti-B	AB

+ shows agglutination
– shows absence of agglutination

The population distribution of blood types varies with location and race throughout the world. In the United States, a typical distribution is

O	A	B	AB
43%	42%	12%	3%

Forensic Characterization of Bloodstains

The criminalist must be prepared to answer the following questions when examining dried blood: (1) Is it blood? (2) From what species did the blood originate? and (3) If the blood is of human origin, how closely can it be associated to a particular individual?

The determination of blood is best made by means of a preliminary color test. The most convenient test for this purpose is the benzidine color test.[1] Its applicability is based on the observation that all blood contains the enzyme peroxidase. This enzyme controls oxidation reactions taking place in the body. In the presence of peroxidase, benzidine, when mixed with hydrogen peroxide, will turn green.[2]

The benzidine test is not a specific test for blood; there are some vegetable materials that also contain peroxidase and will therefore react with benzidine like blood does. These substances include onion, cabbage, and potato stains. However, it is unlikely that such mate-

[1] The test is conducted by adding benzidine dihydrochloride, glacial acetic acid, and hydrogen peroxide to the stained material.
[2] Benzidine is a carcinogen and care must be taken not to breathe its vapor or touch the chemical or its salts. Alternately, the chemical 3, 5, 3', 5' tetramethylbenzidine, reported to be non-carcinogenic, can be substituted for benzidine with equivalent results.

rials will be encountered in criminal situations and thus, from a practical point of view, a positive benzidine test is highly indicative of blood.

There are other color-test reagents available to test for the presence of peroxidase—e.g., phenolphthalein and leucomalachite green; however, these reagents are less sensitive toward blood when compared to benzidine. The luminol test[3] is the most sensitive test for detecting blood. The reagent reacts with blood, causing it to luminesce. When luminol reagent is sprayed onto a suspect item, large areas can be quickly screened for the presence of bloodstains. The sprayed objects must be examined in a darkened area while being looked at for the emission of light (luminescence).

The identification of blood can be made more specific if micro-crystalline tests are performed on the material. There are several tests available; the two most popular ones are the Takayama and Teichmann tests. Both of these depend on the addition of specific chemicals to the blood so that characteristic crystals with hemoglobin derivatives will be formed. The criminalist must be cautioned that crystal tests are far less sensitive than the benzidine color tests for blood's identification and are more susceptible to interferences from contaminants that may be present in the stain.

Once the stain has been characterized as blood, the serologist will have to determine whether the stain is of human or animal origin. For this purpose, the standard test used is the **precipitin test.** Precipitin tests are based on the fact that when animals (usually rabbits) are injected with human blood, antibodies are formed that react with the invading human blood to neutralize its presence. The investigator can recover these antibodies by bleeding the animal and isolating the blood serum. This serum will contain antibodies that specifically react with human antigens. For this reason, the serum is known as **human antiserum.** In the same manner, by injecting rabbits with the blood of other known animals, virtually any kind of animal antiserum can be produced. Currently, antiserums are commercially available for a variety of commonly encountered animals—i.e., human beings, dogs, cats, and deer.

A number of techniques have been devised for performing precipitin tests on bloodstains. The classical method is to layer an extract of the bloodstain on top of the human antiserum in a capillary tube. Human blood, or for that matter, any protein of human origin in the extract, will react specifically with antibodies present

---

[3]The luminol reagent is prepared by mixing 0.1 g 3–amino-phthalhydrazide and 5.0 g sodium carbonate in 100 ml of distilled water. Before use, 0.7 g. of sodium perborate is added to the solution.

in the antiserum, as indicated by the formation of a cloudy ring or band at the interface of the two liquids (Figure 11-3).

Another method, called **gel diffusion**, takes advantage of the fact that antibodies and antigens will diffuse or move toward one another on an agar gel coated plate. Here, the extracted bloodstain and the human antiserum are placed in separate holes opposite each other on the gel. If the blood is of human origin, a line of precipitation will form where the antigens and antibodies meet. Similarly, the antigens and antibodies can be induced to move toward one another under the influence of an electrical field. In the electrophoretic method (see page 84), the electrical potential is applied to the gel medium; a specific antigen-antibody reaction will be denoted by a line precipitation formed between the hole containing the blood extract and the hole containing the human antiserum (see Figure 11-4).

The precipitin test is very sensitive and requires only a small amount of blood for testing. Human bloodstains dried for as long as ten to fifteen years and longer may still give a positive precipitin

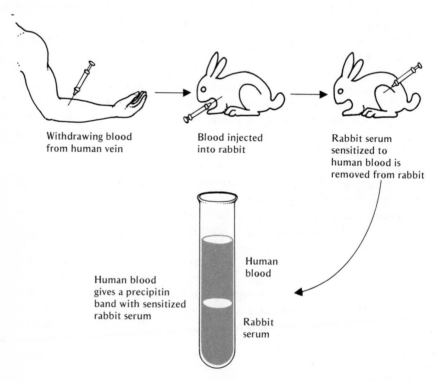

Withdrawing blood
from human vein

Blood injected
into rabbit

Rabbit serum
sensitized to
human blood is
removed from rabbit

Human blood
gives a precipitin
band with sensitized
rabbit serum

Human
blood

Rabbit
serum

FIGURE 11-3.

Antigen and antibody are added to their respective wells.	Antigen and antibody are being moved toward each other	Antigen and antibody have formed a visible precipitin line in the gel between the wells
A	B	C

FIGURE 11-4.

reaction. Even extracts of tissue from mummies 4,000 to 5,000 years old have given positive reactions with this test. Furthermore, experience has shown that human bloodstains diluted by washing in water and left only with a faint color may still yield a positive precipitin reaction (see Figure 11-5).

Once it has been determined that the bloodstain is of human origin, an effort must be made to associate or disassociate the stain with a particular individual. In this situation, however, the forensic

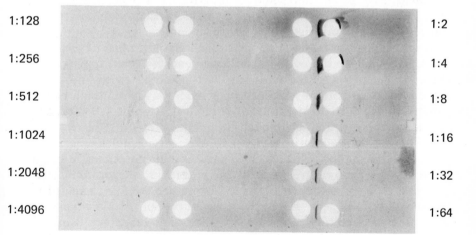

FIGURE 11-5. Results of the precipitin test of dilutions of human serum up to 1 in 4096 against an antihuman rabbit serum. A reaction is visible for blood diluted up to 1 in 512.

Courtesy Millipore Biomedica

serologist is severely limited by the blood factors that survive the drying and aging processes. Stains also vary considerably in purity and quantity, all of which make the analysis of dried blood much more complex than analysis of whole blood. Until recently, existing procedures only permitted the typing of bloodstains by the A-B-O system; however, extensive research efforts have now made the characterization of other blood antigens, as well as some blood enzymes, feasible for routine dried-blood analysis.

In the earlier description of whole-blood typing, the identification of A and B antigens was easily accomplished by directly reacting the blood with anti-A and anti-B serums. This identity of the antigens present was confirmed by visually observing the clumping or agglutination of the red blood cells. Unfortunately, one cannot use the same approach in dried-blood typing, because red blood cells rupture on drying, leaving no cells in the stain to be agglutinated. However, though the cells may have disintegrated, the antigens present on their surfaces remain intact and are still identifiable by indirect means.

Absorption-Elution. The **absorption-elution** technique is the current method of choice for the indirect typing of bloodstains. As illustrated in Figure 11-6, the procedure consists of four steps. Step 1: The antiserum is placed on the bloodstained material, allowing sufficient time for the antibodies to combine with their specific antigens. Step 2: The unreacted serum is removed by being washed off the bloodstained material. Step 3: Once an antibody combines with an antigen, it is possible to break the complex apart by a process known as **elution**. To do this, the stained material must be heated at 55°C. This allows the antibody-antigen bond to break, freeing both. Step 4: When the eluted antibodies are combined with known red blood cells so that the presence or absence of agglutination can be observed, they can be identified. The identification of A-B-O type by the absorption-elution technique is summarized in Table 11-3.

This technique is sufficiently sensitive to type stains on a thread of fiber that is one-half inch in length. In addition, stains as old as eleven years have been typed by the absorption-elution procedure.

The antigens of the A-B-O system are not confined exclusively to the red blood cells. Approximately 80 percent of individuals are classified as **secretors**—which means that their blood-type antigens are found in high concentration in most body fluids (e.g., saliva, semen, vaginal secretions, and gastric juice). In fact, saliva and semen have a higher concentration of A and B antigens than does blood. The value of this observation in criminal investigation is obvious. It is possible, for example, to type semen stains on the clothing of a

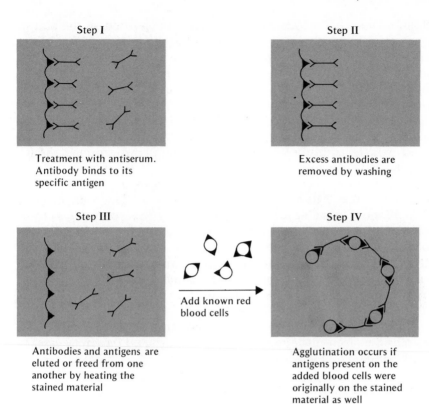

Step I
Treatment with antiserum. Antibody binds to its specific antigen

Step II
Excess antibodies are removed by washing

Step III
Antibodies and antigens are eluted or freed from one another by heating the stained material

Add known red blood cells

Step IV
Agglutination occurs if antigens present on the added blood cells were originally on the stained material as well

FIGURE 11-6. The absorption-elution technique for typing dried bloodstains.

TABLE 11-3. Identification of Blood Types by the Absorption-Elution Technique

Bloodstain Tested with

Anti-A + A Cells	Anti-B + B cells	Antigen Present on Stain	Blood Type
+	−	A	A
−	+	B	B
+	+	Both A and B	AB
−	−	Neither A nor B	O

+ shows agglutination
− shows absence of agglutination

victim of a sexual attack, or even the saliva deposited on the butt of a cigarette. Furthermore, blood-type antigens can be extracted from the tissues and organs. Already it has been demonstrated that hair can be typed, although some criminalists have questioned the reliability of the technique. The A-B-O typing of solid tissue, such as muscle or skin, is also possible.

Further characterization of dried blood can be accomplished by the identification of other antigens located on the surface of the red blood cell. In addition to A-B-O, the M and N antigens and the Rh antigens have received attention from forensic laboratories in this respect. The presence of the M and N antigens in blood was first shown in 1927. Although these antigens can survive in dried blood for nine months under ideal conditions, they have been found to be considerably more difficult to identify under more realistic case conditions. Three blood groups belong to the M-N system: M, N, and MN. Their approximate frequency of occurrence in the white American population is 30 percent for M, 20 percent for N, and 50 percent for MN. Within the Rh system, five antigens, designated as C, D, E, c, and e may be detected in a bloodstain, although their full potential in bloodstain analysis is yet to be realized. The significance of Rh antigens has been made more apparent in disputed paternity cases in which whole blood analysis is involved.

Blood Enzymes

In addition to the antigenic systems discussed above, there are other substances found in the red blood cell which are becoming increasingly important for the individualization of bloodstains. These substances are called **enzymes**. Enzymes are proteins that have important functions in regulating many of the body's chemical reactions. Forensic serologists are particularly interested in enzymes that exist in different forms, or are **polymorphic**. These enzymes can actually be separated into protein components called **iso-enzymes**.

Let's look at one such enzyme, PGM, in order to understand its importance to the forensic serologist. The iso-enzymes of PGM (phosphoglucomutase) can be separated from one another by electrophoresis (see page 84). What is interesting and most important about this separation is the observation that all persons do not have the same PGM iso-enzymes. Actually, as shown in Figure 11–7, there are three common variations or types of PGM: PGM 1, PGM 2-1, and PGM 2. These variations are distributed unevenly throughout the population; PGM 1 is present in approximately 58 percent of the population. PGM 2-1 is in 36 percent and PGM 2 in 6 percent. Thus, the identification of the PGM type in a dried bloodstain provides the for-

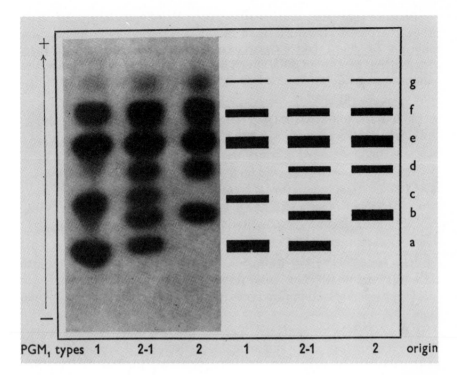

FIGURE 11-7. Photograph and diagram of the separation of PGM isoenzymes accomplished by electrophoresis. PGM can be grouped into one of three types: 1, 2-1, and 2 according to band patterns.

Reproduced from *The Principles of Human Biochemical Genetics*, 2nd ed., by Harry Harris, North-Holland Publishing Co.

ensic serologist with added statistical information with which to reduce the number of possible sources of the bloodstain.

Apparently, there are numerous polymorphic enzymes in red blood cells that offer themselves as potential markers for determining blood origin. However, from a practical point of view, only those enzymes that are capable of surviving the drying and aging processes are of any value to the forensic serologist. At the present time, four enzymes—PGM, AK (adenylate kinase), EAP (erythrocyte acid phosphatase), and EsD (esterase D) seem to be the most applicable for blood characterization. Further research promises to add many more to the list of enzymes suitable for routine dried-blood analysis. In addition, forensic serologists are finding that some of the polymorphic protein systems present in blood—e.g., haptoglobin and hemoglobin — are suitable for the individualization of dried blood.

Because antigens and enzymes occur independently of each other, the probability of a dried bloodstain having a particular combination of these factors is determined by the product of their distribution in the population. Thus, for example, using only the commonest group of the A-B-O system and the four enzymes discussed above, one would get:

Blood and Enzyme Types	Frequency
O	43%
PGM 1	58%
AK 1	91%
EAP-BA	43%
EsD 1	79%

The product of these frequencies shows 8% of the population will have this combination of blood types.

Using the less common types of the same systems, one would find:

Blood and Enzyme Types	Frequency
AB	3%
PGM 2	6%
AK 2-1	9%
EAP-CA	3%
EsD 2-1	19%

In this case, 0.0001% of the population, or one in a million, would be expected to have the same combination of blood types.

Certainly, by expanding its ability to go beyond the A-B-O system, the crime laboratory has taken a significant step towards individualizing human blood, thus increasing the evidential value of bloodstains.

Stain Patterns of Blood

The crime-scene investigator must not overlook the fact that the location, distribution, and appearance of bloodstains and splatters may be useful for interpreting and reconstructing the events that must have occurred to have produced the bleeding. A thorough analysis of the significance of the position and shape of blood patterns with respect to their origin and trajectory is exceedingly

FIGURE 11–8a. Bloodstain from a single drop of blood that struck a plastic wall tile after falling forty-two inches.

Reprinted from *Flight Characteristics and Stain Patterns of Human Blood*, 1971.

complex and requires the services of an examiner who is experienced in such determinations. Most importantly, the interpretation of bloodstain patterns necessitates carefully planned control experiments utilizing surface materials comparable to those found at the crime scene.

A recent in-depth study of this subject was completed by Herbert L. MacDonell and published by the U.S. Department of Justice.[4] Many of Mr. MacDonell's observations and conclusions have important implications for any investigator who seeks to trace the direction, dropping distance, and angle of impact of a bloodstain. Some of them can be summarized as follows:

1. Surface texture is of paramount importance in the interpretation of bloodstain patterns, and correlation between standards and unknowns are valid only if identical surfaces are used. In general, the harder and less porous the surface, the less splatter results. The effect of surface is shown in Figure 11-8.

2. When a blood drop hits a hard, smooth surface it frequently breaks up on impact, casting off smaller droplets. These smaller

[4] Herbert L. MacDonell, *Flight Characteristics and Stain Patterns of Human Blood* (Washington, D.C.: U.S. Government Printing Office, 1971).

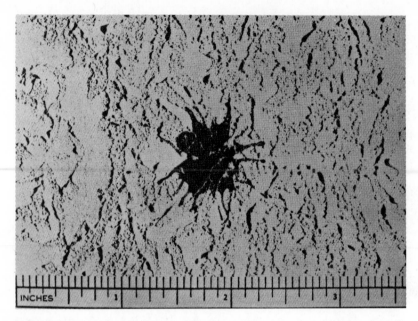

FIGURE 11-8b. Bloodstain from a single drop of blood that struck a heavy irregular textured wallpaper after falling forty-two inches.

Reprinted from *Flight Characteristics and Stain Patterns of Human Blood*, 1971

droplets travel in the same direction as the original drop, ultimately terminating in a pattern that is tadpole-like, with the sharper or pointed end always pointing back toward their origin. An example of this streaking is shown in Figure 11-9. This stain resulted from a drop of blood traveling at about four feet per second, right to left, and falling to the hard, cardboard target at an angle of approximately 56 degrees.

3. It is possible to determine the impact angle of blood on a flat surface by measuring the degree of circular distortion of the stain. A drop of blood striking a surface at right angles gives rise to a nearly circular stain; as the angle decreases, the stain becomes elongated in shape. This progressive elongation is evident in Figure 11-10a and b.

Considerably more detailed information relating to blood patterns is available in MacDonell's treatise, which should certainly be consulted when such determinations are appropriate to an investigation.

Preservation of Blood Evidence

As crime laboratories expand their capability to characterize blood, it is important that field investigators become conscious of

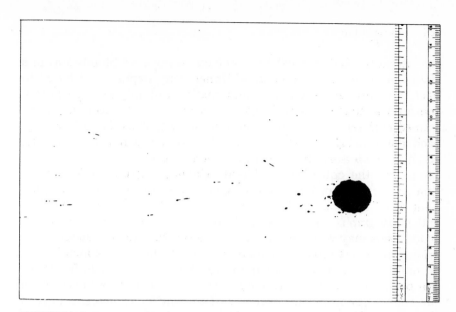

FIGURE 11-9.

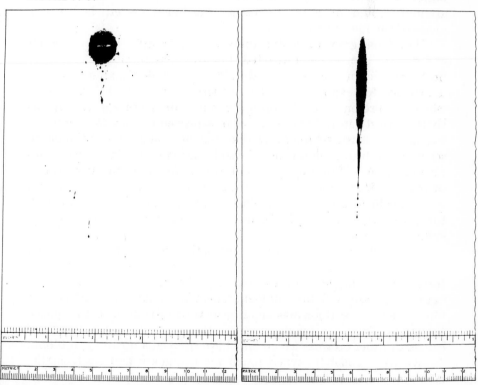

FIGURE 11-10a. Pattern of a single drop of human blood that fell forty-two inches and struck hard, smooth cardboard at 60 degrees.

FIGURE 11-10b. Pattern of single drop of human blood that fell forty-two inches and struck hard, smooth cardboard at 10 degrees.

Reprinted from *Flight Characteristics and Stain Patterns of Human Blood*, 1971

the precautions that must be observed to preserve bloodstains in a stable and uncontaminated state. Unnecessary exposure of blood to heat, moisture, and bacterial contamination will only serve to shorten the survival time of its antigens and enzymes. It is important that all stained material be submitted without delay to the crime laboratory; each day's delay contributes to a loss of antigen and enzymatic activity, and lessens the evidential value of blood.

Before the collection of blood evidence begins, it is important that the bloodstains be photographed close up and their location relative to the entire crime scene recorded through notes, sketches, and photographs. If it is determined that the shape and position of bloodstains may provide information about the circumstances of the crime, an expert must immediately be dispatched to the location for an on-the-spot evaluation of the blood evidence. The significance of the position and shape of bloodstains can best be ascertained when the expert has an on-site overview of the entire crime scene and can better reconstruct the movements of the individuals involved. No attempt should be made to disturb the blood pattern before this phase of the investigation is completed.

Blood has great evidential value when a transfer between victim and suspect can be demonstrated. For this reason, all clothing from both the victim and suspect should be collected and sent to the laboratory for examination. This procedure must be followed even when the presence of blood on a garment does not appear obvious to the investigator. Laboratory search procedures are far more revealing and sensitive than any that can be conducted at the crime scene. In addition, blood should also be searched for in the less-than-obvious places. For example, if it is believed that the perpetrator of the crime may have used a sink to wash his hands free of blood, the water in the sink trap should be removed and sent to the laboratory, because it is possible for diluted blood to remain for a considerable time in the trap.

In the absence of washing facilities, the criminal may have wiped his hands on materials not readily apparent to the investigator. Efforts must be made to find towels, handkerchiefs, or rags that may have been used and then hidden. There is always a possibility that blood shed on a floor may have been wiped or mopped to conceal the crime. Thus, careful attention should be given to examining floor cracks or other crevices which may have trapped a quantity of blood.

Wet blood can be typed much more quickly and easily in the laboratory than dried blood. If a sufficient quantity of liquid blood is found at the scene, it may be collected with a medicine dropper, placed in a glass tube containing an anticoagulant, and kept refrigerated until submission to the laboratory. When the quantity of moist blood is insufficient to be preserved in this manner, it is best to allow the material to thoroughly air-dry out of the presence of direct sunlight or heat.

If feasible, the entire stained article should be packaged and submitted for examination. Otherwise, the dried blood must be scraped with a disposable scalpel blade onto a clean sheet of paper. A portion of the unstained surface material near the recovered stain must likewise be removed and placed in a separate package. The forensic examiner will use the unstained material as a control to confirm that the results of the tests performed were brought about by the stain and not by the material on which it was deposited. An alternative procedure in such situations is to absorb the blood onto a clean cotton swab or filter paper dampened with physiological saline solution (0.9 percent sodium chloride in distilled water). Whenever stains are recovered in this manner, clean swabs or filter paper dampened with the same solution must also accompany the evidence to act as controls.

The packaging of blood evidence in plastic or airtight containers must be avoided, because the accumulation of residual moisture could contribute to the growth of blood-destroying bacteria and fungi. Preferably, each stained article should be packaged separately in a paper bag or a well-ventilated box.

When the typing of a bloodstain is undertaken, it is helpful to the forensic serologist to have control blood samples from all the victims and suspects involved in the case. For this purpose, 5 cc of whole blood should be drawn from these individuals by a qualified medical person and an anticoagulant (e.g., EDTA) added to it. Where legal or other case circumstances prevent the taking of a blood sample, the investigator should check hospital or military records for the individual's blood type.

Principles of Heredity

All of the antigens and enzymes that have been described in the previous sections are genetically controlled traits. That is, they are inherited from parents and become a permanent feature of a person's biological makeup from the moment he or she is conceived. Determining the identity of these traits, then, not only provides us with a picture of how one individual agrees or differs from another, but it gives us an insight into the basic biological substances that determine our overall makeup as human beings and the mechanism by which they are transmitted from one generation to the next.

The transmission of hereditary material is accomplished by means of microscopic units called **genes**. The gene is the basic unit of heredity. Each gene by itself or in concert with other genes controls the development of a specific characteristic in the new individual; the genes determine the nature and growth of virtually every body structure.

The genes are positioned on **chromosomes**, threadlike bodies that appear in the nucleus of every body cell. All human cells contain 46 chromosomes, mated in 23 pairs. The only exceptions are the human reproductive cells, the egg and sperm, which contain only 23 unmated chromosomes. During fertilization, a sperm and egg combine so that each contributes chromosomes to form the new cell (zygote). Hence, the new individual begins life properly mated with 23 chromosome pairs. Because the genes are positioned on the chromosomes, the new individual inherits genetic material from each parent.

Actually, two dissimilar chromosomes are involved in the determination of sex. The egg cell always contains a long chromosome known as the X chromosome, but the sperm cell may contain either a short one, known as the Y chromosome, or a long X one. When an X-carrying sperm fertilizes an egg, the new cell is XX and develops into a female. A Y-carrying sperm produces an XY fertilized egg and develops into a male. Because it is the contribution of the sperm cell that ultimately determines the nature of the chromosome pair, we can say that the father biologically determines the sex of the child.

The discovery of a specific stain for the detection of the Y chromosome has made the sexing of human cells a distinct possibility in the forensic laboratory. Investigators can now visualize the Y chromosome by soaking cells in a solution of magnesium chloride and staining with the chemical quinacrine hydrochloride. Under these conditions, the Y chromosome is observed under a microscope as a fluorescent bright spot. Using this approach, criminalists have in some situations been able to differentiate male and female bloodstains with a high degree of certainty.[5] Further experimentation using this approach brings nearer the possibility that the sexing of human hair will be a reliable technique performed in forensic laboratories in the near future.[6]

Just as chromosomes come together in pairs, so do the genes they bear. Genes that govern a given characteristic are similarly positioned on the chromosomes inherited from the mother and father. Thus, a

[5] A. P. Phillips and G. Gitshan, "The Identification of Male Bloodstains by Y Chromosome Fluorescence," *Journal of the Forensic Science Society*, 14 (1974), 47.
[6] A. P. Phillips and P. Parkinson, "Hair Sexing in Forensic Science," Central Research Establishment Report No. 102, Aldermaston, England.

gene for eye color on the mother's chromosome will be aligned with a gene for eye color on the corresponding chromosome inherited from the father. Genes which influence a given characteristic and are aligned with one another on a chromosome pair are known as **alleles**. Another rather simple example of allele genes in man is that of blood types belonging to the A-B-O system. Inheritance of the A-B-O type is best described by a theory which utilizes three genes designated A, B, and O.

A gene pair made up of two similar genes—e.g., AA and BB—is said to be **homozygous**, and a gene pair made up of two different genes—e.g., AO—is said to be **heterozygous**. If the chromosome inherited from the father carried the A gene and the chromosome inherited from the mother carried the same gene, the offspring would have an AA combination. Similarly, if one chromosome contained the A gene and the other had the O gene, the genetic makeup of the offspring would be AO.

When an individual inherits two similar genes from the parents, there is no problem in determining the blood type of that person. Hence, an AA combination will always be type A, a BB type B, and an OO type O. However, when two different genes are inherited, one gene will be dominant. It can be said that the A and B genes are **dominant** and that the O gene is always **recessive**—that is, its characteristics remain hidden. For instance, with an AO combination, A is always dominant over O and the individual will be typed as A. Similarly, a BO combination is typed as B. In the case of AB, the genes are co-dominant and the individual's blood type will be AB. The recessive characteristics of O will only appear when both recessive genes are present. Hence, the combination OO is typed as O.

A pair of allele genes together constitutes the **genotype** of the individual. However, there is no laboratory test known that can determine an individual's genotype. For example, a person's outward characteristic or **phenotype** may be that of type A, but this does not tell us whether his genotype is AA or AO. The genotype can only be determined by studying the family history of the individual. If the genotypes of both parents are known, that of their possible offspring can be forecast.

An easy way of figuring this out is by constructing a so-called Punnet Square. To do this, write along a horizontal line the two genes of the male parent, and in the vertical column the two kinds of female genes present, as shown below. In our example we'll assume the male parent is type O and therefore has to be an OO genotype; the female parent is type AB and can only be AB genotype.

	male genotype	
	O	O
A		
B		

(female genotype label on left side)

Next, write in each box the corresponding gene contributed from the female and then from the male. The result will be that the squares contain all the possible genotype combinations that the parents can produce in their offspring.

	O	O
A	AO	AO
B	BO	BO

Hence, in this case, 50 percent of the offspring are likely to be AO and the other 50 percent BO. These are the only genotypes possible from the above combination. Because O is recessive, 50 percent of the offspring will likely be type A and 50 percent type B. **From this example we can see that no blood-group gene can appear in a child unless it is present in at least one of the parents.**

In the same way, the genotypes of our parents determine the identity of all blood-group systems, as well as the polymorphic enzymes of their offspring. For example an individual whose blood carries the enzyme EAP-BA has two allelic genes determining this trait. One gene corresponds to EAP-B, the other to EAP-A. When paired these genes are co-dominant.

Although the genotyping of blood factors has useful applications for studying the transmittance of blood characteristics from one generation to the next, it actually has no direct relevance to criminal investigations. It does, however, have important implications in disputed paternity cases, which are normally encountered in civil and not criminal courts.

Many cases of disputed parentage can be resolved when the suspected parents and their offspring are related according to their A-B-O, Rh, and M-N blood systems. When all three systems are utilized, the chance of excluding a man who has been falsely accused of paternity is 56.4 percent. If there are no discrepancies in any of the blood systems tested between offspring and suspect parent, the most that can be said is that the suspect *could* be the father of the child; this does not prove, however, that he is in *fact* the father.

SEMINAL STAINS

Forensic Characterization

A great number of cases received in a forensic laboratory involve sexual offenses, making it necessary to examine exhibits for the presence of seminal stains.

The normal male releases 2.5 to 6 milliliters of seminal fluid during an ejaculation. Each milliliter contains 100 million or more spermatozoa, the male reproductive cell. The forensic examination of articles for seminal stains can actually be considered a two-step process. First, before any tests can be conducted, the stain must be located. Considering the number and soiled condition of outergarments, undergarments, and possible bed clothing submitted for examination, this may in itself prove to be an arduous task. Once located, the stain will have to be subjected to tests that will prove its identity; possibly, it may even be tested for the blood type of the individual from whom it originated.

Often, seminal stains are readily visible on a fabric because they exhibit a stiff, crusty appearance. However, reliance on such appearance for locating the stain is at best unreliable and is only useful to a criminalist when the stain is present in a rather obvious area. Certainly, if the fabric has been washed or contains only minute quantities of semen, visual examination of the article will offer little chance of detecting the stain. The best way to locate and at the same time characterize a seminal stain is to perform the **acid phosphatase color test.**

Acid phosphatase is an enzyme that is secreted by the prostate gland into seminal fluid. Its concentrations in seminal fluid are up to 400 times greater than those found in any other body fluid. Its presence can easily be detected when it comes in contact with an acidic solution of sodium alpha-naphthylphosphate and fast black K dye.

The utility of the acid phosphatase test is apparent when it becomes necessary to search numerous garments or large fabric areas for seminal stains. If a filter paper is simply moistened with water and rubbed lightly over the suspect area, acid phosphatase, if present, will be transferred to the filter paper. Then, when a drop or two of the sodium alpha-naphthylphosphate and fast black K solution are placed on the paper, the appearance of a purple color will be indicative of the acid phosphatase enzyme. In this manner, any fabric or surface can be systematically searched for seminal stains. If it is necessary to search extremely large areas—e.g., a bed sheet or carpet—the article can be tested in sections, narrowing the location of the stain with each successive test. A negative reaction can be interpreted as meaning the absence of semen.

Though some vegetable juices (e.g., cauliflower and watermelon), fungi, contraceptive creams, and vaginal secretions do give a positive response to the acid phosphatase test, none of these substances react with the speed of seminal fluid. A reaction time of less than 30 seconds is considered a strong indication for the presence of semen. This finding may be further reinforced by subjecting the suspect stain to electrophoretic analysis. Acid phosphatase, like many other enzymes, can be made to migrate across a gel coated plate under the influence of an electrical potential. Under the proper conditions, the rate of migration of human seminal acid phosphatase will be different from that of vaginal acid phosphatase or for that matter acid phosphatase derived from other animal or vegetable sources.[7]

Semen can be unequivocally identified by the presence of spermatozoa. When spermatozoa are located through a microscopic examination, the stain is definitely identified as having been derived from semen. Spermatozoa are slender, elongated structures 50 to 70 microns long, with a head and a thin flagellate tail (see Figure 11-11). The criminalist can normally locate them by immersing the stained material in a small volume of water. Rapid stirring of the liquid will transfer any spermatozoa present into the water. A drop of the water is then dried onto a microscope slide, stained and examined under a compound microscope at a magnification of approximately 400X.

Considering the extremely large number of spermatozoa found in seminal fluid, one would think the chance of locating one would be very good; however, this is not always true. For one, spermatozoa are extremely brittle when dry and easily disintegrate if the stain is washed or when the stain is rubbed against another object, as can

---

[7]Three different electrophoretic methods suggested for the identification of seminal acid phosphatase are: (a) S. J. Baxter, "Immunological Identification of Human Semen," *Medicine, Science, and the Law*, 13 (1973), 155. (b) E. G. Adams and B. G. Wraxall, "Phosphatases in Body Fluids: The Differention of Semen and Vaginal Secretion," *Forensic Science*, 3 (1974), 57. (c) J. Sutton and P. H. Whitehead, "Iso-electric Focusing of Seminal, Faecal and Vaginal Acid Phosphatases," *Forensic Science*, 6 (1975), 109.

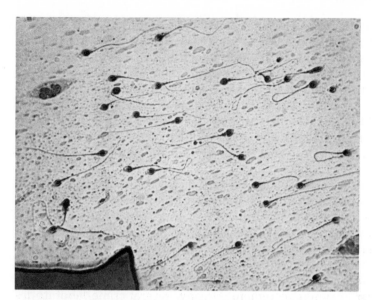

FIGURE 11-11. Photomicrograph of human spermatozoa (420X).
Courtesy Linda Jankowski

frequently happen in the handling and packaging of this type of evidence. Furthermore, sexual crimes may involve males who have an abnormally low sperm count, a condition known as **oligospermia**, or they may involve individuals who have no spermatozoa at all in their seminal fluid (**aspermia**). Significantly, aspermatic individuals are increasing in numbers due to the increasing popularity of vasectomies. In all these circumstances, a conclusive finding of seminal acid-phosphatase is required for the forensic identification of human semen.

Another chemical test for semen involves the detection of choline. Choline is also present in other biological materials, but, like acid-phosphatase, in much lower concentrations than what is found in seminal fluid. Two procedures for the identification of choline utilize microcrystalline tests. The Florence test uses potassium triiodide, and the Barberios test uses picric acid for crystallizing reagents. Thin-layer chromatography may also be applied for the analysis of choline.[8]

We have already observed that nearly 80 percent of the population are secretors having high concentrations of their blood-type antigens in most body fluids. Hence, for a substantial segment of the male population, seminal fluid and/or stains can yield the identity of an individual's blood type. Often this information can provide important corroborative evidence that supports a suspect's involvement in a sexual assault. Likewise, such an identification can serve to

[8] R. R. Hallock, "Spermine and Choline Identification by Thin-Layer Chromatography," *Journal of Forensic Sciences*, 20 (1974), 172.

exonerate someone unjustly accused of committing such a crime. However, the determination of blood type from semen is not without its problems, especially under conditions that normally accompany a sexual assault. Often, the semen stains found on the victim's garments will be mixed with sweat and/or vaginal secretions. Since it is just as probable for a female victim to secrete her blood-type antigens as it is for the male suspect, it becomes important to establish whether the victim and suspect are both secretors and their respective blood types. This information can readily be obtained in the laboratory by a determination of the concentration levels of A, B, and H antigens present in saliva. The saliva of secretors will yield higher levels of blood antigens than that of non-secretors. Naturally, if both the victim and suspect are secretors having the same blood type, the examiner must be especially cautious in typing a seminal stain, taking special care to make sure that the stain is free of any possible contaminants.

As with blood, forensic serologists have been successful in finding polymorphic enzymes in semen. Already, several crime laboratories are engaged in typing the enzyme PGM in semen as a means of extending its individuality beyond the A-B-O system. As research progresses in the detection and characterization of other polymorphic enzymes present in semen, the possibility increases that this body fluid can be made to yield a sufficient number of individual characteristics to become a unique marker for human identification.

The persistence of seminal constituents in the vagina is frequently of considerable importance in the examination of the victims of alleged sexual offenses. As part of the investigation, vaginal swabs must be obtained and placed in dry test tubes by a physician. Additionally, vaginal washings, using no more than 5 to 10 ml of distilled water, should also be taken. In the living subject, spermatozoa *may* be found in the vagina up to three days after intercourse and occasionally up to six days. The likelihood of finding seminal acid phosphatase in vaginal swabs and washings markedly decreases with time following intercourse. But there is little chance of identifying this substance 48 hours after intercourse.[9]

Collection and Preservation of Semen Evidence

In cases involving sexual assaults, there is a distinct possibility that physical contact between the victim and suspect will have resulted in an exchange of relevant physical evidence—i.e., body fluids, hairs, and fibers. To protect this type of evidence, all the outer- and

[9]Anne Davies and Elizabeth Wilson, "The Persistence of Seminal Constituents in the Human Vagina," *Forensic Science,* 3 (1974), 45–55.

undergarments from the involved parties should be carefully removed and packaged separately so that the transfer of evidential material from one item to another will be prevented. But seminal stains found on the clothing of male suspects have by themselves little evidential value. This observation has been reinforced by a recent study carried out by the Central Research Establishment. One hundred pairs of men's trousers obtained from a dry cleaning establishment, all of which were apparently unrelated to a crime, were screened for the presence of acid phosphatase-containing stains. The results show that 37 had stains characteristic of semen. The size and number of seminal stains found in this survey certainly seems to indicate that the finding of semen on a man's trousers is of questionable evidential value. Interestingly, of 100 men's jackets and 100 pairs of trousers examined for blood, 5 jackets and 16 trousers show the presence of bloodstains.[10]

Items suspected of containing seminal stains should be handled carefully. Folding an article through the stain may cause it to flake off, as will the rubbing of the stained area against the surface of the packaging material. If, under unusual circumstances, it is not possible to transport the stained article to the laboratory, the stained area should be cut out and it should be submitted with an unstained piece acting as a control.

In cases relating to the typing of seminal stains, laboratory submissions must include saliva so that the secretor status of both the suspect and victim can be determined. To obtain saliva, the individuals in question should be asked to thoroughly saturate a clean paper towel or three or four cotton swabs with saliva. The saliva should then be air-dried out of direct sunlight or heat. It is best that the donor not have anything in his mouth for an hour before giving this sample—this includes gum, cigarettes, cigars, etc. In addition, a sample of whole blood from both the victim and suspect should be obtained for blood typing.

The fact that individuals may secrete their blood-type antigens in body fluids can be a double-edged sword for the careless investigator. By needlessly touching the suspect area, the investigator may inadvertently transfer his own blood type to the stain through the medium of perspiration. In this respect, it is exceedingly important that stained articles be handled with care, minimizing direct personal contact. In some instances it may be desirable to wear disposable plastic gloves when such evidence must be touched.

A detailed description regarding the collection of evidence relating to sex crimes can be found in Appendix I.

---

[10] G. W. Owen, and K. W. Smalldon, "Blood and Semen Stains on Outer Clothing and Shoes Related to Crime: Report of a Survey Using Presumptive Tests," *Journal of Forensic Sciences*, 20 (1975), 391.

REVIEW QUESTIONS

1. Karl Landsteiner discovered that blood can be classified by its _____ .

2. No two individuals, except for identical twins, can be expected to have the same combination of blood types or antigens. (True, False)

3. _____ is the fluid portion of unclotted blood.

4. The liquid that separates from the blood when a clot is formed is called the _____ .

5. _____ transport oxygen from the lungs to the body tissues and carry carbon dioxide back to the lungs.

6. On the surface of the red blood cells are chemical substances called _____ . It is these substances that impart blood type characteristics to the cells.

7. Type A individuals have _____ antigens located on the surface of their red blood cells.

8. Type O persons have (both, neither) A and B antigens on their cells.

9. It is the presence or absence of the _____ and _____ antigens on the red blood cells that determines a person's blood type in the A-B-O system.

10. The D antigen is also known as the _____ antigen.

11. Serum contains proteins known as _____ which destroy or inactivate antigens.

12. An antibody will react with (any, only a specific) antigen.

13. Agglutination describes the clumping together of red blood cells by the action of an antibody. (True, False)

14. Type B blood contains _____ antigens and anti-_____ antibodies.

15. Type AB blood has (both, neither) anti-A and anti-B.

16. A drug-protein complex can be injected into an animal to cause the formation of specific _____ for that drug.

17. The term _____ describes the study of antigen-antibody reactions.

18. Type AB blood will (be, not be) agglutinated by both anti-A and anti-B serum.

19. Type B red blood cells will agglutinate when added to type (A, B) blood.

20. Type A cells will agglutinate when added to type (AB, O) blood.

21. The distribution of type A blood in the United States is approximately (forty-two, fifteen) percent.

22. The distribution of type AB in the United States is approximately (twelve, three) percent.

23. (All, Most) blood contains the enzyme peroxidase.

24. The _____ color test is the most sensitive test for detecting peroxidase in blood.

25. _____ reagent reacts with blood, causing it to luminesce.

26. Blood can be characterized as being of human origin by the _____ test.

27. Antigens and antibodies (can, cannot) be induced to move towards one another under the influence of an electrical field.

28. The _____ technique is the current method of choice for the indirect typing of bloodstains.

29. Approximately _____ percent of the population are classified as secretors.

30. _____ are proteins that have important functions in regulating many of the body's chemical reactions.

31. Enzymes that exist in different forms in a population are (polymorphic, monomorphic).

32. The shape of bloodstains may provide useful information regarding the direction, dropping distance, and angle of impact of splattered blood. (True, False)

33. Small amounts of blood are best submitted to a crime laboratory in a (wet, dry) condition.

34. Airtight packages make the best containers for blood-containing evidence. (True, False)

35. The basic unit of heredity is the _____ .

36. Genes are positioned on thread-like bodies called _____ .

37. All cells in the human body, except the reproductive cells have _____ pair of chromosomes.

38. The sex of an offspring is always determined by the (mother, father).

39. Genes which influence a given characteristic and are aligned with one another on a chromosome pair are known as _____ .

40. When a pair of allelic genes are identical, they are said to be (homozygous, heterozygous).

41. A (phenotype, genotype) is an observable characteristic of an individual.

42. The combination of genes present in the cells of an individual is called the _____ .

43. A gene (will, will not) appear in a child when it is present in at least one of the parents.

44. A type B person may have the genotype _____ or the genotype _____ .

45. The _____ color test is used to locate and characterize seminal stains.

46. Semen is uneqivocally identified if the presence of _____ is demonstrated.

47. Males having a low sperm count suffer from a condition known as (oligospermia, aspermia).

48. The blood type of a male secretor (can, cannot) be determined from a seminal stain.

49. Finding seminal stains on a man's trousers has by itself (great, little) evidential value.

50. If the typing of seminal stains is desired by an investigator, (saliva, urine) from the suspect and victim must be submitted to the laboratory.

FURTHER READINGS

Culliford, Bryan J., *The Examination and Typing of Bloodstains in the Crime Laboratory*. Washington, D.C.: U.S. Government Printing Office, 1971.

Erskine, Addine G., *The Principles and Practice of Blood Grouping*. St. Louis: C. V. Mosby, 1973.

Kind, S. S., "The Acid Phosphatase Test," in *Methods of Forensic Science*, vol. 3, A. S. Curry, ed. New York: Wiley—Interscience, 1964.

Survey and Assessment of Blood and Bloodstain Analysis Program, vol. 1: Technical Discussion. El Segundo, Cal.: The Aerospace Corp., 1974.

Williams, Ray L., "Forensic Science—The Present and Future," *Analytical Chemistry*, vol. 45 (1973), 1076 A.

Willott, G. M., "The Role of the Forensic Biologist in Cases of Sexual Assault," *Journal of the Forensic Science Society*, 15 (1975), 269.

Audiovisual Presentations

Laboratory Chemistry (filmstrip and audio tape), Robert J. Brady Co., Inc., Bowie, Md.

Fingerprints

chapter 12

HISTORY OF FINGERPRINTING

Since the beginnings of criminal investigation, police have sought an infallible means of human identification. The first systematic attempt at personal identification was devised and introduced by a French police expert, Alphonse Bertillon, in 1883. The Bertillon system relied on a detailed description (portrait parlé) of the subject, combined with full-length and profile photographs and a system of precise body measurements known as anthropometry.

The use of anthropometry as a method of identification rested on the premise that the dimensions of the human bone system remained fixed from the age of twenty until death. Skeleton sizes were thought to be so extremely diverse that no two individuals could have exactly the same measurements. Bertillon recommended the routine taking of eleven measurements of the human anatomy. These included height, reach, width of head, and the length of the left foot.

For two decades this system was considered the most accurate method of identification. It was only in the first years of the new century that police began to appreciate and accept a system of identification based on the classification of finger ridge patterns known as fingerprints. Today, the fingerprint is the pillar of modern criminal identification.

Evidence exists that the Chinese used the fingerprint to sign legal documents as far back as three thousand years ago. However, whether this practice was performed for ceremonial custom or as a means of personal identity remains a point of conjecture lost to history. In any case, the examples of fingerprinting in ancient history are ambiguous and the few that do exist certainly did not contribute to the development of fingerprinting techniques as we know them today.

Several years before Bertillon began work on his system, William Herschel, an English civil servant stationed in India, started the practice of requiring natives to sign their contracts with the imprint of a right hand that had been pressed against a stamp pad. The motives for Herschel's requirement remain unclear until today; it is debatable whether he envisioned fingerprinting as a means of personal identification or just as a method for utilizing the Hindu custom that a trace of bodily contact was more binding than a signature on a contract. In any case, he did not publish anything about his activities until after a Scottish physician, Henry Fauld, working in a hospital in Japan, published his views on the potential application of fingerprinting to personal identification.

In his communication to a scientific publication in 1880, Fauld suggested that skin ridge patterns could be important for the identification of criminals. He related an incident about a thief who left his fingerprints on a whitewashed wall, and how in comparing these prints with those of a suspect, he found that they were quite different. A few days later another suspect was found whose fingerprints compared with those on the wall. When confronted with this evidence, the individual confessed to the crime.

Fauld was convinced that fingerprints furnished infallible proof of identification. He even offered to set up at his own expense a fingerprint bureau at Scotland Yard to test the practicality of the method. But his offer was rejected in favor of the Bertillon system. This decision was reversed less than two decades later.

It was the extensive research into fingerprinting conducted by another Englishman, Henry Galton, that provided the needed impetus that made police agencies aware of its potential application. In 1892, Galton published his classic textbook *Fingerprints*, the first book of its kind on the subject. In the text he discussed the anatomy of fingerprints, and suggested methods for recording and classifying them. Most importantly, the book convincingly demonstrated that no two prints were identical and an individual's prints remained unchanged from year to year. At Galton's insistence, the British government adopted fingerprinting as a supplement to the Bertillon system. The first system for classifying fingerprints to be officially used was developed by an Argentinian, Dr. Juan Vucetich, in 1891. His system is still used in Latin American countries today and is considered by many experts as the most workable one. Most English-speaking countries, including the United States, use a modification of the classification system proposed in 1900 by an Englishman, Sir Edward Richard Henry.

At about this time, Bertillon's system was beginning to fall into disfavor. It was becoming apparent that its results were highly susceptible to error, particularly when the measurements were taken by persons who were not thoroughly trained. The method was dealt its most severe and notable setback in 1903, when a convict, William West, arrived in Fort Leavenworth Prison. A routine check of the prison files startlingly revealed that a Will West, already in the prison, could not be distinguished from the new prisoner by body measurements or even photographs. In fact, the two men looked just like twins and their measurements were practically the same. Subsequently, fingerprints of both prisoners clearly distinguished them.

In the U.S., the first systematic and official use of fingerprints for personal identification was adopted by the New York City Civil Service Commission in 1901. Here the method was used for certifying all civil service applications. Several American police officials received instruction in fingerprint identification at the 1904 World's Fair in St. Louis from representatives of Scotland Yard. After the Fair and the Will West incident, fingerprinting began to be used in earnest in all major cities of the United States. In 1924, the fingerprint records of the Bureau of Investigation and Leavenworth Prison were merged to form the nucleus of the identification records of the new Federal Bureau of Investigation. Presently, the FBI has the largest collection of fingerprints in the world; the total fingerprint records on file approaches 200 million. By the beginning of World War I, England and practically all of Europe had adopted fingerprinting as their primary method of identifying criminals.

THE FUNDAMENTAL PRINCIPLES OF FINGERPRINTS

First Principle: *A fingerprint is an individual characteristic; no two fingers have yet been found to possess identical ridge characteristics.*

The acceptance of fingerprint evidence by the courts has always been predicated on the assumption that no two individuals have identical fingerprints. Early fingerprint experts consistently referred to Galton's calculation showing the possible existence of 64 billion different fingerprints to support this contention. Later, researchers questioned the validity of Galton's figures and attempted to devise mathematical models to better approximate this value. However, no matter what mathematical model one refers to, the conclusions are always the same: the probability for the existence of two identical fingerprint patterns in the world's population is extremely small.

Not only is this principle supported by theoretical calculations, but just as importantly, it is verified by the millions upon millions of individuals who have had their prints classified over the past seventy years; no two have ever been found to be identical.

The individuality of a fingerprint is not determined by its general shape or pattern, but by a careful study of its **ridge characteristics** (also known as minutiae). It is the identity, number, and relative location of characteristics, such as those illustrated in Figure 12-1, that impart individuality to a fingerprint. If two prints are to compare, they will have to reveal characteristics that are not only identical, but have the same relative location to one another in a print. In a judicial proceeding, a point-by-point comparison must be demonstrated by the expert, using charts similar to the one shown in Figure 12-2 in order to prove the identity of an individual.

If an expert were asked to compare the characteristics of the complete fingerprint, no difficulty would be encountered in com-

Ridge Characteristics

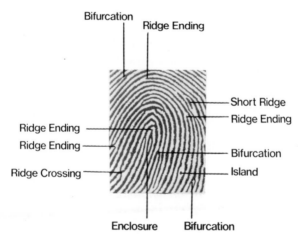

FIGURE 12-1.

Courtesy Police Science Services

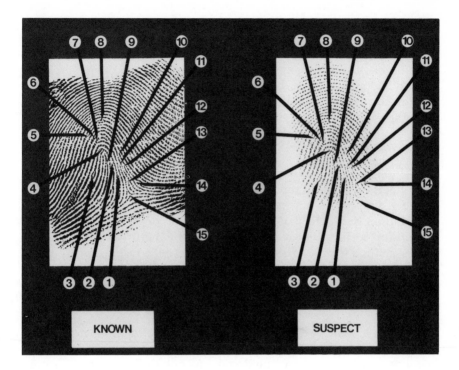

FIGURE 12-2.
Courtesy Police Science Services

pleting such an assignment; there are as many as 150 individual ridge characteristics on the average fingerprint. However, in practice the vast majority of the prints recovered at crime scenes are partial impressions, showing only a segment of the entire print. Under these circumstances, the expert has to be prepared to compare only a small number of ridge characteristics from the recovered print to a known recorded print. For years, experts have debated the question of just how many ridge comparisons are necessary before two fingerprints can be identified as being the same. Numbers that range from eight to sixteen have been suggested as being sufficient to meet the criteria of individuality. However, the difficulty that arises in establishing such a minimum is that no comprehensive statistical study has ever been undertaken to determine the frequency of occurrence of different ridge characteristics and their relative locations. Until such a study is undertaken and completed, no meaningful guidelines can be established for defining the uniqueness of a fingerprint.

In 1973, the International Association for Identification, after a three-year study of this question, concluded that "no valid basis exists for requiring a predetermined minimum number of friction ridge characters which must be present in two impressions in order to establish positive identification.'' Hence, the final determination must be based on the experience and knowledge of the expert, with the understanding that others may profess honest differences of opinion on the uniqueness of a fingerprint if the question of a minimal number of ridge characteristics exists.

Second Principle: *A fingerprint will remain unchanged during an individual's lifetime.*

Fingerprints are a reproduction of friction skin ridges found on the palm side of the fingers and thumbs. Similar friction skin can also be found on the surface of the palms and soles of the feet. Apparently, these skin surfaces have been designed by nature to provide our bodies with a firmer grasp and a resistance to slippage. A visual inspection of friction skin reveals a series of lines corresponding to hills (ridges) and valleys (grooves). It is the shape and form of the skin ridges that one sees as the black lines of an inked fingerprint impression.

Actually, skin is composed of layers of cells; those nearest the surface make up the outer portion of the skin known as the **epidermis.** The inner skin is known as the **dermis.** As one looks at a cross-section of skin (Figure 12-3), a boundary of cells separating the epidermis and dermis is noted. It is the shape of this boundary, made up of **dermal papillae,** that determines the form and pattern of the ridges on the surface of the skin. Once the dermal papillae develop in the human fetus, the ridge patterns will remain unchanged throughout life except to enlarge during growth.

Each skin ridge is populated with a single row of pores that are the openings for ducts leading from the sweat glands. It is through these pores that perspiration is discharged and deposited on the surface of the skin. Once the finger touches a surface, perspiration, along with oils that may have been picked up by touching the hairy portions of the body, is transferred onto that surface, thereby leaving an impression of the finger's ridge pattern (a fingerprint). Prints deposited in this manner are invisible to the eye and are commonly referred to as ''latent'' or hidden fingerprints.

Though it is impossible to change one's fingerprints, there has been no lack of effort on the part of some criminals to obscure them. If an injury reaches deeply enough into the skin and damages the dermal papillae, a permanent scar will form. However, for this to happen, such a wound would have to penetrate 1 to 2 millimeters beneath the skin's surface. Indeed, efforts at intentionally scarring

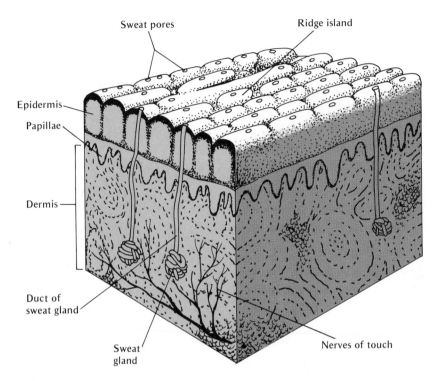

Sweat pores

Ridge island

Epidermis

Papillae

Dermis

Duct of
sweat gland

Sweat
gland

Nerves of touch

FIGURE 12-3.

the skin can only be self-defeating, for it would be totally impossible to obliterate all the ridge characteristics on the hand, and the presence of permanent scars serve as new characteristics for identification.

Perhaps the most publicized attempt at obliteration was that of the notorious gangster John Dillinger, who attempted to destroy his own fingerprints by applying a corrosive acid to them. Prints taken at the morgue after he was shot to death compared with fingerprints recorded at the time of a previous arrest, proving that his efforts had been fruitless (see Figure 12–4).

Third Principle: *Fingerprints have general ridge patterns that permit them to be systematically classified.*

All fingerprints are divided into three classes on the basis of their general pattern: **loops, whorls, and arches.** Sixty to sixty-five percent of the population has loops, thirty to thirty-five percent are whorls, and about five percent are arches. These three classes form the basis for all the ten-finger classification systems presently in use.

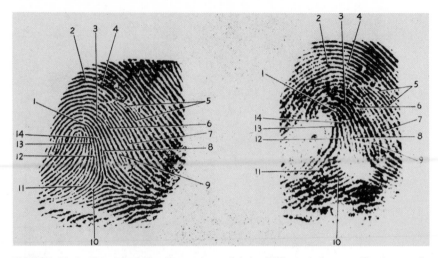

FIGURE 12-4. The right index impressions of John Dillinger before scarification on the left and afterwards on the right. Comparison is proved by the fourteen matching ridge characteristics.

Courtesy Institute of Applied Science

A typical loop pattern is illustrated in Figure 12-5. A loop must have one or more ridges entering from one side of the print, recurving, and exiting from the same side. If the loop opens toward the little finger it is called an **ulnar loop**; if it opens toward the thumb it is a **radial loop**. The pattern area of the loop is surrounded by two diverging ridges known as *type lines*. The ridge point nearest the type-line divergence is known as the *delta*. To many, a fingerprint delta resembles the silt formation that builds up as a river flows into the entrance of a lake; hence the analogy to the geological formation known as a delta. All loops must have one delta. The *core*, as the name suggests, is the approximate center of the pattern.

Whorls are actually divided into four distinct groups, as shown in Figure 12-6: plain whorl, central pocket loop, double loop, and accidental whorl. All whorl patterns must have type lines and a minimum of two deltas. A plain whorl and the central pocket loop have at least one ridge that makes a complete circuit. This ridge may be in the form of a spiral, oval, or any variant of a circle. If an imaginary line is drawn between the two deltas contained within these two patterns, and if the line touches any one of the spiral ridges, the pattern is a plain whorl; if no such ridge is touched, the pattern is a central pocket loop.

As the name implies, the double loop is made up of two loops

LOOP

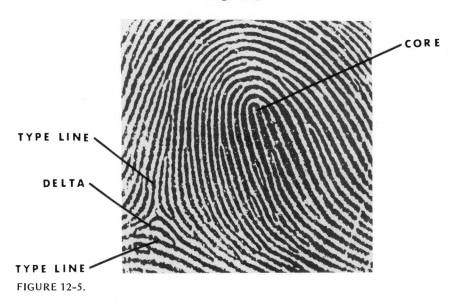

CORE

TYPE LINE

DELTA

TYPE LINE

FIGURE 12-5.

combined into one fingerprint. Any print classified as an accidental either contains two or more patterns (not including the plain arch) or is a pattern not covered by other categories. Hence, an accidental may consist of a combination loop and plain whorl, or a loop and tented arch.

Arches, the least common of the three general patterns, are sub-divided into two distinct groups: plain arches and tented arches, shown in Figure 12-7. The plain arch is the simplest of all fingerprint patterns; it is formed by ridges entering from one side of the print and exiting on the opposite side. Generally, these ridges tend to rise in the center of the pattern, forming a wavelike pattern. The tented arch is similar to the plain arch, except that instead of rising smoothly at the center, there is a sharp upthrust or spike, or the ridges meet at an angle that is less than 90 degrees.[1] Arches do not have type lines, deltas, or cores.

With a knowledge of basic fingerprint pattern classes, we may now begin to develop an appreciation for fingerprint classification systems. However, the subject is far more complex than can be described in a textbook of this nature. The student seeking a more

---

[1] A tented arch is also any pattern that resembles a loop, but lacks one of the essential requirements for classification as a loop.

Whorl patterns

Plain

Central pocket loop

Double loop

Accidental

FIGURE 12-6.

detailed treatment of the subject would do well to consult references cited at the end of the chapter.

THE HENRY SYSTEM

The original Henry system, as it was adopted by Scotland Yard in 1901, converts ridge patterns on all ten fingers into a series of letters and numbers arranged in the form of a fraction. However, the system as it was originally designed could only accommodate files of up to

Arch patterns

Plain   Tented

FIGURE 12-7.

100,000 sets of prints; thus, as collections grew in size it became necessary to expand the capacity of the classification system. In the United States, the FBI, faced with the problem of filing ever-increasing numbers of prints, expanded its classification capacity by modifying and adding additional extensions to the original Henry system. These modifications are collectively known as the FBI system and are used by most agencies in the United States today.

The Primary Classification

Though we will not discuss all of the different divisions of the FBI system, a description of just one part, the primary classification, will provide an interesting insight into the process of fingerprint classification.

The primary classification is part of the original Henry system and provides the first classification step in the FBI system. Using this classification alone, all of the fingerprint cards in the world could be divided into 1,024 groups. For the purpose of obtaining the primary classification, each finger on the hand is assigned a numerical value (shown below in parenthesis) and placed either in the numerator or denominator of a fraction in the following order:

$$\frac{\text{R. Index (16), R. Ring (8), L. Thumb (4), L. Middle (2), L. Little (1)}}{\text{R. Thumb (16), R. Middle (8), R. Little (4), L. Index (2), L. Ring (1)}}$$

The presence of whorls in any of the ten finger impressions is used as the basis for the determination of the primary classification. If the pattern is a loop or arch, it is assigned a value of zero and placed in its proper position in the fraction. If the pattern is a whorl, it is assigned a value of one and placed in its proper place in the fraction.

After values for all ten fingers are obtained in this manner, they are totaled and one is added to both the numerator and denominator. The fraction thus obtained is the primary classification. As an example, if the right index and right middle fingers are whorls and all the others are loops, the primary classification is:

$$\frac{16 + 0 + 0 + 0 + 0 + 1}{0 + 8 + 0 + 0 + 0 + 1} = \frac{17}{9}$$

Approximately 60 percent of the population falls into the 1/1 category—that is, all their fingers have either loops or arches.

A fingerprint classification system cannot in itself unequivocally identify an individual; it will merely provide the fingerprint examiner with a number of candidates, all of whom have an indistinguishable set of prints in the system's file. The identification must always be made by a final visual comparison of the questioned and file print's ridge characteristics; only these features can impart individuality to a fingerprint. Though ridge patterns impart class characteristics to the print, it is the type and position of ridge characteristics that give it its individual character.

The Henry and FBI classification systems are ten-finger classification schemes useful only for processing a full set of fingerprints. Unfortunately, it is a rarity when the crime scene yields anything more than a single partial print of a suspect. Under such circumstances, a ten-finger file will only be of value when the investigator has the names of known suspects in hand. By going through a name index, fingerprint cards of suspects on file can now be removed and compared to the recovered crime-scene print. However, some police departments have established a single-fingerprint collection to aid them in their search for suspects. Here, each fingerprint is filed on a separate card and is independently classified. Unfortunately, this approach becomes much to cumbersome when too many individuals are included in the file. Experience shows that single-print collections are only useful for agencies that restrict its members to active criminals who are most likely to engage in crimes that provide the best chance for recovery of fingerprints—e.g., house burglaries and car thefts.

COMPUTERIZED FINGERPRINT
SEARCH SYSTEMS

Since the early 1960s, police agencies in most industrialized countries of the world have been trying to harness the power of the computer to classify and search their bulging fingerprint files. Now police forces are on the verge of making important technological break-throughs that will make this goal a reality. Present plans call for a computer system in England by 1978 that will automatically read, classify, and match against records fingerprints found at crime scenes. The West German Bundeskriminalamt is scheduled to start computer retrieval and matching of latent fingerprints against its collection of 17 million prints in 1976. At the end of 1973, the Canadian Mounted Police completed the conversion of its file to a computer-based system, and Sweden's automated computerized fingerprint system became operational in 1975. In the U.S., the FBI is proceeding with its ambitious program of developing a system to automatically read, classify, and match fingerprints; it expects to have portions of its system operating by 1977.

The computerized systems being developed independently by the British Home Office and the FBI both incorporate automatic scanning devices that can read and code fingerprint characteristics directly from standard fingerprint cards. Both systems read the print with a flying spot scanner that measures light reflected from the print and converts the image into digital data. This digital data is then transferred into a computer, where it is classified and held in storage for future matching against incoming fingerprints.

The FBI automatic fingerprint reader system, known as FINDER II (FINgerprint reaDER), will record fingerprint data in an average processing time of one-half second per fingerprint. There are two types of digital information generated by the FINDER—minutiae and ridge-direction data. Minutiae data describes certain ridge characteristics by locating areas where ridges terminate (ridge endings) and where ridges branch into two ridges (bifurcations). Ridge-direction data are samplings of the average direction of ridge flow at regular selected intervals across a fingerprint, and basically describe the general pattern of the print.

FINDER classifies a print by comparing the ridge-direction data of the search fingerprint to standard or to prototype direction data stored in the computer's memory. The prototype pattern that compares most closely with the search fingerprint determines the classification of the fingerprint. A composite of the classification of eight fingers (the little fingers are omitted) is used to determine the overall classification for a fingerprint card. Once a set of fingerprints has been classified and stored in the computer, it can be matched against any existing set of prints previously entered into the computer. The system matches prints by comparing the position of minutiae; i.e., bifurcations and ridge endings. Possible matches are printed out by the computer and a technician searches through these to complete the identification.

As it is presently envisioned, the FBI system will not have the capability of automatically processing single latent prints recovered at crime scenes. In theory, FINDER'S files could be organized to search each individual fingerprint entered into it; however, even though the speed of digital computers would make such an extensive search possible, there are practical limitations to this approach. Therefore, rather than attempt to search latents against the whole criminal fingerprint file, it appears to be more practical to follow the traditional approach and to establish a special file on known criminals for searching single-print latents. The file could be organized according to offense categories: for example, kidnapping, forgery, and bank robbery. Such a fingerprint file would be much larger and consequently more valuable than any presently existing manual single-fingerprint file.

One of the problems that any computerized latent print system will have to overcome is the fact that most latents are of such poor quality that they cannot be read and computer-coded automatically. To overcome this problem, present FBI plans call for the development of a semi-automatic coding device that a latent fingerprint examiner would use to encode the print for the computerized search.

METHODS OF DETECTING
FINGERPRINTS

Through common usage, the term "latent fingerprint" has come to be associated with any fingerprint discovered at a crime scene. Sometimes, however, prints found at the scene of a crime are quite visible to the eye, and the word "latent" is a misnomer. Actually, there are three kinds of crime-scene prints: **visible prints** are made by fingers touching a surface after the ridges have been in contact with a colored material such as blood, paint, grease, or ink; **plastic prints** are ridge impressions left on a soft material such as putty, wax, soap, or dust; **true latent** or **invisible prints** are impressions caused by the transfer of body perspiration or oils present on finger ridges to the surface of an object.

Locating the visible or plastic print at the crime scene normally presents little problem to the investigator, because these prints are usually distinct and visible to the eye. Locating the latent or invisible print is obviously a much more difficult task and does require the utilization of techniques that will visualize the print. Though the investigator is presented with a number of alternate methods for visualizing a latent print, the method of choice will depend on the type of surface that is being examined.

Hard and nonabsorbent surfaces (e.g., glass, mirror, tile, and painted wood) require different development procedures from those which are soft and porous (e.g., papers, cardboard, and cloth). Prints on the former are preferably developed by the application of a powder, while the latter generally require treatment with a chemical.

Fingerprint powders are commercially available in a variety of compositions and colors. These powders, when applied lightly to a nonabsorbent surface with a camel's-hair brush, will readily adhere to perspiration residues and/or deposits of body oils left on the surface. Experienced examiners find that gray and black powders are adequate for most latent print work; the examiner will select the powder that affords the best color contrast with the surface being dusted. Hence, the gray powder, composed of an aluminum dust, is used on dark-colored surfaces. It is also applied to mirrors and metal surfaces that are polished to a mirrorlike finish, because these surfaces will photograph black. The black powder, composed basically of black carbon or charcoal, is applied to white or light-colored surfaces.

Of the chemical methods used for visualizing latent prints, iodine fuming is the oldest. Iodine is a solid crystal which, upon being heated, is transformed into a vapor without passing through a liquid phase; such a transformation is called **sublimation**. Latent prints that contain fatty oils will preferentially absorb iodine vapors. Most often, the suspect material is placed in an enclosed cabinet along with iodine crystals (see Figure 12-8). As the crystals are heated, the resultant vapors will fill the chamber and chemically combine with the fatty oils, making the latent print visible. Unfortunately, iodine prints are not permanent and begin to fade once the fuming process is stopped. It is necessary, therefore, for the examiner to photograph the prints immediately upon development in order to retain a permanent record.

The development of latent prints with ninhydrin is dependent on its chemical reaction with amino acids and proteins present in trace amounts in perspiration. Ninhydrin (triketohydrindene hydrate) is commonly sprayed onto the porous surface from an aerosol can. A solution is prepared by mixing the ninhydrin powder with a suitable

FIGURE 12-8. A heated fuming cabinet.
Courtesy Sirchie Laboratories

solvent such as acetone or ethyl alcohol; a 0.6 percent solution appears to be effective for most applications. Generally, prints begin to
appear within an hour or two after ninhydrin application; however,
weaker prints will be visualized after 24 to 48 hours. The development can be hastened if the treated specimen is heated in an oven or
on a hotplate at a temperature of 80 to 100°C. The ninhydrin method has developed latent prints on paper as old as fifteen years.

After the moisture from perspiration has evaporated, a substantial portion of the latent print residue will consist of common salt (sodium chloride). In the presence of the chemical silver nitrate, the chloride ion of the salt will react to form silver chloride. Though silver chloride is colorless, it will be transformed by ultraviolet light into silver. Silver shows the latent print up as black or reddish-brown in color. Commonly, a 3 percent solution of silver nitrate in water is brushed onto a paper or cardboard object suspected of containing a print. The prints are then developed by being exposed to the light.

For most fingerprint examiners, the chemical method of choice is ninhydrin. Its extreme sensitivity and ease of application has all but eliminated the use of iodine for latent print visualization. However, in those instances in which ninhydrin fails, development with silver nitrate may provide identifiable results. In any case, application of silver nitrate will wash away any traces of fatty oils and proteins from the object's surface; consequently, it is necessary to fume with iodine and process with ninhydrin before treatment with silver nitrate.

The use of powders and chemicals may interfere with physical and chemical analysis, particularly in the case of blood, fabrics, and documents. Therefore, in cases involving items with material adhering to their surfaces and/or which will require further laboratory examinations, fingerprint processing should not be performed at the crime scene. Rather, the items should be submitted to the laboratory, where they can be processed for fingerprints in conjunction with other examination that have to be undertaken.

PRESERVATION OF DEVELOPED PRINTS

Once the latent print has been visualized, it must be permanently preserved for future comparison and possible court evidence. A photograph must be taken before any further attempts at preservation are made. Actually, any camera equipped with a close-up lens will do; however, many investigators prefer to use a camera specially designed for fingerprint photography. Such a camera comes equipped with a built-in illuminator and a fixed focus to take photographs on a 1:1 scale when the camera's open end is held exactly flush against the print's surface (see Figure 12-9). In addition, photographs must be taken to provide an overall view of the print's location with respect to other evidential items at the crime scene.

Once photographs have been secured, one of two procedures is to be followed. If the object is small enough to be transported without

FIGURE 12–9. Fingerprint camera and its resultant photo.
Courtesy Sirchie Laboratories

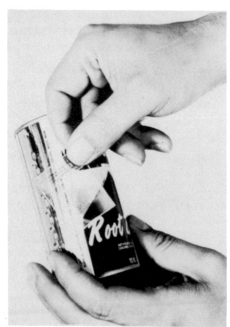

FIGURE 12–10. "Lifting" a fingerprint.
Courtesy Sirchie Laboratories

destroying the print, it should be preserved in its entirety; the print should be covered with cellophane so it will be protected from damage. On the other hand, prints on large immovable objects that have been developed with a powder can best be preserved by "lifting." The most popular type of lifter is a broad adhesive tape similar to scotch tape. If the powdered surface is covered with the adhesive side of the tape and pulled up, the powder will be transferred to the tape. Then the tape is placed on a properly labeled card that offers a good background contrast with the powder.

A variation of this procedure is the use of an adhesive-backed clear plastic sheet which is preassembled to a colored cardboard backing. Before it is applied to the print, a celluloid separator is peeled from the plastic sheet to expose the adhesive lifting surface. The tape is then pressed evenly and firmly over the powdered print and pulled up (see Figure 12-10). The sheet containing the adhering powder is now pressed against the cardboard backing to provide a permanent record of the fingerprint.

REVIEW QUESTIONS

1. The first systematic attempt at personal identification was devised and introduced by _____ .

2. A system of identification relying on precise body measurements is known as _____ .

3. The fingerprint classification system used in most English-speaking countries was devised by _____ .

4. The first systematic and official use of fingerprints for personal identification in the United States was adopted by the New York City Civil Service Commission. (True, False)

5. The individuality of a fingerprint (is, is not) determined by its pattern.

6. A point-by-point comparison of a fingerprint's _____ must be demonstrated in order to prove identity.

7. _____ are a reproduction of friction skin ridges.

8. The form and pattern of skin ridges are determined by the (epidermis, dermal papillae)

9. A permanent scar will form in the skin only when an injury damages the _____ .

10. Fingerprints (can, cannot) be changed during a person's lifetime.

11. The three general patterns into which fingerprints are divided are _____ , _____ , and _____ .

12. The most common fingerprint pattern is the _____ .

13. Approximately five percent of the population have the _____ fingerprint pattern.

14. A loop pattern that opens toward the thumb is known as a(n) (ulnar, radial) loop.

15. The pattern area of the loop is enclosed by two diverging ridges known as _____ .

16. The ridge point nearest the type-line divergence is known as the _____ .

17. All loops must have (one, two) deltas.

18. The approximate center of a loop pattern is called the _____ .

19. If an imaginary line drawn between the two deltas of a whorl pattern touches any of the spiral ridges, the pattern is classified as a (plain whorl, central pocket loop).

20. The simplest of all fingerprint patterns is the _____ .

21. Arches (have, have no) type-lines, deltas or cores.

22. The presence or absence of the _____ pattern is used as a basis for determining the primary classification in the Henry system.

23. The largest category in the primary classification system is (1/1, 1/2)

24. A fingerprint classification system (can, cannot) unequivocally identify an individual.

25. The FINDER system matches prints by comparing the position of bifurcations and ridge endings. (True, False)

26. A fingerprint left by a person with soiled or stained fingertips is called a _____ .

27. _____ fingerprints are impressions left on a soft material.

28. Fingerprint impressions that are not readily visible are called _____ .

29. Fingerprints on porous surfaces are best developed with _____ treatment.

30. _____ vapors will chemically combine with fatty oils to visualize a fingerprint.

31. Fingerprints on hard and non-absorbent surfaces are best developed by the application of a _____ .

32. The chemical _____ visualizes fingerprints by its reaction with amino acids.

33. Chemical treatment with _____ visualizes fingerprints by combining with the salt residues of perspiration.

34. A latent fingerprint is first treated with silver nitrate followed by ninhydrin. (True, False)

35. Once a fingerprint has been visualized, it must first be preserved by _____ .

FURTHER READINGS

Allison, Harrison C., *Personal Identification*. Boston: Holbrook 'Press, 1973.

Banner, Conrad S., and Robert M. Stock, "The FBI's Approach to Automatic Fingerprint Identification—Part I," *FBI Law Enforcement Bulletin*, January 1975, p. 2.

———, "The FBI's Approach to Automatic Fingerprint Identification—Part II," *FBI Law Enforcement Bulletin*, February 1975, p. 26.

Moenssens, André A., *Fingerprint Techniques*. Philadelphia: Chilton Book Co., 1971.

The Science of Fingerprints. Washington, D.C.: U.S. Government Printing Office, 1973.

Audiovisual Presentations

Fingerprints (eighty 35 mm slides and audio tape). Police Science Services, Arlington, Va.

Macroscopic Examination (filmstrip and audio tape). Robert J. Brady Co., Inc., Bowie, Md.

Firearms, Toolmarks and Other Impressions

chapter 13

Just as natural variations in skin ridge patterns and characteristics provide a key to human identification, minute random markings on surfaces can impart individuality to inanimate objects. Structural variations and irregularities caused by scratches, nicks, breaks, and wear permit the criminalist to relate a bullet to a gun, a scratch or abrasion mark to a single tool, or a tire track to a particular automobile. Individualization, a goal so vigorously pursued in all other areas of criminalistics, frequently becomes an attainable reality in firearm and toolmark examination.

Though a portion of this chapter will be devoted to the comparison of surface features for the purposes of bullet identification, a complete description of the services and capabilities of the modern forensic firearms laboratory cannot be restricted just to this one subject, important as it may be. The high frequency of shooting cases has necessitated that the science of firearms identification extend beyond the mere comparison of bullets to include knowledge of the operation of all types of weapons, the restoration of obliterated serial numbers on weapons, the detection and characterization of gunpowder residues on garments and around wounds, the estimation of muzzle-to-target distances, and the detection of powder residues on hands. Each of these functions will be discussed in the following sections of this chapter.

FIREARMS

Bullet Comparisons

It is the inner surface of the barrel of a gun that leaves its markings on a bullet passing through it. These markings are peculiar to each gun. Hence, if one bullet found at the scene of a crime and another test-fired from a suspect's gun show the same markings, the suspect is linked to the crime. Because it is these inner surface striations that are so important for bullet comparison, it is important to know why and how they originate.

The gun barrel is produced from a solid bar of steel that has been hollowed out by drilling. The microscopic drill marks left on the barrel's inner surface are randomly irregular and would in themselves serve to impart a uniqueness to each barrel. However, the manufacture of a barrel requires the additional step of impressing its inner surface with spiral *grooves*, a step known as rifling. As a fired bullet travels through a barrel, it engages the rifling grooves; these grooves will then guide the bullet through the barrel, giving it a rapid spin. This is done because a spinning bullet will not tumble end over end on leaving the barrel, but will remain instead on a true and accurate course. It is the rifling process that produces the spiral grooves in the barrel of a gun (see Figure 13-1). The surfaces of the original bore remaining between the grooves are called *lands*.

The diameter of the gun barrel, sketched in Figure 13-2, measured between opposite lands, is known as the **caliber** of the weapon. Caliber is normally recorded in hundreths of an inch or in millimeters—e.g., .22, .38, and 9 mm. Actually, the term "caliber," as it is commonly applied, is not an exact measurement of the barrel's diameter; for example, a 38 (.38 inches) caliber weapon might actually have a bore diameter that ranges from 0.345 to 0.365 inches.

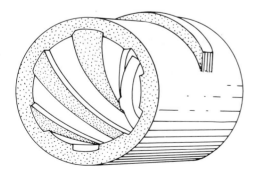

FIGURE 13-1. Interior view of a gun barrel showing the presence of lands and grooves.

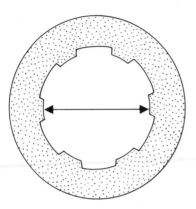

FIGURE 13-2. The cross-section of a barrel with six grooves. The diameter of the bore is the caliber.

Before 1940, barrels were rifled by having one or two grooves at a time cut into the surface with steel hook cutters. The cutting tool was rotated as it passed down the barrel so that the final results were grooves spiraling either to the right or left. However, as the need for increased speed in the manufacture of weapons became apparent, newer techniques were developed that were far more suitable for the mass production of weapons. The broach cutter, shown in Figure 13-3, consists of a series of concentric steel rings, with each ring slightly

FIGURE 13-3. A segment of a broach cutter.

Courtesy New Jersey State Police

larger than the preceding one. As the broach passes through the barrel it simultaneously cuts all the grooves into the barrel at the required depth. The broach is rotated as it passes through the barrel, giving the grooves their desired direction and rate of twist. In contrast to the broach, the button process involves no cuttings. Here, a steel plug or "button" impressed with the desired number of grooves is forced under extremely high pressures through the barrel. A single pass of the button down the barrel forces the metal to flow into the grooves of the button, creating lands and grooves that are negatives of those on the button. The button is rotated to produce the desired direction and rate of twist (Figure 13-4).

Every firearms manufacturer chooses a rifling process that is best suited to meet the production standards and requirements of his product. Once the choice is made, however, the class characteristics of the weapon's barrel will remain consistent; each will have the same number of lands and grooves with the same approximate width and direction of twist. For example, .32 caliber Smith and Wesson revolvers have five lands and five grooves twisting to the right. On the other hand, Colt .32 caliber revolvers exhibit six lands and grooves twisting to the left. Although these class characteristics may prove

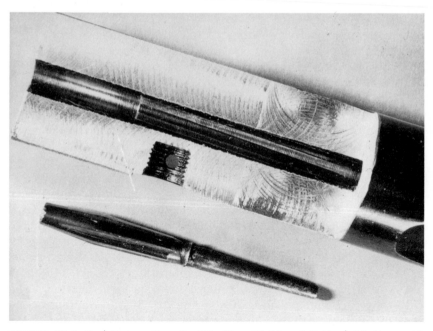

FIGURE 13-4. Top) Cross-section of a .22 caliber rifled barrel. Bottom) A button used to produce the lands and grooves in the barrel.

Courtesy New Jersey State Police

to be of some value in permitting the examiner to distinguish one type or brand-name weapon from another, they will certainly not impart individuality to any one barrel; no class characteristic can do this.

If one could cut a barrel open lengthwise, a careful examination of the interior would reveal the existence of fine lines or striations, many running the length of the barrel's lands and grooves. These striations are impressed into the metal as the negatives of minute imperfections found on the rifling cutter's surface, or they are produced by minute chips of steel pushed against the barrel's inner surface by a moving broach cutter. The fact is that the random distribution and irregularities of these marking are impossible to duplicate exactly in any two barrels. **No two rifled barrels, even those manufactured in succession, will have identical striation markings.** These striations form the individual characteristics of the barrel.

As the bullet passes through the barrel, its surface is impressed with the rifled markings of the barrel. The bullet, in effect, emerges from the barrel carrying the impressions of the bore's interior surface; these impressions reflect both the class and individual characteristics of the barrel (see Figure 13–5). Because there is no practical way of making a direct comparison between the markings on the fired bullet and those found within a barrel, the examiner must obtain test bullets fired through the suspect barrel for comparison. In order to prevent damage to the test bullet's markings and to facilitate the bullet's recovery, test firings are normally made into a recovery box filled with cotton or into a water tank.

The number of lands and grooves, and their direction of twist, are obvious points of comparison during the initial stages of the examination. Any differences in these class characteristics will immediately serve to eliminate the possibility that both bullets traveled through the same barrel. A bullet having five lands and grooves could not possibly have been fired from a weapon of like caliber having six lands and grooves, nor could one having a right twist have come through a barrel impressed with a left twist. Once it has been ascertained that both bullets carry the same class characteristics, the effort must begin to match the striated markings on both bullets. It is an effort that can only be made with the assistance of the comparison microscope (see Chapter 6).

It is no coincidence that modern firearms identification began with the development and utilization of the comparison microscope. This instrument is the single most important tool at the disposal of the firearms examiner. The test and evidence bullets are mounted on cylindrical adjustable holders beneath the objective lenses of the microscope, each pointing in the same direction (see Figure 13–6).

FIGURE 13-5. A bullet impressed with the rifling markings of the barrel after it emerges from the weapon.

Courtesy New Jersey State Police

Both bullets are observed simultaneously within the same field of view, and the examiner rotates one bullet until a well-defined land or groove comes into view. Once the striation markings are located, the other bullet is rotated until a matching region is found. Not only must the lands and grooves of the test and evidence bullet have identical widths, but the longitudinal striations on each must coincide. When a matching area is located, the two bullets are simultane-

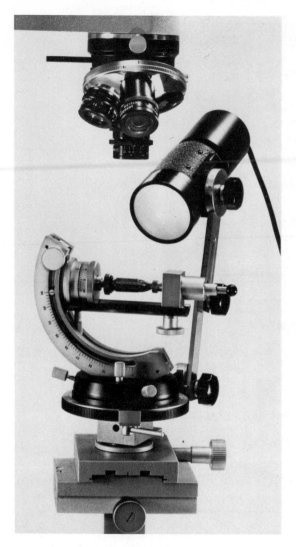

FIGURE 13-6. Bullet holder beneath the objective lens of a comparison microscope.
Courtesy Ernst Leitz

ously rotated to obtain additional matching areas around the periphery of the bullets. Figure 13-7 shows a typical photomicrograph of a bullet match as viewed under a comparison microscope.

Unfortunately, the firearms examiner infrequently encounters a situation in which a perfect match exists all around the bullet's periphery. The presence of grit and rust can to some degree alter the markings on bullets fired through the same barrel. More commonly,

FIGURE 13-7. Photomicrograph of a bullet comparison through a comparison microscope. Test bullet is on the right; the questioned bullet is on the left.

Courtesy Philadelphia Police Dept. Laboratory

recovered evidence bullets may become so mutilated and distorted on impact as to yield only a small area with intact markings. Furthermore, striation markings on a barrel are not permanent structures; they are subject to continuing change and alteration through wear as succeeding bullets traverse the length of the barrel. Fortunately, in most cases, these changes are not dramatic ones and will not prevent the matching of two bullets fired by the same weapon. As with fingerprint comparison, there are no hard and fast rules governing the minimum number of points required for a bullet comparison. The final opinion must be based upon the judgment, experience, and knowledge of the expert.

Frequently, the firearms examiner is presented with a spent bullet without any accompanying suspect weapon and is requested to provide information with regard to the caliber and possible make of the weapon. If the bullet appears not to have lost any of its metal, a probable determination of its caliber can usually be made from its weight. In some instances, the number of lands and grooves, the direction of twist, and the width of lands and grooves are useful class characteristics for eliminating certain makes of weapons from consideration. For example, a bullet that has five lands and grooves and twists to the right could not come from a weapon manufactured by Colt, because Colts are not manufactured with these class characteristics. Sometimes a bullet will have rifling marks that sets it apart from most other manufactured weapons, as in the case of Marlin rifles. These weapons are rifled by a technique known as "micro-grooving," and may have eight to twenty-four grooves impressed into their barrels; few others weapons are manufactured in this fashion. In most cases, however, the firearms examiner will be more successful at eliminating a weapon from consideration rather than at identifying a weapon's make or model solely from class characteristics.

Unlike a rifled firearms, a shotgun has a smooth barrel. It therefore follows that projectiles passing through a shotgun barrel will not be impressed with any characteristic markings that can later be related back to the weapon. Shotguns generally fire small lead balls or pellets contained within a shotshell (see Figure 13-8). A paper or plastic wad pushes the pellets through the barrel upon ignition of the cartridge's powder charge. By weighing and measuring the diameter of the shot recovered at a crime scene, the examiner can usually determine the size of shot used in the shotshell. The size and shape of the recovered wad may also reveal the gauge of the shotgun used and, in some instances, indicate the manufacturer of the fired shotshell.

The diameter of the shotgun barrel is expressed by the term "gauge."[1] The higher the gauge number, the smaller the barrel's diameter. For example, a 10–gauge shotgun has a bore diameter of 0.775 inches as contrasted to 0.662 inches for a 16–gauge shotgun. The exception to this rule is the .410–gauge shotgun, which refers to a barrel .410 inches in diameter.

Cartridge Cases

The act of pulling a trigger serves to release the weapon's firing pin, causing it to strike the primer, which in turn ignites the powder. The expanding gases generated by the burning gunpowder propel the bullet forward through the barrel, simultaneously pushing the spent cartridge case or shell back with equal force against the breechblock. Although the bullet is marked by its passage through the barrel, the shell is also impressed with markings as a result of its contact with

[1]Originally the number of lead balls with the same diameter as the barrel that would make a pound. For example, a 20 gauge shotgun is one having an inside diameter equal to the diameter of a lead ball which weighs 1/20 of a pound.

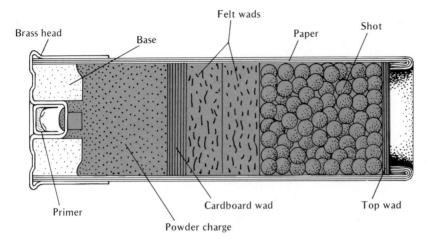

FIGURE 13-8. Cross-section of a loaded shotgun shell.

the metal surfaces of the weapon's firing and loading mechanisms. As with bullets, these marking can be reproduced in test-fired cartridges to provide distinctive points of comparison for individualizing a spent shell to a weapon.

The shape of the firing pin will be impressed into the relatively soft metal of the primer on the cartridge case, revealing the minute distortions of the firing pin. These imperfections may be sufficiently random to individualize the pin impression to a single weapon. Similarly, the cartridge case in its rearward thrust is impressed with the surface markings of the breechblock. The breechblock, like any machined surface, is populated with random striation markings that become a highly distinctive signature for individualizing its surface. Other distinctive markings that may appear on the shell as a result of metal-to-metal contact are caused by the ejector and extractor mechanism, the magazine or clip, as well as imperfections on the fire chamber walls. Photomicrographs in Figure 13-9a and b reveal a comparison of the firing pin and breechblock impressions between evidence and test-fired shells.

Firing pin, breechblock, extractor, and ejector marks may also be impressed onto the surface of the brass portion of shells fired by a shotgun. These impressions provide just as valuable points for individualizing the shell to a weapon as do cartridge cases discharged from a rifled firearm. Furthermore, in the absence of a suspect weapon the size and shape of a firing pin impression, and/or the position of ejector marks in relationship to extractor and other markings may provide some clue as to the type or make of the weapon that may have fired the questioned shell, or at least eliminate a large number of possibilities.

FIGURE 13-9a.

FIGURE 13-9b. Comparison microscope photomicrograph showing a match between (a) firing pin impressions and (b) the breach block markings on two shells.

Courtesy New Jersey State Police

Gunpowder Residues

In incidents involving gunshot wounds, it is often necessary to determine the distance from which the weapon was fired. The degree of importance attached to such a determination is dependent on the severity of the wound and the facts surrounding the shooting. Often in incidents involving a shooting death, the individual apprehended and accused will plead self-defense as the motive for the attack. Such claims are fertile grounds for firing-distance determinations because finding the proximity of the parties involved in the incident is necessary to establish the true facts of the incident. Similarly, a careful examination of the wounds of victims who have supposedly committed suicide usually reveal characteristics associated with a very close-range gunshot wound. The absence of such characteristics is a strong indication that the wound was not self-inflicted and signals the possibility of foul play.

Modern ammunition is propelled toward a target by the expanding gases created by the ignition of smokeless powder or nitrocellulose in a cartridge. Under ideal circumstances, it would be expected that all of the powder would be consumed in the process and converted into rapidly expanding gases. However, in practice this is not the case, because the powder is never totally burned. When a firearm is discharged, unburned and partially burned particles of gunpowder, in addition to smoke, are propelled out of the barrel along with the bullet toward the target. If the muzzle of the weapon is sufficiently close, these products will be deposited onto the target. It is the distribution of gunpowder particles and other discharge residues around the bullet hole that permits an assessment of the distance from which the gun was fired.

The accuracy of a distance determination varies according to the circumstances of the case. In instances in which the investigator is unable to recover a suspect weapon, the best that the examiner can do is to state whether or not a shot could have been fired within some distance interval from the target. More exact opinions are possible only when the examiner has the suspect weapon in hand and has knowledge of the type of ammunition used in the shooting.

The precise distance from which a weapon has been fired must be determined by means of a careful comparison of the powder-residue pattern located on the victim's clothing or skin against test patterns made when the suspect weapon is fired at varying distances from a target. A white cloth or a fabric comparable to the victim's clothing may be used as a test target (see Figure 13-10). Because the spread

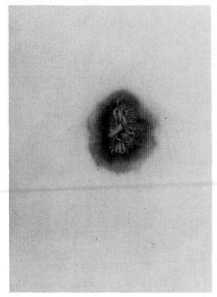

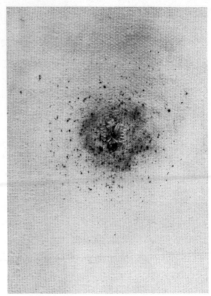

FIGURE 13-10a.   FIGURE 13-10b.

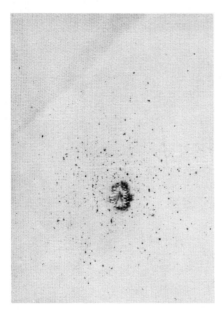

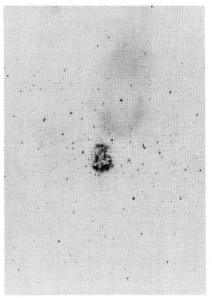

FIGURE 13-10c.   FIGURE 13-10d.

The test powder patterns were made with a .38 Special Smith and Wesson revolver. The muzzle of the weapon was fired at the following distances from the target: a) contact, b) six inches, c) twelve inches, d) eighteen inches.

and density of the residue pattern varies widely between weapons and ammunition, such a comparison is only significant when it is made with the questioned weapon and ammunition, or ammunition of the same type and make. By comparing the test and evidence patterns, the examiner may find enough similarity in shape and density upon which to base an opinion as to the distance from which the shot was fired.

Without the benefit of a weapon, the examiner is restricted to looking for recognizable characteristics around the hole. Such findings are at best approximations made as a result of general observations and knowledge that the examiner has accumulated over an extended period of time spent in firearms examination. There are some noticeable characteristics to be looked for. For instance, in the case in which the weapon is held in contact with or less than one inch from the target, a star-shaped tear pattern may be present (see Figure 13-11). Often, loose fibers surrounding a contact hole will also show scorch marks from the flame discharge of the weapon.

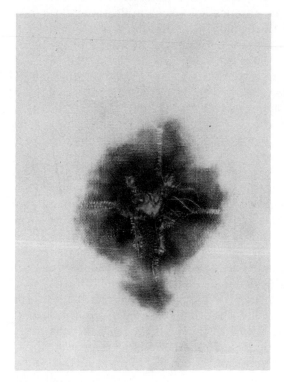

FIGURE 13-11. A contact shot.
Courtesy New Jersey State Police

Carbonaceous smoke or soot deposited around a bullet hole is normally indicative of a discharge 12 to 18 inches or less from the target. The presence of scattered specks of unburned and partially burned powder grains without any accompanying soot can often be observed at distances up to approximately 25 inches. However, occasionally, scattered gunpowder particles will be noted at a firing distance as far out as 36 inches. Finally, a weapon that has been fired more than 3 feet from a target will usually not deposit any powder residues onto the target's surface. In these cases, the only visual indication to characterize the hole as being made by a bullet is a dark ring, known as bullet wipe, around the perimeter of the entrance hole. Bullet wipe consists of a mixture of carbon, dirt, lubricant, primer residue, and lead wiped off the bullet's surface as it passes through the target.

When they are received in the crime laboratory, garments and the surfaces of other evidence relevant to a shooting are first examined microscopically for the presence of gunpowder residue. These particles are readily identifiable by their characteristic color, sizes, and shapes. However, the absence of visual indications does not preclude the possibility that gunpowder residue is present. Sometimes the lack of color contrast between the powder and garment, or the presence of heavily encrusted deposits of blood, can obscure the visual detection of gunpowder. Often, an infrared photograph of the suspect area will overcome the problem. Such a photograph may enhance the contrast, thus revealing soot and powder particles deposited around the hole (see Figure 13-12). In other situations this may not help, and the analyst will need to use a chemical test to detect gunpowder residues.

Nitrites are one type of chemical product that arises from the incomplete combustion of smokeless (nitrocellulose) powder. One test method for locating powder residues involves transferring particles embedded on the target surface to chemically treated gelatin-coated photographic paper. The examiner presses the photographic paper onto the target with a hot iron; once the nitrite particles are on the paper, they are made easily visible by chemical treatment.[2] In addition, comparing the developed nitrite pattern to nitrite patterns obtained from test firings at known distances can be a useful technique for determining the shooting distance from the target.

The determination of firing distances involving shotguns must again be related to test firings performed with the suspect weapon, using the same type of ammunition known to be used in the crime.

[2]P. C. Maiti, "Powder Patterns Around Bullet Holes in Bloodstained Articles," *Journal of the Forensic Science Society*, 13 (1973), 197.

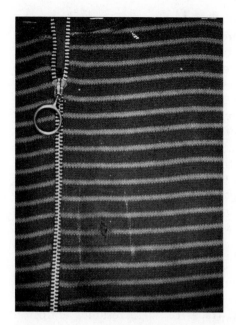

FIGURE 13-12a. Normal photograph of shirt bearing a powder stain.

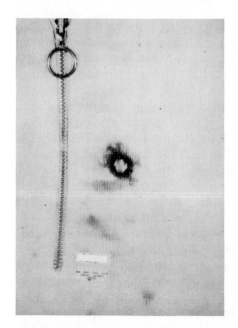

FIGURE 13-12b. Infrared photograph of the same shirt.
Courtesy New Jersey State Police

In the absence of a weapon, the muzzle to target distance can be estimated by measuring the spread of the discharged shot. With close-range shots varying in distance up to 4 or 5 feet, the shot charge enters the target as a concentrated mass, producing a hole somewhat larger than the bore of the barrel. As the distance increases, the pellets progressively separate and spread out. Generally speaking, the spread in the pattern made by a 12-gauge shotgun is increased 1 inch for each yard of distance. Thus, a 10-inch pattern would be produced at approximately 10 yards. Of course, this is only a rule of thumb; normally there are a great number of variables that can affect the shot pattern. Other factors to be taken into consideration include the barrel length, the size and quantity of the pellets fired, the quantity of powder charge used to propel the pellets, and the choke of the gun under examination.

Primer Residues on the Hand

The firing of a weapon not only propels residues toward the target; gunpowder and primer residues are also blown back in the direction of the shooter. As a result, traces of these residues are often deposited on the firing hand of the shooter and their detection can provide valuable information pertaining to whether or not an individual has recently fired a weapon.

Early efforts at demonstrating powder residues on the hands centered on chemical tests that could detect the presence of unburned gunpowder or nitrates. For many years the "dermal nitrate test" enjoyed popularity as such a test. It required the application of hot paraffin or wax to the suspect's hand with a paint brush. After drying into a solid crust, the paraffin was removed and tested with the chemical diphenylamine. The presence of a blue color was taken as an indication of a positive reaction for nitrates (see Table 10-3). However, during recent years the dermal nitrate test has fallen into disfavor with law enforcement agencies owing mainly to its lack of specificity. Common materials such as fertilizers, cosmetics, urine, and tobacco are all known to give positive reactions which are indistinguishable from that obtained for gunpowder by this test.

Current efforts to identify a shooter are now centered on the detection of primer residues deposited on the hand of a shooter at the time of firing. With the exception of most .22 caliber ammunition, primers presently manufactured contain a blend of lead styphnate, barium nitrate, and antimony sulfide. Residues from these materials are most likely to be deposited on the thumb web and the back of the firing hand of a shooter, because these areas are in closest proximity to gases escaping along the side or back of the gun during discharge. In addition, individuals who handle a gun without firing it may have primer residues deposited on the palm of the hand coming in contact with the weapon.

Determination of whether or not a person has fired or handled a weapon is normally made by calculating the amount of barium and antimony on the relevant portions of the suspect's hands. A variety of materials and techniques are now utilized for removing these residues. The most popular approach, and certainly the most convenient from the field investigator's point of view, is to remove any residues present by swabbing both the firing and nonfiring hands with cotton that has been moistened with 5 percent nitric acid. The front and back of each hand is separately swabbed. All four swabs, along with a moistened control, are then forwarded to the crime laboratory for analysis (see Appendix I for a detailed description of residue collection procedures). Another approach involves dipping each hand into a plastic bag filled with dilute nitric or hydrochloric acid. Some investigators advocate using a paraffin lift for removing the barium and antimony. A rather novel method is to apply cellulose acetate mixed with a plasticizer to the suspect's hands. This mixture, known as a "film-lift," is spread by the examiner onto both hands of the suspect; the solution is squeezed out of the nozzle of a polyethylene container.The material dries into a hard film in 3 to 4 minutes and can readily be peeled off.[3]

In any case, once the hands have been treated for the collection of barium and antimony, the collection medium must be analyzed for the presence of the elements. The demonstration of high barium and antimony levels on the suspect's firing hand as compared to the nonfiring hand is a strong indication that that person fired or handled a weapon. Because these elements are normally present after a firing in small quantities (less than 10 micrograms), only the most sensitive of analytical techniques can be used for their detection.

Unfortunately, up until the present time major difficulties have been encountered in examiners' attempts to detect primer residues on suspects' hands. This is reflected by a relatively low rate of positive findings, even though most specimens submitted for this type of analysis are from individuals who are strongly suspected of having fired a gun.

The major difficulty appears to be the short time that primer residues remain on the hands. These residues are readily removed by intentional or unintentional washing or wiping, and even if they are left untouched will be lost through natural absorption into the skin over a period of two hours.[4] Furthermore, the absence of

[3] K. K. S. Pillay, W. A. Jester, and H. A. Fox, "Gunshot Residue Collection Using Film-Lift Techniques," *Forensic Science*, 4 (1974), 145.
[4] J. W. Kilty, "Activity After Shooting and its Effect on the Retention of Primer Residues," *Journal of the Forensic Sciences*, 20 (1975), 219-30.

barium or antimony in .22 rimfire ammunition excludes this common type of projectile from detection.

Until recently, neutron activation analysis (see Chapter 5) was the only method available that demonstrated a sensitivity sufficiently high to be suitable for such a determination. However, the necessity for having access to a nuclear reactor limited this technique to a small number of crime laboratories. Recently, the advent of flameless atomic absorption spectrophotometry has changed this situation (see page 105). Flameless atomic absorption has a sensitivity comparable to that of neutron activation for detecting barium and antimony in hand swabs or washings. Furthermore, the instrument can be purchased at a cost well within the budgets of most crime laboratories. As a result of this development, the immediate future promises to see more crime laboratories expanding their capabilities to perform primer-residue determinations on hands, utilizing the atomic absorption technique.

Recently, a rather novel approach to primer-residue detection has been suggested by researchers at Aerospace Corporation in California.[5] Their analysis procedure requires the application of adhesive tape to the hand's surface in order to remove any adhering residue particles. Microscopic size primer and gunpowder particles on the tape are then located with the aid of a scanning electron microscope (SEM). These particles have a characteristic size and shape which readily distinguishes them from other contaminants present on the hands. When the SEM is linked to an X-ray analyzer (see page 129), an elemental analysis of the particles can be conducted. A finding of any two of the elements lead, barium, and antimony, confirms that the particles did indeed originate from a fired gun.

Whether or not this approach represents an improvement over previous efforts at primer-residue detection remains a question still to be answered.

Serial Number Restoration

Today many manufactured items, including automobile engine blocks and firearms, are impressed with a serial number for identification. Increasingly, the criminalist is requested to restore such a number when it has been removed or obliterated by grinding, filing, or punching.

Serial numbers are usually stamped on a metal body or frame, or on a plate, with hard steel dies. These dies strike the metal surface with a force that allows each digit to sink into the metal at a pre-

[5] R. S. Nesbitt, J. E. Wessel, and P. F. Jones, *Conclusive Detection of Gunshot Residue by the Use of Particle Analysis* (El Segundo, Cal.: Aerospace Corp., 1974).

scribed depth. Restoration of serial numbers can be accomplished because the metal crystals in the stamped zone are placed under a permanent strain that extends a short distance beneath the original numbers. When a suitable etching agent is applied, the strained area will dissolve at a faster rate as compared to the unaltered metal, thus permitting the etched pattern to appear in the form of the original numbers. However, if the zone of strain has been removed, or if the area has been impressed with a different strain pattern, it is usually not possible to restore the number.

Before any treatment with the etching reagent, the obliterated surface must be thoroughly cleaned of dirt and oil and polished to a mirrorlike finish. The reagent is best applied when the polished metal is swabbed with a moistened cotton ball. The choice of etching reagent will depend on the type of metal surface being worked on. A solution consisting of hydrochloric acid (120 ml), copper chloride (90 g.), and water (100 ml) generally works well for steel surfaces.

Collection and Preservation of Firearm Evidence

The protection of class and individual markings on bullets, cartridges, and barrels must be the primary concern of the field investigator who is handling such evidence. Thus, extreme caution is to be exercised when a lodged bullet must be removed from a wall or other object. If the bullet's surface were accidentally scratched during this operation, valuable striation markings could be obliterated. It is best to free bullets from their target by carefully breaking away the surrounding support material while avoiding direct contact with the projectile.

The Hollywood image of an investigator picking up a weapon by its barrel with a pencil or stick is one that must be avoided. This practice will only serve to disturb powder deposits, rust, or dirt lodged in the barrel, and consequently may alter the striation markings on test-fired bullets. If the recovery of latent fingerprints is a primary concern, it is best to hold the weapon by the edge of the trigger guard or by the checkered portion of the grip, which usually does not retain identifiable fingerprints.

Just like any other type of physical evidence recovered at a crime scene, firearm evidence must be marked for identification and a chain of custody must be established. Therefore, when firearms are recovered, an identification tag should be attached to the trigger guard. The tag should be marked to show appropriate identifying data, including the weapon's serial number, make, model, and the investigator's initials. The firearm itself may be further identified by being marked directly with a sharp-pointed scriber in an inconspicuous area of the weapon—e.g., the inside of the trigger guard. This practice will avoid any permanent defacement of a weapon.

Bullets recovered at the crime scene are scribed with the investigator's initials either on the base or the nose of the bullet (Figure 13-13). Again, the obliteration of striation markings that may be present on the bullet must be scrupulously avoided. If the bullet is badly deformed and there is no apparent place for identification, it should just be placed in a container that is appropriately marked for identification. In any case, the investigator must protect the bullet by wrapping it in tissue paper before placing it in a pill box or an envelope for shipment to the crime laboratory. Similarly, a fired casing must be marked in a manner that will avoid the destruction of marks impressed on it from the weapon. This is best marked for identification with the investigator's initials, placed either near the outside or inside mouth of the shell (see Figure 13-14). Discharged shells from shotguns are initialed with ink or indelible pencil on the paper or plastic tube remaining on the shell, or on the metal nearest the mouth of the shell. In addition, in situations in which semi-automatic or automatic weapons have been fired, the ejection pattern of the casings can help establish the relationship of the suspect to his victim. For this reason, the exact location of the place a shell casing was recovered is important information that must be noted by the investigator.

Before any weapon is sent to the laboratory, all precautions must be taken to prevent an accidental discharge of a loaded weapon in transit. In most cases, it will be necessary to unload the weapon. If this is done, a record should first be made of the weapon's hammer and safety position; likewise, the location of all fired and unfired ammunition in the weapon must be recorded. When a revolver is

FIGURE 13-13. Discharged evidence bullets should be marked on the base or the nose. When there is more than one bullet a number should accompany the initials. NEVER mark bullets on the side.

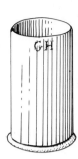

FIGURE 13-14. Discharged evidence shells should be marked on the outside or inside as close to the mouth of the shell as possible. Discharged shotgun shells should be marked on the brass close to the paper or plastic: NEVER mark the shells where the firing pin strikes the primer.

recovered, the chamber position in line with the barrel should be indicated by a scratch mark on the cylinder. A diagram should also be made to show the chamber position of each cartridge or cartridge casing as it is removed from the weapon. Knowledge of the cylinder position of a cartridge case may be useful for later determining the sequence of events, particularly in shooting cases where more than one shot was fired.

When a weapon is recovered from underwater, no effort must be made to dry or clean it. Instead, the firearm should be transported to the laboratory in a receptacle containing enough of the same water necessary to keep it submerged. This procedure will prevent rust from developing during transport.

TOOLMARKS

A toolmark is considered to be any impression, cut, gouge, or abrasion caused by a tool coming into contact with another object. Most often, toolmarks are encountered at burglary offenses that involve the forcible entry into a building or safe. Generally, toolmarks occur in the form of indented impressions into a softer surface or as abrasion marks caused by the tool cutting or sliding against another object.

Typically, an indented impression is left on the frame of a door or window as a result of the prying action of a screwdriver or crowbar. A careful examination of these impressions can reveal important class characteristics—i.e., the size and shape of the tool. However, they rarely reveal any significant individual characteristics that could permit the examiner to individualize the mark to a single tool. Such characteristics, when they do exist, usually take the form of discernible random nicks and breaks which the tool has acquired through wear and use (Figure 13-15).

Just as the machined surfaces of a firearm are impressed with random striations during its manufacture, the edges of a pry bar, chisel, screwdriver, knife, and cutting tool will likewise display a series of microscopic irregularities having the appearance of ridges and valleys. Such markings are left as a result of the machining processes used to cut and finish the tools. The shape and pattern of such minute imperfections are further modified by damage and wear during the life of the tool. Considering the unending variety of pat-

FIGURE 13-15. A comparison of a toolmark with a suspect screwdriver. Note how the presence of nicks and breaks on the tool's edge helps individualize the tool to the mark.
Courtesy New Jersey State Police

terns that the hills and valleys can assume, it is highly unlikely that any two tools will be identical. Hence, it is the presence of these minute imperfections that imparts individuality to each tool.

If the edge of a tool is scraped against a softer surface, it may cut a series of striated lines that reflect that pattern of the tool's edge. Markings left in this manner are compared in the laboratory through a comparison microscope with test toolmarks made from the suspect tool. The result can be a positive comparison, and hence a definitive association of the tool with the evidence mark, when a sufficient quantity of striations match between the evidence and test markings.

One of the major problems associated with toolmark comparisons is the difficulty in duplicating in the laboratory the toolmark left at the crime scene. A thorough comparison requires the preparation of a series of test marks obtained by applying the suspect tool at various angles and pressures to a soft metal surface (lead is commonly used). This approach gives the examiner ample opportunity to duplicate many of the details of the original evidence marking. A photomicrograph of a typical toolmark comparison is illustrated in Figure 13–16.

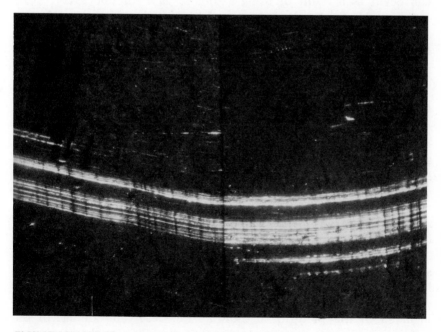

FIGURE 13-16. A photograph of a toolmark comparison seen under a comparison microscope.

Courtesy Ernst Leitz

Whenever it is practical, the entire object or the part of the object bearing a toolmark should be submitted to the crime laboratory for examination. When removal of the toolmark is impractical, the only recourse left to the field investigator is to photograph the marked area to scale and make a cast of the mark. Under these circumstances, liquid silicone casting material or dental plaster has been found to be the most satisfactory for reproducing most of the fine details of the mark. However, even under the most optimum conditions, the clarity of many of the toolmark's minute details will be lost or obscured in a photograph or cast. Of course, this will reduce the possibility that the criminalist could individualize the mark to a single tool.

The suspect tool and mark must be packaged in separate containers, with every precaution taken to avoid contact between the tool or mark with another hard surface. Failure to properly protect the tool or mark from damage could result in the destruction of their individual characteristics. Furthermore, the investigator must bear in mind that the tool or its impression may contain valuable trace evidence. Chips of paint adhering to the mark or tool provide perhaps the best example of how the transfer of trace physical evidence can occur as a result of using a tool to gain forcible entry into a building. Obviously, the presence of trace evidence greatly enhances the evidential value of the tool or its mark, and requires that special care be taken in the handling and packaging of the evidence to avoid the loss or destruction of these items.

OTHER IMPRESSIONS

From time to time impressions of another kind are left at a crime scene. This evidence may take the form of a shoe, tire, or fabric impression, and may be as varied as a shoe impression left on a piece of paper at the scene of a burglary (Figure 13-17), a hit-and-run victim's garment that has come into violent contact with an automobile (Figure 13-18), or the impression of a bloody shoeprint left on a floor or carpet at a homocide scene (Figure 13-19).

The primary consideration in collecting impressions at the crime scene is the preservation of the impression or its reproduction, for later examination in the crime laboratory. Before any impression is moved or otherwise handled, it must be photographed (a scale is included in the picture) to show all the observable details of the impression. Several shots are to be taken directly over the impression as well as at various angles around the impression. The skillful use of side lighting for illumination will help highlight many ridge details

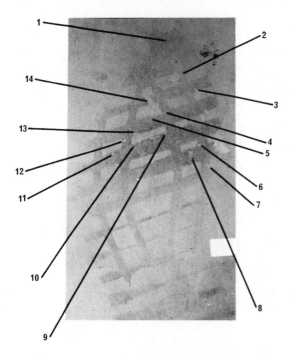

FIGURE 13-17a. Impression of shoe found at the crime scene.

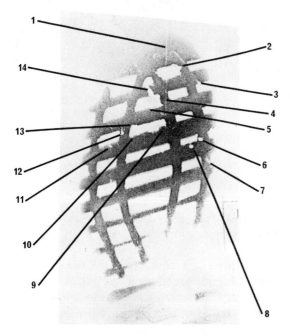

FIGURE 13-17b. Test impression made with suspect shoe.
Courtesy New Jersey State Police

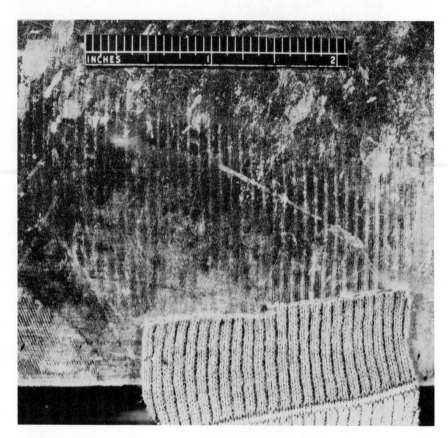

FIGURE 13-18. A small child was found dead at the edge of a rural road near a railroad crossing, the victim of a hit-and-run driver. A local resident was suspected, however he denied any knowledge of the incident. The investigating officer noted what appeared to be a fabric imprint on the bumper of the suspect's automobile. The weave pattern of the clothing of the deceased was compared with the imprint on the bumper and found to compare. When the suspect was confronted with this information he admitted his guilt.

Courtesy The Centre of Forensic Sciences

that may otherwise remain obscured. Photographs should also be taken to show the position of the questioned impression in relation to the overall crime scene.

While photography is an important first step in preserving an impression, it still must only be considered as a backup procedure that is available to the examiner if the impression is damaged before reaching the crime laboratory. Naturally, it is far more preferable for the examiner to receive the original impression for comparison to the suspect shoe, tire, garment, etc. In most instances where the impression is on a readily recoverable item, such as glass, paper, or floor

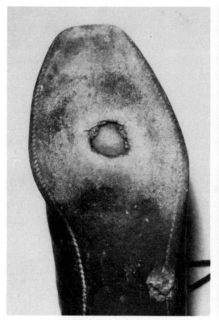 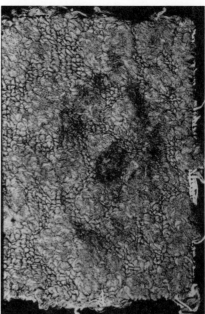

FIGURE 13-19a.   FIGURE 13-19b.

A bloody imprint of a shoe was found on the carpet in the home of a homicide victim. The suspect's shoe shown above made the impression. Note the distinctive impression of the hole present in the shoe's sole.

Courtesy Dade County Crime Laboratory, Miami, Florida

tile, little or no difficulty is presented in transporting the evidence intact to the laboratory.

If an impression is encountered on a surface that cannot be submitted to the laboratory, the investigator may be able to preserve the print in a manner that is analogous to lifting a fingerprint. This is especially true of impressions made in light deposits of dust or dirt. Here wide strips of clear adhesive tape placed over the impression will permit the investigator to lift the impression off the surface. Following this, the tape is placed on a cardboard backing whose color is chosen to provide the best contrasting background to the material composing the impression.

When shoe and tire marks are impressed into soft earth at a crime scene, their preservation is best accomplished by photography and casting. The most frequently used medium for casting is plaster of Paris. A liquid silicone rubber compound is also gaining popularity as a casting material.

Whatever the circumstances, the laboratory procedures used for examining any type of impression remains the same. Of course a comparison is only possible when an item suspected of having made the impression is recovered. Test impressions may be necessary to compare the characteristics of the suspect item with the evidence impression. The evidential value of the impression will be determined by the number of class and individual characteristics that the examiner finds. Agreement with respect to size, shape, or design may permit the conclusion that the impression *could* have been made by a particular shoe, tire, or garment; however, one cannot entirely exclude other possible sources from having the same class characteristics. More significant is the existence of individual characteristics arising out of wear, cuts, gouges, or other damage. A sufficient number or the uniqueness of such points of comparison will support a finding that both the evidence and test impressions originated from one and only one source.

REVIEW QUESTIONS

1. The _____ is the original part of the bore left after rifling grooves are formed.

2. The diameter of the gun barrel is known as its _____ .

3. The number of lands and grooves is a (class, individual) characteristic of a barrel.

4. The (individual, class) characteristics of a rifled barrel are formed by striations impressed into the barrel's surface.

5. The single most important instrument for comparing bullets is the _____ .

6. If bullets were fired in succession from the same weapon, all the individual characteristics would always be identical. (True, False)

7. It is (always, sometimes) possible to determine the make of a weapon by examining a bullet it fired.

8. A shotgun has a (rifled, smooth) barrel.

9. The diameter of a shotgun barrel is expressed by the term _____.

10. Shotgun pellets can be individualized to a single weapon. (True, False)

11. A cartridge case (can, cannot) be individualized to a single weapon.

12. The shape of the indentation caused by the firing pin may be a characteristic peculiar to a firearm. (True, False)

13. The distribution of gunpowder particles and other discharge residues around a bullet hole permits a determination of the distance from which the gun was fired. (True, False)

14. Without the benefit of a weapon, an examiner can make an exact determination of firing distance. (True, False)

15. Carbonaceous smoke or soot deposited around a bullet hole is normally indicative of a discharge _____ to _____ inches from the target.

16. An _____ photograph may help visualize gunpowder deposits around a target.

17. As a rule-of-thumb the spread in the pattern made by a 12-gauge shotgun is increased 1 inch for every _____ of distance from the target.

18. Current methods for identifying a shooter rely on the detection of (primer, gunpowder) residues on the hands.

19. Determining whether or not an individual has fired a weapon is done by measuring the elements _____ and _____ present on the hands.

20. Restoration of serial numbers is possible because in the stamped zone the metal is placed under a permanent strain that extends beneath the original numbers. (True, False)

21. It (is, is not) proper to insert a pencil into a barrel in picking up the weapon.

22. Recovered bullets are initialed either on the _____ or _____ of the bullet.

23. Cartridge cases are best marked at the base of the shell. (True, False)

24. A _____ is any impression caused by a tool coming into contact with another object.

25. Toolmarks compare only when a sufficient number of _____ match between the evidence and test markings.

26. A wear pattern can impart (class, individual) characteristics to a shoe.

FURTHER READINGS

Abbott, J. R., and A. C. Germann, *Footwear Evidence*. Springfield, Ill.: Charles C. Thomas, 1964.

Barnes, F. C., and R. A. Helson, "An Empirical Study of Gunpowder Residue Patterns," *Journal of the Forensic Sciences*, 19 (1974), 448.

Davis, J., *Tool Marks, Firearms and the Striagraph*. Springfield, Ill.: Charles C. Thomas, 1958.

Kirk, Paul L., *Crime Investigation*, 2nd ed. John I. Thornton, ed. New York: Wiley & Sons, 1974.

Moenssens, André A., Ray E. Moses, and Fred R. Inbau, *Scientific Evidence in Criminal Cases*. Mineola, N.Y.: Foundation Press, 1973.

Wessel, J. E., P. F. Jones, Q. Y. Kuan, R. S. Nesbitt, and E. J. Rattin, *Equipment Systems Improvement Program—Gunshot Residue Detection*. El Segundo, Cal.: The Aerospace Corp., 1974.

Wilhelm, Russell M., "General Consideration of Firearms Identification and Ballistics," in *Medicolegal Investigation of Death*, Werner U. Spitz and Russell S. Fisher, eds. Springfield, Ill.: Charles C. Thomas, 1973.

Audiovisual Presentations

Comparative Micrography (filmstrip and audio tape), Robert J. Brady Co., Inc., Bowie, Md.

Document and Voice Examination

chapter 14

DOCUMENTS

Ordinarily, the work of the document examiner involves the examination of handwriting and typewriting to ascertain the source or authenticity of a questioned document. However, document examination is not just restricted to a mere visual comparison of words and letters. The document examiner must know how to utilize the techniques of microscopy, photography, and even such analytical methods as chromatography to successfully uncover all efforts, both brazen and subtle, designed to change the content or meaning of a document. Alterations of documents through overwritings, erasures, or the more obvious crossing-out of words must be recognized and characterized by the examiner as efforts intended to alter or obscure the original meaning of a document. It is the special skills of the document examiner that are relied upon to reconstruct the written contents of charred or burned paper, or to uncover the meaning of indented writings found on a paper pad after the top sheet has been removed.

Any object that contains handwritten or typewritten markings whose source or authenticity is in doubt may be referred to as a "questioned document." Such a broad definition certainly covers all of the written and printed materials that are normally encountered in our daily, social, and business activities. Letters, checks, drivers' licenses, contracts, wills, voter registrations, passports, petitions, and even lottery tickets are the more common specimens received in crime laboratories to be examined. However, we need not restrict our examples to paper documents. Questioned documents may include writings or other markings found on walls, windows, doors, or any other objects.

It must be emphasized that document examiners possess no mystical powers or scientific formulas for identifying the authors of writings. Their success is predicated on applying knowledge gathered through years of training and experience to recognizing and comparing the individual characteristics of questioned and known authentic writings. For this purpose the gathering of documents of known authorship or origin is critical to the outcome of the examination. Collecting known writings may entail considerable time and effort, and their collection may be further hampered by uncooperative or missing witnesses. However, the uniqueness of handwriting makes this type of physical evidence, like fingerprints, one of few definitive individual characteristics available to the investigator; a fact that certainly justifies an extensive investigative effort.

Handwriting Comparisons

Document experts continually testify to the fact that no two individuals write exactly alike. This is not to say that there cannot be marked resemblances between two individuals' handwritings, for there are many factors that comprise the total character of a person's writing. Perhaps the most obvious feature of writings to the layman is its general style. As children we all learn to write by attempting to copy letters that match a standard form or style shown to us by our teachers. The style of writing acquired by the learner is that which is fashionable for the particular time and locale. In the United States, for example, the two most widely used systems are the Palmer, first introduced in 1880, and the Zaner-Bloser, introduced in about 1895. To some extent, both of these systems are taught in nearly all of the fifty states.

The early stages that accompany the learning and practicing of penmanship are characterized by a conscious effort on the part of the student to copy standard letter forms. It is not surprising that many pupils in handwriting class tend at first to have writing styles that are similar, with minor differences attributable to skill in copying. However, as initial writing skills improve, a child normally passes through stages in which the nerve and motor responses associated with the act of writing become subconscious efforts. Writing now begins to take on innumerable habitual shapes and patterns that distinguishes it from all others. It is precisely these unique writing traits that the document examiner looks for.

The unconscious handwriting of two different individuals can never be duplicated. Individual variations associated with mechanical, physical, and mental functions make it extremely unlikely that all these factors can be exactly reproduced by any two individuals. Thus, variations are expected in angularity, slope, speed, pressure, letter and word spacings, relative dimensions of letters, connections, pen movement, writing skill, and finger dexterity. Furthermore, many other factors besides pure handwriting characteristics are to be considered. The arrangement of the writing on the paper may be as distinctive as the writing itself. Margins, spacings, crowding, insertions, and alignment are all results of personal habits. Spelling, punctuation, phraseology, and grammar can be personal, and if so, combine to individualize the writer.

In a problem involving the authorship of handwriting, all characteristics of both the known and questioned documents must be considered and compared. Dissimilarities between the two is a strong indication of two writers, unless these differences can logically be accounted for by the facts surrounding the preparation of the documents. Because any single characteristic, even the most unique one, may be found in the handwriting of other individuals, no one single handwriting characteristic can by itself be taken as basis for a positive comparison. The final conclusion must be based on a sufficient number of common characteristics between the known and questioned writings to effectively preclude the chance of their having originated from two different sources.

What constitutes a sufficient number of personal characteristics? Here again, there are no hard and fast rules for making such a determination. This is a judgment that can only be made by the expert examiner in the context of each particular case.

When the examiner is presented with a reasonable amount of known handwriting for comparison, there is usually little difficulty in finding sufficient evidence to determine the source of questioned document. Frequently however, circumstances may prevent a positive conclusion, or may only permit the expression of a qualified opinion. Such situations usually develop when an insufficient number of known writings are made available for comparison. Although nothing may be found that definitely points to the questioned and known handwriting being of a different origin, there may not be enough personal characteristics present in the known writings that are consistent with the questioned materials.

Difficulties may also arise when the examiner is presented with questioned writings containing only a few words, all deliberately written in a crude unnatural form, or all very carefully written and thought out so as to disguise the writer's natural style—this is a situation usually encountered with threatening or obscene letters. It is extremely difficult to compare a handwriting that has been very carefully prepared to a document written with such little thought for structural details that it only contains the subconscious writing habits of the writer. However, though it may be relatively easy to change one's writing habits for a few words or sentences, the task of maintaining such an effort grows more difficult with each additional word. When there is an adequate amount of writing available to the examiner the attempt at total disguise may fail. This was illustrated in the recent attempt by Clifford Irving to forge letters in the name of Howard Hughes in order to obtain lucrative publishing contracts for Hughes' life story. Figure 14-1 shows the forged signatures of

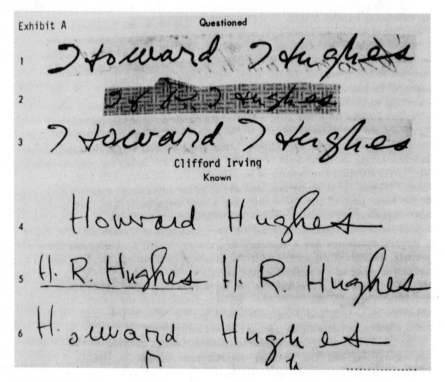

FIGURE 14-1.

Reprinted by permission of the American Society and Materials from The Journal of Forensic Sciences, copyright 1975.

Howard Hughes along with Clifford Irving's known writings. By comparing these signatures, document examiner R. A. Cabbane of the U.S. Postal Inspection Service detected many examples of Irving's personal characteristics in the forged signatures. For example, note the formation of the letter "r" in the word "Howard" on line 1 and 3, as compared with the composite on line 6. Observe the manner in which the terminal stroke of the letter "r" has a tendency to terminate with a little curve at the baseline of writing on Irving's writing and the forgery. Notice the way the bridge of the "w" drops in line 1 and also in line 6. Also, observe the similarity in the formation of the letter "g" as it appears on line 1 as compared with the second signature on line 5.

The document examiner must also be aware of the fact that writing habits may be altered beyond recognition by the influence of drugs or alcohol. Under these circumstances, it may be impossible to obtain known writings of a suspect written under conditions comparable to those in existence at the time the questioned document was prepared.

The Collection of Handwriting Exemplars

It should be fairly obvious by now that the collection of an adequate number of known writings is most critical for determining the outcome of the comparison. Generally, known writings of the suspect furnished to the examiner should be as alike as possible to the questioned document. This is especially true with respect to the writing implement and paper. Styles and habits may be somewhat altered if a person switches from a pencil to a ballpoint pen or to a fountain pen. The way the paper is ruled, or the fact that it is unruled, may also affect the handwriting of a person who has become particularly accustomed to one type or the other. Known writings should also contain some of the words and combinations of letters present in the questioned document.

The known writings must be adequate in number to show the examiner the range of natural variations in a suspect's writing characteristics. No two specimens of writing prepared by one person are ever identical in every detail. Variation is an inherent part of natural writing. The amount and kind of variation differs among writers. In fact, a signature forged by the tracing of an authentic signature can readily be detected if the original and tracing are shown to coincide exactly. No one ever signs two signatures exactly alike.

There are a great many sources to which the investigator can refer in the collection of genuine writings of a suspect. One hundred and six common sources of handwritings are listed in Appendix I ("Guide to the Collection of Physical Evidence"). However, an important consideration in selecting such writings is the age of the genuine document relative to the questioned one. It is important to try to find standards that date closely in time to the questioned document. For most typical adults, basic writing changes are comparatively slow. Therefore, material written within two or three years of the disputed writing are usually found satisfactory for comparison; but, as the age difference between the genuine and unknown specimens becomes greater, the standard has a tendency to become less representative.

Despite the many potential sources of handwriting exemplars, it may be difficult or impossible to obtain an adequate set of collected standards. In these situations handwriting may have to be obtained voluntarily or under court order from the suspect. There is ample case law to support the constitutionality of taking handwriting specimens. In the case of *Gilbert* v. *California*[1] the Supreme Court upheld the taking of handwriting exemplars before the appointment of counsel. The Court reasoned that handwriting samples are identifying physical characteristics that lie outside the protection privileges of the Fifth Amendment. Furthermore, in the case of *United States* v. *Mara*[2] the Supreme Court ruled that the taking of handwriting did not constitute an unreasonable search and seizure of a person and hence was not in violation of the Fourth Amendment rights.

As opposed to nonrequested specimens, written without the thought that they may someday be used in a police investigation, requested writings may not be a totally subconscious effort on the part of the writer. However, the investigator can take certain steps to minimize attempts at deception. The requirement of several pages of writing will normally provide the examiner with enough material that is free of attempts at deliberate disguise or nervousness to permit a valid comparison to be made. In addition, the writing of dictation yields exemplars best representative of the suspect's subconscious style and characteristics.

Other steps that can be taken to minimize a conscious writing effort, as well as to insure conditions approximating those of the questioned writing, can be summarized as follows:

1. The writer should be allowed to write sitting comfortably at a desk or table and without distraction.

2. The suspect should not under any conditions be shown the questioned document or be provided with instructions on how to spell certain words or what punctuation to use.

[1]388 U.S. 263 (1967).
[2]410 U.S. 19 (1973).

3. The suspect should be furnished a pen and paper similar to those used in the questioned document.

4. The dictated text may be the same as the contents of the questioned document, or at least should contain many of the same words, phrases, and letter combinations found in the document. In handprinting cases, the suspect must not be given any instruction on whether to use upper-case (capital) or lower-case (small) lettering. If, after writing several pages, the writer fails to use the desired type of lettering he can then be instructed to include it. All together, the text must be no shorter than a page.

5. Dictation of the text should take place at least three times. If the writer is making a deliberate effort to disguise his writing, noticeable variations should appear between the three repetitions. Discovering this, the investigator must insist upon continued repetitive dictation of the text.

6. Signature exemplars can best be obtained when the suspect is required to combine other writings with a signature. For example, instead of compiling a set of signatures alone, the writer might be asked to completely fill out twenty to thirty separate checks or receipts, each of which includes a signature.

7. Before requested exemplars are taken from the suspect, a document examiner should be consulted and shown the questioned specimens.

Typewriting Comparisons

The most common mechanical writing device the document examiner encounters is the typewriter. The two requests most often made of the examiner in connection with the examination of these machines are: (1) Can the make and model of the typewriter used to type the questioned document be identified, and (2) Can a particular suspect typewriter be identified as having prepared the questioned document?

To answer the first request, the examiner must have access to a complete reference collection of past and present typefaces used by typewriter manufacturers. The two most popular typeface sizes are "pica" and "elite." Though there may be a dozen manufacturers, for example, utilizing a pica typeface, many of these are readily distinguishable when a comparison is made of the individual type character's style, shape, and size.

As is true for any mechanical device, use of a typewriter will result in wear and damage to the machine's moving parts. These changes will occur in a fashion that is both random and irregular, thereby imparting individual characteristics to the typewriter. Variations in the vertical alignment and spacing of the characters, as well as defects in each typeface, are most valuable for proving the identity of a typewriter (see Figure 14-2).

The method of associating a particular typewriter with a typewritten document requires the comparison of the questioned document to exemplars prepared from the suspect typewriter. As with handwriting, the collection of proper standards is the foundation of such comparisons. In this respect, it is preferable if the investigator can directly supply the document examiner with the questioned typewriter. This arrangement gives the examiner the opportunity to prepare an adequate number of exemplars as well as allowing for a direct examination of the machine's typefaces. In the case of IBM Selectric typewriters, the problem of securing the entire typing mechanism is made more difficult because the interchangeability of type-head spheres. Here the typewriter as well as the suspect sphere must be secured for examination.

If the investigator has to prepare standards from the questioned machine, a minimum of one copy in full word-for-word order of the questioned typewriting must be obtained. In preparing standards from a machine with an adjustable touch control, partial copies of the questioned text should be typed in light, medium, and heavy

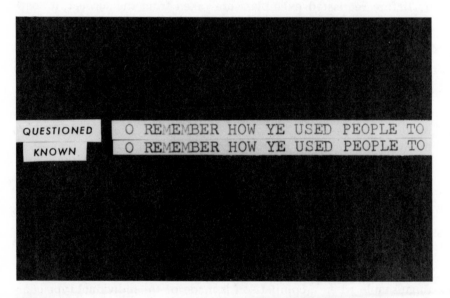

FIGURE 14-2. A portion of a typewriting comparison points to the conclusion that the same machine typed both specimens. Besides the similarity in the design and size of the type, note the light impression consistently made by "M". Also "E" slants to the right almost touching "D" in the word "USED" in both specimens.

Courtesy New Jersey State Police

touches, respectively. One point that is not to be overlooked by either the investigator or the document examiner is the condition of the ribbon. Replacing a worn ribbon with a fresh one makes a significant difference in the typewritten copy. A lightly inked ribbon tends to emphasize slight defects; a well-inked ribbon is likely to obscure them. If exemplars prepared with the ribbon in use differ substantially from the questioned document with respect to inkings, additional standards which more nearly duplicate the questioned document may have to be prepared after consultation with a document examiner. In addition, samples of each character on the keyboard should be typed without the ribbon. To do this, the investigator sets the typewriter in the stencil position and types directly on carbon paper placed over bond paper. This step eliminates any apparent type deformities that may be caused by the condition of the ribbon. Furthermore, an examination of the type impressions left on a ribbon may make it possible to find the portion of the ribbon on which a particular text was typed.

In situations in which apprehension of the suspect typewriter is not possible, the investigator must set about gathering known writings that have been typed on the suspect machine. Ideally, material should be selected that contains many of the same combinations of letters and words found on the questioned document. The individual defects that may characterize a typewriter develop and change as the machine is used; some may have altered during the period of time between the preparation of the questioned and standard material. Hence, if a large quantity of specimens is available, those prepared near the time of the disputed document should be collected.

Alterations, Erasures, and Obliterations

On many occasions, documents are altered or changed after preparation so that their original intent may be hidden or so a forgery may be perpetrated. Documents can be changed in several ways, and for each, the application of a special discovery technique is necessary.

One of the most common ways to alter a document is to try to erase parts of it, using an India rubber eraser, sandpaper, razor blade, or knife to remove writing or type by abrading or scratching the paper's surface. All such attempts at erasure disturb the upper fibers of the paper. These changes are readily apparent when the suspect area is examined under a microscope using direct light or by allowing the light to strike the paper obliquely from one side (side lighting). Although microscopy may reveal whether or not an erasure has been made, it will not necessarily indicate the original letters or words present. Sometimes so much of the paper has been removed that it is impossible to identify the original contents.

In addition to abrading the paper, the perpetrator may also choose to obliterate words with a chemical erasure. In this case, strong oxidizing agents are placed over the ink; a reaction occurs which produces a colorless reaction product. Though such an attempt may not be noticeable to the normal eye, examination under the microscope will reveal a discoloration on the treated area of the paper. Sometimes examination of the document under ultraviolet or infrared lighting will reveal the chemically treated portion of paper.

The fraudulent changing of words or numbers, whether to replace erased material or to change words or numbers (for example, adding zeros to increase the value of a number), is best detected by examination under a microscope. Such an examination will show up small differences in the colors of ink used or in the style of writing. Photography with infrared film may also reveal that the forgery was prepared with an ink different from what was used in the original (see Figure 14-3).

Close examination of a questioned document sometimes reveals crossing strokes or strokes across folds or perforations in the paper that are not in a sequence that is consistent with the natural preparation of the document. Again, these differences can be shown by microscopic and/or photographic scrutiny.

The intentional obliteration of writing by overwriting or crossing out is seldom used for fraudulent purposes because of its obviousness. Nevertheless, such cases may be encountered in all types of documents. Success at permanently hiding the original writing will depend on the material that is used to cover the writing. If it is done with the same ink as was used to write the original material, recovery will be difficult, if not impossible. However, if the two inks are of a different chemical composition, photography with infrared-sensitive film may reveal the original writing. Infrared radiation may pass through the upper layer of writing while being absorbed by the underlying area (see Figure 14-4).

Photography is sometimes successfully used to reveal the contents of a document that has been accidentally or purposely charred in a fire. A common way to decipher charred documents involves reflecting light off the paper's surface at different angles in order to contrast the writing against the charred background. (see Figure 14-5).

Other Document Problems

Indented writings are the partially visible depressions appearing on a sheet of paper underneath the one on which the visible writing

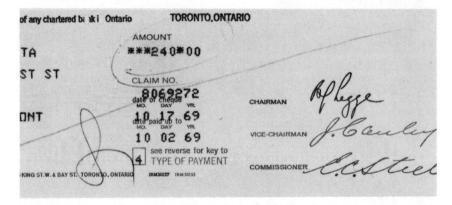

FIGURE 14-3a.

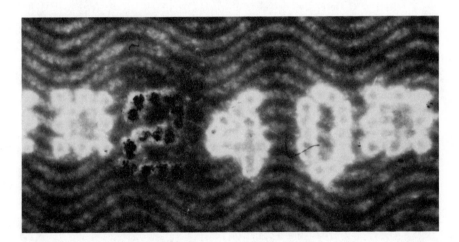

FIGURE 14-3b. A number of checks were stolen from a government agency and altered by an employee. Part of one check as it appears to the naked eye is shown in (a). An infrared luminescence photograph was prepared of the amount figures at a magnification of 10X (b). This clearly shows that the number "2" was added with a different ink. The accused pleaded guilty.

Courtesy The Centre of Forensic Sciences

was done. Such depressions are due to the application of pressure on the writing instrument and would appear as a carbon copy of a sheet if carbon paper had been inserted between the pages.

In certain situations, indented writings have proved to be valuable evidence. For example, the top sheet of a bookmaker's records may have been removed and destroyed, but it still may be possible to determine the writing by the impressions left on the pad. These impressions may contain incriminating evidence supporting the charge of illegal gambling activities. When paper is studied under

FIGURE 14-4a. The top photograph shows an area of a document which has been blacked out with a heavy layer of ink overwriting. Below, the covering ink has been penetrated by infrared photography to reveal the original writing.

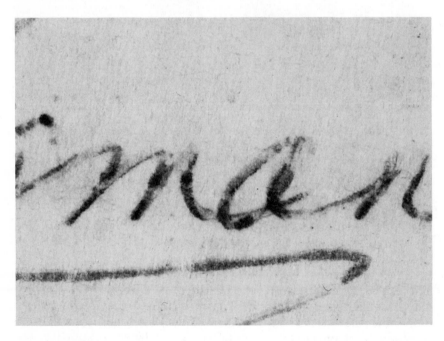

FIGURE 14-4b.

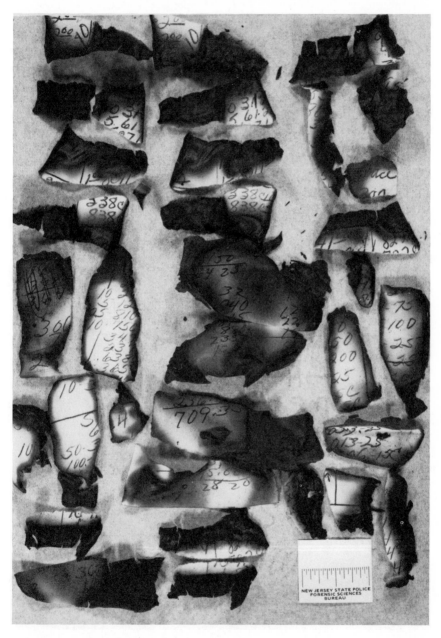

FIGURE 14-5. Decipherment of charred papers seized in the raid of a suspected book-making establishment. The charred documents were photographed with reflected light. Courtesy New Jersey State Police

343

oblique or side lighting, its indented impressions are often readable (see Figure 14-6).

A study of the chemical composition of writing ink present on documents may verify whether or not known and questioned documents were prepared by the same pen. Thin-layer chromatography is particularly suitable for ink comparisons. Most commercial inks, especially ballpoint inks, are actually mixtures of several organic dyes. These dyes can readily be separated on a properly developed thin-layer chromatographic plate. The separation pattern of the component dyes is distinctly different for inks having different dye compositions, and thus provides many points of comparison between a known and a questioned ink.

Ink can be removed from paper with a hypodermic needle with a blunted point to punch out a small sample from a written line. About ten plugs or microdots of ink are sufficient for chromatographic analysis. For several years, the Bureau of Alcohol, Tobacco and Firearms Laboratory in the U.S. Treasury Department has been actively engaged in gathering a complete library of all commercial pen inks. These inks have been systematically catalogued according to dye patterns developed by thin-layer chromatography (see Figure 14-7). On several occasions this approach has been used to prove

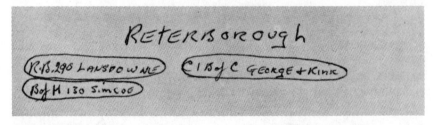

FIGURE 14-6a.

FIGURE 14-6b. A suspect forger was arrested. In his car were found written lists of the victims he intended to defraud. Some of these writings are shown in (a). A writing pad found in his house had indentations on the top page of the pad (b). These indentations corresponded to the writings found in the car further linking the suspect to the writings.

Courtesy The Centre of Forensic Sciences

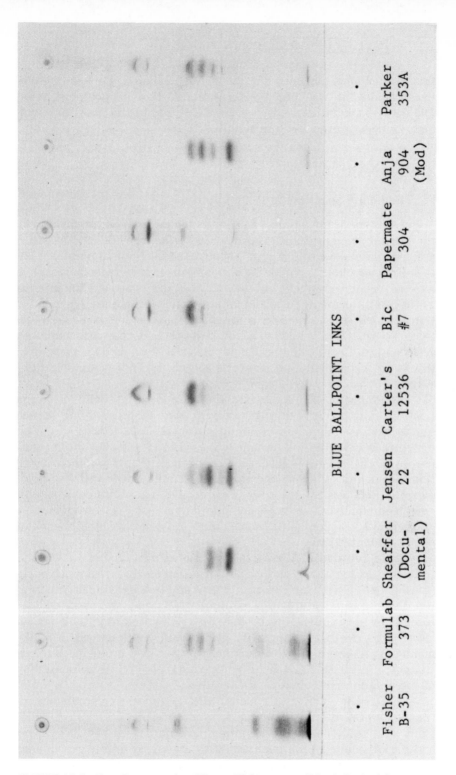

FIGURE 14-7. Chart Demonstrating different TLC patterns of blue ballpoint inks.

Courtesy Alcohol, Tobacco and Firearms Laboratory, U.S. Treasury Department

that a document has been fraudulently back-dated. For example, in one instance, it was possible to establish that a document dated 1958 was back-dated because a dye identified in the questioned ink had not been synthesized until 1959.

VOICE EXAMINATION

The Sound Spectrograph

In this era of telephone, radio, and tape recorder communications, the human voice may often prove to be valuable evidence for associating an individual with a criminal act. The telephoned bomb threat, the obscene phone call, or tape recorded kidnap ransom messages have all become frequent enough occurrences to warrant the interest of law enforcement officials in scientific techniques capable of transforming the voice into a form suitable for personal identification. To this end a good deal of research and casework has been generated as a result of the development of the sound spectrograph; this is an instrument that converts speech into a visual graphic display.

The sound spectrograph was first developed at Bell Telephone Laboratories in 1941 during research devoted to studying speech signals as they related to communication services. During the years of World War II, the instrument was used to identify for intelligence purposes the voices broadcast by German military communications. Following the war and during his employment with the company, a Bell System engineer, Lawrence Kersta, worked with this new technique and became convinced that voice spectrograms, or "voiceprints," as he called them, could provide a valuable means of personal identification.

Kersta contended that each voice has its own unique quality and character arising out of individual variations in the vocal mechanism (see Figure 14-8). The probability that any two individuals will have the same size vocal cavities (throat, nasal, and two oral cavities formed by positioning the tongue) and will coordinate their articulators (lips, teeth, tongue, soft palate, and jaw muscles) in a like manner is so small as to make the human voice a unique personal trait. According to Kersta, the voiceprint is simply a graphic display of the unique characteristics of the voice.

As a result of Kersta's claim, the sound spectrograph has attracted great interest among criminal investigators. Since 1966, many law enforcement laboratories have purchased the instrument and various courts have been asked to accept its results as evidence of an individual's participation in a crime. Although Kersta's theory has not yet been proved conclusively owing to the relatively recent

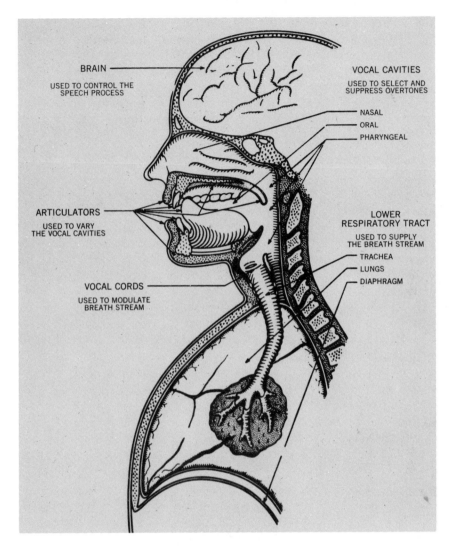

FIGURE 14-8. Schematic of the vocal mechanism.

Courtesy Base Ten Systems, Inc.

use of the sound spectrograph in criminal investigations, there is adequate experimental data to indicate that its reliability is quite high.[3] However, at this time, there are still conflicting opinions in

[3] In 1970, Dr. Oscar Tosi (Michigan State University) completed a study aimed at testing the accuracy and reliability of spectrographic voice identification. The study involved 34,996 separate voice identification attempts, each using 10 to 40 known voices subjected to a variety of speaking conditions—e.g., a noisy telephone line. The overall success rate of properly matching a speaker to a voiceprint was greater than 90 percent. However, though this value is quite high, it does not fully support Kersta's contention of the uniqueness of a voiceprint. (See *Voice Identification Research* (Washington, D.C.: U.S. Government Printing Office, 1972).)

the courts as to whether the voiceprint has gained a sufficient degree of "general acceptance" within the scientific community to satisfy the Frye criteria (see page 13) for admissibility as scientific evidence.

The sound spectrograph, shown in Figure 14-9, converts sound into a visual display called a voiceprint. The first step in making the identification is to obtain tape recordings of both the suspect and known voices for comparison. The magnetic tape containing the

FIGURE 14-9. The sound spectrograph.

Courtesy New Jersey State Police

message to be analyzed is fastened to a scanning drum which holds a 2.5-second segment of tape time. With each revolution of the drum, a variable electronic filter permits only a certain band of frequencies to be recorded. The selected frequencies are converted into electrical energy and recorded by a stylus onto specially prepared chart paper. As the drum revolves, the variable filter moves to higher and higher frequencies while the stylus simultaneously records the intensity of each selected frequency range. Upon completion of the analysis, a print is produced that represents 2.5 seconds of tape time and contains a pattern of closely spaced lines showing all the audible frequencies in the tape segment.

Figure 14-10 demonstrates a typical voiceprint. The spectrum portrays three parameters of speech: time (horizontal axis); frequency (vertical axis); and the relative intensity or volume of the different frequencies. Intensity is proportional to the degree of darkness within each spectrographic region. Hence, in this manner, frequency patterns of identical or like-sounding words are obtained from both the questioned and the known voice for visual comparison. When sufficient similarity exists between the two, a positive conclusion is justified that both voices could have emanated from the same person.

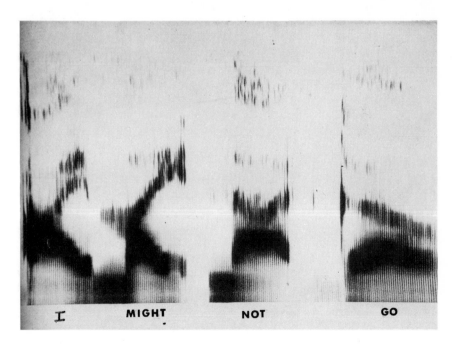

FIGURE 14-10. A voiceprint.

Courtesy New Jersey State Police

The voiceprints depicting the word "you" are shown in Figure 14-11. As an exercise in voiceprint comparison, the reader can attempt to match the questioned voiceprint on the upper left to the voice of one of the five suspects.

Recent notable applications of voiceprint technology has served to increase the public awareness of this technique. For example, voiceprints played a part in Howard Hughes' refutation of Clifford Irving's purported autobiography of Hughes. A few days after McGraw-Hill and *Life Magazine* announced their intent to publish

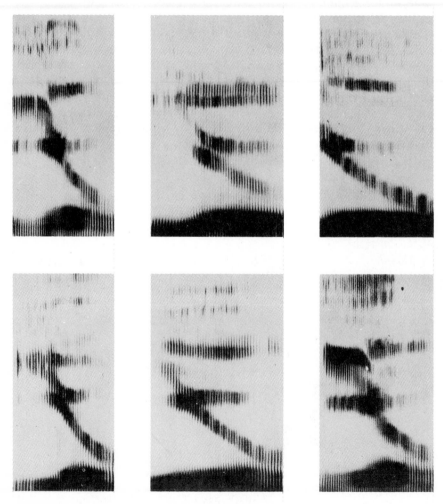

FIGURE 14-11. Voiceprints of five male speakers uttering "You" (The upper left and lower right voiceprints are of the same person).

Courtesy Base Ten Systems, Inc.

Irving's work, Hughes Tool Company officials arranged for a telephone interview between the reclusive Howard Hughes in the Bahamas and a group of newspaper, radio, and TV reporters assembled in Los Angeles. At the request of one of the major TV networks, spectrographic comparisons of the voice from the Bahamas was made against a known sample of Hughes' voice recorded in 1947. The results proved beyond a doubt that the reporters had been conversing with Howard Hughes and not with an imposter. In another case, a perpetrator called the police to report that he had killed a woman and to reveal the location of the body. He gave his name as that of an acquaintance. During the course of the investigation, the man whose name was used was eliminated as the caller and the perpetrator was identified through voiceprint comparisons. Based on that identification, he was found guilty and sentenced to prison.

FURTHER READINGS

Brunelle, Richard L., and A. A. Cantu, "Ink Analysis—A Weapon Against Crime by Detection of Fraud," in *Forensic Science*, Geoffrey Davies, ed. Washington, D.C.: American Chemical Society, 1975.

Hall, Malcolm D., "The Current Status of Speaker Identification by Use of Speech Spectrograms," *Journal of the Canadian Society of Forensic Science*, 7 (1974), 153.

Harrison, W. R., *Suspect Documents*. New York: Praeger, 1958.

Hilton, Ordway, *Scientific Examination of Questioned Documents*. Chicago: Callaghan, 1956.

Moenssens, André A., Ray E. Moses, and Fred R. Inbau, *Scientific Evidence in Criminal Cases*. Mineola, N.Y.: Foundation Press, 1973.

Nash, Ernest W., "Voice Identification with the Aid of Spectrographic Analysis," *Journal of the Association of Official Analytical Chemists*, 56 (1974), 944.

The Future

chapter 15

In 1949, Charles O'Hara and James Osterburg, noted authors of criminalistics, wrote: "The present position of criminalistics among the sciences may properly be compared with that of chemistry in the nineteenth century." Certainly the changes that have taken place since this observation was made are nothing short of revolutionary. Forensic science may still have many shortcomings, but it has successfully shed the distinction of being a nineteenth-century science.

Crime laboratories have now become the major benefactors of enormous advancements in scientific technology. Chromatography and spectrophotometry have already had a tremendous impact on forensic methodology. The future promises even more progress. Mass spectroscopy, atomic absorption, and high-speed liquid chromatography, among other developments, are rapidly gaining recognition as essential forensic tools. The scanning electron microscope is already enhancing the application of microscopy to the examination of trace physical evidence. An even more promising tool is the scanning electron microscope linked to an X-ray microanalyzer. This combination gives forensic scientists the ability to examine very small samples nondestructively while plotting the elemental composition of the specimen in view.

Not only will the practitioners of forensic science continue to see the development of new instruments and techniques suitable for solving their unique problems, but the old workhorses of the crime laboratory—i.e., the gas chromatograph and the spectrophotometer— are in store for a major facelift, thanks to a revolutionary development in electronics called the microprocessor. The microprocessor contains thousands of microscopic transistors, diodes, capacitors, and the like—all hooked together on a quarter-inch chip. The electronic components of a computer that once filled a full room can now be reduced to the size of a few microprocessor chips. Already, instrument manufacturers are taking advantage of this development to link mini-computers to many types of analytical instrumentation (see Figure 15-1). This will help to further automate and speed the collection of data in the crime laboratory.

However, the unabated progress of analytical technology must not obscure the fact that the profession of forensic science has reached a critical juncture in its history. The preoccupation with equipping a crime laboratory with elaborate and sophisticated hardware has left a wide gap between the skill of the scientist and the ability of the criminal investigator to recognize and preserve physical evidence at the crime scene. The crime scene is the critical first step

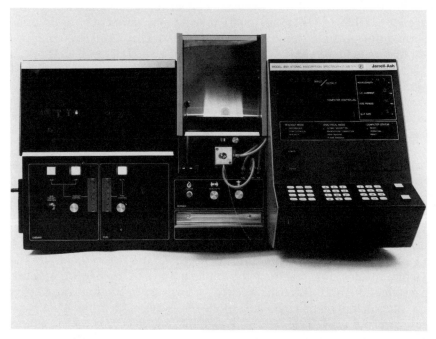

FIGURE 15-1. An atomic absorption spectrophotomer equipped with a microprocessor mini-computer.

Courtesy Fisher Scientific Co.

in the process of utilizing scientific services in a criminal investigation. All the expertise and instrumentation that any crime laboratory can muster will be rendered totally impotent if evidence has been left lying unrecognized or ignored on the ground, or if the evidence has been inadvertently destroyed by careless investigators or curiosity-seekers. Yet recent studies confirm that this is precisely what is happening to evidence at many crime scenes (refer to the first four references at the end of this chapter).

The theme that there is a need for trained and knowledgeable evidence collectors at crime scenes has been a recurring one throughout this text. Once again this requirement must be reiterated. How is the evidence collector or investigator to gain the skill and appreciation for recognizing the value of physical evidence? The trend of events seems to be one of conceding past failings and acknowledging the need for creating specialists to perform evidence collection functions. In growing numbers, police agencies are training and equipping "evidence-collection technicians" to assist criminal investigators in retrieving evidence at the crime scene.

If this program is to have any significant impact on investigative procedures, immediate steps will have to be taken that go beyond the mere designation of an evidence-collection unit within a police agency's table of organization. The effectiveness of such a program should not be measured by the number of oversized and overequipped mobile vans at the unit's disposal; instead, a staff of dedicated operators and administrators trained and experienced in evidence collection has to be assembled. This unit must be recognized as the essential first step in forensic analysis and must become an integral part, both administratively and functionally, of the total forensic service offered by a law enforcement agency.

The education of evidence collectors and investigators is a very critical factor in improving the quality of the crime scene investigation. Although advanced in-depth training by forensic scientists is an essential ingredient for the success of such a program, many agencies, for lack of space, time, or desire, have not implemented this training. It is therefore gratifying that colleges and universities are emerging as centers of education for law enforcement personnel. Criminal justice or law enforcement programs offer themselves as viable forums for teaching the philosophy and theory of criminal investigation and forensic science. However, academia must strive to supplement, not supplant, police in-service training. Police administrators now have the responsibility for selecting the personnel to perform investigative functions. These administrators cannot abdicate their responsibility to create and foster training programs that will assure the competent performance of the investigator's mission.

Whether a college degree will some day be required by all police is still a subject of debate; but the trend is certainly in that direction. Already, nearly 675 higher-education institutions in the United States offer some kind of law enforcement program. It is from the ranks of these students that future generations of criminal investigators and police administrators will be recruited. For the forensic scientist, participation in these programs offers a unique opportunity to teach, develop, and put into practice the philosophy that science is an integral part of criminal investigation.

Of course education alone is not sufficient for assuring the professional conduct of the criminal investigator or evidence collector. Experience, perceptive skill, persistence, and precise judgment are all ingredients essential to the makeup of the successful investigator and evidence collector. Combine all these with a careful selection process designed for choosing only those who qualify for this role, and the end result will be a substantial enhancement of the quality of criminal investigative services.

I don't want to leave the reader with the impression that crime laboratories are not being used, or that forensic scientists have difficulty in justifying a full day's work. To the contrary, these facilities are overworked and understaffed. Just the demand imposed on them to complete the examination of drug evidence and blood alcohol is enough to inundate and preoccupy all but the larger crime laboratories. Most facilities can barely keep their heads above water and are literally drowning in a sea of drugs. Unfortunately, the disproportionate burden placed on the skills, time, and equipment of the laboratory by drug and blood alcohol evidence has had a detrimental effect on the capacity of the law enforcement system to process physical evidence generated by more serious crimes.

The solution to the problem may seem obvious; more people, larger facilities, and of course more money. In this respect, the crime laboratories must stand in line with other components of the criminal justice system. For the simple truth of the matter is that skyrocketing crime rates have overburdened our police, courts, and correctional institutions. In light of public and political outcries, criminal justice administrators have sought programs geared to producing quick and dramatic reductions in crime rates. In this kind of atmosphere, hiring more scientists or buying a mass spectrometer or a gas chromatograph may hardly seem to many to be an effective or appealing remedy to the problem of crime reduction.

I'm not advocating a crash program for building crime laboratories, or, for that matter, a crash program aimed at improving the lot of any one segment of the criminal justice community at the expense of the others. The reduction of crime will only come about with a balanced approach to criminal justice, as well as the alleviation of social injustices. In this respect, we must keep the future role of the crime laboratory in its proper perspective while examining the goals and performance that we expect from all components of our criminal justice system.

It must be emphasized to criminal justice planners and administrators that the size and effectiveness of a crime laboratory directly mirrors the capability of the investigative agencies that it services. If all or even most of the burglaries, homicides, assaults, rapes, and other types of major offenses were investigated with the thoroughness expected of a proper criminal investigation, the quantity of physical evidence collected would necessitate the existence of adequately staffed and equipped crime laboratories.

I need only illustrate this point by observing that the single most important impetus behind the expansion of crime laboratory services in the United States since 1966 has been the large influx of drug specimens. A required chemical analysis of these confiscated materials has made the laboratory's participation in prosecution proceedings mandatory. The criminal justice system, faced with the prospect of unreasonable delays due to understaffed laboratories, quickly moved to expand these facilities in order to keep pace with the ever-increasing number of drug seizures. Unfortunately, this same kind of pressure has not yet developed in relation to the collection and the analysis of other types of physical evidence related to crimes just as serious as drug offenses, if not more so.

Although the commitment of police to improve the quality of the crime-scene investigation is essential, it must be accompanied by a simultaneous effort to improve the caliber of crime laboratory services. Certainly the thorough collection of crime-scene evidence will necessitate the employment of more forensic scientists to handle the increasing caseloads. However, it would be a mistake for forensic scientists to be lulled into a false sense of security by believing that the tremendous strides made in the development of analytical instruments and techniques during the past twenty years is alone sufficient to meet the needs and goals of their profession. In truth, progress can be expected in the future only if crime laboratories are assured of staffs composed of trained and knowledgeable scientists. Unfortunately, because the rapid expansion of criminalistic services has created unprecedented demands for more forensic scientists, it has become exceedingly difficult to locate, train, and assimilate competent individuals into existing crime laboratory operations.

At present, few colleges and universities offer courses or degree programs in criminalistics. For the most part, crime laboratories have to recruit new employees from the ranks of college graduates who have received their formal education in chemistry, biology, geology, or physics. Though some of these individuals may have textbook knowledge of the techniques utilized in forensic analysis, few arrive at the crime laboratory possessing an understanding of the practical aspects of applying scientific theory and techniques to the problems of criminal investigation. This deficiency necessitates a prolonged and time-consuming period of intensive training under the direction of trained criminalists. Not only must the new criminalist learn to apply specialized skills to the responsibilities and objectives of a working crime laboratory, he or she must also acquire a familiarity with all phases of crime laboratory operation.

The extent and depth of versatility expected of the forensic scientist is usually determined by the size of the crime laboratory's staff. Scientists in smaller laboratories are often expected to be generalists, performing a wide variety of tasks in order to fulfill the varied objectives of the laboratory. Their counterparts in larger facilities enjoy the luxury of working in specialized areas, relying on a teamwork approach to provide the spectrum of scientific skills needed for the comparison or identification of physical evidence.

In addition to his/her technical responsibilities, the newly trained criminalist must discover and master the role of the expert witness. Courtroom demeanor and the ability to communicate thoughts and ideas in clear, concise terms are absolutely essential if the scientist's examination and conclusions are to be properly and effectively presented at hearing or in court.

The present momentum of forensic research could very well falter unless individuals who possess relevant knowledge and skills are attracted to careers in forensic science. The recognition by a sufficient number of colleges and universities of the need for fostering undergraduate and graduate programs in this field is essential for assuring an ample supply of scientists to meet the anticipated manpower needs of the profession. Furthermore, the establishment of forensic education programs, especially at the graduate level, will be accompanied by the formation of new academic research programs dedicated to investigating fertile areas of research that are pertinent to the expanding role of forensic science in criminal justice. In a university environment, these research programs can be pursued in an atmosphere unaffected by the pressures of everyday casework, a burden that presently weighs heavily on the shoulders of the working forensic scientist.

The most serious shortcoming of modern forensic science is the lack of statistical data to support the technical advances that have been made in recent years. Gathering statistical data is tedious and undramatic work; some may even characterize it as deadly dull. However, the fact remains that this requirement goes to the very heart of forensic science.

Thousands of dollars and immeasurable amounts of time and effort are presently being spent to develop new methods for testing physical evidence. New instruments and techniques have allowed scientists to penetrate sensitivity limits thought unattainable just a few years ago. Yet it seems most illogical to pursue the scientific analysis of evidence without knowing the statistical value of the results generated.

Unfortunately, in spite of the fact that crime laboratories are equipped with expensive and sophisticated instruments, seldom can a forensic scientist report to a police officer or a jury that a scientific examination of the evidence has in itself solved a case. More often than not, a conclusive comparison of evidential and control material will not be able to exclude other possible sources. To further complicate matters, the statistical data available to support such conclusions are usually sketchy or nonexistent. In these situations, a heavy reliance must necessarily be placed on the experience and opinion of the expert in interpreting the significance of the forensic examination.

Even though physical evidence for corroborating investigative findings is an important contribution to any criminal case, situations like these certainly do not motivate investigators to go all out in their search for physical evidence. It is no coincidence that the items most sought at the crime site are those which possess potential individual characteristics—i.e., fingerprints, firearms, bullets, toolmarks, and track impressions—for these are more likely to have the greatest impact on an investigation. Once these avenues have been exhausted, there seems to be little desire to progress any further. Clearly, future research will have to concentrate on defining the value of the much larger category of class evidence so that these items can become statistically more meaningful and attractive to scientist and investigator alike. Forensic science will only thrive as a scientific discipline by supplementing the personal experiences and views of experts, no matter how impartial they may be, with vigorous proof supported by sound experimental data.

Realistically, the prospects for individualizing many types of physical evidence in the near future are not good; nonetheless, the major thrust of forensic research must concentrate on defining the most distinctive properties of evidence and relating these properties to statistics that measure their frequency of occurrence. The creation of data banks to collect, store, and disseminate this kind of information will facilitate the task. In England, such a prototype system is already in operation. Glass refractive index data collected by all of the British forensic regional laboratories are transmitted to a central computer located at the Central Research Establishment, where they are compiled and stored. Forensic scientists at the regional laboratories can now query the computer and receive within minutes the frequency of occurrence of a particular type glass of a given refractive index or a range of indices.

Data storage relating to other types of evidence is starting to be accumulated, but on a much smaller scale. For example, at the Metropolitan Police Laboratory in London, thousands of paint samples retrieved from crime-site scenes are being coded and filed on punched cards according to topcoat color and layer structure. It is anticipated that this collection will facilitate the matching of paint collected in future investigations to those already on file. Such a system could prove invaluable in linking suspects to past crimes. Additionally, all blood specimens presently received by this laboratory are being typed and classified according to the many antigens and polymorphic proteins detectable in bloodstains. This project holds the promise that very shortly blood will join the fingerprint as a mark of human identity.

Because the responsibility for providing forensic services is spread among more than 200 independent government laboratories in the United States, the task of accumulating meaningful statistical data applicable to the entire country or to large regions is exceedingly difficult. Future progress will depend on the willingness of all crime laboratories to enter into cooperative programs that will insure uniform standards of analysis as well as the collection and dissemination of analytical and statistical data. Although progress in this area has been exceedingly slow, recent developments give reason for optimism.

The establishment of the American Society of Crime Laboratory Directors in 1974 provides local, state, and federal crime laboratory directors with a forum in which to discuss and plan common strategy. A planned Criminalistics Laboratory Information System (CLIS) holds the promise that all U.S. laboratories will one day be joined by terminals linked to a central computer. The Forensic Science Foundation, the research arm of the American Academy of Forensic Sciences, is supporting a program designed to measure the proficiency of all crime laboratories in the examination of common items of physical evidence. The National Bureau of Standards is collecting and disseminating to American crime laboratories automobile paint chips for current domestic models. NBS is also developing a collection of automobile headlight characteristics as well as photographic reproductions of various manufactured lenses. The FBI has made new commitments to train criminalists throughout the United States, and is endeavoring to foster an atmosphere of cooperation among fellow crime laboratories. Already hundreds of inexperienced as well as seasoned forensic scientists have participated in courses and seminars being conducted at the FBI's training academy.

A foundation of cooperation has been laid; much now remains to be accomplished. How successful our profession will be in fulfilling its present and future obligations to justice will be dependent on the skill, dedication, and ingenuity of its practitioners.

FURTHER READINGS

Gurgin, V. A., B. Parker, and S. J. Betsch, "Criminalistics: Today and Tomorrow," *Journal of Forensic Sciences*, 19 (1974), 518.

Kingston, C. R., and J. L. Peterson, "Forensic Science and the Reduction of Crime," *Journal of Forensic Sciences*, 19 (1974), 417.

Parker, B., and J. L. Peterson, *Physical Evidence Utilization in the Administration of Criminal Justice*, Washington, D.C.: U.S. Government Printing Office, 1972.

Peterson, Joseph L., *The Utilization of Criminalistics Services by the Police*, Washington, D.C.: U.S. Government Printing Office, 1974.

——, "LEAA's Forensic Science Research Program," in *Forensic Science*, Geoffrey Davies, ed. Washington, D.C.: American Chemical Society, 1975.

Walls, H. J., "What Is 'Reasonable Doubt'? A Forensic Scientist Looks at the Law," in *Forensic Science,* Joseph L. Peterson, ed. New York: AMS Press, Inc., 1975.

Williams, R. L., "Forensic Science—The Present and Future," *Analytical Chemistry*, 45 (1973), 1076A.

Readings

R. v PAYNE

J. M. Cameron, MD, PhD, MRCPath, DMJ

Reader in Forensic Medicine at the London Hospital Medical School

The case which we are about to relate is one illustrating brilliant detective work finally clinched by indisputable forensic scientific evidence. It is our intention to describe the scene and background of this ghastly "motiveless" murder, and then to produce the scientific evidence which triumphantly settled the case beyond all reasonable doubt. On 23 November, 1947, Claire Jacqueline Parvin was born. Twenty years later on 30 September 1967, she married Bernard Daniel Josephs. At 8.05 P.M. on Wednesday, 7 February, 1968, after approximately five months of married bliss Bernard returned home to Flat 15, Deepdene Court, Kingswood Road, Shortlands, Bromley, Kent, where they had lived since 25 October, 1967, to find his bride brutally murdered in the bedroom. She was wearing among other clothing a cerise woollen dress. This had been a Christmas present from her husband in 1966.

Approximately 18 months prior to her marriage, Claire Josephs

Reprinted by permission from the *Medico-Legal Journal*, vol. 40, part I, 1972.

became friends at work with a young girl who subsequently married Roger John Payne on 7 October 1966—a marriage which Claire and her mother attended. The two girls continued their friendship by correspondence, Claire getting advice concerning matters in con-nexion with her forthcoming marriage—on one occasion Claire could well have met Roger John Payne. On 7 January, 1968, Mrs. Payne visited Claire at Deepdene Court and Roger Payne was shown around the flat when he came to pick up his wife. On this occasion Claire was wearing a brown skirt and green jumper. The significance of this will be appreciated when reference is made later to the scientific evidence of certain fibres found on Payne's overcoat. A week after the visit of Mr. and Mrs. Payne to the Josephs' flat, namely January 15, 1968, Claire Josephs started work as a telephonist at West Wickham. Again the significance of this will become apparent when reference is made to the scientific evidence, for only after this date did Claire start to wear the cerise woollen dress which had been kept in a suit-case since mid-1967 and in which she was found dead.

On the morning of Wednesday, February 7, 1968, Bernard Josephs and his wife Claire had breakfast together before setting off to their respective jobs. Bernard helped his wife to tidy up the flat and put away their breakfast dishes and generally tidy up the kitchen. Claire Josephs was driven to and from her work by a girl friend who on February 7 picked up Claire at 9.05 A.M.; both girls left work at 5.30 P.M. Claire dressed in a pink dress, blue raincoat and chiffon scarf, being dropped off at approximately 5.40 P.M. So it would be reasonable to assume that she arrived at her flat at about 5.45 P.M. This was confirmed by Claire's mother-in-law who phoned at 5.30 P.M. and got no reply but when she phoned at 5.45 P.M. she spoke to Claire for 12–15 minutes giving her instructions as how to make a lemon soufflé. This was the last occasion on which Claire Josephs is known to have been alive. As far as Claire's husband is concerned, he finished work in Barking at 6.00 P.M., went to a nearby public house with a friend where he drank until 7.00 P.M. when both men and his friend's fiancée commenced the journey home. At 7.50 P.M. the three went to a public house in Shortlands where they bought six bottles of beer before driving Bernard Josephs to Deepdene Court. His friend remarked that all the lights in the flat were out and, think-ing that Claire might be at her parents' address, offered to wait and drop Mr. Josephs there. His offer was declined and Bernard made his way to the flat.

He let himself in, to find the house in darkness. He switched on the lights, and put his raincoat and briefcase on the settee—so far all was neat, tidy and undisturbed. He looked into the kitchen, walked into the hall and then into the bedroom. Switching on the light he saw his wife's legs protruding beyond the end of the bed, the curtains were drawn to leave a small gap. She was lying face downwards slightly turned to the right. He gently lifted her head and saw a ghastly wound across her neck. Horrified he ran from the bedroom and in a distressed state telephoned his wife's parents, and his own parents, but failed to call the police or ambulance. His father-in-law was the first to arrive and notified at 8.13 P.M. the police and ambulance who arrived at 8.18 P.M. Among the next to arrive at 8.25 P.M. was the family doctor who certified the girl to be dead. It was approximately 10 minutes later at 8.35 P.M. on the arrival of Detective Sergeant Peck that any order was put into practice, for it must be appreciated that before 8.35 P.M. some twelve or more people were milling about the flat, thus reducing the possibility of finding fingerprints or other useful clues. There can be no recrimination or justifiable criticism of Bernard Josephs' initial action on finding his wife.

Det. Supt. John Cummings arrived at 9.15 P.M. to take charge of the inquiry into what was to be his final and probably most successful case. He noted that the flat revealed little or no evidence of disorder or disturbance and there had been no forcible entry. The deceased's right slipper was by the wall between the kitchen and the lounge doors, an indication of its having dropped off while she ran or stumbled. In the kitchen a mixing machine still set at No. 2 was plugged in but switched off at the point. In the bowl a soufflé mixture was partly made with eggs, butter and lemons on the right side, and a recipe lying on the left side. This indicated that she had probably been interrupted by a call at the door. On the draining board was a cup and saucer containing coffee, while on the sill was a matching plate containing six shortbread biscuits taken from a packet which had been broken open and was lying on the sideboard. This suggested to Det. Supt. Cummings that the caller was not well known hence the more formal offer of a biscuit on a plate rather than from a packet. No weapon was found at the flat but the next morning a "Peerage" bread-knife with a 4½ in. plastic handle and a 8 in. blade with a serrated cutting edge was noted to be missing. Despite diligent and exhaustive searches, the bread-knife was never found.

At autopsy later that night she was found to have fourteen incised wounds in front of the neck, partially undercut from below up and four stab wounds of the neck—one of which penetrated muscles on the right side of neck through the right side of the base of the tongue to reach the right side of the front of the spine (2nd cerebral vertebra). Over the voice-box were areas of bruising and marks intermittently extending round the neck which in conjunction with fine petechiae were suggestive of constriction of the neck with a degree of asphyxia at or shortly before death. Marks on the right side of the mouth could have been caused by finger nails. If assaulted from behind they would be consistent with having been caused by the left hand, leaving the right hand free. The linear incised wounds in front of the neck were consistent with having been caused by a knife with a serrated edge. The marks could have been caused either by a left-handed person from in front or a right-handed person from behind or by a right-handed person from above the head with the body on the floor. The defence type wounds on the right hand are also consistent with having been caused by a similar serrated knife. Superposition of such a knife on scale photographs and a cast of the right hand showing identical markings particularly the wound in the first web of the hand and tip of right little finger.

None of the numerous linear wounds in the front of the neck were fatal as they were either partial or full skin thickness extending only as far as underlying muscle. There were four stab wounds directly inwards and slightly upwards in direction, which could have been caused by an assault from behind with the victim upright or above the head if the body lay on the ground. These stab wounds had penetrated the neck vessels with the introduction of air into the circulation with the development of air embolism and subsequent haemorrhage, death being rapid thereafter. The cause of death was attributed to air embolism and haemorrhage due to wounds of the neck. Taking into consideration the various factors the time of death would centre on 7.15 P.M. approximately. There was no evidence of a sexual assault.

As there had been no forcible entry to the flat inquiries were concentrated on relatives, friends and acquaintances who could have been entertained by Mrs. Josephs. This necessitated long and laborious routine inquiry which eventually resulted in Roger John Payne being interviewed for the first time on February 12. Payne was a 26-year-old bank clerk living near Maidstone, Kent. When seen there were numerous scratches on both his hands and a bruise on his forehead. He alleged they had been produced by his wife during a quarrel over a cat on Sunday, February 4. On February 7 Payne had to appear in London for a medical examination and interview in connexion with his work. He commenced work at 9 A.M., left at 11.30 A.M., changed into a newly pressed suit straight from the cleaners and drove in his motor car (a pale blue Morris 1100) to London for his medical examination. At about 3.30 P.M. he left his interview and went to an address in Sutton arriving about 4.20 P.M. and leaving about 5.15 P.M. He next apparently went to a fish and chip shop, although no evidence to support this statement could be found, before driving to his mother's home (approximately 2¼ miles away). On the way his car broke down and whilst repairing it the bonnet apparently fell on his head. His mother stated initially he only stayed a few minutes between 6 and 7 P.M. although in a second statement he said he arrived about 6.30 P.M. and left about 7.30 P.M. He then drove home and again his car broke down when he alleged he got mud on his overcoat. When he arrived home about 9.15 P.M. his wife saw blood on his head. The next day Payne again took his suit to the cleaners. Payne was arrested on February 24, he appeared at Bromley Magistrate's Court on March 18 and 19, 1968, when the case for the DPP was put by Mr. Nugent and Payne was represented by his counsel Mr. Gordon Graeme. He was committed to the Central Criminal Court where on May 15 before Mr. Justice Cooke, Payne pleaded not guilty. The case for the Crown was put by Mr. John Bussard, QC, assisted by Mr. W. Richardson while for the defence appeared Mr. Wilfred Fordham, QC, and Mr. Gordon Graeme. After the defence objected to one women juror the case commenced. He was found guilty of the murder on May 24, by a majority of 11 to 1 after a retirement of 3¾ hours, and sentenced to life imprisonment. After the jury had returned their verdict it was stated Payne had a number of previous convictions. In November 1959, at the age of 17, he was placed on probation for three years at Surrey Assizes for breaking into a girl's house armed with a knife, placing a hand over her mouth and attempting sexual intercourse with her. In April 1965, at Maldon and Surbiton Magistrates Court he was sentenced to 3 months' imprisonment for assault occasioning actual bodily harm, when at 2.45 A.M. he entered the bedroom of a middle-aged woman. He held her by the wrists, placed his hand over her mouth and injured her as she struggled (*Daily Express* 25.5.68).

Leave to appeal was rejected when Mr. Roger Frisby, QC, put his case before Lord Justice Salmon who sat with Lord Justice Megaw and Mr. Justice O'Connor.

Miss Margaret Pereira, BSc

Senior Principal Scientific Officer, Metropolitan Police Forensic Science Laboratory

The Metropolitan Police Forensic Science Laboratory became involved in this case on Friday, February 9, 1968, when clothing and post mortem samples from the deceased were brought to the laboratory. At the same time, items were received from a suspect who was soon to be eliminated from the case as the result of police inquiries. Contrary to reports in certain newspapers, the dead girl's husband had been eliminated before the laboratory became involved in the case. Three days later, garments were accepted from a second suspect and, on February 13, a number of items were received relating to Roger John Payne. These included a hat, overcoat, suit and a blood sample. There was a request from the police for urgent examination of apparent blood stains on the hat and overcoat. The following day it was reported that these stains were of the same group as Payne himself and different from that of Claire Josephs. Attention was then given to the clothing of the second suspect and nothing of an incriminating nature was found.

On Monday, February 19, the coffee cup from the kitchen was brought to the laboratory. It was felt that, in the absence of finger prints, useful evidence might be obtained if saliva on the rim could be grouped. The following day the presence of saliva of Group A was reported. This was of the same group as Payne but as not of great significance as 42% of the British population are of this group. However, on the same day the examination for evidence of contact between the clothing of the dead girl and Payne was started. It was found that the dress Claire was wearing was of a fluffy woollen fabric and was of an exceptionally bright cerise colour. A few fibres exactly matching those of this dress were found on the hat and overcoat of Payne. This information was quickly reported to Bromley C.I.D.

After this, Det. Superintendent Cummings asked that the clothing of the deceased should be examined for fibres which might have come from Payne's clothing and this aspect was given special attention. Both his overcoat and suit contained a variety of colours and neither was of pure wool. Because of the variety of types of fibre present in these garments this examination took several days but resulted in the detection, on Claire's raincoat, of a number of fibres which could have come from Payne's overcoat and others which matched his suit. All of the fibres matching these garments were of fairly common occurrence. Because of the fluffy nature of the dress it was unsuitable for examination for contact fibres.

Priority was also given to a man's handkerchief which was found at the flat and was not the property of Bernard Josephs. It was bloodstained and tests revealed the presence of blood of two different groups, AB, MN (Claire Joseph's group) and A, M (Payne's group and present in approximately 12% of the British population). Fibres were also found on this handkerchief matching Payne's overcoat, his suit and Claire's dress. This information was given to Det. Superintendent Cummings on Friday, February 23, and it was decided that it was necessary to know the blood group of Bernard Josephs. A sample was obtained and tested that evening and found to be group O, N. Clearly, the blood present on the handkerchief did not originate from him.

Superintendent Cummings said that he intended to arrest Payne on the following day and also to search his house. During the examination of the clothing of Payne and Claire and also of the handkerchief it had become apparent that there were fibres in all these items which probably had a common source. These were rayon fibres and the majority were plain red and others were combinations and permutations of red, black, pale yellow and blue. It was obvious that these fibres came from a rayon printed fabric in which the background was red. It was therefore suggested that there might be an item of this nature, perhaps a tie, at Payne's home.

On the following Monday, many items belonging to Payne were received. These included several ties, a cravat and a scarf. The latter was in a very frayed condition and was of red printed rayon. The fibres matched exactly with those found previously. In addition, there were eight red wool fibres on the scarf which matched those of Claire's dress. Also amongst the items received was a man's handkerchief of the same pattern as the one found in the flat. It was however slightly larger but was woven in a similar manner.

Payne's Morris 1100 was also brought to the laboratory. Det. Superintendent Cummings thought it highly likely that when the murderer left the flat he took the knife away with him and dispose of it later. If the person was driving away in a Morris 1100, the most likely place to have secreted the weapon would be inside the pocket on the driver's door. Accordingly, this was the first part of the car to be examined and blood staining was found in the bottom corner of the pocket. It was later tested and found to be of group AB but MN grouping failed. However in the PGM system, the blood stain was also the same type as Claire Josephs (PGM 2-1) and the combination of AB, PGM 2-1 is found in approximately one person in eighty. It was apparent that the inner surface of the driver's door had been washed but very faint human blood staining was detected in various places in the washed area. At a later stage, the debris on the floor of the car was examined and several fibres matching the nylon carpet in the girl's flat were found together with a few fibres matching her dress.

Further work on Payne's clothing revealed a total of sixty-one fibres matching Claire's dress on his overcoat, twenty-two on his hat, six on his jacket and none on his trousers. As previously stated, the suit had been cleaned and it was interesting that the fibres found on the jacket were not lying on the surface but were embedded in the interstices of the cloth. Fortunately, these fibres were brilliantly fluorescent and were easily detected by examining the garments under ultra-violet light.

Twenty rayon fibres matching Payne's scarf were found on Claire's raincoat and eight were present on the handkerchief found in the flat. There was also a single red and black rayon fibre matching the scarf on the left thumb nail of the deceased.

Evidence of these findings was given at the committal at Bromley Magistrates Court and later Dr. Barbara Dodd attended the Metropolitan Police Laboratory when she took samples of the significant blood stains and subsequently examined them on behalf of the defence.. Dr. Julius Grant also came to the laboratory on behalf of the defence and examined all of the fibres which were of relevance. Neither of these two experts gave evidence at the trial.

The trial commenced on May 15, 1968, and on May 17, Mr. Norman Roper carried out a further examination of the fibres on behalf of the defence. Later, he gave evidence at the trial where he agreed in principle with the prosecution witness about the similarity of the fibres concerned but disagreed as to their significance.

From a forensic scientist's point of view this was a case in which Locard's principle that "Every contact leaves its trace" was borne out to a remarkable degree. It was of course a matter of pure chance that there were fibres involved which shed rapidly and were very characteristic as was the fact that the dead girl's blood group was relatively uncommon. However, the possibility of obtaining such evidence of contact purely by chance must be infinitesimal.

THE ATTEMPTED ASSASSINATION OF ARCHBISHOP MAKARIOS: A FORENSIC SCIENCE CASE STUDY

Julius Grant, MSc, PhD, FRIC

Paper read to the Medico-Legal Society, January 13, 1972

At about 7.05 A.M. on the morning of Sunday, March 8, 1970, the President of the Republic of Cyprus, Archbishop Makarios, boarded his personal helicopter in the courtyard of the archbishop's palace in Nicosia, in order to fly to Macheras Monastery to officiate at a memorial service. He sat on the left of the pilot, Major Zacharias Papadoyiannis. The helicopter took off, and when it had attained the height of the Archbishopric, it made a turn of 150 degrees, still climbing. At a point about 10 metres above the roof of the Archbishopric (Fig. 1), a shot was heard from the left and rear, and a burst of machine gun-fire came from the same direction. The Archbishop was not hit, but his pilot sustained a severe wound in the abdomen. With great difficulty in view of his wound, the damage

Reprinted by permission from the *Medico-Legal Journal*, vol. 40, part 2, 1972.

FIGURE 1.

caused to the helicopter and the proximity of buildings and electric
cables, the pilot managed to land on an open space on the corner of
two neighbouring streets, out of range of the firing (Fig. 2). The
Archbishop and pilot dismounted from the helicopter and ran away
from it, having in mind the possibility of an explosion. However, the
pilot collapsed and was taken to hospital where, after a critical illness, he eventually recovered.

The Presidential Guard at the Archbishopric was conscious that
the firing came from the roof of the Pancyprian Gymnasium opposite
the Archbishop's palace, and they fired in that direction (Fig. 1).
Shortly, after the firing occurred, early risers in Thysseos and Othellos
Streets, which adjoin the high side wall of the Pancyprian Gymnasium,
saw four men climbing over the wall of the school into Thysseos
Street. One spectator asked what was happening, but received no
reply; he called out to the men to stop or he would shoot them. One
then held his hands to his face, and turned back and said to one of
the others who was coming up behind him and was holding a pistol,
"They are shooting at us." All four then turned into Othellos Street.
The spectator and other onlookers then saw the four men board a

FIGURE 2.

car waiting nearby and drive off. The first spectator telephoned the police and subsequently identified the car by appearance, although he was unable to note the number. Other spectators were able to provide confirmatory evidence regarding the car, although the evidence of identification of the four persons was weak. However, eventually it seems to have been established that the car was of a light blue colour with a white line and was a Fiat, Model 850, registration number ZDR 320. In the meantime the police had been informed of the incident. They entered the Pancyprian Gymnasium, and took possession of the firearms and other exhibits found on the roof.

In another part of Nicosia, at a distance of about a mile from the scene of the attempt, a merchant opening his shop at about 8.30 in the morning noticed a self-drive car having the above description. As this had not been moved by 11.30 A.M. he telephoned the police. On Sunday, March 8, the day of the attempt, at 8.30 in the morning, one G. A. Taliadoros went to the Larnaca Road police station and reported that the car which he had hired on February 12 had been stolen from a parking place. His agitated condition and confused replies to questions aroused suspicion, and he was questioned about the circumstances of the theft of his car as well as about his own movements. In due course two associates of Taliadoros were also detained. They were questioned as to their whereabouts at the relevant time, and as their answers were deemed to be unsatisfactory they were held in custody. Further arrests were made subsequently, and six persons, as follows, were ultimately detained, namely (Fig. 3):

Adamos Haritonos, 23, student; an associate of Taliadoros
Georghios Alexandrou Taliadoros, 33, estate agent
Antonakis Prokopi Solomonodos, 32, former inspector of police
Antonakis Petrou Yenagritis, 28, police constable
Costas Polykarpou Ioannides, 32, newspaper editor
Polikarpos Antoni Polykarpou, 32, police constable

Monday, March 9, was a holiday and when on Tuesday, the 10th, Maria Constantinou, a cleaner of the Pancyprian school unlocked the toilets, she found below an aperture in the wall two dirty blankets in a heap. One was light grey in colour and the other a darker colour, rather brownish. These also were taken by the police for examination.

The police force acted with great promptitude and efficiency under the direction of Chief Supt. G. Hadjiloizou of the C.I.D. They

Solomonodos

Haritonos

Yenagritis

Taliadoros

FIGURE 3.

took possession of the weapons found on the roof of the Pancyprian school and a number of other articles from the school roof, and also the blankets referred to above. At about the same time a shepherd found a cache of arms, also wrapped in two blankets, hidden in a ditch near Nicosia; and these were taken by the police. They were similar to the arms found on the roof of the Gymnasium and fingerprints were obtainable from them.

Shortly after the above events I received a telephone call from the High Commissioner for Cyprus in London asking me if I could fly to Cyprus at once; he hinted at the reason. A few days later I attended a Cabinet meeting at the Presidential Palace, where I met the President, and I was formally invited to be responsible for the forensic investigation of the assassination attempt. The resources of the police force and Government Analyst were placed at my disposal, and I take pleasure in paying tribute to the assistance and hospitality I received.

The activities of the police had resulted in the following list of articles of potential importance to be investigated:

> From the school: weapons; two blankets; cigarette ends; button; faecal matter.
>
> From the arms cache: weapons; two blankets.
>
> From the car: dust from floor; dust from boot; fingerprints; cigarette ends.
>
> From the persons detained: all outer clothing; also some 50 articles of other miscellaneous clothing; dust from a car and blankets from the homes of the persons detained.
>
> Miscellaneous: revolver holster; newspapers; car cover; etc.

The forensic examination of the above is now dealt with in order of importance. The jacket worn by Taliadoros, when he was arrested, bore a smear of white dust on the right shoulder approximately 3 × 2 cm. in dimensions, and similar in colour to that of the whitewashed walls of the school. Taliadoros said that he picked it up while sitting on a bench and leaning against the wall of the police station where he was originally detained. The police had assiduously taken samples of plaster from the walls of the school along the escape route of the gunmen from the roof to the wall of Thysseos Street, but it was apparent that the mark on the jacket was a surface rubbing, and was a top coat of whitewash and not plaster. In view of the importance of this smear and the lack of wholly positive other forensic evidence concerning Taliadoros, I thought it advisable to make a fresh examination of the scene. Surface rubbings were, therefore, first taken from the areas from which the plaster had been removed. An attempt was then made to reconstruct the early stages of the escape after the shots had been fired.

It will be seen from Fig. 1 that the gunmen must have climbed down from the flat roof where they had fired at the President on to an open air passage flanked on the right by the high whitewashed wall shown in Fig. 4. Free passage down the area was prevented on the left by the pitched skylights (four in number) which serve the classroom below and which are apparent in the photograph. It was found that the most convenient way of travelling along this passage in a hurry was to pass between the wall and the skylight, a distance of only 40 cm. This is too small to accommodate a man facing the direction in which he was running. Indeed there was a natural instinct, I found, to half-turn to the left, i.e., away from the wall, on passing between the narrow gaps. If this was done the right shoulder did not necessarily touch the wall but, as a runner emerged from the gap, there was a distinct probability that his right shoulder would rub against the square-section vertical drain pipes from the roof, which project from the wall to the extent of about 10 cm. When this happened a smear could be produced on the shoulder of the same size and type and in the same location as that found on Taliadoros's jacket.

FIGURE 4.

A surface rubbing was, therefore, taken from one of the drain pipes at shoulder level, and it was found that the superficial coating was apparently unlike ordinary whitewash but was consistent with a mixture of whitewash and a white emulsion paint. A likely explanation of this is that it had been found that the whitewash would not cover the metal drainpipe as well as on the actual wall, and a top-coating of emulsion paint had, therefore, been applied over it. The claim that the smear had come from the police station was easily disposed of, because the bench on which Taliadoros had sat had a wooden back separating the sitter from the wall; and moreover, the whitewash on the wall was not pure white but a pale yellow colour. Below are shown in tabular form the spectroscopic analysis of all the powders collected, from which it will be seen that the powder from the coat and that from the drainpipe matched perfectly; moreover they have no counterpart in any of the other samples, which are characteristic of an ordinary lime wash. The presence of both calcium and titanium is consistent with the use of a paint of good covering power, with the limewash on the pipe; and this occurs also on the coat.

Sample	J	1	2	3	4	5
Aluminum	Minor	Absent	Trace	Minor	Trace	Minor
Barium	Minor	Major	Trace	Minor	Trace	Major
Calcium	Major	Major	Major	Major	Major	Major
Chromium	Trace	Trace	Trace	Trace	Trace	Trace
Iron	Trace	Minor	Trace	Trace	Trace	Trace
Magnesium	Minor	Major	Major	Minor	Major	Major
Silicon	Major	Minor	Trace	Major	Trace	Minor
Titanium	Major	Absent	Absent	Major	Absent	Absent
Zinc	Absent	Minor	Absent	Absent	Trace	Trace

Key

J—Taliadoros's jacket.
1—Landing outside classroom door.
2—Lavatory outside wall.
3—Drainpipe on roof.
4—Lavatory wall where blankets were found.
5—Column at foot of staircase near classroom.

In the course of the hearing the defence pointed out that in Nicosia all the drainpipes of the houses are of this rectangular type, so that the rubbing could have come from one of hundreds in the town. Having foreseen this argument I had spent nearly two hours roaming the streets of the town and rubbing my jacket against drainpipes—often to the mystification of passers-by! Out of many in various parts of the town I found that about 60% were whitewashed, with the whitewash often partly rubbed off, and the remainder were painted with a gloss paint which could not be rubbed off. I did not find one which had the appearance or effect of the drainpipes in the roof corridor at the school. The Court regarded this as significant, according to the Presiding Judge in his summing-up.

Coming now to the two blankets found by the lavatories, these consisted of a grey blanket, torn, with bloodstains and dark stains resembling grease. There was also a brown blanket with several holes, also with dark stains resembling grease. The majority of the fibres comprising it were of wool, and were of a rather unusual shade of brown. The grease stains were extracted, and it was possible to show that the substance present was similar to a type of greasy lubricant in the stores of the Police Department; and that both were similar to the grease on the weapons, which doubtless was used to prevent them from rusting. Infra-red spectroscopy was used for this purpose. There was nothing characteristic about this grease and this evidence, though contributory, was not in itself conclusive. However, an interesting fact noted was that the grease stains on the blanket and the grease on the weapons, while alike, were completely dissimilar from four other types of oil or grease also kept in the police store. Thus, although the weapons were not police weapons, the grease on them could have come from the police store.

It has been mentioned that bloodstains were found on the grey blanket. These were of human blood. It was thought at first that they were associated with the observation that one of the fugitives seen climbing over the wall had his hand against his face. However, none of the men arrested had any wounds, and examination of the bloodstains showed that they were of the drop rather than of the smear type to be expected from a wound. Medical examination showed no evidence of recent nose-bleeding from any of the men detained. As the stains were old it was not possible to carry out a grouping test. It was felt that they could have produced before the relevant date and this aspect of the evidence was not pursued further.

So far as the weapons found on the scene were concerned, these are shown in Fig. 1. They comprised a Bren gun, a Lee Enfield rifle, and an M6 rifle; 39 spent cartridges were found, and there were about the same number unused. The only features of importance were the grease referred to above, and fingerprints in the grease. On the weapons were found two prints each having 13 points of diagnostic identity with the right forefinger of Haritonos; one was on the magazine of the Bren gun. On some ammunition was found a print which had 16 points of diagnostic identity with the print from the right forefinger of Yenagritis. On other ammunition was found a print which had 16 points of identity with a print from the left thumb of Solomonodos. On further items of ammunition was found a print which had 16 points of diagnostic identity with a print from the left thumb of Yenagritis. Other prints were found, but were not produced in evidence. On the loaded Bren gun magazine and ammunition found on the roof of the Gymnasium were two prints having 16 points of diagnostic identity with a print from the right thumb of Solomonodos. Other fingerprint evidence attributable to Taliadoros, Haritonos and Yenagritis was found on the car. Some of these were found near the top edge and on the outside of one of the windows; indicating that the door had been pulled shut, using the partly opened window, by the owner of the print who was sitting inside.

In England 16 points of identity are taken as conclusive evidence of the identity of origin of two fingerprints. In Cyprus, in general the courts accept the same standards as in this country. It will be seen that except in one case the requisite 16 points were obtained. In the case of Haritonos only 13 such points per print were obtained but points from different parts of more than one print from the same finger can be added together to make the necessary 16. It could be claimed that the lack of further points of identity was due to the poor character of the prints found on the scene in this instance and that there were no dissimilarities between the two prints which could not be accounted for in the same way. Solomonodos, who had been a police officer, accepted that the prints found could have been his. Both he and Yenagritis were in the National Guard in 1963-67, and they stated that they had been in the habit of handling arms and ammunition. In mid-1969 the Police authorized the collection of arms surrendered by civilians. Yenagritis and Solomonodos claimed to have been involved in this operation; no Bren guns were among the arms then collected. Haritonos was in the National Guard in 1968 and said that he had handled Bren guns within nine months of the assassination attempt.

This gave rise to a lively controversy as to the age of the fingerprints, which is always difficult to determine with certainty. Supt. Dekatris, the capable fingerprint expert of the Cyprus C.I.D., held the view that the sharpness of the prints indicated recent origin. This was contested by the defence, but I felt that I could support the prosecution's argument because the prints were made in grease, which in the hot climate of Cyprus tends to run; and under these conditions fingerprints became blurred rapidly. An experiment in which prints made in grease on metal were kept at 20°C and 30°C (the summer temperature in Cyprus) for a few days, showed a distinct difference in sharpness when developed.

The defence called an expert, formerly of the Greek police force, but he was unable to convince the Court that the fingerprints were old or that the blurring on ageing theory was untenable, especially bearing in mind that at least nine months had elapsed since the alleged handling of the weapons and the discovery of the arms. In any case this referred only to the presence of the fingerprints of Solomonodos and Yenagritis, and not to those of their associates.

Fingerprint evidence was also sought from the cigarette ends. These were found on the scene, in the car, and in the police station after detention. Practically all were of the same make and had been smoked in the same way, i.e., to the extent of two-thirds of their length. They were then stubbed out in a similar way by being bent almost at right-angles. It was hoped that the stubbing-out operation would have left a fingerprint on the cigarette paper, but unfortunately nothing that could be satisfactorily used as evidence was found when we used the ninhydrin test. On the other hand experiments in which we produced similar stubs did leave fingerprints. The reason for this difference may have been the greater heat of burning in the case of the cigarette ends believed to have been associated with the accused; or because the smoker was one of the few people whose fingerprints do not respond to the ninhydrin test. It would have been interesting to have tested the fingerprints of the six men on paper to check this. A saliva grouping test on the cigarette ends might also have been helpful, but facilities were not available.

Much of the forensic work concerned fibres. The objective was to link the fibres from one or more blankets with one or more of the accused. This applied both to the fibres of which the blankets were made and to adventitious fibres found on the blankets. To this end a large collection from the wardrobes of the six men was seized and thoroughly examined, including the pocket linings—since the latest style in trousers can apparently contain as many as seven pockets! In all some 60 outer garments, including shoes, were tested; also included were contents of cars and blankets from the homes of the accused, which the defence alleged were the source of certain of the fibres found. This was extremely laborious work but was fully justified. The connecting links in the evidence were small in number but important. In my evidence on this aspect I thought it advisable to make clear the significance and limitation of evidence based on fibres. This disarmed some anticipated cross-examination.

In making a comparison between fibres found on a suspect and fibres found at the scene of a crime or on an article associated with it, there are three principal criteria to be taken into account, namely:

(a) the material of which the fibre is made;
(b) the colour of the fibre;
(c) its dimensions, i.e., shape and size.

1. Now, if one has two single fibres, one from the scene and one from the suspect, and they are alike in all the three above respects, then one can say that the fibres could have come from the same source, but that there is no certainty that they did so.
2. On the other hand if the fibres being compared are unusual in some respect as well as being alike, then the chance that they come from the same source is greater.
3. Finally, if one is examining groups of fibres, i.e., tufts of fibres of different kinds and different colours, then if the two groups contain the same fibres in the same proportions, then the possibility that they come from the same source is very high indeed; but one still cannot say with absolute certainty that they did so.

On the jacket belonging to Taliadoros, which had the white smear referred to above, I found a number of fibres which were not part of the composition of the jacket, i.e., extraneous fibres. On the left shoulder of the jacket was such a brown fibre, which matched closely the principal fibres of the brown blanket found at the scene of assassination attempt. Since this was an unusual fibre I placed it in category 2 above. This could not be regarded as conclusive evidence, because the brown fibre could have come from some other source. However, as stated, the shade of the colour was unusual and it is interesting to note that although some hundreds of fibres from various items of clothing, car dust, etc. were examined, in no case did a brown fibre similar to that from the blanket occur except on the left shoulder of Taliadoros's jacket. It should be added that the police took a multi-coloured blanket from the home of Taliadoros. It contained brown fibres, which were said to have accounted for the fibre on his jacket; there was a superficial resemblance, but microscopical methods showed the fibres to be quite different.

In the righthand pocket of the trousers of Taliadoros I found a tuft of fibres which was similar to the fibres comprising one of the blankets used to wrap the weapons. Since this consisted of no less than four fibres of different colours and types in each case, I placed this in the third category, representing the strongest possibility of identity.

On a pullover belonging to Yenagritis I found a human hair which was similar to a human hair which I found on one of the blankets from the school lavatory. It is impossible to say with complete certainty that two human hairs are or are not identical. However, these were alike in colour; they were both relatively long, too long for a male hair, even in these days; and I felt that the possibility that they came from the same source was strong. This was another link between Yenagritis and the blanket.

On the left arm of the jacket of Polykarpou I also found a tuft of fibres similar to those of one of the blankets, and the nature of these was such as to put them in the third category, of the strongest possibility. I also examined debris I collected from the body and boot of the car of Solomonodos and here I found a tuft of fibres similar to those of one of the blankets presumably used to wrap the guns. Here again the nature and the proportions of the fibres placed them in the category of maximum possibility.

The forensic evidence established links as follows:

Linking:

> Arms to blankets—grease.
> Arms to accused—fingerprints.
> Blanket to accused—fibres.
> Scene to accused—white smears (Taliadoros).
> Car to accused—fingerprints and fibres.

The preliminary enquiry was heard in Nicosia starting April 15, 1970, with Mr. A. Frangos, Senior Counsel of the Republic, for the prosecution. Ninety-five witnesses were called by the prosecution; cross-examination was reserved.

The subsequent trial was held in the assize court room of Nicosia in October, 1970. The prosecution was conducted by Mr. Talarides, Senior Counsel, and Mr. Frangos. In Cyprus legal procedure resembles that of England except that there is no jury, the verdict resting with the three presiding Judges. In a small country such as Cyprus this is regarded as a more desirable procedure. Apart from the prosecution forensic evidence, testimony was largely concerned with the actions, behaviour and alleged alibis of the accused. The Defence sought to establish alibis and to prove reasonable doubt as to the forensic evidence, but the combined effect of the latter apparently convinced the Judges. The charge against Polykarpou was withdrawn at the first hearing due to lack of evidence; only that from the fibres being available. Ioannides was acquitted owing to insufficient evidence; he was expelled from Cyprus. The remaining four were sentenced to 14 years' imprisonment in Nicosia and, according to the press, they subsequently confessed that theirs was one of several plots which were due to take place at the time of the attempted assassination and which undoubtedly would have done so had it not been for the prompt action of the authorities. The accused instructed their respective Counsel not to place any factors in mitigation before the Court; Haritonos stated that he did not pray for leniency.

The author is indebted to the Government of Cyprus for permission to reproduce the illustrations; and to Chief Supt. Hadjiloizou for his co-operation in the preparation of this paper.

TEAMWORK IN THE FORENSIC SCIENCES:
REPORT OF A CASE

L. W. Bradford and A. A. Biasotti

*Director and Supervising Criminalist, respectively, Laboratory of
Criminalistics, San Jose, California*

The scene in which the following events occurred is a single story
dwelling in a quiet residential neighborhood where the victim lived.
The victim was a 45-year-old woman who lived in the second house
on a particular cul-de-sac street next to a red house on the corner
(which is of later significance). A street light is situated here.

The investigative events began with the discovery of the victim
lying faceup over the foot of her bed with the top of her head completely blown off. Tissue debris covered both walls and the ceiling
surrounding the victim. The gruesome discovery was made and reported immediately at 2:30 A.M. by an elderly male boarder who
rented one bedroom in the victim's house. The boarder had entered
the house, using his key, at about 1:15 A.M. after working as a bar-
tender since 4 P.M. the previous day. He went directly to his bedroom and read for about an hour. When ready to retire, he noticed
lights in the victim's bedroom and kitchen. Investigating, he discovered the victim. The first patrol unit arrived at the scene within
minutes. The patrol officer found no weapon and, after a quick
search for a possible intruder on the premises, called for assistance.

The detective team arrived at the scene within ten minutes and
was followed within the hour by a team of four investigators who
were immediately deployed to interview neighbors for possible leads.
A more detailed search of the scene revealed that:

1. All doors were locked and there were no signs of forced entry.
2. The victim's clothing was neatly arranged on a chair next to her bed.
3. There was no indication of a struggle prior to the fatal shot.
4. Valuables appears to be intact and undisturbed.

After photographing the victim and the scene, the body was removed; and a search was made for the projectile which caused the
extensive trauma to the victim. A high velocity weapon was assumed
to be the cause of death.

The major portion of a 150 grain, military type, jacketed bullet
was recovered in the wall space back of the headboard of the victim's

bed. A projection of the bullet path through the mattress, headboard, and wall, in conjunction with the position of the body, an apparent "defense" type wound on the lower right wrist of the victim, and the lack of powder residues indicated that the victim was shot while sitting on the end of the bed, leaning back at about a 30-degree angle, and holding her right arm held in defensive fashion over her face. Class characteristics of the rifle impressed on the .30 caliber bullet indicated the possibility of Remington Rifles, Model numbers 721 to 760.

This fatal bullet was destined to be the vital link in connecting the suspect with the victim, but in a very unusual manner. The second vital link, discovered later in the investigation, was a cancelled check, which will be discussed separately.

Canvassing of the immediate neighbors developed several witnesses who on the evening before:

1. Heard a loud "bang" or "back fire" between 10:15 P.M. and 10:30 P.M.
2. Saw a red station wagon with white top, round tail lights, and loud muffler start up and drive out of cul-de-sac within a few minutes after hearing the "loud bang." The license number was not obtained.
3. Described the driver of the vehicle as a male—without further details.

It was also learned from persons in the neighborhood that a vehicle similar to the described station wagon had been parked near the scene on several previous occasions.

Careful and methodical interrogation of all the neighbors, known friends, and former husband (amicably separated) of the victim continued until such time that a conference was called by the detective-in-charge to summarize and evaluate the information assembled. Logical suspects, including the boarder, the former husband, and several known acquaintances, were quickly eliminated because alibis were confirmed by investigation. One lead, however, needed to be followed. It was learned from friends that the victim frequented a local commercial dance studio. Questioning of persons present during Wednesday afternoon at the dance studio indicated that most of the victim's dancing lessons had been with a part-time instructor who would be in a position to give more information about the victim's acquaintances and habits than anyone else.

Through further leads and contacts, the address of this man was found to be an apartment in an adjacent city. The instructor was 23 years old and married with two children. Two detectives upon arriving at the suspect's apartment, noted a red and white 1955 Ford Station Wagon parked in the stall of the apartment. Upon knocking and identifying themselves they were invited into the living room by

the instructor. While questioning him about the victim, her acquaintances, and his actions the night of the murder, the detectives noted a
marble topped coffee table, end table, and lamp which fitted the
description of furniture taken in a burglary of the victim's residence
several months prior. When asked about this furniture, the instructor
said that he had purchased it somewhere at a department store. He
later changed his story indicating that it was given to him by a friend.
The suspect further stated that he had visited the victim the previous
week to borrow $50; but instead he sold her a painting for $140. He
denied any knowledge of the murder or of owning a caliber .30 rifle.

He had a good alibi for the night of the murder. He had taken his
wife (a waitress) to work early Wednesday evening, taking their
children (girl, age 5; boy, age 3) with them and returned home to
baby-sit, clean house, and watch TV until about 12:30 A.M. when he
departed, leaving the children at home alone, to pick up his wife at
work.

As the result of this initial questioning, during which the suspect
had changed some of his story, and considering the presence of the
stolen furniture, the investigators asked the suspect to go to police
headquarters for further questioning, which he did willingly. Further
interrogation of the suspect at headquarters, and interrogation of his
wife, separately, strengthened the investigators' suspicions that the
suspect was not telling the truth and knew more about the murder
than he had admitted. At the conclusion of these interviews, the man
and wife accepted the police opinion that the furniture was stolen
property and allowed it to be taken from their apartment. The man
was released at this time after agreeing to a polygraph examination
the following day.

Shortly after midnight when the investigators arrived at the suspect's apartment to recover the furniture, they learned from a neighbor adjacent to the suspect's apartment that their apartment had
been burglarized about three weeks earlier while she and her husband
were away for that weekend. This burglary had been investigated and
revealed a forced entry by cutting a screen over the bathroom window and entry through an unlocked window. Reported stolen were a
Remington .30-'06 Model 760 Gamemaster rifle and $10 in cash.
With this information in hand, a warrant to search the suspect's
apartment and station wagon was obtained and executed on Friday
afternoon, the second day following the murder.

The search of the suspect's apartment brought forth the following:

1. A paper target with bullet holes which appeared to be about .30 caliber.
2. One fired caliber .30-'06 cartridge case (established by laboratory examination to be not connected with the stolen rifle).

3. A caliber .22 rifle, a .410 gauge shotgun and a caliber .25 pistol.
4. An electric shaver identified as belonging to the boarder living in the victim's house and reported stolen in a burglary.
5. A pair of stained trousers (lab examination revealed no blood or human tissue on these trousers).

The search of the suspect's station wagon developed the following:

1. Cuff links identified as taken with the electric shaver found in the apartment.
2. A large "gunshot" penetration from interior to exterior at about a 45 degree angle in the right side with the entry in line with the top of the rear-seat cushion.

The "gunshot" hole in the suspect's vehicle was an unexplained event which later developed into yet another interesting speculative aspect of this case. From an examination of the penetration, powder, pattern, and lead pellets found in the vehicle, it was determined that this hole was consistent with the firing of a .410 gauge shotgun. It was found that this single shot, bolt action Mossberg, Model 173 A, .410 gauge shotgun found in the suspect's apartment would fire when dropped on its butt with the thumb safety in the "fire" position. This information at the time did little more than add mystery to the investigation. About 19 days after the murder, however, this event assumed new significance when one of the investigators in checking out the neighborhood near the scene observed what appeared to be a pellet pattern on the sidewalk next to the curb in front of the house on the corner next to the victim's residence. This was the area in which the red and white station wagon had been observed parked on previous occasions. Examination of the pattern in conjunction with the hole in the vehicle indicated that the pattern, size, shape, shot imprints, and angle were all consistent with the hypothesis that the suspect's .410 shotgun discharged through the right side while parked at the curb. No statements had been given by the suspect to the point of this evidence.

When again questioned about the items recovered in the search and his alibis, the suspect refused to answer most questions without his attorney. He did, however, attempt to explain the target with the caliber .30 bullet holes by saying that he had recently been to a local outdoor shooting ranch where he was shooting a "large caliber rifle" which he described as "more than a .22 and smaller than a cannon." This statement, which must have been an inadvertent "slip" by the suspect, provided a useful clue.

All information thus far obtained pointed to a connection between the suspect and the victim, the burglaries, and possibly the murder; but a direct link with the crime was not a matter of established fact. Based upon these tenuous developments and on the advice of the District Attorney of Santa Clara County, the suspect was arrested and charged with Burglary, Receiving Stolen Property, and Murder. After the arrest the chief detective found a key in the personal property taken from the suspect at the time of booking which appeared to be identical with the house key to the victim's residence. The suspect when questioned about the key said that it was for a prior residence in the area and gave an address. A check of this alibi address revealed that the suspect and his wife had lived at that address. The locks had not been changed after they had moved, and the key taken from the suspect and matching the victim's key did not open any of the locks at the alibi address; but it did open the entrance door to the victim's house. How or when the suspect obtained this key has never been determined, but it was known that the victim stored her wraps and purse in the cloak room at dancing periods when the suspect was present. Consequently, he had the opportunity to make a duplicate.

At this point, a service station attendant was located who tentatively identified the suspect as one who had stopped at his gas station in the vicinity of the death scene on the night of the murder.

The suspect, when faced with all of the apparent contradictions to his alibis, accused the police of lying and attempting to falsely implicate him and refused to answer further questions. When the time for an agreed polygraph examination arrived, he refused to undergo the examination. From this point on, no further information was obtained directly from the suspect which would aid in the solution of the case.

Two days after the murder, the police were faced with an array of alibis, contradictions, and facts which appeared to be pieces of a puzzle, but which defied fitting together in any logical way. It was again time for reflection and contemplation before planning the next move. A review of the progress to date indicated that the next two main lines of investigation should be:

1. To contact the neighbors of the suspect who resided in the apartment adjacent to the suspect to determine whether any fired components from the caliber .30-'06 Remington Model 760 rifle were available from the period prior to the time of the burglary in which the rifle was taken.
2. To investigate the shooting range for spent bullets where the suspect indicated that he may have fired a rifle.

The neighbors were contacted first and three fired .30-'06 cartridge cases were obtained which had been fired from the rifle before it was stolen (Fig. 3). When asked when and where the rifle had last been fired, the neighbor replied that it had been at a pine tree during the recent fall deer hunting season in the Sierra Nevada mountains located about 150 miles from his apartment. This occurred while he was hunting with a friend and a nephew. The neighbor had his .30-'06 Remington Model 760 rifle; the friend had a .30-'06 Springfield, Model 1903 rifle; and his nephew had a .30-30 Winchester Model 94 rifle. He said that he and his nephew had sighted in their rifles with targets placed against a large pine tree at a distance of about 150 feet from a clearing near a road. Several shots were fired. He thought that he could locate the tree. Four days after the murder, the neighbor guided investigators to a pine tree approximately 100 feet tall and about 30-in. in diameter. A small section surrounding one apparent bullet hole was cut out, and a jacketed bullet was recovered and returned to the laboratory in San Jose for examination. This bullet was found to be from a caliber .30 weapon of six right hand riflings with a land width consistent with the Model 94 Winchester used by the neighbor's nephew. A second trip to the pine tree was made; and with permission and assistance of the U.S. Forest Service, the tree was felled. A five-foot section of the trunk was returned to Santa Clara County where it was split and dissected. With the aid of X-ray equipment, a second bullet was recovered. The bullet was fully mushroomed, leading to a cover over the rifling marks which had preserved the class and individual characteristics on the base portion of the metal jacket. The bullet proved to be a soft point fired from a caliber .30 weapon with class characteristics consistent with a Remington Model 760 rifle. These class characteristics were the same as as those of the fatal bullet. Further study revealed a significant similarity of individual characteristics between the fatal bullet and the bullet from the tree indicating that both had been fired by the neighbor's stolen rifle (Figs. 1 and 2).

The next phase of the investigation proceeded to the shooting range where it was believed that the suspect may have fired a rifle prior to the murder. Nine days after the murder the range master of the Sunnyvale Rod and Gun Club was contacted, and it was determined that the range had opened about a month prior to the murder after renovating the sandstone-shale embankment which served as a backstop at 100 yards from the firing point. The range had been closed for about three months while the embankment was scraped and cleared. When shown a photo of the suspect and asked if he recognized the person, the range master stated that the photo resembled a person using the range during the past month who was shooting a .30-'06 Remington Model Gamemaster, "pump-action" rifle. Entries on the sign-in register required for all persons using

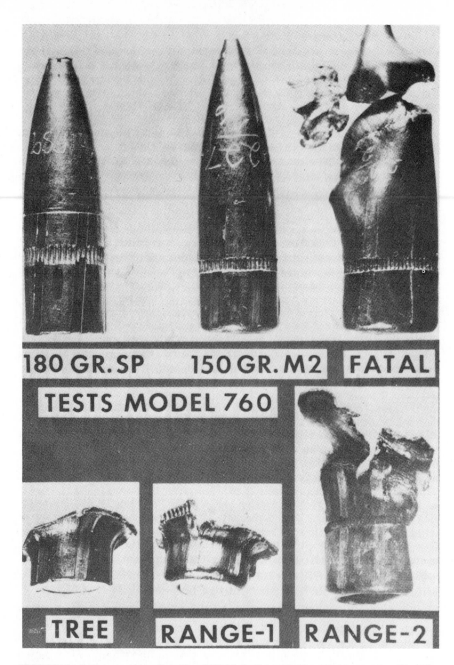

FIGURE 1. Bullets used to link the FATAL bullet with the missing murder rifle. The FATAL bullet and the two RANGE bullets are metal jacketed, spitzer, 150 grain M2 ball (U.S. Army) military type. The bullet from the TREE is a 180 grain soft point corresponding to ammunition possessed by the owner of the stolen rifle. The two TESTS were *not* fired by the murder weapon and are included solely for the purpose of illustrating bullet type and class characteristics of rifling marks.

386

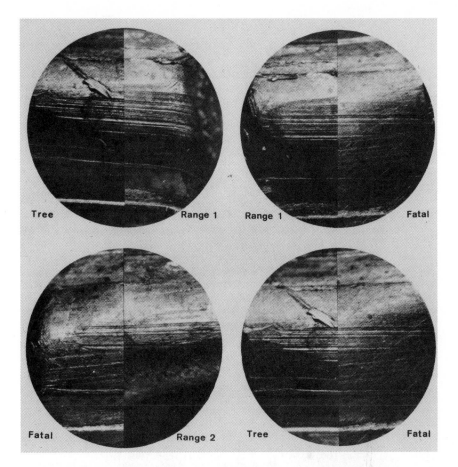

FIGURE 2. Comparison photomicrographs demonstrating the identification between the bullets shown in Figure 1.

the range were hastily searched for the name and address of the suspect. None being found, the list was submitted to the Laboratory of Criminalistics for a handwriting examination to determine whether or not the suspect could have signed the register using an assumed name.

When the register was examined at the Laboratory, the only immediately available authentic specimen of handwriting of the suspect was his endorsement on a $140 check which he had earlier mentioned in connection with the purported sale of a painting to the victim. An examination of the complete range record revealed the name of the suspect one week later than the date first indicated by the range master. This name was identified with the writing on the check endorsement. There was further examination of the check which will

FIGURE 3. Comparison photomicrographs demonstrating the identification between cartridge cases recovered near tree to cases from the owner of stolen rifle.

be discussed separately. The signature on the range record was dated three days prior to the murder. The register indicated that he was assigned to firing Point # 29. Point # 30 was the last firing position. A man and his son assigned lanes 27 and 28 and another person assigned lane 30 were immediately contacted and questioned. Lanes 29 and 30 were customarily the only targets used for high velocity weapons.

The man and his sons shooting lanes 27 and 28 identified the suspect from a photograph and said he was firing a .30-'06 Remington Model 742 or 760 in lane 29. Also that he was firing military type ammunition and when asked if they could have his brass, the suspect replied that he was saving it for a friend. They further noted that a girl, about 5 and a boy, about 3, accompanied the suspect at the range. Based upon this information the embankment covering targets # 28, 29 and 30 was searched with the aid of a screen. Several buckets of metal jacket fragments were recovered. The buckets of projectiles were taken to the laboratory where rapid sorting based on gross class characteristics eliminated all but a few jackets and jacket fragments with class characteristics similar to the fatal bullet (Fig. 1).

A detailed comparison microscope examination was now begun which revealed that two bullet jackets from the range had class and individual characteristics that established an identity between the .30 caliber bullet from the tree and the fatal bullet (Figs. 1 and 2). Thus, about three weeks after the murder, the two bullets from the range provided the needed missing link between the stolen rifle and the fatal bullet. Without this evidence a connection between the stolen rifle and the fatal bullet would never have been established because the rifle had not been found. The physical evidence had now provided a link between the murder weapon and the suspect and the fatal bullet. To strengthen this link further, a third trip was made to the area from which the neighbor had fired at the pine tree. With the aid of a metal detector, three fired .30-'06 cartridge cases were found. Microscopic comparisons of breech bolt marks on these cases led to an identification with the three fired cases previously obtained from the neighbor (Fig. 3).

Returning to the subject of the $140 check, the endorsement was of interest as an exemplar of the defendant's signature for the purpose of comparison with the range record. Much to the surprise of the investigators during the preliminary examination of this document at the laboratory, it was discovered that the entire face of the check was traced. It was further determined that the payer signature was traced from an authentic victim's signature and the remainder of the check was traced from authentic writing of the suspect, including his own name as payee.

The document examiner, upon this finding, asked the detectives to obtain the victim's check stubs for the period involved with the $140 check.

It was found that the traced check was numbered in a sequence different from those covering the period of her stubs. The traced check was number 330. A new group of five personalized check books had recently been received from the bank by mail. Four of these were found by the detectives in an opened bank envelope on the victim's desk. The fifth book containing checks No. 325 through 349 were missing. Speculate now as to the reason that check No. 330 was cashed by the defendant rather than Nos. 325, 326, 327, 328, and 329.

The prosecutor charged first degree murder. The defendant was found guilty and was sentenced to life. The prosecutor used the following lines of argument following the presentation of all the evidence:

1. The victim was a lonely woman who had spent several thousand dollars for dancing lessons over a period of years as a form of recreation.
2. The defendant gained a knowledge of the victim's habits, address, and situation through frequent association as a dance instructor.
3. Through access to the defendant's wraps and purse while at dancing sessions, the defendant gained possession of a key by either replication or theft.
4. Using this illicit key, the defendant had made visits to the victim's home while she was attending dance sessions in other areas. He had taken property from this home on several occasions. This included the furniture, boarder's cuff links, and the check book.
5. The defendant had burglarized his neighbor's apartment and had taken the .30-'06 rifle. When entering the victim's home, he was armed, first with the .410 gauge shotgun, later with the .30-'06 rifle. The long-barreled weapons were concealed by placing them on the floor behind the driver's seat of the vehicle. On one of these occasions, while the vehicle was parked near the victim's home, the shotgun was accidentally discharged while in the act of placing or removing it from this position.
6. The defendant traced the victim's signature on check No. 325, using the technique of carbon paper; however, when he covered the tracing with ink, it was a different color than his freehand writing on the remainder of the check face. He continued practicing the forgery until he learned that tracing the entire check face was the only method of avoiding a difference in appearance of the ink color between the payer line and remaining entries. In this way he used up checks Nos. 325, 326, 327, 328, and 329, and finally perfected the forgery on check No. 330.
7. After cashing the check, the defendant waited until the day that he thought cancelled checks through the mail would arrive at the victim's house, at which time he again entered the home armed with the rifle intending to remove the cancelled check No. 330 and destroy it in order to conceal the forgery; he unexpectedly encountered the victim and killed her.

The case is bizarre for several reasons:

1. The connection of the fatal bullet with the suspect without the rifle is exceptionally uncommon.
2. The fact of a defendant tracing his own name is very peculiar.
3. The good fortune of finding exemplar bullets in examinable condition from the tree and range under the circumstances described is unlikely.

It is to the credit of the investigators, examiners, and prosecutors that they recognized the value and significance of all of the facets of the evidence and were able to communicate with each other in a manner which made the most effective use of all of it.

Glossary

Acid— A compound capable of donating a hydrogen ion (H^+) to another compound.

Agglutination— The clumping together of red blood cells by the action of an antibody.

Allele— Any of several alternative forms of a gene located at the same point on a particular pair of chromosomes. For example, the genes determining the blood types A and B are alleles.

Alpha Ray— A type of radiation emitted by a radioactive element. The radiation is composed of helium atoms minus their orbiting electrons.

Alveolus— A small sac in the lungs through whose walls air and other vapors are exchanged between the breath and the blood.

Amorphous Solid— A solid in which the constituent atoms or molecules are arranged in random or disordered positions. There is no regular order in amorphous solids.

Analagesic— A drug or substance that lessens or eliminates pain.

Anthropometry— A system of identification of individuals by measurements of parts of the body, developed by Alphonse Bertillon.

Antibody— A protein that destroys or inactivates a specific antigen. Antibodies are found in the blood serum.

Anticoagulant— A substance which prevents coagulation or clotting of the blood.

Antigen— A substance, usually a protein, that stimulates the body to produce antibodies against it.

Antiserum— Blood serum in which there are specific antibodies.

Artery— A blood vessel that carries blood away from the heart.

Atom— The smallest unit of an element; not divisible by ordinary chemical means. Atoms are made up of electrons, protons, and neutrons plus other subatomic particles.

Atomic Mass Number— The sum of the number of protons and neutrons in the nucleus of an atom.

Atomic Number— The number of protons in the nucleus of the atom. Each element has its own unique atomic number.

Base— A compound capable of accepting a hydrogen ion (H^+).

Becke Line— A bright halo that is observed near the border of a particle immersed in a liquid of a different refractive index.

Beta Ray— A type of radiation emitted by a radioactive element. The radiation consists of electrons.

Birefringence— A difference in the two indices of refraction exhibited by some crystalline materials.

Black Powder— Normally, a mixture of potassium nitrate, carbon, and sulfur in the ratio 75/15/10.

Caliber— The diameter of the bore of a rifled firearm. The caliber is usually expressed in hundreds of an inch, or millimeters; e.g., .22 caliber, and 9mm.

Capillary— A tiny blood vessel across whose walls exchange of materials between the blood and the tissues takes place; receives blood from arteries and carries it to veins.

Catalyst— A substance that accelerates the rates of chemical reactions but is not itself permanently changed by the reaction.

Celsius Scale— The temperature scale using the melting point of ice as 0 and the boiling point of water as 100, with 100 equal divisions or degrees between.

Chemical Property— Describes the behavior of a substance when it reacts or combines with another substance.

Chromosome— A rodlike structure in the cell nucleus, along which the genes are located.

Combustion— The rapid combination of oxygen with another substance accompanied by the production of noticeable heat and light.

Compound— A collection of similar kind of molecules formed from two or more elements.

Continuous Spectrum— A type of emission spectrum showing a continuous band of colors all blending into one another.

Crystalline Solid— A solid in which the constituent atoms have a regular arrangement.

Density— A physical property of matter that is equivalent to the mass per unit volume of a substance.

Depressant— A substance used to depress the functions of the central nervous system. Depressants calm irritability and anxiety, and may induce sleep.

Detonating Cord— A cordlike explosive containing a core of high-explosive material, usually PETN. Also called primacord.

Dispersion— The separation of light into its component wavelengths.

Egg— The female reproductive cell.

Ejector— The mechanism in a firearm which throws the cartridge or fired case from the firearm.

Electron— A very light, negatively charged particle which is one of the fundamental structural units of the atom.

Electron Orbitals— The pathway of electrons as they move around the nuclei of atoms. Each orbital is associated with a particular electronic energy level.

Element— A collection of atoms all having the same atomic number. An element cannot be broken down into simpler substances by chemical means.

Emission Spectrum— Light emitted from a source and separated into its component colors or frequencies.

Endothermic Reaction— A chemical transformation in which heat energy is absorbed from the surroundings.

Energy— The combined ability or potential of a system or material to do work. Some forms of energy are heat energy, chemical energy, and electrical energy.

Enzyme— A type of protein that acts as a catalyst for certain specific reactions.

Erythrocyte— A red blood cell.

Extractor— The mechanism in a firearm by which a cartridge of a fired case is withdrawn from the chamber.

Exothermic Reaction— A chemical transformation in which heat energy is liberated.

Explosion— A chemical or mechanical action resulting in the rapid expansion of gases.

Fahrenheit Scale— The temperature scale using the melting point of ice as 32° and the boiling point of water 212°, with 180 equal divisions or degrees between.

Flash Point— The minimum temperature at which a liquid fuel will produce enough vapor to burn.

Fluoresce— To emit visible light when exposed to light of a shorter wavelength—i.e., ultraviolet light.

Frequency— The number of waves that pass a given point per second.

Gamma Ray— A high-energy form of electromagnetic radiation emitted by a radioactive element.

Gas— A state of matter in which the attractive forces between molecules is small enough to permit them to move with complete freedom.

Gauge— Size designation of a shotgun; originally the number of lead balls with the same diameter as the barrel that would make a pound. For example, a 12-gauge shotgun would have a bore diameter of a lead ball 1/12 of a pound in weight. The only exception is the .410 shotgun, in which bore size is .41 inch.

Gene— A unit of inheritance located on a chromosome.

Genotype— The particular combination of genes present in the cells of an individual.

Glowing Combustion— Burning at the fuel air interface. Examples are a red-hot charcoal or a burning cigarette.

Hallucinogen— A substance which induces changes in mood, attitude, thought, or perception.

Heat of Combustion— The heat evolved when a substance is burned in oxygen.

Hemoglobin— A red blood cell protein responsible for transporting oxygen in the bloodstream and the red coloring of blood.

Heterozygous— Having two different allelic genes on two corresponding positions of a pair of chromosomes.

High-Energy Explosive— Explosive with a velocity of detonation greater than 1,000 meters per second. For example, dynamite and RDX.

Homozygous— Having two identical allelic genes on two corresponding positions of a pair of chromosomes.

Hydrocarbon— Any compound consisting only of carbon and hydrogen.

Ignition Temperature— The minimum temperature at which a fuel will spontaneously ignite.

Inorganic Compound— A chemical compound not based on carbon.

Ion— An atom or molecule bearing a positive or negative charge.

Iso-enzymes— Multiple molecular forms of an enzyme, each having the same or very similar enzyme activities.

Isotope— An atom differing from another atom of the same element in the number of neutrons it has in its nucleus.

Line Spectrum— A type of emission spectrum showing a series of lines separated by black areas. Each line represents a definite wavelength or frequency.

Liquid— A state of matter in which molecules are in contact with one another but are not rigidly held in place.

Low-Energy Explosive— Explosive with a velocity of detonation less than 1,000 meters per second. For example, black powder and smokeless powder.

Mass— A constant property of matter which reflects the amount of material present.

Matter— All things of substance. Matter is composed of atoms or molecules.

Microcrystalline Tests— Tests to identify specific substances by the color and morphology of the crystals formed when the substance is mixed with specific reagents.

Mineral— A naturally occurring crystalline solid.

Molecule— Two or more atoms held together by chemical bonds.

Monomer— The basic unit of structure from which a polymer is constructed.

Narcotic— Analgesic substances that depresses vital body functions such as blood pressure, pulse rate, and breathing rate. The regular administration of narcotics will produce physical dependence.

Neutron— A particle having no electrical charge which, along with the proton, is a basic unit in the structure of the nucleus of an atom.

Nucleus— The core of an atom in which the protons and neutrons exist.

Organic Compound— Substances composed of carbon and hydrogen, and often, smaller amounts of oxygen, nitrogen, chlorine, phosphorus, or other elements.

Oxidation— The combination of oxygen with other substances to produce new products.

Oxidizing Agent— A substance that supplies oxygen to a chemical reaction.

Parfocal— Construction of a microscope such that when an image is focused with one objective in position, the other objective can be rotated into place and the field will remain in focus.

pH— A symbol used to express the basicity or acidity of a substance. A pH of 7 is neutral; lower values are acidic, higher values basic.

Phase— A uniform piece of matter. Different phases are separated by definite visible boundries.

Phenotype— The physical manifestation of a genetic trait such as shape, color, and blood type.

Photon— A small packet of electromagnetic radiation energy. Each photon contains a unit of energy equal to the product of Plank's constant and the frequency of radiation—E = hf.

Physical Dependence— Physiological need for a drug that has been brought about by its regular use. Dependence is characterized by withdrawal sickness when administration of the drug is abruptly stopped.

Physical Evidence— Any object that can establish that a crime has been committed or can provide a link between a crime and its victim or a crime and its perpetrator.

Physical Property— Describes the behavior of a substance without reference to any other substance.

Plane-Polarized Light— Light confined to a single plane of vibration.

Plasma— The fluid portion of unclotted blood.

Polymer— A substance composed of a large number of atoms. These atoms are usually arranged in repeating units or monomers.

Polymorphism— The occurrence in a population of two or more common alleles producing a variety of phenotypes. For example, blood types are examples of polymorphism. Similarly, some enzymes exist in different forms and are therefore polymorphic.

Precipitin— An antibody which reacts with its corresponding antigen to form a precipitate.

Preservative— A substance added to blood in order to inhibit the growth of micro-organisms. Sodium fluoride is a common preservative.

Proteins— Polymers of amino acids that play basic roles in the structures and functions of living things.

Proton— A positively charged particle that is one of the basic structures in the nucleus of an atom.

Psychological Dependence— The conditioned use of a drug caused by underlying emotional needs.

Pyrolysis— The decomposition of organic matter by heat.

Radioactivity— The particle and/or gamma ray radiation emitted by the unstable nucleus of some isotopes.

Real Image— An image formed by the actual convergence of light rays upon a screen.

Refraction— The bending of a light wave as it passes from one medium to another.

Refractive Index— The ratio of the speed of light in a vacuum to its speed in a given substance.

Ridge Characteristics— Ridge endings, birefractions, enclosures, and other ridge details which must match in two fingerprints in order for their common origin to be established. Also call minutiae.

Safety Fuse— A cord containing a core of black powder. It is used to carry a flame at a uniform rate to an explosive charge.

Secretor— An individual who secretes his/her blood type antigen(s) in body fluids. Approximately 80 percent of the population are secretors.

Serology— The study of antigen-antibody reactions.

Serum— The liquid that separates from the blood when a clot is formed.

Smokeless Powder (double-base)— An explosive consisting of a mixture of nitrocellulose and nitroglycerin.

Smokeless Powder (single-base)— An explosive consisting of nitrocellulose.

Solid— A state of matter in which the molecules are held closely tobether in a rigid state.

Sperm— The male reproductive cell.

Spontaneous Combustion— A fire caused by a natural heat-producing process in the presence of sufficient air and fuel.

Stimulant— A substance taken to increase alertness or activity.

Sublimation— A physical change from the solid directly into the gaseous state.

Titration— The analytical operation of adding a reagent until a reaction is complete, and then measuring the volume so added.

Vein— A blood vessel that transports blood toward the heart.

Virtual Image— An image that cannot be seen directly. It can only be seen by a viewer looking through a lens.

Wavelength— The distance between crests of adjacent waves.

Weight— A property of matter that depends both on the mass of a substance and the effects of gravity on that mass.

X Chromosome— The female sex chromosome.

X-ray— A high-energy, short-wavelength form of electromagnetic radiation.

Y Chromosome— The male sex chromosome.

Appendices

Appendix I
Guide to the Collection of Physical Evidence
New Jersey State Police

Specimen	Packaging	Amount Required		Collection Procedure
		Control	Evidence	
AMMUNITION
Cartridges (unfired)	Place in small clasp type envelope.		Submit separately those found in gun from all other evidence cartridges.	Initial on case near bullet end.
Discharged bullets	Same as above. (Separate envelope for each specimen).		All found.	Initial on base or nose, never on side.
Discharged shells	Place in small clasp type envelope. (Separate envelopes if found at different locations, mark each envelope.)		All found.	Initial on outside of case near open end. (Never mark where firing pin strikes.)
Shotgun shells	Same as above.		All found	Initial on brass near paper or plastic.
Pellets	Same as above.		All found.	Not necessary to mark pellet. Mark envelope with initials.
Wadding	Same as above, if taken from body, dry before submitting. Place in		All found.	Mark envelope with initials.

ARSON ACCELERANTS

	Packaging	Amount	Remarks
	clasp type envelope, mark outside.		
Gasoline, Kerosene, etc.	Metal or glass container with airtight seal.	One Pint	Volatile liquids must be poured into clean containers and sealed. Submit original container.
Residues	Metal or glass container with airtight seal.	Identical material uncontaminated with suspect accelerant.	Collect specimens which have an odor or trace of fluid, or those which are capable of absorbing the suspect accelerant.

BLOOD
(See Toxicology)

	Packaging	Amount	Remarks
Dry stains not on fabrics.	Solid container or druggist fold. Wrap each stain separately.	5cc of whole blood containing an anticoagulant (the anticoagulant EDTA is recommended) collected from suspect and like amount from victim.	On small objects—send entire stained object. On large objects—scrape stain onto clean paper using a clean blade for each stain. **DO NOT** add preservative to control blood.
Stained clothing, fabrics, etc.	Place in clean paper bags. **DO NOT USE PLASTIC BAGS** (causes mildew). Wrap separately.	As above 5cc of whole blood from suspect and like amount from victim.	If wet, air-dry thoroughly. **DO NOT** use heat to dry. **DO NOT** add a preservative to control blood.

(continued)

Specimen	Packaging	Amount Required		Collection Procedure
		Control	Evidence	
CLOTHING	Place in clean paper bag. **DO NOT USE PLASTIC BAGS.** Wrap or bag each item separately.		All	Leave clothing whole, **DO NOT** cut out suspect area. **AIR DRY WET CLOTHING.**
DOCUMENTS Anonymous letters, extortion letters, bank robbery notes.	Plastic sheet protector.	Original documents in document cases, reproductions are unacceptable. (See *Footnote**)	All original documents.	**DO NOT** handle with bare hands. Place in proper enclosure envelope and seal with cellophane tape. Specify if evidence is to be treated for latent prints.
Charred or burned paper.	Solid container.		All	**DO NOT** handle with bare hands.
Checks	Envelopes.	(See *Footnote**)	All	As with Anonymous letters. Advise what parts questioned or known. Furnish physical description of suspect.
Check protector, rubber stamp and dater stamp sets, known standards.	Plastic sheet protectors.	Obtain several in full. (complete series of numbers)	All	As with Anonymous letters. **DO NOT** disturb inking mechanisms on printing devices. **SEND ACTUAL DEVICE WHEN POSSIBLE.**
Handwriting and handprinting, known standards.	Same as above.	(See *Footnote**)	All	See Anonymous letters.

Obliterated, eradicated or indented writing.		Same as above. **DO NOT** fold.	All	Advise if bleach or staining method may be used.
Typewriting, known standards	Obtain minimum of one copy in full word for word order of questioned typewriting. Include partial copies in light, medium, heavy touch. Also carbon samples of each character on keyboard.	Same as above.	All	See Anonymous letters. Examine ribbon for evidence of questioned message thereon. For carbon paper samples, either remove ribbon or place in stencil position and type directly on carbon paper placed over bond paper.
EXPLOSIVE RESIDUES	All	Solid sealed container.	All	Collected debris and bomb fragments around suspected origin or explosion. The laboratory **WILL NOT** accept potentially explosive bombs or chemicals. These items should be deactivated by the nearest bomb disposal unit.
FIBERS	Entire garment or other cloth items.	Individual fibers are packaged in a druggist fold, pill box or vial. **DO NOT** place loose in an envelope.	All	Package separately, fibers collected from different sources; whenever possible submit the entire article on which the fibers have been observed. **DO NOT** use Tape to collect fibers.

(continued)

Specimen	Packaging	Amount Required		Collection Procedure
		Control	Evidence	
FINGERNAIL SCRAPINGS	Druggist fold or plastic vial.		All available.	A clean knife blade should be used to scrape under each fingernail. A separate druggist fold or vial should be used for each finger and clearly marked identifying the finger or fingers.
FIREARMS Automatic Pistols	Unload weapon unless the presence of other evidence prohibits handling; i.e., blood, hairs, fibers, prints. Weapon can be placed in a heavy duty envelope and the outside of the envelope marked **"LOADED"** or **"UNLOADED."**		All found.	Attach a tag indicating the name, caliber and serial number of the weapon along with the investigators initials. Special care should be exercised to preserve other evidence on the weapon; i.e., blood, hair, fibers, latent prints. Should these items be present, the weapon should be carefully packaged in a cardboard box. Exterior of the carton or box marked, **"LOADED"** or **"UNLOADED."** Request for examination should specify the weapon is to be examined for other types of

			evidence—blood, hairs, fibers, latent prints.
			Initials of the investigator should be placed in the magazine well and under the slide.
Revolvers	Same as for Automatic Pistols.	All found.	Procedure same as automatic pistols. Initial under top strap.
Rifles and Shotguns	Unload weapon unless the presence of other evidence prohibits handling; i.e., blood, hairs, fibers, prints.

Weapons not involving other types of physical evidence may be hand carried.

Weapons requiring examination of other physical evidence—blood, hair, fiber, prints must be carefully packed in a cardboard box or carton to preserve the evidence.

Indicate whether **"LOADED"** or **"UNLOADED."** | All found. | Attach a tag indicating the name, caliber and serial number of the weapon along with the investigators initials.

Initials of the investigator should be placed inside the trigger guard. |

| Specimen | Packaging | Amount Required | | Collection Procedure |
		Control	Evidence	
GLASS Fragments	Place questioned and known fragments in separate solid containers. Avoid breakage.	All	All	All glass found at crime scene should be recovered and submitted.
Particles	Place in pill box, druggist fold or vial. Seal and protect against breakage. **DO NOT** place loose in envelope.	3" piece of broken item.	All	Forceps can be used to collect glass particles, whenever possible submit the entire article on which the particles have been observed.
HAIR	Druggist fold, pill box or vial. **DO NOT** place loose in envelope.	Several dozen or more full length hairs **PULLED** not clipped from different parts of body/or head.	All	Package separately, hairs collected from different sources. Label location from which taken. Whenever possible, submit the entire article on which the hairs have been observed.
NARCOTICS AND DANGEROUS DRUGS Liquids	Solid container.	All	All	Separate drugs and package individually.
Powders, tablets and	Druggist fold, pill box	All	All	Same as above.

Specimen	Amount Required	Method of Packaging	Special Instructions
capsules.		or vial, glassine envelope (aluminum foil is acceptable for powders).	
Vegetation	All	Plastic or paper bag.	Package vegetation separately. If wet, air dry thoroughly before submission. Smoking instruments are packaged individually to prevent contamination.
ORGANS *(See Toxicology)*			
PAINT (Paint chips or scrapings)	At least ½ square inch of solid, with all layers represented. / All. Recover all the layers.	Druggist fold, pill box or vial. DO NOT place loose in envelope or in plastic bag.	Whenever possible, submit the entire article on which the paint has been observed. Otherwise, use a clean knife blade to remove all the layers of paint from the object. DO NOT use tape to collect paint.
SEMINAL STAINS *(See "Specific Method of Collecting Evidence in Sex Crimes" on page 414)*	All		
SOIL	Collect a quantity approximating 1–2 teaspoons of / All	Solid container or druggist fold. DO	Package separately soil collected at different areas. Whenever pos-

(continued)

Specimen	Packaging	Amount Required		Collection Procedure
		Control	Evidence	
SOIL (cont.)	**NOT** place loose in envelope.	soil at crime scene (top layer only) as well as representative samples in a 200-foot radius of the crime scene.		sible, submit the entire article on which the soil has been observed. Label all samples with proper location (approximately 8 to 10 representative samples).
TOXICOLOGY (Living)				
Blood	Clear test tube or vial.		25cc of blood for drug determination. 5cc of blood for alcohol.	Physician taking blood sample should add anticoagulant (e.g., sodium oxalate) and preservative (e.g., sodium fluoride). Refrigerate until delivery to laboratory.
Urine	Clean bottle or vial.		All voided.	Refrigerate until delivery to the laboratory.
Stomach Washing	Same as above.		All	Same as above.
TOXICOLOGY (Dead)				
Blood	Clean test tube or vial.		25cc for drugs. 5cc for alcohol.	Add anticoagulant and preservative. Refrigerate until delivery to laboratory.
Brain	Plastic container.		300 grams.	Keep refrigerated until delivery to laboratory.

Bile		All	Same as above.
Liver		300 Grams.	Same as above.
Kidney		All	Same as above.
Urine		All in bladder.	Same as above.
Skin around puncture marks		All	Same as above.

TOOLMARKS

	Solid container package in order to prevent damage to area of toolmark.	Submit suspect tool. Package in a separate container. Whenever possible, submit entire object containing the toolmark.	**DO NOT** attempt to reproduce marking by casting a mold unless that is the only method by which the evidence can be preserved.

VOICEPRINT

Magnetic Tape Recordings ¼"	Use containers that original tape came in. Properly marked and initialed.	Suspect(s) must repeat identical words appearing in questioned tape.	All original recording or best copy available.
Cassette Recordings are acceptable.			Obtain best recording by eliminating background noise (Typewriters, telephones, air conditioners, conversation, etc.) (See *Footnote***)

Document Examination

*Duplicate the original writing conditions as to text, speed, slant, size of paper, size of writing, type of writing, instrument, etc. Do not allow suspect to see questioned writing. Give no instructions as to spelling, punctuation, etc. Remove each sample from sight as soon as completed. Suspect should fill out blank check forms. In hand printing cases, both upper case (capital) and lower case (small) samples should be obtained. In forgery cases, obtain sample signatures of the person whose name is forged. Have writer prepare some specimens with hand not habitually used. Obtain undictated handwriting when feasible. In certain investigations, it may not be possible to have suspect prepare specimen writings. For this purpose a list has been prepared giving the investigator sources for obtaining standards for comparison.

Sources of Handwriting Specimens

1. Account books
2. Affidavits
3. Application forms
4. Assignments
5. Autographs
6. Automobile insurance applications
7. Automobile license applications
8. Automobile title certificates
9. Bank deposit slips
10. Bank safe deposit entry slips
11. Bank savings withdrawal slips
12. Bank signature cards
13. Bank statements, receipts for
14. Bible entries
15. Bills of sale
16. Bonds
17. Books, signatures of owner in
18. Building "after hours" registers
19. Corporation papers
27. Corporation papers
28. Criminal records
29. Credit applications
30. Credit cards
31. Deeds
32. Deeds of trust
33. Depositions
34. Diaries
35. Dog license applications
36. Drafts
37. Drive-it-yourself applications
38. Drivers' licenses and applications
39. Druggists' poison registers
40. Employment applications
41. Envelopes
42. Fishing licenses
43. Funeral attendance registers
44. Gas service applications
45. Gasoline mileage records
46. Gate records at defense plants
47. Greeting cards, Christmas, etc.
54. Leases, real property
55. Letters
56. Library card applications
57. Light company applications
58. Life insurance applications
59. Loan applications
60. Mail orders
61. Manuscripts
62. Marriage records
63. Membership cards
64. Memoranda of all kinds
65. Military papers
66. Mortgages
67. Motor vehicle records
68. Newspaper advertisement copy
69. Occupational writings
70. Package receipts
71. Parent's signatures on report cards
72. Partnership papers
73. Pawn tickets
81. Postal cards
82. Probate court papers
83. Promissory notes
84. Property damage reports
85. Recipes
86. Receipts for rent, etc.
87. Registered mail return receipts
88. Release of mortgages
89. Rental contracts for equipment
90. Reports
91. Retail store sales slips
92. School and College papers
93. Social security cards and papers
94. Sport and game score cards
95. Stock certificates, endorsements
96. Surety bond applications
97. Tax estimates and returns
98. Telegram copy
99. Telephone service applications
100. Time sheets
101. Traffic tickets

19. Business license applications
20. Charity pledges
21. Check book stubs
22. Checks, including endorsements
23. Church pledges
24. Convention registration books
25. Contracts
26. Cooking recipes

48. Hospital entry applications, etc.
49. Hotel and motel guest registers
50. Hunting license
51. Identification cards
52. Inventories
53. Jail records

74. Passports
75. Payroll receipts
76. Pension applications
77. Permit applications
78. Petitions, referundum, etc.
79. Photograph albums
80. Pleadings

102. Vehicle rental forms
103. Voting registration records
104. Water company service applications
105. Wills
106. Workman's compensation papers.

**It is recommended that the investigator phone the Voiceprint Unit before obtaining voice recordings of the suspect(s).

SPECIFIC METHODS OF COLLECTING
EVIDENCE IN SEX CRIMES

This segment of the Physical Evidence Manual provides specific instructions on how rape and other sex-related crime evidence should be submitted to the various laboratories of the Forensic Science Bureau.

It must be noted that the Forensic Science Bureau **will not** analyze any specimen for venereal disease. Any specimen collected (Thayer-Martin, Urine, etc.) for that purpose must be submitted to a local office of the Department of Health or hospital having proper incubation equipment for this type of analysis.

A. Collection, Preservation and Packaging of Semen Evidence.

   1. Stains

      a. Items must be dry before packaging.

         (1) Clothing—submit each item in a separate paper bag. Handle the clothing as little as possible and DO NOT touch or fold areas where there are suspected seminal stains.

         (2) Blankets—sheets, bedding, rugs, seat covers, etc., package properly and submit entire object.

         (3) Vehicles

            (a) Submit the entire seat.

            (b) If it is necessary to examine the vehicle, consult with the laboratory in advance.

B. Human Orifices

   1. Evidence Samples

      a. Victim should be advised against washing out the violated area. Washing may destroy any evidence.

      b. Samples should be obtained by a qualified medical practitioner.

   2. Vaginal Specimens

      a. The complainant should be examined as soon as possible for the presence of motile (active or alive) spermatozoa.

         (1) Inactive sperm can be found in the vagina for extended periods after intercourse.

b. Smear(s): Should be taken only by qualified personnel. A thin smear is prepared and allowed to dry. **Do Not** use sprays or glazes of any kind on these smears. Upon drying, a cover glass may be placed over the smear and labeled as such. The smear should be placed in a slide holder to prevent against contamination and breakage. All smears and/or holders should be labeled with all pertinent data; type of smear, from whom taken, by whom, location and date.

c. The doctor should rinse the vaginal vault, using a minimum amount of liquid (preferably not more than 5-10 ml of distilled water).

d. All swabs should be placed in dry test tubes. All test tubes should be properly labeled and initialed for future identification.

e. The test tubes should be refrigerated until submitted to the laboratory

3. Rectum

a. In appropriate cases, obtain swabs and place in dry test tubes properly labeled.

b. Same as 2. b., above.

4. Oral Cavity

a. In appropriate cases, swabs should be taken from all areas of the mouth and placed in dry test tubes properly labeled.

b. Same as 2. b., above.

C. Controls

1. It may be possible to determine the **ABO** blood group of seminal material. In order to do this, it will be necessary to know the secretor status and blood group of the people involved. This will always include all suspects and victims, but may also involve others the victim may have had intercourse with within twenty-four (24) hours of the examination and taking of samples.

2. Collect both blood and saliva as controls from all the necessary people. If a blood sample cannot be directly obtained from a person, an official record—i.e., hospital, military, medical, etc.—of his blood type should be substituted.

a.   Saliva from a living donor

(1)   Be certain that the donor has a good supply of saliva generated in the mouth prior to spitting or have the donor spit in the same area more than once. It is best that the donor not have anything in his mouth for an hour prior to the giving of the sample. (Including cigarettes, cigars, etc.).

(2)   Have the donor spit into a clean, absorbent paper towel and outline the area of the saliva before it dries. The instrument used to outline the area must not come in contact with the spit. Be careful to avoid transfer of perspiration from the hands of the person collecting the sample. Handle edges only.

(3)   Air dry, initial, fold and place the paper towel into a properly marked envelope and seal.

3.   Saliva from a deceased individual

a.   Have the medical examiner swab the inside of the dead person's mouth. At least four (4) samples are needed from four different areas in the mouth. Do not swab areas that have been contaminated by blood. (If seminal fluid is suspected in the mouth, have the examiner swab an area which he feels may be uncontaminated).

b.   Place swabs in appropriately marked, dry, clean test tubes.

D. Pubic Hairs

1.   The victim's pubic hair should be combed with a clean comb to collect any loose hairs that may have been transferred from the male.

2.   Twenty-four or more hairs from various areas of the pubic region from both the victim and suspect are to be obtained. It is preferred that these hairs include the roots.

E. Other Evidence

1.   All other evidence encountered, e.g., blood, head hairs, fibers, must be submitted to the laboratory according to procedures outlined in the Guide to the Collection of Physical Evidence (see pages 402–413).

ATOMIC ABSORPTION ANALYSIS FOR
GUNSHOT RESIDUE

This test is presently conducted by the U.S. Treasury Department, Forensic Laboratory, Washington, D.C.. Specimens should be submitted directly to their National Laboratory by **registered mail**:

Information on Gunshot Residue

The presence of two chemical elements, barium and antimony, on test swabs is considered indicative of gunshot residue (GSR). The two elements are present in most cartridge primers, and antimony is often found in the bullet lead as well.

It has been found that cotton swabs are quite useful for collecting GSR, but because the amounts of these elements deposited on the firing hand is quite small, contamination of the swab by either barium or antimony from other sources may prevent GSR detection. Of particular concern is the quality of the collection materials themselves. Only plastic shafted cotton swabs packaged after use in plastic containers such as vials or self-sealing bags are suitable.

There are situations in which the National Laboratory will not accept hand swabs for analysis because the analysis would not be meaningful. A list of these reasons is given below:

1. A .22 caliber weapon was used, but not with FEDERAL brand ammunition.
2. Six or more hours elapsed between the weapon firing and the hand swabbing.
3. The subject's hands were washed or fingerprinted between the time the weapon was fired and the hands were swabbed.
4. The swabs are obviously contaminated (e.g., by blood), have been exposed to contamination by container breakage, or have had prolonged contact with foreign materials such as paper labels.
5. Unsuitable collection materials were used (e.g., gauze, swabs with wooden shafts).
6. Specimens are not labeled.
7. Specimens are packaged in other than plastic containers.
8. Transmittal letter is missing or inadequate.

COLLECTION, PACKAGING AND TRANSMITTAL
OF GUNSHOT RESIDUE SPECIMENS

A. Collection and Packaging

1. When **not** to collect residues

    a. If more than six (6) hours have elapsed since the weapon was fired. (**Exception:** Suicide victims whose hands have been protected with plastic bags).

    b. If the subject's hands have recently been washed or fingerprinted.

    c. If .22 caliber ammunition (other than Federal Brand) was used.

2. What materials to use? (**Do not substitute!**)

    a. **Single-tipped** cotton swabs on **plastic** shafts.

    b. A 5% solution of nitric acid ("Reagent" grade) using distilled or demineralized water.

    c. Plastic (polyethylene, polypropylene, or polystyrene) vials with tight-fitting plastic caps, or plastic evidence bags (with interlocking closure), preferably not larger than 3" X 4".

3. How to collect and package?

    a. Thoroughly wash **your** hands or cover them with clean plastic gloves.

    b. Apply four drops of 5% Nitric Acid to **each** of two swabs.

    c. Using both swabs simultaneously, **thoroughly** swab the back of the left hand and its fingers.

    d. Place both swabs in a new plastic bag or vial. Seal the bag or cap the vial. Label the container "Left Back of (Suspect's name)" and mark with your initials and the date.

    e. Repeat steps (b) through (d) separately for Left Palm, Right Back, and Right Palm.

    f. Swab the cartridge case, if available, with a single dry or water moistened swab. Package and label.

    g. Prepare "Control" swabs by performing step (b). Package immediately and label.

B. Transmittal

1. Prepare a transmittal letter containing **as much** of the following information as is available to you at time of writing. Please acknowledge all requested items of information. For example, if the gun type, or caliber, or brand of ammunition is not known, include in your letter a statement of that fact.

a. Date of your letter.
b. Your case number
c. Subject's full name
d. Date and time of shooting
e. Date and time of swabbing
f. Type and caliber of gun

g. Brand of ammunition
h. Subject's occupation
i. Subject's hobbies
j. Is subject right-handed or left-handed?
k. Brief description of incident

2. Attach the original copy of your transmittal letter to the outside of the evidence mailing container, place another copy inside the container, and send by **registered** mail to the National Laboratory.

Appendix II
Chromatographic and Spectrophotometric Parameters for Figures Contained within the Text.

1. *Figures 4-6a and b*
   $3' \times 1/4''$ glass column; 3% OV-17 on Varaport 30, 80/100 mesh.
   T (injection port) = 280°C, T(detector) = 280°C, T(column) = 200°C
   Carrier Gas: Nitrogen at 50 ml/min

2. *Figure 4-7*
   $8' \times 1/8''$ stainless steel, 15% carbowax 20M, AW-DMCS treated 80/100 mesh chromosorb W plus $3' \times 1/8''$ stainless steel, 10% silicone D.C. 200 in series.
   Temperatures unknown
   Carrier Gas: Nitrogen

3. *Figure 4-8*
   Absorbent: Silica Gel G
   Developing Solvent: Benzene
   Visualizer: Fast Blue B Salt

4. *Figure 4-9*
   Absorbent: Silica Gel G
   Developing Solvent: Chloroform-Diethylamine (9:1)
   Visualizer: Iodoplatinate

5. *Figure 4-13*
   Solvent: 0.1N HCL

6. *Figure 4-14 a*
   Heroin hydrochloride in KBr

7. *Figure 4-14 b*
   Secobarbital (free acid) in KBr

8. *Figure 7-11*
   Acrylic fibers ground in KBr

9. *Figure 7-13 a and b*
   1.83 m X 0.32 cm stainless steel column, 20% carbowax 1540 on 60/80 mesh chromosorb W.
   Pyrolysis temperature unknown
   T(injection port) = 250°C, T(detector) = 250°C, T(column) - programmed at 2 minutes initial hold at 50°C, then 10°C/minute to 180°C, hold for 25 minutes
   Carrier Gas: Argon at 50 ml/min.

10. *Figure 7-16 a and b*
    Same as Figure 4-7.

11. *Figure 8-8*
    Solvent: 0.1N HCL

12. *Figure 9-6*
    Ethanol in whole blood analyzed by "head space" technique.
    A porous polymer column was used.
    T(injection port) = 132°C, T(detector) = 132°C, T(column) = 132°C
    Carrier Gas: Helium (Thermal conductivity detector was used).

13. *Figure 10-5 a and b*
    2.44 m X 0.32 cm. o.d. stainless steel column, 7% Bentone 34 + 10% di-n-decylphthalate on chromosorb W, 60/80 mesh.
    T(injection port) = 150°C, T(detector) = 150°C, T(column) = 100°C
    Carrier Gas: Nitrogen at 25 ml/min

14. *Figure 10-8*
    RDX in KBr

15. *Figure 14-7*
    Absorbent: Silica Gel
    Developing Solvent: Ethyl acetate, absolute ethanol, water (70:35:30)

Answers

CHAPTER 1

1. forensic science
2. Sherlock Holmes
3. Alphonse Bertillon
4. Francis Galton
5. Leone Lattes
6. Calvin Goddard
7. Albert Osborn
8. Hans Gross
9. Edmond Locard
10. California
11. regional
12. drug
13. FBI, Drug Enforcement Administration, Bureau of Alcohol, Tobacco and Firearms, and U.S. Postal Service
14. federal, state, county and municipal
15. physical science unit
16. biology unit
17. firearms unit
18. toxicology unit
19. evidence collection unit
20. Frye v. United States
21. specialization

22. Coppolino v. Florida
23. expert witness
24. True
25. training

CHAPTER 2

1. physical evidence
2. True
3. photograph, sketch
4. systematic
5. carriers
6. victim's clothing, hair, blood, and fingernail scrapings
7. scientific integrity
8. is not
9. False
10. is not
11. control
12. chain of custody
13. False
14. identification
15. comparative
16. probability
17. individual
18. class
19. True
20. natural variations

CHAPTER 3

1. physical
2. chemical
3. metric
4. meter, gram, liter
5. 1/100
6. 1/1000
7. 200
8. milliliter
9. True
10. 453.6 grams
11. True
12. Temperature
13. 180
14. 100
15. mass
16. equal-arm balance
17. density
18. float
19. refraction
20. refractive index

21. True
22. amorphous
23. birefringence
24. dispersion
25. glass
26. individual
27. density, refractive index
28. flotation
29. Becke line
30. radial
31. narrower
32. True
33. will
34. False
35. minerals
36. density-gradient
37. True

CHAPTER 4

1. matter
2. elements
3. 105
4. periodic
5. atom
6. compounds
7. molecule
8. solid
9. has no
10. sublimation
11. less
12. phases
13. organic
14. Inorganic
15. qualitative, quantitative
16. spectrophotometry
17. chromatography
18. True
19. higher
20. True
21. gas chromatography
22. retention time
23. pyrolyzed
24. thin-layer chromatography
25. visualized
26. R_f
27. False
28. electrophoresis
29. True
30. wavelength
31. False
32. electro-magnetic

33. lower
34. photons
35. True
36. less
37. can
38. Beer's
39. spectrophotometer
40. monochromator
41. infrared
42. mass spectrometry

CHAPTER 5

1. oxygen, silicon
2. ten
3. trace
4. absorb, emit
5. emission spectrum
6. True
7. line
8. is
9. False
10. emission spectrometer
11. laser beam
12. atomic absorption spectrophotom-
    etry
13. does
14. False
15. antimony
16. proton, neutron, electron
17. are not
18. positive
19. is
20. protons
21. atomic number
22. True
23. True
24. light
25. atomic mass number
26. isotopes
27. False
28. alpha rays, beta rays, gamma rays
29. electrons
30. gamma rays
31. neutrons
32. neutron activation analysis
33. crystalline

CHAPTER 6

1. lenses
2. virtual

3. compound
4. objective lens
5. eyepiece or ocular lens
6. virtual
7. True
8. transmitted
9. vertical or reflected
10. condenser
11. parfocal
12. binocular
13. magnifying power
14. 200×
15. numerical aperture
16. field of view
17. decreases
18. depth of focus
19. decreases
20. comparison
21. True
22. stereoscopic
23. False
24. working distance
25. plane-polarized
26. perpendicular
27. polarizing
28. birefringent
29. scanning electron
30. X-rays

CHAPTER 7

1. hair follicle
2. cuticle, cortex, medulla
3. True
4. cortex
5. medulla
6. medullary index
7. 1/3, 1/2
8. absent
9. animal
10. cannot
11. comparison
12. 100
13. is
14. False
15. neutron activation analysis
16. Natural
17. cotton
18. True
19. synthetic fibers
20. False
21. Polymers

22. monomer
23. Proteins
24. True
25. double refraction or birefringence
26. pyrolysis gas chromatography
27. pigment, binder
28. color
29. layer structure
30. acrylic lacquers
31. acrylic enamels
32. False
33. binder
34. inorganic
35. True

CHAPTER 8

1. True
2. high
3. physical
4. True
5. False
6. regular
7. analgesics, depressive
8. Opium
9. morphine
10. heroin
11. True
12. hallucinogens
13. Hashish
14. tetrahydrocannabinol (THC)
15. True
16. liquid hashish
17. lysergic acid
18. depresses
19. Barbiturates
20. long
21. Methaqualone (Quaalude)
22. Tranquilizers
23. False
24. Amphetamines
25. intravenous
26. clandestine
27. Cocaine
28. sniffed
29. Controlled Substances Act
30. five
31. one
32. four
33. False
34. Marquis
35. Marquis

36. marihuana
37. cocaine
38. Microcrystalline
39. chromatography
40. infrared
41. cystolith
42. chain of custody

CHAPTER 9

1. ethyl alcohol
2. False
3. is
4. True
5. stomach, small intestine
6. faster
7. 30, 90
8. watery
9. oxidation, excretion
10. oxidized
11. liver
12. breath
13. 0.015
14. artery, vein
15. pulmonary
16. alveoli
17. 2,100
18. lower
19. Breathalyzer
20. potassium dichromate
21. absorption
22. catalyst
23. gas chromatography
24. decline
25. 0.10
26. Schmerber v. California
27. morphine
28. blood, urine
29. Marihuana, LSD
30. acids, bases
31. greater
32. acidic
33. pH
34. False
35. carbon monoxide
36. percent saturation

CHAPTER 10

1. False
2. oxidation

3. False
4. Energy
5. chemical, mechanical
6. breaking, formation
7. absorb, liberate
8. liberate
9. exothermic
10. heat of combustion
11. endothermic
12. True
13. ignition
14. gaseous
15. flash point
16. Pyrolysis
17. Glowing combustion
18. increases
19. oxygen
20. potassium nitrate, charcoal, sulfur
21. True
22. porous
23. Airtight
24. Spontaneous combustion
25. gas chromatograph
26. cannot
27. thin-layer chromatography
28. explosion
29. low-energy
30. High energy
31. black powder, smokeless powder
32. confined
33. False
34. initiating, non-initiating
35. is not
36. RDX
37. PETN
38. initiating
39. crater
40. collection
41. microscopic
42. acetone
43. color spot tests, thin layer chromatography
44. infrared spectrophotometry
45. X-ray diffraction

CHAPTER 11

1. type
2. True
3. Plasma
4. serum

5. Red blood cells
6. antigens
7. A
8. neither
9. A, B
10. Rh
11. antibodies
12. only a specific
13. True
14. B, A
15. neither
16. antibodies
17. serology
18. be
19. A
20. O
21. forty-two
22. three
23. All
24. benzidine
25. Luminol
26. precipitin
27. can
28. absorption-elution
29. 80
30. Enzymes
31. polymorphic
32. True
33. dry
34. False
35. gene
36. chromosomes
37. 23
38. father
39. alleles
40. homozygous
41. phenotype
42. genotype
43. will
44. BB, BO
45. acid phosphatase
46. spermatozoa
47. oligospermia
48. can
49. little
50. saliva

CHAPTER 12

1. Alphonse Bertillon
2. Anthropometry

3. Sir Edward Richard Henry
4. True
5. is not
6. ridge characteristics
7. Fingerprints
8. dermal papillae
9. dermal papillae
10. cannot
11. loop, whorls, arches
12. loop
13. arch
14. radial
15. type lines
16. delta
17. one
18. core
19. plain whorl
20. plain arch
21. have no
22. whorl
23. 1/1
24. cannot
25. True
26. visible fingerprint
27. Plastic
28. latent fingerprints
29. chemical
30. iodine
31. powder
32. ninhydrin
33. silver nitrate
34. False
35. photography

CHAPTER 13

1. land
2. caliber
3. class
4. individual
5. comparison microscope
6. False
7. sometimes
8. smooth
9. gauge
10. False
11. can
12. True
13. True
14. False
15. 12, 18
16. infrared

17. yard
18. primer
19. barium, antimony
20. True
21. is not
22. base, nose
23. False
24. toolmark
25. striations
26. individual

Index

Haptoglobin, 261
Hashish, 171, 173, 188
Hashish oil, 188
Headlight filaments, 60
Heat of combustion, 222, 222 (*table*)
"Heavy Metals", 214
Hemoglobin, 215, 255, 261
Henry, William, 75
Henry's Law, 75, 200
Henry system of fingerprint classification, 288-90
Heredity, 267-71
Heroin:
  administration of, 168-69
  analysis of, 81-82, 90, 93, 95, 184-85, 187
  diluents of, 169-70
  effect of, 169
  legal control of, 171-72, 182
  metabolism of, 211
  physical dependence on, 166
  psychological dependence on, 165
  synthesis of, 168
Herschel, William, 280
High energy explosive (*see* Explosives)
Hofmann, Albert, 175
Holmes, Sherlock, 3
Hoover, J. Edgar, 6
Hughes, Howard, 334-35, 350-51
Hydrocarbons, analysis of, 231-33
Hydrogen, isotopes of, 110

Identification of physical evidence, 29-30
Ignition temperature, 223, 224 (*table*), 225
Immersion method, 53-55, 127
Immunological assay for drugs, 252-53
"Implied consent" law, 209
Indented writings, 340-41, 344
Individual characteristics, 30-32
Infrared photography, 314, 340
Infrared spectrophotometry:
  description of, 88-93
  of drugs, 187
  of explosives, 242
  of fibers, 148-49
  of paints, 157
Initiating explosives, 237
Inks, 340, 344, 346
Inorganics, definition of, 73
Iodine fuming, 293
Ion, 93
Irving, Clifford, 334-35, 350-51
Iso-enzymes (*see* specific enzymes), 260-62
Isotopes:
  definition of, 110
  of hydrogen, 110
  synthesis of, 111-12

Kersta, Lawrence, 346
Kirk, Paul, 6
Kriminologie, 5

Landsteiner, Karl, 4, 247
Laser beam, use in emission spectroscopy, 103

Latent fingerprints, 12, 292-95
Lattes, Leone, 4
Lead, 106, 318
Leucomalachite color test, 255
Librium, 177, 182
Lie-detector (*see* Polygraph)
Light:
  absorption of, 73, 87-88, 202
  dispersion of, 50, 89
  emission of, 109
  frequency of, 85, 87, 108-09
  plane polarized, 126
  refraction of, 47, 117
  speed of, 85
  theory of, 84-87
  wavelength of, 85
Line spectrum, 101
Liquid, definition of, 72
Liquid hashish, 173
Locard, Edmond, 5-6
Loop patterns, 286
Los Angeles Police Dept., 6
Low energy explosives (*see* Explosives)
Luminol test, 255
Lyons, France, 5
Lysergic acid diethylamide (LSD):
  analysis of, 184, 253
  detection in body, 212, 253
  effects of, 175
  legal control of, 182
  physical dependence on, 166
  psychological dependence on, 175
  synthesis of, 174-75

MacDonell, Herbert L., 263
Man-made fibers, 142-44, 143 (*table*)
Marihuana:
  analysis of, 81, 128, 184, 188
  botanical features of, 188
  description of, 172
  detection in body, 212
  effects of, 173-74
  history of, 171-72
  legal control of, 164, 168, 171-72, 182
  physical dependence on, 166
  psychological dependence on, 165-66, 173
  THC content of, 172-73
Marquis reagent, 39, 184
Mass, 43
Mass spectrometry:
  applications of, 93-95, 214
  chemical ionization, 95
  theory of, 93-95
Matter:
  classification, 72-73
  definition of, 68
  states of 69, 72
Medulla of hair, 135, 137, 139-40
Medullary index of hair, 135, 137, 139
Mercury, 214
Mescaline, 174
Metals:
  as physical evidence, 98-99
  poisonous, 214-15
  serial number restoration on, 318-19
  trace elements in, 100-01, 112

Methadone, 170-71
Methamphetamine (see Amphetamines)
Methaqualone (Quaalude), 176-77, 182
Metric system, 39-41
Metropolitan Police Laboratory (London), 6, 248, 359
Microcrystalline tests:
  blood, 255
  choline, 273
  drugs, 185, 213
Microprocessor, 353
Microscope:
  applications for, 54-55, 61, 137-39, 148, 154, 185, 241-42, 272, 304-06, 323, 340
  comparison, 4, 123-24, 139, 304-06, 323
  compound, 117-22, 135
  hot-stage, 54-55
  polarizing, 126-27, 148
  scanning electron (SEM), 34, 127-30, 135, 318, 352
  stereoscopic, 124-26, 154, 241
Minerals, 61-62, 127
Minutiae (see Ridge characteristics)
M-N bloodgroup system, 249, 260, 271
"Mobile crime laboratories", 26
Molecule, definition of, 69
Monochromator, 88-89, 105
Monomers, 144-45
Morphine:
  analysis of, 184
  in body tissues, 211
  legal control of, 171-72
  source of, 168

Nalline test, 14
Narcotics:
  definition of, 168
  types of, 168-71
National Bureau of Standards, 359
Natural fibers, 142
Natural gas;
  analysis of, 244
  collection of, 244
  low energy explosive, 237
Neutron activation analysis:
  applications of, 111-12, 318
  of hair, 141
  theory of, 110-11
Neutrons:
  charge of, 106
  number in nucleus, 110-11
  size of, 106
  source of, 111
  symbol of, 107
New Jersey State Police Laboratory, 8
Ninhydrin, 293-94
Nitrocellulose (see Smokeless powder)
Nitroglycerin (see also Dynamite)
  chemical structure of, 226-27
  detection of, 242
  in dynamite, 238
  in smokeless powder, 236
Nobel, Alfred, 238
Non-initiating explosives, 237-39
Nucleus:

composition of, 107, 109-10
structure of, 109-10
Numerical aperture, 122
Nylon, 142, 144, 147-48

Odds (see Probability)
Odontology, 2
O'Hara, Charles, 352
Oligospermia, 273
Opiates, 170
Opium, 164, 168, 182
Organics, definition of, 73
Organized Crime Control Act, 9
Osborn, Albert, 4-5
Osterburg, James, 352
Oxidation, 220
Oxidizing agents, 226, 236, 340

Paint:
  analysis of, 10, 80, 103, 156-57
  automobile, 155-56
  collection and preservation of, 159-60
  composition of, 154
  data collection for, 359
  evidential value of, 32, 157, 159
  trace elements of, 103, 112, 157
Paternity tests, 271
Pathology, 2
People v. Williams, 14
Periodic table, 69, 71 (table), 107
Peroxidase, 254-55
PETN (pentaerythritol tetranitrate):
  classification of, 236-37
  detection of, 242
  uses of, 239
pH, 213
Phases:
  in chromatography, 74-76, 81
  definition of, 72
Phencyclidine (PCP), 174, 182
Phendimetrazine, 180
Phenmetrazine, 180
Phenolphthalein color test, 255
Phenotypes, 269-70
Phosphoglucomutase (PGM), 260-61, 274
Photography:
  crime scene, 24
  infrared, 314
  laboratory services for, 12
  uses of, 295, 314, 324, 326, 340
Photons, 87, 89
Physical dependence on drugs, 166, 167 (table)
Physical evidence (see specific types of evidence):
  admissibility, 13-14
  class characteristics of, 32-34
  collection of, 13, 16-18, 27-28
  common types of, 22-23
  comparison of, 30-34
  definition of, 21
  identification of, 29-30
  individual characteristics of, 30-32
  laboratory services for examination, 10-12
  marking of, 28

definition of, 73
theory, 87-88
Spermatozoa, 268, 272-73
Spontaneous combustion, 229, 231
Stereoscopic microscope, 124-26, 154, 241
Stimulants, 178-81
Study in Scarlet, A (Doyle), 3
Sublimation, 72, 293
Succinylcholine chloride, 14
Synthetic fibers, 144

Takayama test, 255
Teichmann test, 255
Temperature, 41-42
Tetrahydrocannabinol (THC), 172-73, 253
Tetryl (2, 4, 6-trinitrophenylmethyl-nitramine), 237
Textiles (*see* Fibers)
Thallium, 214
Thin-layer chromatography:
  application of, 186, 188, 232-33, 242, 273, 344, 346
  description of, 81-84
Tire impressions, 324-28
TNT (trinitrotoluene):
  classification of, 236, 237
  uses of, 238-39
Toolmarks:
  collection and preservation, 324
  collection of paint from, 160, 324
  comparison, 323
  definition, 321
  individual and class characteristics of, 321-23
Toxicology:
  analytical techniques used, 212-16
  classification of drugs for, 212-13
  collection of specimens for, 211-12
  forensic aspects of, 210-12
  laboratory services for, 12
  poison detection by, 214-16
Trace elements:
  in brass, 100 (*table*)
  in bullets, 106
  in copper wires, 112, 112 (*table*)
  in drugs, 112

in fibers, 101
in glass, 51, 101
in hair, 101, 112, 141
in metals, 100-01, 112
in paint, 103, 112, 157
significance of 100-01
in soil, 101
Tranquilizers, 177
Tritium, 110
Turin, Italy, 4
Type lines, 286
Typewriters:
  collection of exemplars from, 338-39
  identification of make and model, 338
  individual characteristics, 337-38
  typefaces of, 337

Ultraviolet spectrophotometry, applications of, 88-93, 186-87
United States Postal Inspection Service, 335
United States v. Mara, 336

Vacuum sweeper, 25
Valium, 177, 182
Van Urk test, 184
Virtual image, 117
Visible spectrophotometry (*see also* Breathalyzer), 88-93
Voice examination, 12-13, 346-51
Vollmer, August, 6
Vucetich, Juan, 281

Wavelength, 85
Weight, 42-43
Whorl patterns, 286
Wood, 10
Working distance, 125

X-rays:
  emission by elements, 129-30, 318
  nature of, 85, 87
X-ray diffraction:
  application of, 112-13, 215, 242, 244
  theory of, 113

Zygote, 268